Money and Power in Provincial Thailand

NORDIC INSTITUTE OF ASIAN STUDIES

RECENT AND FORTHCOMING STUDIES ON SOUTHEAST ASIA

Elections in Indonesia
Hans Antlöv and Sven Cederroth (eds)

Lee Kuan Yew: The Beliefs Behind the Man
Michael D. Barr

Atlas of Laos
Bounthavy Sisouphanthong and Christian Taillard

Historical Atlas of Indonesia
Robert Cribb

Authority Relations and Economic Decision-Making in Vietnam
Dang Phong and Melanie Beresford

Indonesian Politics in Crisis
Stefan Eklöf

Where China Meets Southeast Asia
Grant Evans, Chris Hutton and Kuah Khun Eng (eds)

Thailand and the Southeast Asian Networks of the Vietnamese Revolution, 1885–1954
Christopher E. Goscha

The House in Southeast Asia
Signe Howell and Stephen Sparkes (eds)

Thailand in Crisis
Pasuk Phongpaichit and Chris Baker

Entrepreneurship in Vietnam
Per Ronnås and Bhargavi Ramamurthy (eds)

Democracy in Malaysia
Francis Loh Kok Wah and Khoo Boo Teik (eds)

The Nordic Institute of Asian Studies (NIAS) is funded by the governments of Denmark, Finland, Iceland, Norway and Sweden via the Nordic Council of Ministers, and works to encourage and support Asian studies in the Nordic countries. In so doing, NIAS has published well in excess of one hundred books in the last three decades.

MONEY & POWER IN PROVINCIAL THAILAND

edited by

Ruth McVey

NIAS

First published in 2000 by NIAS Publishing
Nordic Institute of Asian Studies
Leifsgade 33, DK–2300 Copenhagen S, Denmark
tel: (+45) 3254 8844 • fax: (+45) 3296 2530
E–mail: books@nias.ku.dk
Website: http://nias.ku.dk/Books/

British Library Cataloguing in Publication Data

Money and power in provincial Thailand

1. Local government - Thailand 2. Local finance - Thailand 3. Thailand - Economic conditions 4. Thailand - Politics and government
I. McVey, Ruth Thomas II. Nordic Institute of Asian Studies
320.9'593

ISBN 87-87062-67-4 (hardback)
ISBN 87-87062-70-4 (paperback)

Simultaneously published in North America
by the University of Hawai'i Press
and in Asia by the Institute of Southeast Asian Studies, Singapore
and by Silkworm Books, Chiang Mai

Typesetting by the Nordic Institute of Asian Studies
Printed and bound in Singapore by Prime Packaging Industries Pte Ltd

Contents

Preface ... vii

Editor's Note ... viii

Contributors ... ix

1. Of Greed and Violence, and Other Signs of Progress ... 1
   Ruth McVey

2. *Chao Sua, Chao Pho, Chao Thi:* Lords of Thailand's Transition ... 30
   Pasuk Phongpaichit and Chris Baker

3. Local Godfathers in Thai Politics ... 53
   Sombat Chantornvong

4. The Rise of Local Power in Thailand: Provincial Crime, Elections and the Bureaucracy ... 74
   James Ockey

5. Market Society and the Origins of the New Thai Politics ... 97
   Michael J. Montesano

6. The Local Dynamics of the 'New Political Economy': A District Business Association and Its Role in Electoral Politics ... 123
   Daniel Arghiros

7. The Entrepreneurs of Khorat ... 154
   Yoko Ueda

8. Developing Provincial Capitalism: A Profile of the Economic and Political Roles of a New Generation in Khon Kaen, Thailand ... 195
   Kevin Hewison and Maniemai Thongyou

9. Beyond Bangkok: The Provincial Middle Class in the 1992 Protests ... 221
   James P. LoGerfo

Select Bibliography ... 271

Index ... 284

Tables

7.1 Variation in value of economic activities in Nakhon Ratchasima province, the Northeast and Thailand ... 155

7.2 Factories in the manufacturing sector of Nakhon Ratchasima province, 1989 ... 157

7.3 Economic growth rate in Thailand, the Northeast and Nakhon Ratchasima province, 1975–1989 ... 160

7.4 Share in GDP, population and per-capita GDP in Nakhon Ratchasima province, the Northeast, Bangkok and Thailand, 1975–1990 ... 161

7.5 Occupations of interviewees ... 162

7.6 Ethnicity and dialect groups of interviewees ... 164

7.7 Generation of Chinese immigrants and Chinese descendants ... 165

7.8 Attendance of Chinese school by Chinese immigrants and Chinese descendants ... 166

7.9 Birth place of Chinese immigrants and Chinese descendants ... 166

7.10 Birth place of Chinese immigrants and Chinese descendants, analysed by generation ... 167

7.11 Self-made Men – Chinese immigrants and Chinese descendants ... 168

7.12 Self-made Men – Chinese immigrants and Chinese descendants, analysed by generation ... 169

7.13 School career of Chinese immigrants and Chinese descendants ... 169

7.14 School career of Chinese immigrants and Chinese descendants, analysed by generation ... 170

7.15 Father's occupation ... 172

7.16 Experience in local elections ... 184

8.1 Business people and electoral politics ... 200

8.2 Regional productivity, 1993 ... 203

8.3 Growth Rates in Khon Kaen, 1984–1992 ... 204

8.4 Business activities of respondents and families ... 207

8.5 Reported association memberships ... 209

8.6 Perceptions of economic significance in Khon Kaen ... 211

8.7 Politically influential persons ... 212

9.1 Occupational background of PollWatch volunteers, 22 March 1992 elections ... 229

9.2 State-sponsored pro-Suchinda rallies, 15 May 1992 ... 235

9.3 Protest actions outside Bangkok province, 5–21 May 1992 ... 237

9.4 Protest actions by region ... 239

9.5 Selected characteristics of Patthalung, Nakhon Si Thammarat and Songkhla provinces ... 244

9.6 Selected characteristics of Buriram, Sisaket and Chiang Mai provinces ... 245

9.7 Size of the middle class nationwide and in selected provinces, 1970 and 1990 ... 254

9.8 Growth of the professions nationwide and selected provinces, 1970 and 1990 ... 255

PREFACE

This volume had its distant origins in a panel which Robert Taylor and I organized for the Third International Conference on Thai Studies, held at the University of London's School of Oriental and African Studies in 1993. At that time, we had been struck by the fact that research on Thailand had addressed itself almost entirely to the national scene or the peasantry. Almost nothing appeared to link village and capital, yet it was evident that with the country's rapid economic development intermediate nodes of power and growth would assume a critical role.

The debates at that meeting made apparent the increasing importance of provincial centres, and the emergence in them of powerful leaders whose influence was based on a combination of political and economic activities. Their behaviour reflected Thailand's particular history and traditions and was also shaped by global economic and cultural forces. The present volume represents a further exploration of this theme (about half the contributions here were developed from papers presented to the panel). It attempts to place provincial leadership in the context of a rapidly changing Thai capitalist polity, and aims more generally at furthering our understanding of the nexus between local and global forces in the transition from agrarian to industrial society.

I am very grateful to Robert Taylor for his work in formulating and organizing the initial discussions and his wise advice in the later stages of the project. I should also like especially to thank Chan Heng Chee, who made possible a stay at Singapore's Institute of Southeast Asia Studies, where much of the editorial work was accomplished. I benefitted greatly from discussions with colleagues in Singapore, and in particular from the cheerful helpfulness of Ch'ng Kim See of the ISEAS library. Finally, my thanks to Gerald Jackson of the Nordic Institute of Asian Studies for his patience and attention in seeing the volume through the press.

EDITOR'S NOTE

There is no universally accepted system for the transliteration of Thai, and the names of many well-known Thai are spelled idiosyncratically in the international press. Since those spellings are most likely to be familiar to the readers of this volume, we have opted for common journalistic practice as exemplified in the *Far Eastern Economic Review* for the names of public figures. For other Thai names, we have followed personal preference where known, and otherwise a modified version of the Library of Congress transliteration system. Common journalistic practice is also followed in rendering political party names in their Thai or English-language versions. Thai book titles and so on are transliterated in the modified Library of Congress system.

CONTRIBUTORS

Daniel Arghiros is Lecturer in the Social Anthropology of Development in South-East Asia at the Department of Politics and Asian Studies, University of Hull, UK. He is the author of *Political Structures and Strategies: a Study of Electoral Politics in Contemporary Rural Thailand* (Hull: Centre for South-East Asian Studies, 1995), and 'The Rise of Indigenous Capitalists in Rural Thailand: Profile of Brickmakers in the Central Plains', in M. Rutten and C. Upadhya (eds), *Small Business Entrepreneurs in Asia and Europe: Towards a Comparative Perspective* (New Delhi: Sage, 1997), as well as *Democracy, Development and Decentralization in Provincial Thailand* (Richmond, Surrey: Curzon Press, forthcoming 2001).

Chris Baker is a freelance researcher, writer, and translator based in Bangkok. He is co-author, with Pasuk Phongpaichit, of *Thailand's Crisis* (Chiang Mai: Silkworm Books and Copenhagen: NIAS, 2000), *Thailand's Boom and Bust* (Chiang Mai: Silkworm Books, 1998) and *Thailand: Economy and Politics* (Kuala Lumpur: Oxford University Press, 1995).

Kevin Hewison holds the Foundation Chair in Asian Languages and Societies at the University of New England, Australia, and is Director of that university's Asia Centre. He has edited *Political Change in Thailand. Democracy and Participation* (London: Routledge, 1997) and is author of *Power and Politics in Thailand: Essays in Political Economy* (Manila: Journal of Contemporary Asia Publishers, 1989) and 'Emerging Social Forces in Thailand: New Political and Economic Roles', in Richard Robison and David S.G. Goodman (eds), *The New Rich in Asia.* (London: Routledge, 1996).

James P. LoGerfo is an equity research associate at Bank of America Securities, New York; he is the author of 'Thailand: towards Democratic Consolidation,' *Journal of Democracy* 7 (1996) (with David King).

Maniemai Thongyou is Lecturer in the Department of Sociology and Anthropology at Khon Kaen University, Thailand. Earlier, she worked with human rights and development NGOs before becoming Deputy Director of the Research and Development Institute, Khon Kaen University.

Ruth McVey is Emeritus Reader in Southeast Asian Politics at the University of London (School of Oriental and African Studies). She has written widely on Southeast Asian politics and has previously edited *Southeast Asian Capitalists* (Ithaca: Cornell Studies on Southeast Asia, 1992).

Michael Montesano is Assistant Professor in the Southeast Asian Studies Programme of the National University of Singapore. His doctoral thesis is on 'The Commerce of Trang, 1930s–1990s: Thailand's National Integration in Social-Historical Perspective' (Cornell University, 1998).

James Ockey is a Senior Lecturer in the Department of Political Science, Canterbury University, New Zealand. He is the author of 'Crime, Society and Politics in Thailand', in Carl Trocki (ed.), *Gangsters and Democracy: Electoral Politics in Southeast Asia* (Ithaca NY: Cornell University Southeast Asia Program, 1998).

Pasuk Phongpaichit is Professor at the Faculty of Economics, Chulalongkorn University, Bangkok. In addition to the works co-authored with Chris Baker, she has edited, with Sungsidh Piriyarangsan *Chon chanklang bon krasae prachathipatai thai* [The Middle Class in the Course of Thai Democracy]. Bangkok: Chulalongkorn University Political Economy Centre, 1993; *Rat, thun, chao pho thongthin kap sangkhom thai* [State, Capital, and Local Godfathers in Thai Society] (Bangkok: Chulalongkorn University Political Economy Centre, 1992), and *Corruption and Democracy in Thailand* (Bangkok: Chulalongkorn University Political Economic Center, 1994).

Sombat Chantornvong is Associate Professor at the Faculty of Politicial Science, Thammasat University, Bangkok. He has written *Luak tang wikrit: panha lae tang ok* [Thai Elections in Crisis: Fundamental Problems and Solutions] (Bangkok: Kopfai Publishing Program, 1993), and is co-author of 'Constitutional Rule and the Institutionalization of Leadership and Security in Thailand', in Stephen Chee (ed.), *Leadership and Security in Southeast Asia: Institutional Aspects* (Singapore: Institute of Southeast Asian Studies, 1991).

Yoko Ueda is Associate Professor at the Faculty of Commerce, University of Marketing and Distribution Sciences, Kobe, Japan. She is the author of *Local Economy and Entrepreneurship in Thailand: A Case Study of Nakhon Ratchasima* (Kyoto: Kyoto University Press, 1995) and of 'Sino–Thai Entrepreneurs and the Development of Provincial Economies in Thailand', in Chan Kwok Bun (ed.), *Alternative Identities: The Chinese of Contemporary Thailand* (Singapore: Times Academic Press, 2000).

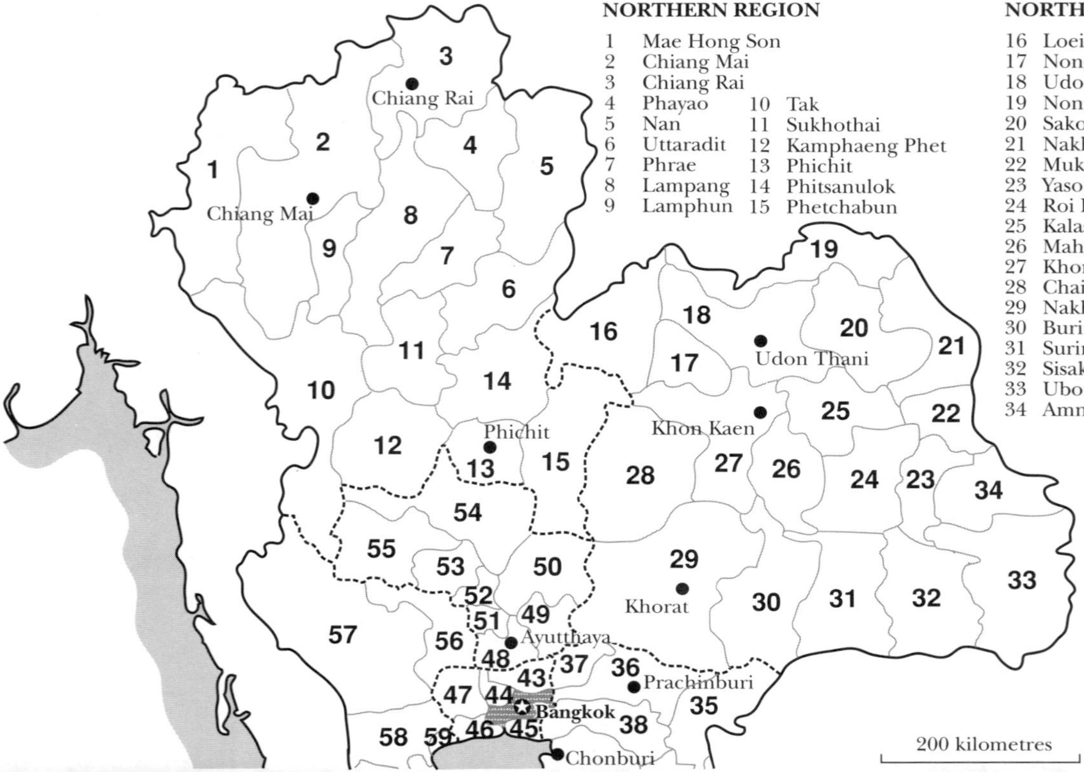

NORTHERN REGION

1 Mae Hong Son
2 Chiang Mai
3 Chiang Rai
4 Phayao
5 Nan
6 Uttaradit
7 Phrae
8 Lampang
9 Lamphun
10 Tak
11 Sukhothai
12 Kamphaeng Phet
13 Phichit
14 Phitsanulok
15 Phetchabun

NORTHEASTERN REGION

16 Loei
17 Nong Bualamphu
18 Udon Thani
19 Nong Khai
20 Sakon Nakhon
21 Nakhon Phanom
22 Mukdahan
23 Yasothon
24 Roi Et
25 Kalasin
26 Mahasarakham
27 Khon Kaen
28 Chaiyaphum
29 Nakhon Ratchasima
30 Buriram
31 Surin
32 Sisaket
33 Ubon Ratchathani
34 Amnat Charoen

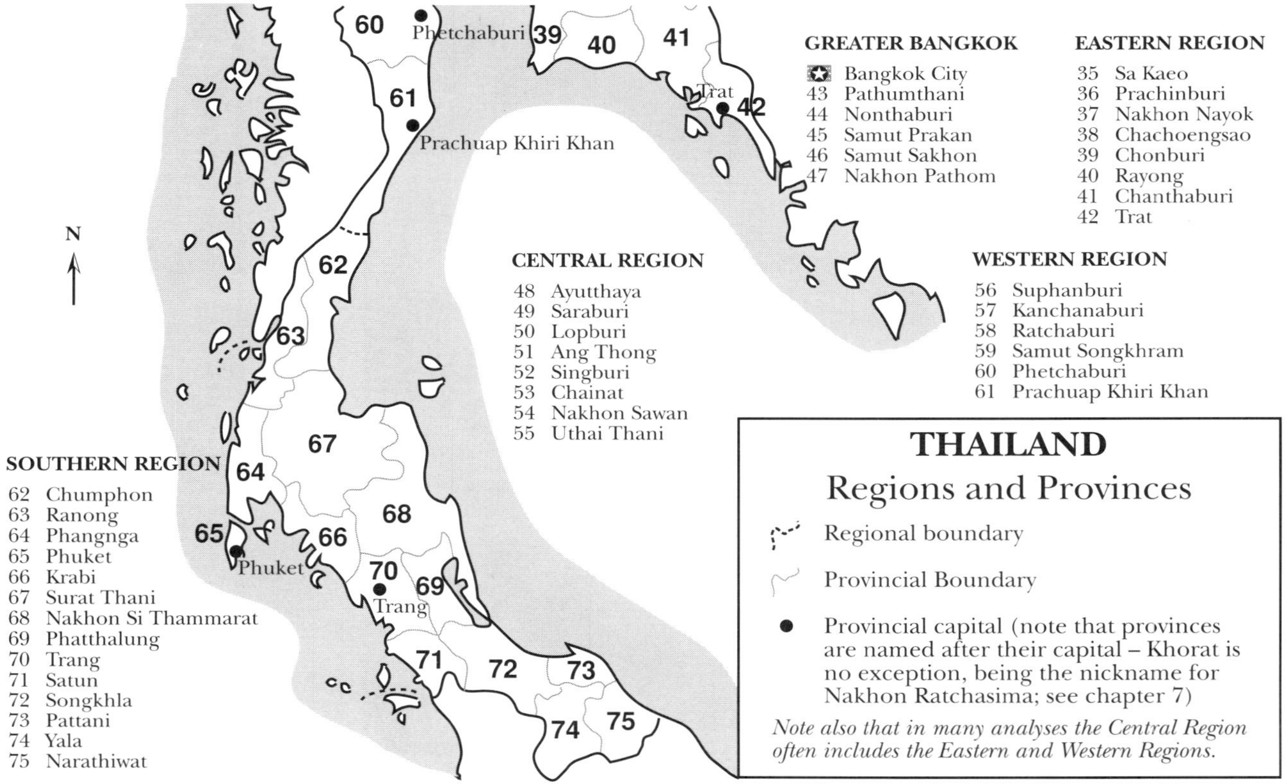

N
60
Phetchaburi
39
40
41
Trat
42
61
Prachuap Khiri Khan
62
63
64
65
Phuket
66
67
68
70
Trang
69
71
72
73
74
75
GREATER BANGKOK
Bangkok City
43 Pathumthani
44 Nonthaburi
45 Samut Prakan
46 Samut Sakhon
47 Nakhon Pathom
EASTERN REGION
35 Sa Kaeo
36 Prachinburi
37 Nakhon Nayok
38 Chachoengsao
39 Chonburi
40 Rayong
41 Chanthaburi
42 Trat
CENTRAL REGION
48 Ayutthaya
49 Saraburi
50 Lopburi
51 Ang Thong
52 Singburi
53 Chainat
54 Nakhon Sawan
55 Uthai Thani
WESTERN REGION
56 Suphanburi
57 Kanchanaburi
58 Ratchaburi
59 Samut Songkhram
60 Phetchaburi
61 Prachuap Khiri Khan
SOUTHERN REGION
62 Chumphon
63 Ranong
64 Phangnga
65 Phuket
66 Krabi
67 Surat Thani
68 Nakhon Si Thammarat
69 Phatthalung
70 Trang
71 Satun
72 Songkhla
73 Pattani
74 Yala
75 Narathiwat
THAILAND
Regions and Provinces
Regional boundary
Provincial Boundary
Provincial capital (note that provinces are named after their capital – Khorat is no exception, being the nickname for Nakhon Ratchasima; see chapter 7)
Note also that in many analyses the Central Region often includes the Eastern and Western Regions.

ONE

OF GREED AND VIOLENCE AND OTHER SIGNS OF PROGRESS

Ruth McVey

Not so very long ago, 'Southeast Asia' evoked rice fields and water buffaloes. Some might imagine this scene embellished with ancient monuments, others with guerrillas in black pyjamas; but few indeed would have seen the marks of industrialization. But by the 1990s, mention of the region could conjure up skyscrapers, their outlines softened by smog, their bases garlanded with gridlocked traffic, their precincts filled with people shopping, shopping, shopping.

In some respects, Southeast Asia was the jewel in the crown of the Asian-Pacific economic transformation of the late twentieth century: not essential to its existence, but a splendid decoration that confirmed the glory of the whole. For if a region which so recently appeared to be resolutely agrarian, sunk in neotraditional torpor or torn by revolutionary crisis, could acquire the energy and focus needed for spectacular capitalist take-off, did this not reflect the particular genius and general promise of East Asian capitalism?

Responding to this, most studies of Southeast Asia's economic change looked at big business as the engine of the region's growth and considered especially its relationship to international capitalism and to overseas Chinese business networks and values. When in mid-1997 the region's boom was suddenly threatened by collapse, analysts' attention remained riveted on the macro-economic sources of cause and effect: overborrowing, banking mismanagement, crony capitalism, lack of regulation and transparency, the potential regional and global knock-on effects.

This emphasis on big business, international linkages, and state policy is undoubtedly important, but it is not the only way of understanding Southeast Asian capitalism. Indeed, it tends to divert our attention from what is ultimately a more important question for the countries of the region, namely the depth and effect of capitalist change on the Southeast Asian society. Thus far, this has been considered in piecemeal fashion at best. Like the blind men and the elephant, Southeast Asia specialists have examined various parts of their subject, from diverse ideological, disciplinary, and temperamental angles, and on the basis of this have constructed very different creatures. Thus some have stressed not the accomplishments of Southeast Asian capitalism but its social and environmental impact, showing villages emptied by migration, local economies and cultures crushed by tourist development and agribusiness, landscapes destroyed by the plundering of natural resources. Most notably, very few analysts have looked at society's middle distance between capital and countryside. It is as if we see the region through a telephoto lens, ricefield and skyscraper pressed flat against each other.

In part this reflects ideological and disciplinary currents in global scholarship, but it also reveals a certain Southeast Asian reality. There has been a superconcentration of wealth and enterprise in the region's principal cities, which are now literally choking on excess population, traffic, and (at least until the crash) capital. Outside the metropolitan complexes, industrial development has centred on designated zones, which minimize contact with the life around them, and on areas of natural resource, whose exploiters' main concern with the local inhabitants is how to be rid of them. Yet the existence and dynamics of provincial enterprise are very relevant to the continuing argument about whether Southeast Asia's capitalist upsurge is 'genuine' or merely a spin-off of East Asian economic energies, and the development of middling nodes of urban life is critical for the region's general prospects for social and political stability.[1]

The contributors to this book have attempted to redress this imbalance by concentrating on the intermediate level of economic, political, and social life – the world of provincial cities and market towns. We have taken Thailand as the locus of our search, in part because that country presents a particularly vivid contrast between images of Southeast Asian stagnation and dynamism. Portrayed only a few years before as the quintessential non-modernizing 'bureaucratic polity', by the 1980s Thailand had transformed itself into the paladin of Southeast Asia's capitalist take-off. In 1997 its economy was the first of the region to crash, and foreign observers have anxiously watched the country's subsequent struggles as auguries for the future of the Asia-Pacific region and the world.

Thailand has also displayed to an extreme degree Southeast Asia's imbalance between capital and provinces, and therefore illustrates the consequences of this sharply. Bangkok is a prototypical primate city, possessing a huge preponderance of the country's wealth and political power. Until quite recently, most Thai towns – they could hardly be called cities – were little more than administrative nodes linking Bangkok to the countryside, and they could scarcely be imagined to have an impact on metropolitan life.[2]

From the mid-1980s, however, the rise of a frequently violent competition for business and political leadership in the Thai provinces, and the growing importance of provincial support for national power-holders, drew attention to the way in which these urban centres were being transformed by capitalist development. The more spectacular competitions of provincial bosses focused attention on lawlessness and excess, but also caused concerned scholars to reflect on its relationship to Thai culture and history, and to look at the economic and social environment in which these leaders flourished. Our volume brings together some of the research inspired by this, drawing on a variety of disciplinary approaches, national backgrounds, and sites of study.

The studies were made before the economic crisis of 1997 and so do not deal with its impact. As I shall argue below, it is unlikely that the downturn – which in any case appeared to abate in 1999 – will radically change the emerging pattern of provincial economic and political power, short of complete social collapse. No doubt, however, it will encourage Thai political and economic entrepreneurs to a less exuberant expression of their power, a process of sobering that was already becoming evident as the newly rich began to seek respectability for themselves and their heirs.

The individual essays in this volume are sufficiently transparent and clearly inter-related that it is not necessary, I think, for me to point out their significance and connection by way of introduction.

What I should like to do instead is to consider some of the questions they raise concerning ideological and social change, and to draw attention to certain consequences of provincial capitalist transformation for the relationship between city and countryside.

OFFICIAL REALITY, LOCAL EXIGENCY

In order to see how Thai provincial society has altered, and why particular expressions of that change have aroused much controversy, we need to examine what might be called the received view of Thai culture and social structure. Until quite recently there was a good deal of agreement between the Thai/Siamese state's own presentation of its society and that portrayed by foreign and domestic academic observers. Both envisioned a bureaucratic elite ruling over but detached from an undifferentiated, autonomous, and generally passive peasantry. The country folk were seen to live largely self-sufficient lives; the market was not absent, but it was far from central to their existence, and it certainly presented no source of authority or goal for ambition.[3]

Villagers were, however, reminded of their subordination to mightier affairs by the presence of nearby exemplary centres. The buildings that contained the government's district (*amphoe*) and provincial offices were both centrally located and symbolically set apart from the rest of the town. The people who worked in them dressed distinctively, in uniforms that emphasized their gradations of rank (and the common people's lack of any). Standard Thai had to be used in official precincts, and the countryman who had only mastered dialect was humiliated and quite possibly ignored if he could not express his needs in the appropriate language. Senior officials were almost always from other areas and were transferred before they developed local roots and interests.

In short, government centres were not user-friendly, nor were they meant to be. They were intended instead to convey the majesty and distance of the state, reminding country folk that they were relatively uncivilized and therefore rightfully without power. Over time government came to offer certain frugal signs of the state's paternal regard, in the form of schools, health centres, and development offices; and better-off villagers had the prospect of attaching themselves to the skirts of state power by gaining enough schooling to become a teacher or member of the local government staff. However, official imagery continued to convey the idea of an absolute gap between state and populace, and stressed that there was no legitimate source of power outside the state and its representatives.

Officials were said to have *amnat,* the power of authority. Non-officials might have at best influence – *itthiphon* – which was inherently illegitimate because power was properly located only in the state. Indeed, the only adjective used to modify *itthiphon* was *muet,* dark, for benign influences were hardly conceivable in a context which viewed influence itself as contesting the authority of the state.[4]

This model of a monolithic, centralized bureaucracy with no gradations between itself and an undifferentiated peasant mass was not the heritage of an ancient Oriental despotism, but a late nineteenth-century ideological construction aimed at denying the very different Siamese political arrangements that had existed prior to King Chulalongkorn's programme of bureaucratic modernization.[5]

Before that reform, Bangkok had related to its subjects through a series of local and regional chiefs, whose power – especially in the peripheral areas of the kingdom – was based as much on local sources of support as on the capital's endorsement. In some areas, particularly the Northeast, prominent families retained popular regard for a long time after their power was broken, and could be seen, in Thailand's fitful experiments with electoral politics, through the appearance of their descendants as champions of local interests.

Seeking to expunge such separate loyalties, the modern Thai state imposed a pattern for official behaviour which both emphasized the state's absolute authority and made it peculiarly hard for officials to relate to what was actually going on at the local level. To prevent officials from engaging in the older system of 'eating' the surplus they had extracted from the populace under their authority rather than subsisting on a centrally provided salary, post-reform Bangkok generally allowed senior officials at the district and provincial levels to stay only a few years in one place. And to keep local attachments from interferring with state exactions, the Ministry of the Interior avoided placing its officials in localities with which they had personal connections.

Compliance with this model left incoming administrators with a problem. They could, of course, go through the rites of office with little regard for what these yielded in terms of popular response; but Bangkok required some evidence of local cooperation. Moreover, the system intended that such officials' incomes would be restricted to their salaries. Unfortunately, government pay was often late and always inadequate.[6] The head of even the smallest bureaucratic empire had to keep his staff content with acts of generosity, since staff co-operation was necessary to his reputation as an effective administrator. He also had to convince his superiors and patrons higher in the bureaucracy that he was a loyal supporter who should be considered for a posting closer to Bangkok. Such reminders were most effectively conveyed through gifts. Consequently, a new official would nearly always find and cultivate local sources of wealth and power, however absent these might be from the official version of things.

The most evident source of local wealth was the marketplace; every district town had one, however humble. This was a covered space devoted to weekly trade, flanked by the shops of the merchants who carried on business in the district. In the provincial and larger district towns the market areas formed a quite substantial 'downtown', which often threatened to deprive the official centre of its social if not architectural pre-eminence. The petty traders in the market were usually Thai, but the merchants in the shops were Sino-Thai or Chinese. Especially after the great influx of Chinese immigrants to the provinces in the 1920s and early 1930s, the Chinese presence in Thai towns was strong enough, and its economic activity significant enough, to give rise to a distinct entrepreneurial sub-culture.[7]

While the shopkeepers' alien customs and insularity set them apart from ordinary Thai, rural folk found them generally much more approachable than government officials. The common people were the shopkeepers' customers, after all, and merchants made an effort to establish relations of trust with their more important clients. Some, particularly rice millers and dealers in local products, provided the closest available approximation of a banking service, and villagers were likely to come to them rather than government officials for assistance in dealing with the wider world.

Merchants and officials in district and provincial towns had an uneasy but symbiotic relationship with one another. They were in tacit competition, for the marketplace and the government complex presented two radically different images of what was right behaviour and what constituted success. For officials, the market and the entrepreneur were always to some degree illegitimate, inasmuch as they implied power outside the state, while to businessmen, the bureaucrats were hindrances and parasites. On the other hand, officials needed money, and businessmen required permits and concessions; and so deals were struck for mutual profit.

Though bureaucrats found in merchants a ready source of wealth, they did not always have the best access to and influence over the population. To secure local compliance, officials therefore had to look to people who were recognized in surrounding communities as sources of leadership.

Thai rural society was not highly stratified, but neither was it as atomized and 'loosely structured' as anthropologists once imagined. As Pasuk and Baker point out below, the historical fluidity and autonomy of Thai rural life meant that it developed leaders of its own, who were largely independent of the state once the old hierarchy of supra-local rulers was ended. People who were natural leaders – or who came from families locally acknowledged as sources of power – offered protection, advice, and sustenance to those who gave them loyalty and labour. The greater a notable's following, the higher his standing; indeed, repute rather than material goods was his acknowledged goal. Such a man might not possess the official authority of *amnat*, but his reputation as a generous patron and counsellor might give him the still higher claim to moral grace, or *barami*.

Such men of prowess – *phu yai* or big men – could achieve official recognition by being elected as *phuyaiban* or village head. The most influential among these might aspire to be chosen by his fellows as *kamnan* or chief of the *tambon* (subdistrict or commune, the village cluster that constituted the highest level of local government). *Phuyaiban* were elected by villagers in open meetings; until the 1970s, when a retirement age was set, they served for life, and the post was frequently handed down within one or two leading families.[8]

It was these acknowledged notables with whom district officials formally dealt. They were rewarded with pay (miniscule at best; at worst, often non-existent), with honour, and most importantly through access to the state bureaucracy. From the officials' point of view, such local chiefs served to convey the government's will to the people; from the popular viewpoint, the headman's duty was to defend local interests against state intrusion. In situations where the financial rewards of local office were few and bureaucratic pressures were increasing, indigenous men of power often preferred to avoid any official recognition and to exercise their influence on a purely private basis. State endorsement was not really necessary for enforcing their will, as they could rely on informal arrangements made with officials, on the network of personal and business relationships that linked locally prominent families, and if need be, on the muscle available from their entourage.

Such leaders' proclaimed concern with repute did not mean they disdained riches; on the contrary, financial power was essential to the accumulation of a following. A patron had to succour his clientele, show generosity, fend off challenges by rivals and officials; and all this required wealth. It was considered a sign of a notable's puissance that resources flowed to him, above all through the labour and gifts of those who were in his debt or sought his favour.It was thought natural that officials seeking local cooperation would first of all offer opportunities for enrichment to such men of influence.

It was by no means unusual for notables to include gangsters among their close following. Law was a matter for the state, not the common people; it was distant, incomprehensible, and generally available only to those who had the right connections and price. The police were quartered in the district and provincial towns; their ventures into the countryside were sporadic and usually punitive or extortionary, and people generally thought it best to stay as far away from them as possible. Justice and protection were not to be found in government and the law but in personal relationships, and local leaders were looked to for this. Social pressure might suffice for enforcement where a community was still compact and unchallenged by outside forces or new ideas, but where a larger arena was involved, a man of influence had to make sure that he commanded his own means of physical enforcement.

Moreover, there was a folk hero's glamour in the traditional idea of the rural tough or *nak leng,* who irreverently flaunted established authority and won out through the strength of his own character. Local big men sometimes cultivated a *nak leng* style to emphasize their dynamism and independence; most famously, the manner was adopted by Field Marshal Sarit Thanarat, whose dictatorship instigated Thailand's turn to free-market capitalism at the beginning of the 1960s.[9] One should not, however, confuse such an assumption of the *nak leng* style with the actual role of the rural tough; real leaders gained their prominence through shrewdness and manipulation rather than muscle.

The *phu yai* pattern presented a third social model, a cultural style and source of power distinct from the bureaucracy and the market. In practice, the boundary was often blurred, especially in areas where urban influences were more strongly felt. Sometimes *phu yai* were officials who had served in the area earlier, established local relationships in spite of state policy, and returned to pursue these connections after their retirement. Others were well-rooted Sino-Thai merchants, who had developed followings which went beyond mere trading clienteles. Where economic resources and activity were greater, men of prowess might establish business and political links which gave them informal control over quite significant territory. In such areas officials might find the only practical – or safe – course of action was to seek a *modus vivendi* with local big men, ceding effective control in return for public acknowledgement of their authority and private financial assistance.

THE ARRIVAL OF SERIOUS MONEY

In the 1950s and 1960s, when foreign advisers and observers began to ponder Thailand's slow pace of economic development and institutional modernization, they did not consider such local networks of power. Accepting the official model, they saw the bureaucracy as the only locus of power, dismissed the merchants as dependent on bureaucratic protection, and characterized the rest of Thai society as 'loosely structured' and passive and therefore incapable of placing collective demands. This view was expressed most influentially in the early 1960s by Fred Riggs, who argued that Thailand was a 'bureaucratic polity', in which all power and political contest were located within officialdom. Businessmen were at best 'pariah capitalists' who depended on the favour of officials. There thus seemed nothing to prevent the continuing bureaucratic exploitation of a society that was no longer traditional but was incapable of modernizing itself.[10]

This conclusion rested on the denial of local and non-bureaucratic networks of power. Moreover, while Riggs was writing, Thailand was changing. Under Field Marshal Sarit, restrictions on the ethnic Chinese were lifted, and private enterprise was given preference over state capitalism. Foreign money began to flow, and with the Vietnam War it became a flood. By the 1970s business confidence and the Bangkok middle class were strong enough to bring down an inept military-bureaucratic regime and to undertake an erratic but continuing experiment with parliamentary democracy.

The 1973 'revolution' was an affair of the capital, but the combination of democracy and rapid capitalist development which it entailed profoundly altered the way power was expressed in the provinces.[11] Democracy opened up a way in which local power could be exercised openly and independently of officialdom, a way by which bureaucrats might be made to heed business interests. Rapid economic expansion raised the stakes of local competition, and also brought the provinces much closer to Bangkok.

Banks were the usual harbingers of capital's advance into the Thai countryside. They were overwhelmingly Bangkok-based, for the Bank of Thailand, as concerned for stability and centralization in the financial sphere as the bureaucracy was in the political, did what it could to discourage banks based on local capital.[12] The Bangkok banks, acknowledging their ignorance of the very different provincial environment, initially copied the old European trading practice of putting their interests in the hands of local agents called *compradores*.[13] They were likely to choose for this role a prominent merchant, whose local knowledge and prestige could secure clients and guarantee their solidity. Or the banks might make arrangements with local men of wealth to form an agency, which used the Bangkok bank's name and credit line but operated more flexibly than could a formal branch. In this way the banks endorsed the financial importance of the marketplace, and the local market-based business and social hierarchy, as well as the continuing importance of personal relations and trust in a society where legal recourse was uncertain and slow.

But Bank of Thailand pressure eventually suppressed these intermediate connections. Only proper Bangkok bank branches would do, and in the 1970s these were to be found even in the more remote district towns. They did not attempt to blend into shopkeeperly familiarity, nor did they erect structures imitating the authoritative solidity of government buildings. Rather, they displayed themselves glamorously, as dream palaces proposing a marvellously different future. Their luxurious forms proclaimed to rural folk that the modern world was within reach, that wealth was the key to prestige and success, and that the bank would help them get it. They thus presented a model of civilization very different from the aloof and hierarchical government complex, the alien but homely bustle of the marketplace, or the personal relationships of village life. Along with the expanding medium of television – and increasingly, in the larger provincial centres, the virtual reality of the shopping mall – they brought the flavour and ideology of capitalist modernization to country folk, and made them feel that the affairs of Bangkok were not wholly alien to their own aspirations.

In other ways, the banks undermined the established power and values of provincial merchant society. For one thing, they offered local people a source of credit other than the dealers in rice or other rural products. These began to lose their social centrality and eventually much of their economic importance. In spite of the banks' overall tendency to siphon money from the provinces towards Bangkok, they made possible, at relatively little cost, a great upsurge in rural production and petty industry. The resulting economic ferment spread the sphere of banking interests well beyond the confines of the old marketplace. Consequently, the order based on personal trust and dependence within the market community began to be replaced by credit arrangements with banks, and financial weight became more important than personal repute. It also meant – since legal redress was still a very uncertain matter – that banks and other businesses found their affairs increasingly entangled with provincial strongmen whose power rested not solely on local wealth and influence but was wielded much more widely, by political as well as economic means.

Such men had long existed, particularly in areas whose resources permitted the extraction of a significant surplus. Often from Sino-Thai merchant families, they used their capital, their entrepreneurial know-how, and connections with officials to build up networks of local *phu yai* through relationships of debt and patronage. But before the 1970s such men of influence were largely invisible to the wider world. They had their arrangements, of course, with men of prominent power, especially military-political leaders, and were pleased to have such personal connections known, for they added to their image as men of influence. However, they generally did not seek to express themselves in public affairs, for there seemed little to be gained by it. Parties – when they were allowed to exist – had been simply the followings of Bangkok-based factions. Parliament had little power to allocate money, and party politics was seen as inherently illegitimate by the bureaucratic-military establishment. Though in some cases provincial intellectuals or the remnants of old elites provided a voice for local aspirations, by and large politicians did little to counter accusations that they served no real representational purpose. Nor was public service particularly rewarding. As we have noted, rural big men often preferred not to hold office as *kamnan* or *phuyaiban* because it made them responsible for enforcing unpopular regulations. In the early 1970s this avoidance of local office was common; but less than two decades later such positions were worth killing for.[14]

What made the difference was money. Some of this flowed into the provinces in the 1970s by virtue of rural development and infrastructure programmes, often in the context of counter-insurgency efforts. Some resulted from the new economic activities made possible by improved transportation and consumer demand. *Tambon* development programmes put funds directly into the hands of commune heads. Village and commune officials could use their contacts with officialdom to get advance knowledge of new roads or other initiatives which they could turn to profit through land purchases or other timely actions. Consequently, local office became something worth fighting for and, as parliamentary power increased, parties became worth joining.

The kind of competition that this generated differed from the Thai bureaucratic elite's factional struggles over the spoils of power, for the provincial contestants did not view office as the be-all and end-all of their struggle. Rather, they saw it as simply one of the means of enhancing wealth generated by political and/or economic entrepreneurship. This resulted in contests which were much more public than the bureaucrats' infighting, and which displayed more openly the raw ingredients of force.

DEMOCRACY AND ENRICHMENT

It was no accident that Thailand's economic expansion was accompanied by the replacement of bureaucratic-military rule with a more open politics. The old system had presented businessmen with a relatively small number of potential patrons from which to seek official permissions, favours, and concessions. Once the economy began to take off, this created a serious bottleneck, especially for new economic actors in the provinces, where the range of potential bureaucratic patrons was limited.[15] Particularly stubborn or greedy officials could make life exceedingly difficult for businessmen, and parliamentary control of the bureaucracy offered a way around this. Parties were an alternative source of patronage, one even more sensitive to local interests and the power of money. Consequently, businessmen cultivated Thailand's frail new flower of democracy (unless, as happened periodically, rising popular demands persuaded them that it had become a noxious weed). Increasingly, businessmen stood for public office themselves.

The most direct and obvious economic advantage to be gained by political participation was the acquisition of preference or monopoly. Public contracts, logging or mining concessions, rights of distribution, and the like were sources of great profit, and they were the particular targets of entrepreneurs whose strength was political as much as economic. Such concessions could be sought by businessmen as goods in themselves, or because they made possible the leap in financial resources necessary for investment in more substantial economic ventures.

The earliest businesses to play a notable part in Thailand's politics were the banks, which supported the sophisticated conservatism of metropolitan finance.[16] By the 1980s, however, it was apparent that banking influence on party politics was being challenged by businessmen whose source of power lay largely in their political involvement and who were for the most part based in the provinces. The election of Chatichai Choonhavan as prime minister in 1988 marked the triumph of the tycoon-turned-politician, and needless to say, it was greeted with some hesitation by Bangkok interests. Their unease grew as state resources underwent a massive transfer to politically connected provincial businessmen, and in early 1991 they backed a military coup as the lesser evil. As LoGerfo recounts below, they soon regretted this decision, but the return to democracy a year later saw a revival of provincially based 'money politics' with all its problems.

One reason why Thailand's recent politics has been perceived as particularly corrupt is that it shifted some of the perquisites of power away from those who had commanded them before. What had seemed to the Bangkok elite a gentlemanly flow of benefits among those fit to rule appeared less legitimate in the hands of crass outsiders. The new politics also directed attention to the way in which power was wielded in the provinces, and focused particularly on strongmen who flourished by manipulation and force. Some of these *chao pho* or 'godfathers' engaged in violent contests for turf, particularly in the 1980s and early 1990s, and they generally showed flamboyant disregard for the law.

The *chao pho* became emblematic of the unacceptable face of Thai capitalism, and as a result have been much discussed by journalists, political reformers, and academics. There has been considerable disagreement in the literature as to just which political-business entrepreneurs should be included in this category, and whether or not they were anything more than predators. Needless to say, opinions on this have differed not least on the basis of the analyst's view of capitalism. However, as we will see in the first essays in this volume, the debate has been most useful in that it has caused scholars to reflect on the historical and social origin of provincial big men.

The *chao pho* are not something that sprang unbidden from Thailand's recent economic upsurge. They are clearly related to the local men of influence, in particular those who combine roles in the market with personal followings.[17] Their presence draws attention to certain persistent facts of Thai life: that patronage is important; that justice and protection are to be found more in personal relationships than in the law. They remind us that officials have high status but may in fact be irrelevant to power, or may wield power but by no means in the interest of the state.

It is often pointed out that *chao pho* engage freely in criminal activity; this is taken by reformers as a sign of their basically illegitimate character. It should also cause us to reflect, however, on the problem of defining the boundary between licit and illicit in terms of the way society functions. What the Thai state declares to be illegal is often understood locally as officialdom laying claim to another source of monopoly. The person wishing to exploit such a resource will gain the complicity of the appropriate officials, and the business goes ahead to mutual profit. For those playing the power game, whether bureaucrats or entrepreneurs, the state's rules do not set boundaries as much as they set the price.

The reasons for the illegality or restriction of a particular activity such as gambling, liquor distribution, prostitution, or the exploitation of forest reserve land may be as opaque to ordinary folk as are most other official requirements. The idea of a civically recognized moral boundary between legal and illegal activity is a middle-class urban notion which still has little meaning in provincial Thailand, and hence a *chao pho*'s engagement in criminal activities does not normally prevent ordinary people from seeking his patronage. Indeed, since the realities of political power have generally overridden considerations of law, national figures have shown themselves as ready as the common folk to ignore them.

Engagement in open violence is often cited as an essential *chao pho* attribute, and certainly it was particularly evident in the mid-1980s to mid-1990s. However, the bloody contests for domination between bosses in that decade reflected less an intrinsic urge to fight than the difficulty of maintaining a monopoly of power in a rapidly evolving economy. After all, a 'godfather' aims at becoming the sole channel for the extraction of significant resources in his area: his companies or his agents must have their take. More people entered the contest for power in the newly booming provinces, and many *chao pho* sought to extend their territorial and extractive reach. But as the dust of competition settled and turfs became more clearly demarcated, open violence between bosses has given way increasingly to pressure on those beneath.

This squeeze was applied in particular to local business. It is businessmen, and the middle class generally, who experience the *chao pho* directly as oppressors, and who are the main source of protest against them. Like the military-bureaucratic patrons of old, the *chao pho* stand athwart economic and political links to the outside world; as the economy develops it becomes increasingly difficult and expensive for entrepreneurs to acknowledge their monopoly. Small businessmen chafe ever more at their extortionary demands; businessmen with greater influence find ways around them. At the same time, the increasing complexity of economic activity makes it more difficult to retain control in a single boss's hand. Most of the great *chao pho* of the past decade have been succeeded by several heirs and managers, running different parts of the empires they constructed. In style and function they are more like other businessmen, inclined to pursue advantage by manipulating law and officials rather than through private acts of violence.

Of course, there is a difference in style and scope between the present-day provincial leadership in Thailand and that prevailing before the country's capitalist take-off. New money, as everywhere, is rough and aggressive, forcing back the boundaries of acceptable behaviour. Cash rather than reputation becomes openly the measure of one's worth. Cash, too, has become the basis of provincial leaders' followings, as money becomes more important in people's lives and political candidates offer more of it to buy their votes.

One effect of this has been virtually to wipe out parliamentary participation by the older sources of provincial leadership and allegiance. The older politicians tended to be ethnic Thai, the newer ones usually Sino-Thai from market backgrounds. The current generation of Sino-Thai provincials is quite assimilated in language and behaviour to the urban Thai model (which, especially in Bangkok, has itself been influenced by overseas Chinese culture), so this has not meant a pronounced cultural shift, but it is a further move away from Thai rurality. Nor has the new power of provincial politicians meant a more equitable distribution of wealth between the capital and the provinces. On the contrary, in the late 1990s the already great disparity was still increasing, and the poorest regions were falling even further behind.[18]

In spite of the new emphasis on money, *chao pho* have frequently displayed themselves as patrons in the old manner, for they know that the qualities of personal loyalty and generosity are still highly valued by country folk. The offering of money to voters is not inconsistent with this, for, as Sombat's essay points out, it is taken as a sign of puissance and largesse appropriate to a man of power. And, as Arghiros illustrates below, there are still businessmen-politicians whose primary goal is local fame, and who therefore promote common interests instead of simply reaping personal advantage. Yet Arghiros also observes a decline of control over votes through personal patronage and employer domination: now money must be offered, and compliance is not certain. This, plus the fact that the cultivation of relations in Bangkok has become more important to local political and business leadership than is the encouragement of local followings and reputation, has meant that men of influence rely less on general patronage and generosity than on their ability to pay well for votes.[19]

Money has thus come to dominate politics at all levels: one must have money to run, and one must make money from office too.[20] All parties in Thailand are now basically business parties, and business leaders consider politics a natural extension of their accumulative efforts. This has made politics exceedingly expensive for the candidates and for society. Vote-buying, even more than pork barrel, has little positive economic benefit (though it may well be the only tangible thing most ordinary provincials receive from their rulers). Such a system can easily become too costly to maintain from the viewpoint of a country's ruling elite, and its leaders may eventually prefer to compose their differences and seek an authoritarian solution. This happened in the Philippines' 1972 exchange of a well-established democracy for dictatorship under Ferdinand Marcos, and it was a strong factor in the Bangkok elite's support for the military coup of 1991.[21]

Needless to say, the financial crash of 1997 greatly concentrated elite minds on the matter. Reformers had already been alarmed by the restoration of unabashed money politics after 1992, which reached its apogee in the administration of Banharn Silpa-archa (1995–1996), the first provincial boss to achieve national leadership. Hopes that the resulting tangle of waste and corruption could be eliminated by a military man's decisiveness fed the rise to power of Gen. Chavalit Yongchaiyudh (1996–1997). However, Chavalit led virtually the same coalition as his predecessor, and his tenure was marked likewise by corruption and inertia. Fundamental reform seemed called for, and the recession gave it urgency. The result was the drafting of a new constitution and electoral system, aimed at increasing the honesty and accountability of rule.[22]

The ever-available alternative to democratic reform, viz. dictatorship, is hardly an ideal solution to the money–politics dilemma, for – as the 1991–1992 junta showed – military-bureaucratic power-holders have considerable appetites of their own, and authoritarianism revives the problem of too many business interests pursuing too few sources of patronage. The alternative, within a capitalist system, is to persuade the populace that its interests are served less by cash handouts than by good government and rational development policies, and to provide political leaders who credibly pursue these goals. As can be imagined, this is far easier said than done, not least because an emerging popular consciousness of the possibility of responsible government may result in policy demands that the metropolitan elite finds far from rational.

Keeping the Prize

If all Thai political parties are now business parties, in the sense that they depend financially on business support and frequently put up businessmen as candidates, this does not mean that they reflect alternatives among business interests or particular development strategies. Rather, the parties accumulate business support wherever they can, as part of their general effort to gain financing and influence. Prominent business leaders, and also political business entrepreneurs such as *chao pho,* distribute their favours according to which party seems to offer personally the greatest advantage, and they show no hesitation in switching allegiances. Consequently, the system yields high individual rewards at the cost of overall effectiveness and strategic choice. Although it includes far more businessmen in the power game than did military-bureaucratic rule, it has in important respects simply opened up the pool of patronage without really abandoning old principles.

One way for businessmen to cut the costs of politicking and ensure that their strategic interests are reflected in government policy is to pursue sectoral concerns through business associations and lobbies. There has already been a significant national-level formation of such groups, and analysts have discerned in this an important step away from a patronage-based system towards a more democratic contest of interests.[23] At the national level, increased business specialization and international linkages mean that the need for such association is particularly clear. However, the studies in this collection show little sign of such an evolution in the provinces.

This is not because there is no precedence for provincial businessmen to organize around collective interests: Arghiros describes such an association, noting that it developed in part from a rotating credit society, a long-established means of raising capital among small businessmen and householders in Southeast Asia. None the less, his brickmakers' association soon evolved into a springboard for individual political ambitions rather than the representative of collective sectoral interests. Similarly, the provincial chamber of commerce described by Montesano defines its goals very vaguely and seems to serve principally as a vehicle for its leaders. Ueda's Khorat entrepreneurs have organized into political-business clubs, which concentrate on situating their members advantageously in the existing patronage system.

Other analysts have seen the best chance for political and economic reform to lie in the developing role of the middle class. As elsewhere in Southeast Asia, the Thai 'middle class' is imagined to be a group of increasing significance, but there is little agreement as to its composition. Most commentators have taken the attitudes of intellectuals, professionals, and students as the benchmark, however these may in fact relate to the ideas of small and medium businessmen, lesser bureaucrats and military officers, white-collar employees, and others who might be subsumed in the category.[24] The operative term seems to be 'middle' rather than 'class', the idea being to include those who neither command the politico-economic heights nor are part of the uneducated mass. Thus modern-minded farmers and highly skilled workers are sometimes counted as reflecting middle-class attitudes in spite of their 'blue-collar' employment.

The assumption of such analysis is that as economic structures grow more complex, and educational and technical requirements increase, those in the intermediate economic and social levels will become consciousness of interests which separate them from those at the top, even if they are engaged in the same sectoral pursuit. The middle class, it is commonly thought, will want to open out participation in political decision-making and ultimately to establish a 'civil society' that is not dominated by the state but supervises it.

Although the middle class, even defined at its broadest, is hardly well developed in the Thai provinces, it has shown much more vitality there than have business associations. LoGerfo's contribution to this volume shows how middle-class groups mobilized in the context of the 1992 overthrow of authoritarian rule. Clearly, much of their energy and unity came from the moment, and most of them sank into apathy once their immediate goals were achieved. None the less, they arose from and extrapolated on networks of provincial reformist opinion, and undoubtedly the experience laid the basis for a greater sense of unity and purpose among them.

In addition, the 1992 events emphasize the fact that what counts in the construction of power is not just wealth, following, and political connections, but also ideological flow. Certain expectations begin to form concerning the proper goals of society and the acceptable ways of pursuing them; these may be influenced by economic interest and/or international fashion, but the important thing is that key segments of political opinion come to think of them as valid. Groups that act for these ideals against a regime widely thought to have deviated from them are likely to find support.

Of course, short of truly massive disaffection, such backing is likely to be conditional on not rocking the boat of interests too vigorously – the 1976 rejection of democracy by those who feared it would overturn the social order gave a bloody reminder of this. As if still traumatized by the experience, Thai social and political reformers have since proceeded cautiously in their public manifestations, eschewing the mobilization of the lower classes.

Indeed, mass participation in decision-making is not seen as particularly desirable by most middle-class Thai provincials: what they want is 'good government', not democracy for its own sake.[25] 'Good' means competent and honest, and needless to say, the identification of Thai democracy with venality has done little to convince people of a necessary connection between good government and democracy.[26] Although the new basic law was proclaimed to be a 'people's constitution', the electoral reforms accompanying it betrayed a middle-class preference for good government over popular participation.[27]

Implicit in the reformers' efforts to achieve a transition from patronage-based centralism to 'good government' under Thai capitalism is a drive towards the cultural consolidation of the political and economic elite. At present there is a very visible gap between new money and old, provincial and metropolitan, 'pure' entrepreneur, political businessman of prowess, bureaucrat, and professional. The result is a fluid and colourful but not particularly convincing or dynamic style of rule. If the mass of the population is to be persuaded that those in command have a natural right to govern them, they will have to be confronted with a more homogeneous and authoritative ruling class.

In some respects this upgrading is already underway. The electoral reforms imply a more culturally coherent representative body in their search for rule, if not by the great and the good, at least by the educated and respectable. It is generally agreed that the *chao pho* are a temporary phenomenon, the product of a 'Wild West' phase of Thailand's development. They or their children will seek financial and social security by integration into the respectable elite. If, as Sombat reminds us in his essay, there will always be ambitious followers ready to replace them, it is very likely that as Thai capitalist society becomes more solidly established, these less presentable exponents will be tastefully hidden in the underworld.

Capitalist consolidation is also likely to lead to a new *modus vivendi* between bureaucracy and business. In spite of the decline in bureaucrats' importance as patrons, the state's reach into society is increasing, and at the same time its rules are being changed to accommodate business interests. It is no longer as easy for an entrepreneur simply to ignore regulations, and by the same token it becomes more important for him to see that regulations and regulators suit his interests.[28] Ultimately, therefore, greater cooperation between businessmen in the form of sectoral associations and lobbies would seem likely, in spite of their present weakness in the provinces, and with it a relationship between bureaucracy and business based as much on institutional as personal ties. Quite possibly, fewer entrepreneurs will seek to appear as politicians themselves: Hewison and Maniemai's progressive young businessmen look upon the hurly-burly of Thai political life with some disdain, though no doubt they would consider the discreet influencing of political decisions in their favour to be a valid business activity rather than political involvement.

All things remaining equal (as they seldom do), it seems probable that greed and violence will be exercised more discreetly in the getting of riches, and will be mediated by the law and the state. The general impulse for elite coherence is certainly there: new money desires to become old, provincials seek metropolitan sophistication, all wish to safeguard the exclusivity of their privileges and ensure their children's inheritance.

The increasing coherence of the business and political elite carries its own dangers, however. In particular, it widens the gap between Thailand's haves and have-nots. The gradual replacement of patronage by monetary relationships, the education of *chao pho* heirs, and the eventual prospect of reliance on control over law rather than control over followings makes it more difficult and less necessary for those in the upper reaches of society to relate to those below. At the same time, industrialization and the improvement in communications and education mean that the passivity of the mass of the population can no longer be taken for granted. In the end, not only the middle class but also the great mass of common folk are experiencing change and will respond to it.

The recession that began in mid–1997 will no doubt reveal to what extent Thai provincial capitalism's vitality is its own or depends on pork barrel and excess capital from outside. At the time of writing, the impact of the crash on the provinces is far from clear, but we can be sure it has brought severe business hardship. With the demise of the high-flying days of easy money, spectacular displays of wealth and patronage are less possible. They are also less necessary, for the new uncertainty reminds people that they have no other real insurance than their ties to a man of power. Patron–client networks are likely to become more important in the crisis, and it will cost less for leaders to maintain a client's loyalty.

The drying-up of metropolitan investment and pork barrel may bring a greater reliance on local sources of funding and support, and an increased consciousness of interests separating entrepreneurs in the provinces from the capital. The failure of economically weaker and politically dependent businesses should also lead to a consolidation of entrepreneurship in more powerful provincial hands. Assuming the recession is neither so long nor so deep as to bring a general collapse, it should result in a more self-confident provincial capitalism, conscious of its interests and able to assert them against Bangkok. Certainly, a vigorous and locally oriented provincial entrepreneurship is an important element in bridging the gap between metropolis and countryside, rulers and mass. However, this will not in itself guarantee that popular interests will be served, the more so since, if only the most powerful provincial capitalists survive the crisis, they may well see their future advantage in cementing ties with Bangkok rather than continuing to champion local needs.

Thailand at the end of the twentieth century is undergoing a structural and ideological reorganization as momentous as that which took place at the end of the nineteenth. Then, we remember, Siam drastically reconfigured its principles of rule, in the name of modernization and effective government. King Chulalongkorn was able to put through his changes, after a long and bitter struggle, only because the thinking of Siam's elite had been transformed by the impact of global change from the early years of the nineteenth century. Four decades after Chulalongkorn's reform, the royal absolutism that had been its central goal was toppled by the modern bureaucratic-military elite that had been created as royalty's main instrument. Another four decades, and bureaucratic rule was itself overthrown as an obstacle on Thailand's road to good government and modernity.

There is no reason to suppose that the order that is now emerging will not itself come to seem archaic, the enemy of future visions of modernity and proper rule. Indeed, the new system may not last long. It is, after all, very narrowly based. It ignores the still-numerous peasantry, the emergent urban working class, the claims and opportunities of religion. Its culture is a Sino-Thai and Western version of Thai-ness, alien to the vast part of the population. Its emphasis on material success and its involvement in the global economy make it very vulnerable to hard times, as the current crash is demonstrating; and democracy's egalitarianism beds uncomfortably with capitalism's inequity. The extent to which the new Thai order succeeds in making itself central to the way in which the Thai people imagine their world will depend very much on how it is mediated by those who shape it in the provinces. The essays that comprise this volume will help to reveal the character of this elite, and the background against which it is acting to transform the Thai nation.

NOTES

1. For arguments on the superficiality of Southeast Asian capitalist development, see especially Yoshihara Kunio, *The Rise of Ersatz Capitalism in South-East Asia* (Singapore: Oxford University Press, 1988); also Yoshihara, 'The Ethnic Chinese and Ersatz Capitalism in Southeast Asia', in Leo Soeryadinata (ed.), *Southeast Asia and China: The Politico-Cultural Dimension* (Singapore: Times Academic Press, 1995), pp. 66–86; James Clad, *Behind the Myth: Business, Money and Power in Southeast Asia* (London: Unwin Hyman, 1989).

2. See Yoko Ueda's chapter below for the relative sizes of Thai urban centres. As late as the early 1970s the Bangkok/Thonburi population was thirty times larger than that of the largest provincial town: Visid Prachuabmoh and John Knodel, 'The Longitudinal Study of Social, Economic, and Demographic Changes in Thailand: Review of Findings', *Asian Survey* 14 (1974): 350–363.

3. For critiques of this approach, see Katherine A. Bowie, 'Unraveling the Myth of the Subsistence Economy: Textile Production in Nineteenth Century Northern Thailand', *Journal of Asian Studies* 51 (1992): 77–82; Benedict R. O'G. Anderson, 'Studies of the Thai State: The State of Thai Studies', in Eliezer B. Ayal (ed.) *The Study of Thailand* (Athens: Ohio University Papers in International Studies, 1978), pp. 193–247. Studies of life between the village and the state were striking for their absence: research on market towns only got underway in the 1960s.

4. See the essays by Pasuk and Baker, Sombat, and Ockey below; and Yoshifumi Tamada, 'Itthiphon and Amnat: Informal Aspect of Thai Politics', *Tonan Ajia Kenkyu* 28 (1991): 455–466. For efforts to indoctrinate rural Thai into the state's view, see Charles F. Keyes, 'The Proposed World of the School: Thai Villagers' Entry into a Bureaucratic State System', in

Charles F. Keyes (ed.) *Reshaping Local Worlds: Formal Education for Cultural Change in Rural Southeast Asia* (New Haven: Yale University Southeast Asia Studies, 1991), pp. 89–130; Peter Vandergeest, 'Constructing Thailand: Regulation, Everyday Resistance, and Citizenship', *Comparative Studies in Society and History* 35 (1993): 133–159; Bruce Missingham, 'Local Bureaucrats, Power and Participation: A Study of Two Village Schools in the Northeast', in Kevin Hewison (ed.) *Political Change in Thailand. Democracy and Participation* (London: Routledge, 1997), pp. 149–162.

5. For the principles of the older Thai system, see Stanley J. Tambiah, 'The Galactic Polity', in S. J. Tambiah, *World Conqueror and World Renouncer* (Cambridge: Cambridge University Press, 1976), pp. 102–131; for pre-reform practice see Akin Rabibhadana, 'Clientship and Class Structure in the Early Bangkok Period', in W. William Skinner and A. Thomas Kirsch (eds). *Change and Persistence in Thai Society* (Ithaca: Cornell University Press, 1975), pp. 93–124. For Chulalongkorn's reforms, see Tej Bunnag, *The Provincial Administration of Siam 1892–1915* (Kuala Lumpur: Oxford University Press, 1977); David K. Wyatt, *The Politics of Reform in Thailand* (New Haven: Yale University Press, 1969); Michael Vickery, 'Thailand's Regional Elites and the Reforms of King Chulalongkorn', *Journal of Asian Studies* 29 (1970): 863–881.

6. Pasuk Pongphaichit and Chris Baker remind me (personal communication) that this was not always the case. Prior to the Second World War, top bureaucrats were very well paid, and especially in the provinces counted as rich men. However, official salaries underwent very little change in the postwar years, with the result that officials became increasingly dependent on acquiring unofficial sources of income.

7. See the essays by Montesano and Ueda in this volume; also Michael Montesano, 'Thap Thieng and the Wider World: Six Decades of Entrepreneurship and Economic Change in Trang Town', in Amara Pongsapich *et al. (eds) Entrepreneurship and Socio-Economic Transformation in Thailand and Southeast Asia (*Bangkok: Chulalongkorn University Social Science Research Institute, 1994), pp. 307–321; Chester F. Galaska, 'Continuity and Change in Dalat Plu, a Chinese Middle Class Business Community in Thailand' (diss., Syracuse University, 1969); Preecha Kuwinpant, 'Marketing and the Management of Personal Relations in Wang Thong', in Han ten Brummelhuis and Jeremy Kemp (eds), *Strategies and Structures in Thai Society* (Amsterdam: University of Amsterdam Antropologisch-Sociologisch Centrum, 1984), pp. 139–152; Amara Pongsapich, 'Social Processes and Social Structures in Chonburi Thailand', *Journal of the Siam Society* 44 (1976): 207–236; Chakrit Noranitipadungkarn, *Elites, Power Structures and Politics in Thai Communities* (Bangkok: NIDA Research Center, 1970); Stephen F. Tobias, 'Chinese Religion in a Thai Market Town' (diss., University of Chicago, 1973); Maria Christina Blanc Szanton, 'People in Movement: Mobility and Leadership in a Central Thai Town' (diss., Columbia University, 1982). For the background to Chinese settlement in Thailand, see G. William Skinner,

Chinese Society in Thailand: An Analytical History (Ithaca: Cornell University Press, 1957).

8. For a discussion of *phu yai* and other concepts of informal rank and repute, see Navavan Bandhamadha, 'Reflections on Thai Society from a Language Point of View', *Proceedings of the International Conference on Thai Studies* , vol. 2 (Canberra: Australian National University, 1987), pp. 231–240. For the general importance of men of prowess in Southeast Asia, see O. W. Wolters, *History, Culture and Region in Southeast Asian Perspective* (Singapore: Institute of Southeast Asian Studies, 1982). For discussions of its expression in patronage systems, see Lucien M. Hanks, 'The Thai Social Order as Entourage and Circle', in G. William Skinner and A. Thomas Kirsch (eds), *Change and Persistence in Thai Society* (Ithaca: Cornell University Press, 1975), pp. 172–196; Edward Van Roy, *Economic Systems of Northern Thailand: Structure and Change* (Ithaca: Cornell University Press, 1971); Gehan Wijeyewardene, 'Patrons and Pau Liang', *Journal of the Siam Society* 54 (1971): 229–234; R. A. Hall, 'Middlemen in the Politics of Rural Thailand: A Study of Articulation and Cleavage', *Modern Asian Studies* 14 (1980): 441–464; Ruth McVey, 'Change and Consciousness in a Southern Countryside', in Han ten Brummelhuis and Jeremy Kemp (eds), *Strategies and Structures* (Amsterdam: University of Amsterdam Antropologisch-Sociologisch Centrum, 1984), pp. 109–137.

9. For the role of the *nak leng*, see David B. Johnston, 'Bandit, Nak Leng and Peasant in Rural Thai Society', *Contributions to Asian Studies* 15 (1980): 90–101. The description of the *kamnan* in Lauriston Sharp and Lucien Hanks, *Bang Chan: Social History of a Rural Community in Thailand* (Ithaca: Cornell University Press, 1978), pp. 106–118, is a good example of the manner. For Field Marshal Sarit's assumption of the style, see Thak Chaloemtiarana, *Thailand: The Politics of Despotic Paternalism* (Bangkok: Social Science Association of Thailand and the Thai Kadi Foundation, 1979).

10. Fred W. Riggs, *Thailand: The Modernization of a Bureaucratic Polity* (Honolulu: The East-West Center Press, 1966); the concept of Thai 'loosely-structured society' had been proposed by the anthropologist John Embree in 1950. See also Norman Jacobs, *Modernizaton without Development: Thailand as an Asian Case Study* (New York: Praeger, 1971); William J. Siffin, *The Thai Bureaucracy: Institutional Change and Development* (Honolulu: The East-West Center Press, 1966). However, a far more complex relationship between business and military leaders was shown earlier by G. William Skinner in his magisterial study of *Leadership and Power in the Chinese Community of Thailand* (Ithaca: Cornell University Press, 1958). See also Clark Neher, 'A Critical Analysis of Research on Thai Politics and Bureaucracy', *Asian Thought and Society* 2 (1977): 13–27. The assumptions of the bureaucratic polity concept are far from dead, however; we can see some of them in Krirkkiat Phipatseritham and Yoshihara Kunio, 'Thailand: Industrialization without Development', *East Asian Cultural Studies* 28 (1989): 91–100.

11. For the politics of this period, see David Morell and Chai-anan Samudavanija, *Political Conflict in Thailand* (Cambridge, Mass.: Oelgeschlager, Gunn & Hain, 1981) and John L. S. Girling, *Thailand: Society and Politics* (Ithaca: Cornell University Press, 1981).

12. Yoko Ueda, 'The Development of Commercial Banking and Financial Business in the Provinces of Thailand', *Tonan Ajia Kenkyu* 31 (1994): 385–411.

13. The Thai word is a transliteration of the original Portuguese. See the essays by Ueda and Montesano below; also Alek A. Rozental, 'Branch Banking in Thailand', *Journal of the Developing Areas* 3 (1968): 37–50.

14. Benedict Anderson, 'Murder and Progress in Modern Siam', *New Left Review* 181 (1990): 33–48.

15. There is a good discussion of this problem in Somrudee Nicro-wattanayingyong, 'Development Planning, Politics, and Paradox: A Study of Khon Kaen, a Regional City in Northeast Thailand' (diss., Syracuse University, 1991).

16. For the development of the Thai banking elite and its political role, see Kevin Hewison, *Bankers and Bureaucrats* (New Haven: Yale University Southeast Asia Studies, 1989); Suehiro Akira, *Capital Accumulation in Thailand 1855–1985* (Tokyo: Center for East Asian Cultural Studies, 1989), pp. 245–265; Phanni Bualek, *Wikhro naithun thanakhan phanit khong thai* (Bangkok: Songsan, 1986).

17. Indeed, the historian Nidhi Aeusrivongse has applied the term *chao pho* to all local men of prowess whose power rested on their ability to control local resources Nidhi Aeusrivongse, 'Chao pho withya kap khwam plianplaeng', in Nidhi Aeusrivongse (ed). *Song na sangkhom thai* (Bangkok: Phuchatkan, 1996), pp. 105–108. Nidhi's *chao pho* are those I have described earlier as local 'big men', whose power rests on their ability to monopolize the extraction of local surplus. They frequently hold the post of *kamnan* and are often in a debt/patronage relationship to a *tauke* (prominent businessman, usually a Sino-Thai merchant), who provides them with financial backing and market connections. With the modernization of the Thai economy and communications, such *tauke* patrons began to take a more direct role in controlling local resources, effectively making themselves into provincial *chao pho* and reducing the local strongmen to the role of their agents. Nidhi stressed that ordinary folk did not necessarily experience the *chao pho's* domination as oppressive, because that leader provided something in the way of protection and charity, matters of great importance to people with no other hope of support or justice. For a similar vision, see Van Roy's description of *pho liang* patrons in his *Economic Systems of Northern Thailand.*

18. Ueda, 'The Development of Commercial Banking', argues that in spite of official encouragement of banks to invest in provincial enterprises, their net effect has been to channel investment from the provinces to the

capital. Nipon Poaponsakorn and Belinda Fuller, 'Industrial Location Policy in Thailand: Industrial Decentralization or Industrial Sprawl', in Mayusama Seichi, Donna Vanderbrink, and Chia Siouw Yue (eds), *Industrial Policies in East Asia* (Tokyo/Singapore: Nomura Research Institute/Institute of Southeast Asian Studies, 1997), pp. 145–184, show that in spite of government policies designed to encourage industries to develop outside the metropolitan area, and growing congestion in that region, businesses continue to concentrate around the capital. They argue that the need to gain permissions and to influence decision-making in Bangkok is so important for businessmen that it overrides any other considerations.

19. The relationship between vote-buying, political patronage, and patron–client relationships is lucidly discussed in Daniel Arghiros, *Political Structures and Strategies; a Study of Electoral Politics in Contemporary Rural Thailand* (Hull: University of Hull Centre for South-East Asian Studies Occasional Paper No. 31, 1995).

20. For vote-buying see Eiji Murashima, 'Local Elections and Leadership in Thailand: A Case Study of Nakhorn Sawan Province', *The Developing Economies* 25 (1987): 363–385; William A. Callahan and Duncan McCargo, 'Vote-Buying in Thailand's Northeast', *Asian Survey* 26 (1996): 376–392; Sombat Chantornvong, *Leuktang wikrit: panha lae thang ok* (Bangkok: Kopfai, 1993); Anusorn Limmanee, *Political Business Cycle in Thailand, 1979–1992: General Election and Currency in Circulation* (Bangkok: Institute of Thai Studies, Chulalongkorn University, 1995), pp. 5–8; Arghiros, *Political Structures and Strategies.* Compare R.A. Hall's discussion in 'Middlemen in the Politics of Rural Thailand: A Study of Articulation and Cleavage', *Modern Asian Studies* 14 (1980): 441–464. Writing before the great expansion of Thai capitalism and money politics, Hall noted that members of parliament did not play an important role as mediators between the populace and the elite, and suggested that this was because parliament had too limited a role and low a reputation for ordinary people to look to its members as patrons; parliament's quality and power would therefore have to be strengthened (p. 459). Studies of recent politics indicate that parliament's power has little to do with voting choice. People vote for leaders who are already their patrons by virtue of vote-buying or more substantial ties. What such patrons do in parliament is assumed to be in their own interest, though of course local allies and followers will be encouraged by any pork barrel the politician cares to redistribute.

21. Anusorn Limmanee, *Political Business Cycle in Thailand* (Bangkok: Institute of Thai Studies, Chulalongkorn University, 1995) describes the pattern of a steep rise in currency circulating in periods just before elections between 1986 and 1992, and attributes this to the large demand for notes of small denominations for vote-buying purposes. Vote-buying was generally thought to have been even more significant in the 1995 election; see David Murray, 'The 1995 National Elections in Thailand', *Asian Survey* 36 (1996): 361–375. Arghiros, *Political Structures and Strategies* (p. 37), notes that in the

Central Thai district where he did field research, local banks ran out of 50-baht notes (the then standard payment for votes) in a 1990 *tambon* election. In elections to the provincial council, a candidate spent 120,000 baht in 1985, but had to fork out 750,000 in 1990 and 3,000,000 in 1995 (p. 59).

22. While the 1997/98 reforms promised radical change, they were not without precedent. In response to unrest in the outlying regions, both the democratic governments of 1973–1976 and Prem's long regime of the 1980s promoted rural development programmes aimed at reducing agrarian disaffection. There was, moreover, a growing feeling among the elite that Bangkok's overwhelming dominance of decision-making was in itself old-fashioned and inefficient, and this lent powerful support to the proponents of democratization. Initially, the Ministry of the Interior managed to emasculate decentralizing initiatives or employ them to its own advantage in competing with other bureaucratic hierarchies. It was able to limit the provincial councils' authority largely to the granting of public works contracts (which, however, was what local businessmen-politicians were most interested in, and which meant the bureaucrats' loss of a prime source of patronage). The 1994 establishment of *tambon* councils promised to make the first real dent in the Ministry's power over local government, but its effects were scarcely visible before the even more radical changes called for by the constitutional reforms of 1997–1998. Such was the ideological impetus for decentralization as the key to good, modern government that the Ministry found it could not fight the reforms directly, and it settled instead for what promises to be a long campaign of footdragging. See Michael H. Nelson, 'Comparative Decentralization: Some Observations on Sub-national Governance in Thailand, France, Germany, and the United Kingdom' (paper presented to the Department of Government, Chulalongkorn University, June 1998), pp. 3–25.

23. See especially Anek Laothamatas, *Business Associations and the New Political Economy of Thailand: From Bureaucratic Capitalism to Liberal Corporatism* (Singapore: Institute for Southeast Asian Studies, 1992) and Anek, 'From Clientelism to Partnership: Business–Government Relations in Thailand ', in MacIntyre (ed.), *Business and Government* , pp. 195–215 ; also Richard F. Doner, 'The Limits of State Strength: Toward an Institutionalist View of Economic Policy', *World Politics* 44 (1992): 398–431. For a critical view, Kevin Hewison, 'Liberal Corporatism and the Return of Pluralism in Thai Political Studies', *Asian Studies Review* 16 (1992): 261–265.

24. For views of the middle class, see Surin Maisrikrod, 'The Making of Thai Democracy: A Study of Political Alliance among the State, the Capitalists, and the Middle Class', in Anek Laothamatas (ed.), *Democratization in Southeast and East Asia* (Singapore/Bangkok: Institute of Southeast Asian Studies/Chulalongkorn University Social Science Research Institute, 1997), pp. 141–166; Sungsidh Piriyarangsan and Pasuk Phongpaichit (eds), *Chon chan klang bon krasae prachathibotai thai* (Bangkok: Chulalongkorn University Political Economy Center, 1993); Kevin Hewison, 'Emerging Social Forces in

Thailand: New Political and Economic Roles', in Richard Robison and David S. G. Goodman (eds), *The New Rich in Asia* (London: Routledge, 1996), pp. 137–162; Richard Doner and Anek Laothamatas, 'Thailand: Economic and Political Gradualism', in Stephen Haggard and Steven Webb (eds) *Voting for Reform: Democracy, Political Liberalization, and Economic Adjustment* (Oxford: Oxford University Press/The World Bank, 1994); Richard Robison, *The Emergence of the Middle Class in Southeast Asia* (Murdoch WA: Murdoch University Asia Research Centre, 1995).

25. Jim LoGerfo, this volume, and in 'Attitudes toward Democracy among Bangkok and Rural Northern Thais', *Asian Survey* 36 (1996): 904–923. Hewison, 'Emerging Social Forces in Thailand', likewise emphasizes middle-class preference for effectiveness and stability above democracy.

26. For a discussion of the problem, see Pasuk Phongpaichit and Sungsidh Piriyaransan (eds) *Corruption and Democracy in Thailand* (Bangkok: Chulalongkorn University Political Economic Center, 1994).

27. These required, for example, that all members of parliament have university degrees. It was argued that this stricture would remove the *chao pho* from the parliamentary scene. In practice it was likely simply to hasten the trend for bosses to substitute their offspring or other educated placemen. The 1998 reforms also aimed to increase the accountability of MPs by replacing the system of multi-member constituencies with smaller, single-member ones. To ensure that candidates to electoral office were beholden neither to the bureaucracy nor to criminal bosses, considerable effort was devoted to establishing a hierarchy of electoral vetting committees, whose members were to be educated, financially independent, and free of the taint of corruption. Needless to say, this ensured they would come from the middle (or upper) class.

28. The point is made in Nidhi Aeusrivongse, 'Chao pho withya', p. 108. James Ockey, 'Thai Society and Patterns of Political Leadership', *Asian Survey* 36 (1996): 345–360, observes a recent shift in Thai politicians' manner from the *nak leng* style to that of the *phu di,* or gentleman. We may imagine that this is part of the capitalist elite's gentrification.

TWO

Chao Sua, *Chao Pho*, *Chao Thi*: Lords of Thailand's Transition

Pasuk Phongpaichit and Chris Baker

In a 1990 article, Ben Anderson noted that the increase of gangland-style murders from around 1978 onwards signalled an important change in Thailand's provincial economy and society. New fortunes were being made. New men were emerging. New and violent methods were being used to determine the local allocation of power.[1] Through the 1980s and early 1990s, the emergence of the provincial boss, or *chao pho*, was one of the most prominent features of Thai politics – widely discussed in the press, in academic debate, and among the politicians themselves.[2] This essay sets the rise of these new men into the context of a broader political economy.

As Anderson noted, the rise of the *chao pho* was bound up with the transition from a rural to an industrial economy, and from military rule to representative democracy. In 1970, Thailand was still predominantly an agrarian society; four-fifths of the population lived in the countryside. Agricultural production was double that of industry, and over half of all exports were agricultural crops. By the mid-1990s, however, Thailand had become a proto-industrial country. The manufacturing sector produced three times the value of agriculture, and the principal exports were computer and electronic parts.

Political transition ran parallel to this economic transformation. For almost half a century, from the 1930s to the 1980s, the military had dominated Thai politics. Even though parliamentary institutions were introduced after the 1932 revolution, civilian governments responsible to an elected parliament operated for only two short periods (1944–1947 and 1975–1976). For the remainder of the time, the parliament was either controlled through appointees, intimidated into submission, or disposed of completely. In the 50 years following 1938, a military man occupied the post of prime minister for all but eight years.

After 1979, however, the military's domination waned. An elected parliament lasted 12 years without disruption, establishing for the first time some institutional permanence. An attempt by the military to restore a measure of dominance by coup in 1991 was reversed 15 months later by a popular rising. The office of prime minister slipped gradually out of military hands. Prem Tinsulanonda (1980–1988) was a true military man. Chatichai Choonhavan (1988–1991) had a general's rank but was more businessman than soldier. Chuan Leekpai (1992–1995, 1997–) had no military connections and belonged to the political party with the longest record of opposing military rule. And Banharn Silpa-archa (1995–1996) was a proto-typical provincial businessman-politician. The election of November 1996 brought back to the premiership a retired general, Chavalit Yongchaiyudh, who clearly hankered after the good old days of military rule. But his parliamentary troops, drawn from the ranks of provincial businessmen-politicians, held his praetorian ambitions in check. When he tried to declare a state of emergency to suppress middle-class street protests, the military command refused to cooperate and told him to resign.[3]

The succession to military rule has involved a complex interplay between three major players on the political scene: the established Bangkok business interests with roots going back to the rice, export, and import trades of the 1940s; rising provincial businessmen, many of whom made rapid fortunes from the 1970s onwards through buccaneering methods; and the mass of the peasantry. We shall attempt below to understand the forces and relationships of this triangle in the context of Thailand's transition from an agrarian to an industrial economy.

CHAO SUA: METROPOLITAN BUSINESS AND POLITICS

The rise of Bangkok big business dates from the 1940s. Until that decade, large corporate enterprises were very few: the Siam Cement works, a soap factory, the Boonrawd brewery, and a handful of match factories. The city's major commercial activity, the rice trade, was prone to sharp fluctuations that had wrecked several successive trading dynasties and disrupted the steady accumulation of capital. Bangkok was packed with small shops, workshops, and service businesses. Thai domestic capitalism was stuck at the shophouse stage.[4] Business leaders had supported the 1932 revolution; they wanted more access to political power so that they could orient government policy more in favour of business growth. But after the revolution they were brushed aside by the soldiers, for in this period, they did not yet have the wealth or the numbers to contest for power.[5]

From the 1940s this changed, mainly as the result of three factors. First, colonial enterprise retreated against the background of depression, war, and decolonization, opening up new opportunities in trade, import substitution, and services. Second, from the Korean War boom onwards, Thailand's economy was towed along by the long cycle of growth and trade expansion in the West. Third, in the late 1950s, the Thai government formally resolved to expand the domestic economy by assisting urban enterprise through promotional policies, infrastructure investments, and appropriate macro-management.

The nature of Thailand's urban growth in this post-war phase was shaped by the banks and the country's rulers. Until the 1940s, the capital market had been dominated by foreign banks and had remained very poorly developed. During the Second World War, when the foreign banks were dormant, a handful of small business combines in the city formed new banks. Over the ensuing years, these banks attracted the deposits of thousands of small traders and shopkeepers, and these assets provided a source of capital to found urban enterprises on a larger scale than was previously possible. The three major banking groups themselves floated hundreds of companies to exploit the new opportunities opening up in the post-war economy. Each also attracted a small coterie of friends and associates who deployed the bank's capital into other ventures. Easily the most successful of these groups was that clustered around the Bangkok Bank. The bank grew its asset base at a sustained average annual rate of 20 per cent over 20 years, took a one-third share of the entire banking market, and financed around a third of all overseas trade. Its associates forged into all the leading sectors of the economy from the rice trade, through agribusiness, to textiles, auto assembly, and real estate.[6]

At the same time, Thailand's military rulers came to play a large role in allocating access to economic opportunities. From the 1930s to the 1950s, they followed a policy of state capitalism that effectively allowed them to license and promote selected entrepreneurs, who invested in joint ventures with government capital.[7] From the 1950s, they established a framework of licensing and investment promotion that again allowed them considerable powers of favouritism. On top of these formal systems, the rulers also developed many informal ways of promoting business through political power and patronage: by allocating government contracts, protecting illegal activities such as the drugs trade, selling off state monopolies, and undermining competitors.

In this period, the key axis of the urban political economy ran between the First Army headquarters and the Bangkok Bank. Spectacular success in the growing urban economy was reserved for the small number of business groups that clustered around this axis, or around lesser centres associated with other banks and political figures. Virtually all of these successful groups were of Chinese-immigrant origin. Most were second or third generation, but a few had arrived in the last wave of emigration from China between the onset of world depression and China's 1949 revolution. A few had established some business success in the pre-war period, particularly in the last growth cycle of the rice economy. Most, however, started the move from shophouse to conglomerate during the 1940s.[8] Like many such immigrant groups, they prospered by working hard, amassing savings, and cooperating for mutual advantage. Most of them came from the Teochiu area around Swatow, and the heads of successful families took leading roles in clan associations and business groups. They invested in one another's enterprises to share risks and rewards, and they exchanged marriage partners to strengthen links, often with little reference to traditional boundaries on such alliances.

By the 1970s, there were around 20 families that dominated the urban economy. Each family had usually started in a core business but then used their privileged access to capital and patronage to extend sideways into related fields. Each had come to dominate a conglomerate of multiple companies. The magnates of the new conglomerates were sometimes called *chao sua*, a Thai-ification of a Chinese term for a merchant prince. In earlier centuries it had been applied to the dominant figures of the junk trade, and the new capitalists inherited the term because of their similar Chinese origins and their comparable dominance. Craig Reynolds suggests *chao sua* should be translated as tycoon 'with its connotations of power and influence as well as wealth'.[9]

In the 1970s the mutually beneficial alliance between these business groups and the generals fell apart. In large part this was simply a consequence of the growing wealth and confidence of the businessmen. In their infant stages, they had needed the patronage of the generals, but now they felt strong enough to dominate on their own. In part, too, it resulted from the gradual shift of business focus from the home market to exports. While the generals held some control over the allocation of opportunities in the Thai home market, they had much less when it came to exports. Finally, it was also related to global power shifts: the Thai military was strongly aligned to the US in the prosecution of the Cold War, and as the American venture in Indochina crumbled, many businessmen grew anxious to reorient Thai foreign policy in line with regional strategic concerns and business opportunities.

The business leaders did not attack their old military allies directly; but after the military junta had been felled by a student-led revolt in 1973, businessmen played a strong role in establishing a new political succession. They contributed to the process of writing a new constitution, flooded into the new parliament in far larger numbers than ever before, and took leading roles in the three political parties which dominated parliament from the mid-1970s to the late-1980s. At the core of the Chart Thai Party were some of the business groups that had grown up around the Bangkok Bank/First Army axis of the 1950s and now played a large role in the textile industry. The Social Action Party (SAP, Kit Sangkhom) attracted several leaders connected to the banks and to the agribusiness conglomerates. The Democrat Party (DP, Prachatipat) drew in many middling businessmen from the city and from the port towns of the southern region.[10]

Only a few leading members of the big conglomerate families took a direct political role. Generally these families were not prepared to spare their limited manpower resources for politics. The few who did (such as Surat Osathunakroh from the pharmaceutical-based consumer conglomerate, Osothsapa) found that political prominence rendered both them and their companies too vulnerable. Most of the political players were lesser business associates, or people who had made a career as political brokers for big business. An example of the first was Boonchu Rojanasathien, who had risen from humble provincial origins to high positions in the Bangkok Bank through professional skill. He then went on to become the most articulate advocate of business politics in the parliament.[11] An example of the second was Pramarn Adireksarn, who came from a bureaucratic family and had a military career. In the 1950s and 1960s, he played a key role in brokering deals between the generals, the Bangkok Bank group, and overseas textile firms. From the 1970s onwards, he played a similar but expanded middleman role as a leader of the Chart Thai Party. In general, big business interests exerted their political influence by financing the election of such candidates who would support their interests in the Assembly and in the corridors of government administration.

In the short parliamentary interlude of 1975–1976, and again after parliament was restored in 1979, the business lobby gently but inexorably pressed against the weight of military dominance. They supported the reorientation of foreign policy away from the US Cold War stance and towards friendly relations with China and Indochina. They agitated for a reduction in military budgets in order to free up more public funds to boost the economy and to build infrastructure. They pressed government to dismantle the tangle of licensing controls and miscellaneous red tape that had provided opportunities for the generals to favour their friends. They supported changes in the constitution that would reduce military tutelage over parliament and provide business politicians with greater control over policy-making.[12]

Bangkok business's opposition to military rule was essentially pragmatic. If there was a business advantage to be gained from cooperation with the military, then they would cooperate. Through the 1980s, the business lobby worked directly with the military prime minister, General Prem, to influence economic policy-making.[13] After the 1991 coup, they cooperated enthusiastically with the military-appointed government of Anand Panyarachun, whose cabinet of businessmen and technocrats undertook many reforms in economic policy welcomed by the business lobby. But in the long run, metropolitan business sought to control the machinery of state in order to pursue policies favourable to capital accumulation. In Western countries, industrial revolutions had led to similar political movements, usually directed against the ruling aristocracy. In Thailand, it pitted the businessmen against military rulers who had earlier monopolized political power. However, this contest was complicated by the rise of a new and rather different breed of businessmen in the provinces.

CHAO PHO: PROVINCIAL BUSINESS AND LOCAL INFLUENCE

Whereas the 1940s represented the take-off decade for Bangkok business, in the provinces this change did not come until the 1970s. Until then, most provincial towns were little more than small administrative centres. Most had only a few thousand people; the largest was one-fortieth the size of Bangkok. In the late 1960s and 1970s, several of these towns began to feel the tug of Bangkok's growth, and in them a new and prospering cadre of provincial businessmen began to emerge. They occupied the space that was created between the concentration of economic and political power in Bangkok, on the one hand, and the concentrations of people and resources in the provincial periphery on the other. They grew by straddling the economic and often also the political linkages that connected these two poles.

The character of these major provincial business interests differed from place to place and also from time to time, but there is a rough pattern. Many began by acquiring a major role in extracting resources from the periphery to supply the export demand channelled through Bangkok. Some of the new business leaders began as local rice millers and traders. Others started by buying, processing, and despatching upland cash-crops, whose cultivation spread rapidly from the 1960s onwards. Still others were involved in logging, mining, and fishing. With the connections these entrepreneurs made in Bangkok, they were able to start businesses moving goods and services back from the capital to supply growing demand in the periphery. Typically they set up truck and automobile dealerships, petrol stations, and distributorships for household durables, construction materials, liquor, and luxury goods. Finally, they pursued local opportunities born of rising prosperity, especially real estate, construction, hotels, resorts, and modern retailing.

Two other sorts of business provided especially fast and lucrative returns. The first was public works contracting. Flush with US aid money and nervous about the growth of communist insurgency, the Thai government was rapidly investing in roads, offices, and other public works in the provinces. Some businessmen who specialized in supplying government contracts became spectacularly wealthy. Thus

Banharn Silpa-archa started out supplying gravel for road construction in Suphanburi, extended into various forms of government contracting and supply, and became the uncrowned king of the province. Banharn's cabinet (1995–1996) was nicknamed the *ratthaban phu rap mao*, the contractors' government, because so many of the ministers made their money in the past (and present) from government contracts.[14]

The second form of business comprised various types of illegal enterprise – smuggling, logging, gambling, drugs trading, arms running, and prostitution. The provinces were still lightly policed, the long sea and land borders offered many illicit business opportunities, and the towns harboured lively markets for various kinds of vice. Several provincial businessmen progressed from legitimate trades to the quicker money available on the fringe. *Sia* Leng of Khon Kaen, for instance, made his nest-egg as a provincial crop trader. He then used the same network to run an underground lottery, and progressed from there to managing casinos in the capital.[15] Probably only a minority of the provincial businessmen indulged in illegal businesses; but because the profit rates were so much larger, this minority often emerged as the richest, most prominent, and most powerful in the locality.

Such provincial notables cultivated close links with local officialdom – the district office, the land department, the local military – to secure the licences, permits, land deeds, and other wherewithal to do business, to corner the lucrative government contracts, and to provide cover for their illegal activities. They also built up networks of associates and gangs of subordinates. This was a new and crude business environment, and the methods used could be rough and ready. Some of the most prosperous provincial business centres (especially Chonburi, Petchburi, Chiang Rai, and Khorat) acquired a reputation for hired gunmen, sporadic violence, and regular newspaper reports of murders 'arising out of a business dispute'.

The men who deployed these various talents most successfully became very prominent local figures indeed. Gradually they acquired the popular appellation of *chao pho*. The term traditionally referred to a god or spirit residing in a place thought to harbour supernatural power. It was applied to big provincial businessmen in recognition of their 'supernatural' ability to flout the law. This usage was confirmed after the term was used as the title translation of the film *The*

Godfather; it has often been translated as 'Mafia', and certainly contained overtones of gangsterism and violence.[16] From time to time *chao pho* were removed from the scene in spectacular fashion – blown up by a Claymore mine on the steps of a provincial courthouse; blown off a provincial highway by a rocket launcher in broad daylight; blown away by a hail of gunfire in the Bangkok suburbs.

From the 1970s onwards, the *chao pho* assumed a major role in local and national politics. *Chao pho* who had extensive businesses in areas such as construction contracting, logging, and transportation soon learnt that they could extend their business very quickly by being elected to local office, or by building close connections with political figures.[17] Because of their extensive influence in local business and their wide patronage links with the local populace, the Bangkok-based political parties sought the *chao pho*'s help to organize election campaigns. At first many *chao pho* were prepared to put their local networks at the disposal of Bangkok leaders who needed a provincial seat. In the early 1980s, for instance, the leading banker and national politician Boonchu Rojanasthien was supported by *Kamnan* Poh of Chonburi, perhaps the country's single most famous *chao pho*. But before long, many *chao pho* changed their minds and preferred to stand themselves or put forward a local associate;[18] *Kamnan* Poh cut his links with Boonchu and supported first a group of relatives and business associates, and then his own sons.[19]

For the individual *chao pho*, the attraction of a seat in parliament was obvious. It dramatized his role as a true 'local boss'. Moreover, it strengthened the linkages and contacts with the sources of economic and political power in Bangkok. The *chao pho* quickly discovered that the electoral system offered them splendid opportunities. All but around 30 of the 300 plus parliamentary seats were elected from provincial constituencies. Most of these constituencies were a single province (or half-province), returning two or three members. These large multi-member constituencies favoured those who dominated the provincial headquarters, and this meant the *chao pho* with their extensive control of local business and their links to the local officials who administered the electoral process. Some *chao pho* could claim to control elections across several provinces and constituencies. In the 1988 elections, for instance, *Sia* Yae, one of the major *chao pho* of the central region, claimed to have played a role in the election of between 10 and 25 MPs.[20]

At each successive election in the 1980s, more of the provincial seats were occupied by local figures. By the sheer logic of numbers, they dislodged the Bangkok businessmen from the leadership of the major political parties, a revolution that took place between 1984 and 1988. The old Bangkok-based political leaders fared badly in this intrusion. Many of the Bangkok businessmen who were prominent in the Social Action Party quit politics or, like Boonchu Rojanasthien, floated off into a twilight zone of minor parties.[21] The new party leader was Montri Pongpanich, an Ayutthaya businessman who, like Banharn, had a base in government contracting. The Chart Thai party was similarly transformed, with Banharn eventually becoming party leader in 1994. The Bangkok wing of the Democrats split away to form a separate party which subsequently evaporated, and the base of the Democrats was relocated to the provincial South.

After the shock of the provincial influx, the conflict of *chao sua* and *chao pho* became a strong underlying theme of politics. In part, this conflict was about style and sophistication. The *chao sua* were established figures in the capital; the *chao pho* were new men from the provinces; they often carried the taint of *very* new money and held very provincial attitudes. In part, it reflected their differing business interests. The *chao pho* were traders with a domestic focus and they favoured diverting government funds to provincial development. The *chao sua*, on the other hand, were increasingly involved in manufacture and export and they preferred to channel government funding into major national infrastructure. In part too, the clash reflected differing attitudes to the military. The *chao sua* were extracting themselves from entanglements with military bosses; the *chao pho* were building their personal networks from the local to the national level as quickly as possible and had few qualms about pursuing this through alliance with powerful generals. In part, it reflected direct business competition. The *chao pho* tried to monopolize the new opportunities in their own provincial backyards. Sometimes they had to defend themselves from the inroads of established Bangkok *chao sua*, who saw opportunities to set up hotels, department stores, shopping complexes, entertainment complexes, and real estate businesses in the provincial towns. They felt threatened by Bangkok's more powerful and established businessmen, who had better credit and bigger friends.[22]

The *chao pho/chao sua* distinction is meant to dramatize an important tension amongst businessmen – one that acquired major political significance in the 1980s and early 1990s. In real life, this distinction between Bangkok/provincial *chao sua* and *chao pho* was not clear-cut but more like shades in a spectrum. There were many Bangkok-based businesses that operated on the *chao pho* model, and there were provincial businessmen who had moved into international exporting. Moreover, there were individual firms that straddled both extremes. Charoen Pokphand (CP), for instance, had major export interests and had supported the drive for policy change and bureaucratic decontrol in the 1980s; it also had share issues on the stock exchange, which fluctuated according to the risk and profit assessments of international finance. But at the same time CP also had a real estate arm, for which it cultivated links with generals and bureaucrats. And it was a bidder for infrastructure contracts, for which it allegedly used influence with a variety of generals and *chao pho* politicians.

Of all the established Bangkok politicians, Chatichai Choonhavan dealt most successfully with the provincial influx. He had already established an electoral base in Khorat, where the local *chao pho* were happy to share their provincial constituency with such an illustrious figure.[23] When Chatichai became prime minister in 1988, the change was not only from a military to an elected premier, but also from a cabinet of technocrats and Bangkok businessmen to one heavily weighted with the new men of the provinces.

The political conflict between *chao sua* and *chao pho* heightened after Chatichai's elevation to prime ministerial office. The Bangkok leaders who had been bundled aside by the provincial influx were quick to portray Chatichai's provincially dominated cabinet as unusually corrupt, a charge which offered an opportunity to the military to carry out a coup in 1991.[24] Bangkok business initially welcomed the take-over and the sacking of Chatichai's cabinet, and cheered the military's appointment of Anand Panyarachun, head of one of the Bangkok conglomerates, as the new prime minister. However, *chao sua* enthusiasm for military rule soon waned. After the restoration of parliament in 1992, Bangkok business circles talked about becoming more involved in electoral politics to prevent both the continued interference of the military and total domination by the provincials. Some sponsored the PollWatch body, which attempted to prevent the more wayward tactics employed by provincial candidates. In 1994, the same lobby supported amendments to incorporate such electoral controls in the constitution. And in 1995–1996, in reaction to the blatant corruption of the provincial-dominated Banharn government, Bangkok business supported moves to amend the constitution. Through the early 1990s, there was a series of scandals which seemed orchestrated to undermine some of the richest and most powerful of the *chao pho* politicians. Three provincial MPs were accused of drug-running, two had to resign their seats, and one was subject to extradition proceedings by the US. One provincial MP was caught in a highly unusual raid on a Bangkok casino, and another had to summon up all his powers of rhetoric to explain why a house he owned was being used for illegal gambling. At least four provincial MPs were rumoured to be involved in oil smuggling.

Eventually the *chao sua* and the *chao pho* will probably grow more alike, and such tensions will alleviate. But in the particular stage of the 1980s and early 1990s, their differences underlay business disputes, gangland battles, and political party warfare.

CHAO THI: PEASANTS AND PROTEST

Generals, tycoons, and provincial bosses occupied the political foreground in this period of transition. But the background cannot be ignored. The peasantry still accounted for over half the population, and occupied a special place in the national mythology ('backbone of the nation'). The very fact that they were carefully excluded from formal politics tended to dramatize the fact that they were 'the people' on which a democracy was supposedly founded. For these reasons we dub them the *chao thi*, literally the lords of the place, the general term for the spirits of the locality found all over Thailand.

In other Asian regions, the phase of rapid urban growth reduced the peasantry to a minor portion of the society. Agriculturists represented only 10 per cent of the workforce in Japan by 1980, 18 per cent in Korea by 1986–1989, and 16 per cent in Taiwan by 1979–1985. In Thailand in the early 1990s, when the country was being hailed as the next NIC or Asian Tiger, some 60 per cent of the workforce was still engaged in agriculture. Thailand's large peasantry had been shaped by a long movement of agricultural expansion across an open land frontier. In the early nineteenth century, most of the area of modern Thailand was covered by swamp and forest, and the population may have been as little as one million. From the 1950s to the 1980s, the peasantry cleared some 24 million hectares, reduced the forests to 15 per cent of total area, established some five million farm holdings, and expanded to around 40 million people.[25]

This peasantry had a history of mobility and pioneering. It had also, until recently, been relatively free of the kind of local overlords found in many peasant societies – landlords, revenue officials, and moneylender-traders. In the late nineteenth century, in both Bangkok and the northern state of Lanna, rulers started to create great landed estates in the most fertile rice-growing areas. But these projects were later surpassed by the great movement of pioneer colonization. By the 1980s, only 11 per cent of holdings were held by landlords, most of whom were bureaucrats and absentees. Few lived in a big house in the village, and there was no culture of landlordism.

At the turn of the twentieth century the government had launched a scheme of land taxation following colonial models based on land records and village headmen. But again the scheme crumbled: the work of land survey lagged far behind the expansion of the frontier, the government was nervous about collecting revenue in the face of local opposition and after several years of meagre returns, the whole scheme was abandoned in the 1930s.

Traders did not penetrate deeply into the village economy either. With no land deeds to provide security for loans, and no effective judicial system to enforce debt payments, traders were nervous about extending loans to villagers. Traders could not tie the peasants up with debt to secure the supplies of surplus rice for export, and had instead to tempt them with dried fish and other simple consumer goods.[26] In neighbouring territories where colonial governments provided stronger support for merchant capital, trader-moneylenders acquired large tracts of land used as collateral during the depression of the 1930s. In Siam, there was little land transfer of this kind; instead, many of the traders went bankrupt.

The expansion of Thailand's land frontier nurtured an independent and distinctive peasant culture based on owner-operator family farms with relatively little experience of overlordship. This rural society was jealous of its independence. Government attempts to impose greater control at the turn of the century provoked a series of revolts, but more often the peasantry reacted to impositions from above by evasion, for the open land frontier acted as a refuge and a safety-valve. Until the 1960s, government basically managed the countryside by leaving it alone. It left it to merchant networks to coax a surplus of rice out of the villages for export, raising revenue by taxing this surplus as it passed through the city rather than at its village origin. The state maintained only a sparse administrative presence in the provincial towns, and did little to increase agricultural production beyond some drainage schemes in the Chaophraya delta.

All this changed in the 1960s. Government resolved to accelerate economic growth by increasing both agricultural production and the rate of surplus extraction. It set out to achieve this goal by expanding its own investments in irrigation, crop research, and rural transportation, and by promoting agribusinesses to extract the surplus. The policy was successful, and an eightfold increase in agricultural exports drove economic growth through the 1960s and 1970s. At the same time, the government set out to take greater administrative control over the countryside: it built roads into the villages, sent in teachers and policemen, and tied the village headmen more closely to the bureaucracy. It began taxing things, counting things, and controlling things more than ever before.

In the 1970s, the countryside reacted. The communist insurgency spreading across from Indochina was successful in recruiting villagers in the remoter fringe to oppose the growth of urban exploitation and governmental intrusion. Peasants in the north organized to oppose the rising rents being imposed by the landlords. Peasants in the central plain agitated against growing debt, land transfer, and the insecurity that came from increased dependence on the market.[27] Outside these more organized agitations, there were scattered local movements to exclude government and secede from the market.[28]

The army brought these protests under control with the gun. Then, in the 1980s, the situation of the countryside changed yet again. The trend of decline in world agricultural prices reduced the profitability and growth rate of agriculture, and at the same time rapid industrialization made agriculture a peripheral part of the national economy. Between 1980 and 1990, agriculture was reduced from 21 to 13 per cent of GDP, and from 48 to 20 per cent of total exports. With agriculture stagnant and the urban economy booming, the income gap between town and country rapidly widened.

The frontier movement that had shaped the peasantry now shifted into reverse. To protect the small area of remaining forest, the government gradually closed down the land frontier. In the early 1990s, for the first time in over a century, the cultivated area declined. The rampant and increasingly dominant city intruded into the rural resource base; it demanded land for industrial estates, urban housing, golf courses, and recreational resorts. It took over rivers to generate electricity and act as industrial waste disposal systems. It colonized forest zones to plant eucalyptus trees for the pulp-and-paper industry.

The peasantry also changed very rapidly under growing urban influence. By the mid-1980s, over half of all rural youth travelled to the cities for education, excitement, and employment. Some went only for the space of a dry season; others stayed several years. But a majority still circulated back to the village, carrying new ideas and experiences. The advent of mass television brought urban culture directly into village homes. An urban market culture expanded in the villages, especially in the post-1986 boom, as urban merchants spread retail networks, and as returned migrants invested their savings in a shop or service business. This was no longer a traditional peasantry. Agriculture's contribution to rural incomes fell to under half the total, with migrant remittances and local commerce contributing growing shares. But the majority of the peasants still retained their long-term residence in the village, and clung on to land, family, and community as their social support.

Two kinds of rural agitation swelled through the 1980s and 1990s. The first demanded government action to halt agrarian decline and bolster rural incomes through price support schemes and agricultural extension projects. The second set out to defend the rural resource base against urban inroads. Agitators protested against dam projects, golf courses, eucalyptus planting, factory pollution of the air, soil and water.[29] By the early 1990s, such protests were running at a rate of two per day. By the mid-1990s, these protests had gelled into a movement. Five times, peasants from the Northeast marched on the city demanding government action on a laundry list of problems ranging from land rights to failed development schemes. In 1995 and 1996, they drew in allies from other regions and from the urban slums to form the Assembly of the Poor, which negotiated with government against a background of sustained demonstrations in the heart of the capital. Among the leaders of these new politics, one distinguishing feature was their experience of the city. Most had been rural–urban migrants. Some had been trained in trade union politics. A few had climbed the educational ladder and had built personal networks linked to the urban civil society of NGOs, media, and intellectuals.[30]

The peasantry had the power of numbers and, with the increasing importance of representative institutions, numbers counted. The peasantry also had a sense of their own difference and independence nurtured in the century of frontier expansion, and this feeling gave force to their agitation in defence of resources. The peasantry had also acquired a central role in the ideology of the state: as the main element in the population and the key force in the economy, it had often been dignified as the 'backbone of the nation'. Under growing urban influence, the peasantry had developed new political ideas and leaders. As the peasantry came under pressure in the 1970s and 1980s, intellectuals developed a theoretical platform for peasant defence based on the idea that the peasants were the original occupants of Siam; that the village preceded the state historically, and by implication, ideologically.[31] The peasants were in effect the *chao thi*, the lords or spirits of a place who needed to be placated by whoever wanted to take up residence there.

OFFERINGS TO THE *CHAO THI*: THE POLITICS OF TRANSITION

The new institutions of representative democracy were developed by the city and dominated by the city. The state denied education to the peasantry,[32] undercut any signs of peasant political organization, and rigged the electoral procedures to the prejudice of peasant candidates. Very few peasant representatives found their way into the parliament.[33] Yet the other political players could not ignore them. As one leader of Assembly of the Poor said in 1997: 'The power of the soldier is his gun. The power of the businessman is his money. From our experience, the power of the poor is our feet.'[34]

The strategies that the military, the *chao sua* and the *chao pho* adopted towards the peasantry were very different. During the campaign against the insurgency, the army became deeply involved in policing and organizing the villages. When the insurgency had been contained and the army's political role came under attack from the business politicians, some elements in the army attempted to build the army's rural organizations into bases of support for military rule. In the early 1980s, the army spread a web of propaganda and vigilante organizations through the villages; these were used to campaign against any tendency towards communism and to win support for military politics.[35] Generals such as Chavalit Yongchaiyudh blamed rural problems on exploitation by the urban businessmen who also dominated parliamentary politics, and implied that military rule would provide the peasantry with a better deal. Chavalit also secured funds from the government budget to launch rural development programmes managed by the army. The *Isan Khiew* (Green Northeast) scheme was intended to show that the army was more concerned than civilian politicians were about the idea of rural development, and more efficient in its implementation.

This sort of strategy is in no way unique to Thailand. It contained strong echoes of the strategies of fascist movements in Europe and especially in Japan in the 1930s. It also bore similarities to the policies of some military dictatorships in Latin America in the 1970s and early 1980s. But it failed. In the late 1980s, the army's network of rural organizations withered away. This collapse appeared to be a consequence of the nature of Thailand's peasant society. In the European and Japanese cases, the military built successful fascist alliances with gentry groups, often declining gentry groups opposed to growing urban domination. In the Latin America of the 1970s, the military found allies among landlords who welcomed state help in translating their feudal dominance into the rising urban economy. The Thai military found it much more difficult to build similar alliances with a relatively flat, independent, family-farm-based peasantry which harbours anti-statist traditions formed in a recent movement of frontier settlement.

By contrast, the *chao pho* simply set themselves up as little lords of the locality. *Kamnan* Poh of Chonburi boasted that he was more important to the locality than the formal representatives of government:

> People cannot rely on *kharatchakan* [bureaucrats]. *Kharatchakan* have only small salaries. But I have much and I can distribute much. Whenever I sit in the local coffee shop [*ran kafae*] people can come and consult with me. I am a man of the people already. I am more accessible than *kharatchakan*. On any matter where the *kharatchakan* cannot help, I can. And I do it willingly and quickly. It's all very convenient for the people ... Most of what I do is about giving employment and improving the local facilities.[36]

The *chao pho* cultivated an image of themselves as *phu yai* or 'big men' concerned with the status and welfare of the community. They made donations to local temples; financed various types of religious trips and ceremonies (*thot pha pa, thot kathin*); donated to public projects such as building roads, resting pavilions, bus shelters and bridges; and scattered largesse among the ordinary people:

> Whenever these [ordinary] people have any problems they go to the *chao pho*. School opens, there is no money, they can get it from the *chao pho* ... A pregnant wife about to deliver, has to go to the hospital, no money, go to see the *chao pho*, he gives the money needed ... The extent of their patronage is incredible. People are indebted to their patronage [*bun khun*] up to their necks.[37]

The *chao pho*'s informal influence was a function of the relative poverty of the mass of the people, the relatively poor state of local infrastructure, and the ineffectiveness of local systems for justice and social welfare. With moderate ease, the *chao pho* could provide some measure of security, justice, social welfare, and local infrastructure more speedily and more accessibly than officialdom. When it came to elections, peasants could be persuaded that such local lords would be the best representatives the province could send to the national capital. To intensify such persuasion, the *chao pho* could also mobilize their wealth, their widespread business contacts, and their relations with the officials conducting the polls. *Kamnan* Poh admitted that Chonburi had a high percentage of polls cast because his friends were over-zealous in stuffing the ballot boxes.[38]

The *chao pho*'s dependence on the peasantry was gradually reflected in the vocabulary and theatre of public politics. Banharn devoted his maiden speech as premier to the claim that he wished to be leader of 'all of Thailand, not only of the rich', although his cabinet of contractors showed little interest in realizing this pledge. Chavalit started his bid for the premiership with the claim he would be an agent of 'harmony' between different classes – a rehash of an old military ideal. But as he ascended to the premiership with the backing of the *chao pho* politicians, he repositioned himself as leader of the poor and the peasants. When he came under pressure from urban demonstrations, he trucked in villagers to cheer his speeches claiming leadership of the oppressed. Eventually the gap between theatre and reality engulfed him. His pro-poor, anti-urban rhetoric flirted with the ethnic division between rural Thai and urban Chinese: 'Thai people own this country and allow others to share the land. But ... this second group of people ... want to destroy this land. I want to see my people rise up to protect this country.'[39] His *chao pho* lieutenants were virtually all Thai-Chinese. Chavalit's government crumbled two months later. In the age of transition, the theatre of politics operated within certain limits.

The *chao sua* politicians were more remote from the peasantry. They could relate to the peasantry only through policy and ideology. From the mid-1970s, *chao sua* politicians such as Boonchu had recognized the need for rural development policies to offset potential rural opposition to urban growth, and to prevent isolation of the *chao sua* parties. Boonchu had these policies devised in the research department of the Bangkok Bank. The policies included support for crop prices, better legal protection of land rights, and local development works managed by independent local bodies (the *Tambon* Development Fund). In essence these reforms aimed to make peasants more successful and hence more committed participants in the market economy.

These sorts of rural policies remained on the agenda of the *chao sua* parties through the 1980s and early 1990s. They were extended in various ways, particularly by the administration of Chuan Leekpai (1992–1995), which launched schemes to issue deeds to peasants without proper land title, to extend the structures of local self-government, to increase investment in agricultural development, and to bolster crop price supports.

Yet big business remained fundamentally ambivalent about rural society, and tended to waver between two attitudes. On the one hand, it accepted the need to make rural society a more prosperous ally, or at least an acquiescent partner in its own project to develop the urban economy. Thus it supported schemes such as the *tambon* plan, the National Economic and Social Development Board's poverty plan, and attempts to put more funds behind rural infrastructure and development.[40] On the other hand, it felt that the rural sector acted increasingly as a drag on economic growth, and a complication in politics – the unsophisticated rural electorate provided the vote base for the *chao pho* politicians, who had a tendency to ally with the military residuum and plunder the state. As a result, Bangkok businessmen occasionally wished that the rural sector would simply disappear. During the aggressively self-confident years of spectacular urban growth from 1986–1990, one businessman argued that 'Bangkok is Thailand and Thailand is Bangkok'. Some urban pundits openly speculated that Thailand could grow even faster if it could lose its rural dead weight, rather as Singapore had flourished by shucking off its connection to Malaysia. Perhaps more realistically, other representatives of capital argued for accelerating the commercialization of agriculture and absorbing it within the overall urban transition – in short, developing it out of existence.

CONCLUSION

Thailand is going through a transition, a change of ownership. The generals are leaving by the side exit. Not willingly, not quickly, but leaving all the same. The *chao sua* and the *chao pho* are moving in, and they have brought along their professional and managerial friends to make the place more homely and give it a touch of class. But already it seems like a divided house, a *ban song yaek*.[41]

The *chao sua* and the *chao pho* are squabbling over who gets the front room. In time they will probably be able to get on with one another; but the new owners still have to make their peace with the *chao thi*, the spirits of the place. This is very important. Somehow the previous occupants never quite did it properly; and the spirits of the place always gave them trouble, like *pii*, restless ghosts. The new owners will have to decide whether they want to appease them or drive them away (if they can). Much depends on how well they handle this issue.

NOTES

1. Benedict R. O'G. Anderson, 'Murder and Progress in Modern Siam', *New Left Review*, 181 (1990): 33–48.

2. For the different understandings of *chao pho* in this volume and elsewhere, see the introductory essay, p. 14 ff. [Ed.].

3. Pasuk Phongpaichit and Chris Baker, *Thailand's Boom and Bust* (Chiang Mai: Silkworm Books, 1998), pp. 264–273.

4. Akira Suehiro, *Capital Accumulation in Thailand 1855–1985* (Tokyo: The Centre for East Asian Cultural Studies, 1989).

5. Nakarin Mektrairat, *Kanpatiwat sayam pho.so. 2475* (Bangkok: Munnithi khrongkan tamra sangkhomsat lae manutsayasat, 1992).

6. Kevin J. Hewison, *Bankers and Bureaucrats: Capital and the Role of the State in Thailand* (New Haven: Yale University Southeast Asia Studies, 1989), p. 197; Suehiro *Capital Accumulation*, pp. 157–169, 245–265.

7. Sungsidh Piriyarangsan, *Thai Bureaucratic Capitalism 1932–1960* (Bangkok: Chulalongkorn University Social Research Institute, 1983).

8. Pasuk Phongpaichit and Chris Baker, *Thailand: Economy and Politics* (Kuala Lumpur: Oxford University Press, 1995), Ch. 4.

9. Craig Reynolds, 'Tycoons and Warlords: Modern Thai Social Formations and Chinese Historical Romance', in Anthony Reid (ed.), *Sojourners and*

Settlers: Histories of Southeast Asia and the Chinese (St Leonard's: Allen & Unwin, 1996), p. 140.

10. David Morell and Chai-anan Samudavanija (1981), *Political Conflict in Thailand: Reform, Reaction, Revolution* (Cambridge, Mass,: Oelgeschlager, Gunn & Hain, 1981), Ch. 5.

11. Rathakorn Asadorntheerayuth, *Boonchu Rojanastien* [in Thai] (Bangkok: Dokbia Publishers, 1993).

12. Pasuk Phongpaichit, 'Technocrats, Businessmen and Generals: Politics of Economic Policy Reform in Thailand', in A. MacIntyre and K. Jayasuriya (eds), *The Dynamics of Economic Policy Reform in Southeast Asia and the Southwest Pacific* (Kuala Lumpur: Oxford University Press, 1992).

13. Anek Laothamatas, *Business Associations and the New Political Economy of Thailand: From Bureaucratic Polity to Liberal Corporatism* (Boulder, Col.: Westview Press, and Singapore: Institute of Southeast Asian Studies, 1992).

14. It was also nicknamed the '7-Eleven cabinet', made up of seven parties and eleven factions, and open for business 24 hours a day. See Pasuk and Baker, *Thailand's Boom and Bust*, pp. 258–264.

15. See *The Nation*, 7 April 1991.

16. Chartchai Na Chiangmai, 'Parapolitical Behaviour of Northern Thai Villagers: An Application of Social Network Concepts' (Ph.D. thesis, University of Wisconsin-Madison, 1983); *Matichon sutsapda*, 7 and 25 March 1984; 'Opening the File on Jao Phor Nakornsawan', *Matichon sutsapda*, 25 March 25 1984; *Thai rat*, 18 July 1985; Viengrat Netipoh, 'Turakit nakleng + nakleng thurakit = nak thurakit kung nakleng', *Chotmai khao sangkhomsat*, August–October 1989; Sondhi Limthongkul, 'Chao pho: kan kamnoed lae damrong u yang pen rabop', *Samut sangkhomsat*, January–July 1991; James Ockey, 'Business Leaders, Gangsters and the Middle Class: Societal Groups and Civilian Rule', (Ph.D. thesis, Cornell University, 1992); Sombat Chantornvong, 'Botbat khong chao pho thongthin nai setthakit lae kanmuang thai', in Pasuk Phongpaichit and Sungsidh Piriyarangsan (eds), *Rat thun chao pho thongthin kap sankhom thai* (Bangkok: Political Economy Centre, Chulalongkorn University, 1992).

17. Sixty-two per cent of all the 2,046 *so cho* (members of provincial councils, whose main functions are to pass provincial ordinances, approve provincial budgets, and oversee the work of provincial officials) elected in October 1990 reported their occupations as businessmen/traders. See Somkiat Wanthana, 'Nak thurakit thongthin kap prachathipatai thai', in Sungsidh Piriyarangsan and Pasuk Phongpaichit (eds), *Chon chan klang bon krasae prachathipatai thai* (Bangkok: The Political Economy Centre, Faculty of Economics, Chulalongkorn University, 1993).

18. Sombat Chantornvong, 'Botbat khong chao pho', p. 136.

19. See Chapter 3 for a fuller description of the rise of the *chao pho* and activities of *Kamnan* Poh among others (Ed.).

20. James Ockey, 'Business Leaders', Ch. 4; and see this volume.

21. He later floated back into the Democrat Party and became its rather truculent elder statesman.

22. The spectacular murder with which Ben Anderson rounded off his 1990 article (see fn. 1) probably arose from such a dispute.

23. See the discussion by Yoko Ueda in this volume.

24. Pasuk Phongpaichit and Sungsidh Piriyarangsan, *Korrapchan kap prachathippatai thai* (Bangkok: The Political Economy Center, Chulalongkorn University, 1994).

25. Pasuk and Baker, *Thailand*, Chs. 1–2.

26. Chatthip Nartsupha, *Setthakit muban thai nai adit* (Bangkok: Sangsan Publishing House, 1984), pp. 62–64; Punee Bualek, 'Laksana khong nai thun thai nai rawang songkhram lok khrang thi nung thung song (pho. so. 2457–2483)'. Paper presented at the 5th International Conference on Thai Studies, SOAS, London, 1993.

27. Kanoksak Kaewthep, *Bot wikhro sahaphan chaona chao rai haeng prathet thai* (Bangkok: Chulalongkorn University Social Research Institute, 1986).

28. See for instance, Shigeharu Tanabe, *Nung luang nung dam tamnan khong phunam chaona haeng lanna thai* (Bangkok: Sangsan Publishing House, 1986).

29. Philip Hirsch, *Political Economy of Environment in Thailand* (Manila and Wollongong: Journal of Contemporary Asia Publishers, 1993); Pinkaew Leungaramsri and Noel Rajesh, *The Future of People and Forests in Thailand after the Logging Ban* (Bangkok: Project for Ecological Recovery, 1992).

30. Praphat Pintopteng, *Kan muang bon thong thanon* (Bangkok: Krirk University, 1998)]

31. Chatthip Nartsupha, *Setthakit muban thai nai adid* and 'The "Community Culture" School of Thought', in Manas Chitakasem and Andrew Turton (eds), *Thai Constructions of Knowledge* (London: School of Oriental and African Studies, University of London, 1991); Chatthip Nartsupha and Phonphilai Lertwicha, *Watthanatham mu ban thai [Thai village culture]* (Bangkok: Sangsan Publishing House, 1994).

32. In 1991, 89 per cent of the total employed workforce in the rural area had received six years of education or less; see National Statistical Office, *Report of the Labour Force Survey*, August 1991, Bangkok.

33. The proportion of all MPs returning their occupation as 'farmer' had never risen higher than 9 per cent. In 1992, it was 3 per cent.

34. Wiraphon Sopha quoted in Praphat, *Kan muang bon thong thanon*, p. 150.

35. Chai-Anan Samudavanija, Kusuma Snitwongse and Suchit Bunbongkarn, *From Armed Suppression to Political Offensive* (Bangkok: Institute of Security and International Studies, Chulalongkorn University, 1990); Andrew Turton, *Production, Power and Participation in Rural Thailand: Experiences of Poor Farmers'*

Groups (Geneva: United Nations Research Institute for Social Development, 1987).

36. Viengrat Netipoh, 'Semi-Businessmen, Semi-Gangsters', p. 91.

37. Seri Temiyawait, commenting on Sombat Chantornvong's paper on the roles of local godfathers, in *Rat thun chao pho thongthin lae sangkhom thai,* p. 147.

38. *Matichon sutsapda,* 25 May 1986. Chapter 3 of this volume covers this point in greater detail (Ed.).

39. *The Nation,* 18 September 1997.

40. The 1975 *tambon* scheme allocated funds to local government for infrastructure. The poverty plan, part of the 1982–1986 Fifth Plan, targeted the poorest areas for rapid development.

41. The title of a television drama series, conceived, written, filmed and broadcast between the May 1992 overthrow of military rule and the September 1992 election, to dramatize the key issues of Thailand's rapidly changing political economy in an idiom and on a medium to which the rural audience could relate.

THREE

Local Godfathers in Thai Politics

Sombat Chantornvong

Observers of the Thai social and political scene since the 1980s will certainly agree that one of the kingdom's most colourful phenomena has been that of the *chao pho*, or 'godfathers'. Stories about violent killings by or of these local leaders and their men often make headline news, particularly when, as in most cases, such crimes are executed with gross violence and in clear defiance of the law enforcement authorities. But probably even more visible is the role of local or provincial notables at election time, when (so it seems) all roads lead to the godfather. The extent to which these leaders have made their impact felt by the whole society is evidenced by the fact that, when military leaders seized power from the civilian government in February 1991, one of the first items on their agenda was to draw up special legislation to deal with the *chao pho*.[1]

This paper attempts to trace the evolution and role of local godfathers in Thai politics. It seeks, first of all, to establish the relationship between their economic and political role and their traditional position in the Thai social structure. It will also examine the grounds for the frequently heard accusation that the Thai practice of democracy has contributed to the growing influence of these godfathers.[2] It is hoped that the discussion will shed light on their future role as well.

THE GODFATHER'S ANCESTRY

The word *chao pho* is probably best explained by two other Thai terms: *nak leng* and *phu mi itthiphon*. Used with a qualifier, the word *nak leng* means to be knowledgeable about or highly preoccupied with something; hence one may talk about a *nak leng nang sua* (one who reads a lot or knows a lot about books) or a *nak leng kan panan* (a gambler). Used alone, however, the term signifies a certain personal character. A *nak leng* has to be daring, courageous, honest, and manly. He is someone who will never shy away from a fight or any confrontation.[3] To be a true *nak leng*, as opposed to an ordinary hoodlum, one needs to have certain necessary qualities. A *nak leng* has as his code of conduct the 'virtue' of manliness, which earns him respect from others, especially if he assumes the role of a protector – someone who looks out for his friends and subordinates. In other words, a *nak leng* is someone who is gentle and kind to his friends but at the same time is very tough with his foes.

The word *nak leng* has always been part of the Thai vocabulary, for it is deeply rooted in Thai culture, with its emphasis on a clearly defined hierarchy of power relationships. The inability of the traditional state to enforce order at the village level also contributed to the emergence of *nak leng* as local leaders. Being both feared and respected, a *nak leng* or strongman functioned naturally, more or less, as an informal community leader.[4] Nor was the status of the *nak leng* diminished by the late nineteenth-century reorganization of provincial government, which integrated the villages into the bureaucratic system. This demarcated clusters of hamlets into *muban*, or administrative villages, under official headmen (*phuyaiban*), in the process, a good number of *nak leng* were appointed as official local leaders. This was not surprising – after all, a *nak leng* already had the qualities needed for effective leadership.

Yet, while an average *nak leng* may develop around him an intricate web of followers based on his ability to protect them from outside harassment, this does not cause him to be viewed as possessing *amnat*, or legitimate power. This term has a strong connotation of being derived from official authority.[5] As a person of no official authority, a *nak leng* is said instead to have *itthiphon* or influence, as long as he can exert his power over others. In other words, *itthiphon* is an informal kind of power, and a *nak leng* is someone who, because of his personal qualities, can exercise informal power over those in his community. The principal reason why a *nak leng* becomes 'influential' is therefore cultural in nature, and has nothing to do with economics. An ordinary *nak leng* can therefore be found in just about any setting, rural or urban. Moreover, it is not uncommon for a *nak leng* to break the law in order to protect his group.

But whereas the influence of a *nak leng* is often limited to his immediate community and does not denote power over government officials, a *phu mi itthiphon* (man of influence) is someone who can exert such pressure. This term is of much more recent origin and is used by the authorities to label certain individuals whom they deem to constitute a threat to the country's social, economic, and political stability. The general public, however, has come to prefer the word *chao pho,* popularized by the Hollywood film *The Godfather*. In the old days, *chao pho* meant a divine spirit that aided those who faithfully brought it offerings and prayed for assistance. Nowadays the term is applied most broadly to anyone of influence in any walk of life; thus one may talk about a *chao pho* in the entertainment business, or 'the boss' in professional boxing circles. Second – and politically much more important – the word *chao pho* is used to refer to someone whose influence is recognized not only by his own people but also by high-ranking government officials. In the eyes of the public, a *chao pho* is someone who can use his influence to further his interests in complete disregard of the law.[6] The distinguished politician and cultural authority MR Kukrit Pramoj put it very simply: only those who make a living illegally are entitled to be called *chao pho.*[7]

Like the *nak leng,* the *chao pho* is both feared and loved. He is feared because he has the ability to use violence as the means to achieve his ends; he is loved because he regularly contributes from his surplus of money and services to the well-being of the community. Indeed, the extent to which he gives to his community should be such that its members eventually are willing to forget about his illegal activities.[8] Nevertheless, since the media's use of *chao pho* tends to have very dark connotations, men of influence understandably prefer to be called *nak leng.* Thus *Sia* Leng, a leading *chao pho* from Khon Kaen province, portrays himself as a great *nak leng,* a man who keeps his word: 'I admit that I am a *nak leng* but I am not a gangster. I am a *nak leng* with credibility, with spirit, with promise. I have always observed these principles. That is why I have so many friends.'[9]

While *chao pho* love to have others think of them as traditional *nak leng,* they are actually a lot more than that. The crucial difference lies, first of all, in their economic roles. A *chao pho*'s economic status and role are much higher and quite different from those of the rest of the community. Unlike a *nak leng*, a *chao pho* is primarily engaged in a sizeable business. Yet, more often than not, a *chao pho*'s business is monopolistic in nature, and needs a government licence or concession to operate, like liquor or cigarette dealerships, lumbering or mining concessions, or slaughterhouse operation. The absence of competition makes for big profits, and it is not uncommon for a *chao pho* to increase these by exceeding whatever legal restrictions are set on his enterprise. The resulting financial surplus enables the *chao pho* to make his way into many other economic sectors. We should note, however, that the term *chao pho* has been so loosely used by the media that, from the popular viewpoint, it can also mean those who make a living out of smuggling gold or contraband goods, operating illegal mines or logging enterprises – in other words, people who engage solely in unlawful enterprise. In the provinces, those who run illegal gambling dens, casinos, or underground lotteries, employing a large number of subordinates to safeguard their economic interest and to eliminate opponents, are similarly often called *chao pho*.

It has been suggested that the *chao pho* phenomenon of godfather-businessman began to evolve as early as the turn of the century, when the Thai economy began to change from self-sufficiency to a cash economy.[10] The emergence of a money economy encouraged competitive struggle among early capitalists to gain control of natural resources and tradable goods. It brought the need to open up new territory and the consequent movement of a large number of people from one place to another. All this happened at a time when ownership rights to farmland or to any other productive property were not yet clearly defined. Moreover, there were as yet no established procedures for labour recruitment and control. As a result, it was only natural that in the area largely ignored by the central government, operators of enterprises functioned as both economic bosses and sources of what passed for law, and these were forerunners to the present-day *chao pho*. In the North they are referred to as *pho liang* and in the South *nai hua*; both these terms imply a very high degree of social respectability, as patrons whom others depend on; and they thus differ greatly from the more equivocal *chao pho*.[11]

The modern-day understanding of *chao pho* is of much more recent origin. It emerged under the authoritarian regimes that dominated

Thai politics following the overthrow of the absolute monarchy in 1932, with the appearance of influential businessmen closely linked to the national ruling cliques. Thanks to political and military patronage, such entrepreneurs were granted sole rights to establish banking and other services, as well as to engage in trade and the export of natural resources. In the provinces, local men of influence were granted similar rights by central bureaucrats or were entrusted with monopolistic powers by national-level *chao pho*, for whom they acted as sole agents or representatives for goods and services in the area. The first generation of such provincial *chao pho* was mostly local Chinese merchants who had immigrated to Thailand in search of a better economic life.[12] Being conscious of the vulnerability that their foreign origin entailed, they were highly solicitous of the authorities and sought to cultivate good relationships with local bureaucrats. As Thailand was only formally centralized, and provincial officials were more or less free to interpret and enforce the laws as they saw fit, these bureaucrats could grant their entrepreneurial favourites a free hand in building their economic empires.[13]

The first generation of local *chao pho* needed to buy protection from Thai political elites in order to advance and protect their businesses. But the second generation of politically connected businessmen, who flourished during the 1960s, appeared to be more than just a docile partner in the system of patron–client relationships. Although they still did not have direct access to political power in Bangkok and thus had to depend on provincial patrons, their parents' successes had provided them with the considerable advantage of a strong economic base. They were usually referred to by the title *Sia*, a word that in Teochiu Chinese dialect was used to address a tycoon. Being born to local wealth, they naturally had a certain degree of respect within the community, which they could enhance with charitable activity. They were accustomed to socialize with low-ranking and underpaid provincial officials, whom they often provided with economic benefits. Years later, they could count on the gratitude of those minor officials who made it to the top of the bureaucratic hierarchy.[14]

However, even with a strong economic base, those children of a *chao pho* who had no 'guts' for the kind of things expected from a man of influence could never follow in the paternal footsteps.[15] New talent was always to hand, though, and a good number of second-generation *chao pho* emerged from former employees of the first-generation godfathers. They made good use of the opportunities provided in the 1960s by the rapid expansion of the capitalist economy from Bangkok to the outer provinces. This was the time of military rule under Field Marshal Sarit Thanarat, General Thanom Kittikachorn, and General Praphat Charusathien, when foreign capital was brought in to build US air bases and infrastructure connected with the pursuit of the Vietnam War. Private investment also came to Thailand from the United States and Japan, and war-related activity ensured that much of it got to the more distant provinces. Such an influx of capital naturally had a considerable impact on business sectors in all regions, and led most notably to an expansion of the provincial banking business. It made possible the rise of a new generation of provincial businessmen, whom it provided with new opportunities to make it big, especially in fields allied with construction.[16] Being now economically stronger than even the highest-ranking government officials in the provinces, some of those newly enriched local entrepreneurs were quite ready to assume a larger role as *chao pho*. Officially, the regimes of the 1960s asserted their desire to eliminate the 'dark influence' of the *chao pho*, but in practice the military rulers meant to do away with only those who were not their clients. Thus, each new group of military leaders would see the emergence of a new group of *chao pho*.[17] Indeed, one might even say that military dictatorship was *par excellence* the environment in which the patronage-based granting of business licences and concessions flourished, and this was the necessary condition for the birth of the present-day *chao pho*.

THE WAYS OF THE GODFATHER

But if the emergence of the modern *chao pho* is so closely linked with authoritarian rule, how is one to explain the significant role that is played by local godfathers since Thailand's assumption of the rocky road towards constitutional democracy in the early 1970s? Here, we must consider briefly the fact that businessmen as a group have come to take a new interest in politics. Where once they shied away from any overt involvement, in the past two decades businessmen have generally been very active in electoral campaigns.[18] This change of attitude must be attributed to the fact that the overthrow of the military regime in 1973 marked the beginning of a new era in which military bureaucrats no longer could fully dominate the Thai political scene. Now power struggles, which used to be reserved for the military-bureaucratic cliques, also took place in parliament. An elected MP was no longer powerless under the old 'bureaucratic polity', and business people as a class lost no time in reinforcing their economic influence with political power. Most of the major political parties that have been founded since 1973 are clearly business-dominated parties. Businessmen seek political power by running for election themselves or by giving financial support to candidates or parties of their choice.

It was this entrance to electoral politics by business people, especially those from Bangkok, which originally drew provincial godfathers into politics.[19] Usually, a new candidate for parliament would draw on all available means to win an election, relying most heavily, of course, on his own resources. But even if he has substantial amounts of money to spend, a Bangkok businessman soon finds out that money alone is not enough to procure votes; local connections are equally important. Indeed, they are most crucial for his first victory at the poll. Hence, both party leaders and individual candidates naturally seek support from local godfathers, who have money, manpower, and good-will at their disposal.

In the very beginning, the relationship between a candidate and a local godfather might not be anything other than personal.[20] The candidates would hope that past acquaintance with the godfather would win him over. Indeed, the godfather himself usually made no political demands on candidates he chose to support. Government officials who might have done the godfather some earlier favour might also ask him to support a certain candidate. These bureaucrats knew too well that elected politicians could reward or punish them, and it was in their interest to see that friendly candidates got elected. Any candidates lucky enough to receive support from both the godfather and high-ranking government officials in the area would have a pretty good chance to win.

On the part of the common people, voting for a particular candidate recommended by a local godfather is probably nothing more than paying back a friend's favour. To them, it is nothing compared to what the godfather has done for the community, and they are happy to comply. Political and financial support from the godfather could therefore prove quite crucial for a candidate's chances of elections.

Originally, the sphere of influence of a godfather might be limited to a particular area, not covering the whole constituency or the whole province. Still, a godfather's initial political success can lay the foundations for much wider sphere of influence. A godfather is much more than an ordinary *hua khanaen*, or political canvasser.[21] He can mobilize people and deliver a very substantial number of votes.

The successive general elections since 1979 have also contributed to the rising political influence of the godfathers. The increasingly fierce political party competition which marked these contests added to the significance of the godfather's role as electoral agent, and indeed the political influence of the godfathers seems to have increased with each general election. In return, this new political recognition puts the *chao pho* on very good terms with the highest-ranking government officials – both the ones stationed in the province and those in Bangkok. This easy access to both elected politicians and high-ranking officials enables local godfathers to climb rapidly up the social ladder. Nowadays it is not uncommon to see a godfather, acting in the role of local businessman, get himself openly and actively involved in fund-raising drives for charity organizations or similar public programmes. In many cases, the generous donations made by the godfather melt even the heart of an honest government official.[22] After all, government funding for public services in rural areas is always lacking. It is only natural, therefore, that government officials do not want to be too aggressive in enforcing the law if the godfather is involved. The general public, too, is quick to detect the special regard given the godfather by provincial or district officials.[23]

In the age of information some shrewd godfathers are known to have taken over the ownership of certain newspapers. It is interesting to note that some godfathers have been presented by certain columnists as true *nak leng*, with 'great heart'. They are often described as 'the ones who do nothing but give'.[24] As a rule, a godfather rarely denies the fact that he is an influential person, but he always insists that whatever influence he has within his community is the result of his good deeds, not the opposite. The image he wants to project is of one who gives not only to his immediate followers but also to the public at large, as a true philanthropist. Before *Sia* Yae's brutal murder by a bomb in 1989, he described his social role in the community in the following manner:

> I help people. Whoever is in trouble comes to me. Some people say that I am an influential person. Actually, it is simply the result of the good deeds that I have done all along. I help whoever comes to me. For example, when someone approaches me, I will ask first if he has been unjustly treated. I send my people, for example, a member of the Provincial Assembly, to look into the matter. My people will report to me if that person has really been badly treated or not. If it is true – if he is the victim of injustice – I will help him; but if he turns out to have cheated or injured, robbed, or killed others, I will turn him over to the police ... Each year my expenses on liquor alone run above 600,000 baht. At home I buy foreign whiskey to entertain guests and respected elders, or my friends. I also buy thousands of blankets to give to the monks or to my subordinates who ask me; in the cold season I send them off to whomever comes to my mind. I buy thousands of GQ T-shirts, and I give them away on New Year's Day.[25]

In the final analysis, the most important benefit a godfather receives from cultivating a cordial relationship with the authorities is his capacity to use them as collaborators in pursuing his economic interests. Gaining control of a business that needs special licensing or government concession is still the best way for a local godfather to procure income he can generously share with his deputies. *Kamnan* Poh, the most notorious godfather of the east coast, spoke thus about how he commanded loyalty from his own men:

> It is knowing how to share that matters. With big business, you give 10 per cent, 20 per cent here and there, giving everybody a better living. If you alone are rich while your people are poor, who are going to be your friends? I hold to this, and that's why people help me ... I have a licence for liquor sales in Chonburi province. At the *amphoe* [district] level, I am the sole distributor. At the *tambon* [subdistrict] level, however, I divide it up among my men, depending on the size of the *tambon* and the number of men. Those who do their job well will make 10,000 to 20,000 baht each month. Something like that. As the central dealer, I never use the money I make for myself. Whatever profit I make, I use to help out those who are in trouble. I myself have many other businesses.[26]

More often than not, the 'other businesses' owned by a local godfather are not only large in scale but also highly profitable. Before the Gulf War broke out in 1991, for example, it was not uncommon for a local godfather to be actively engaged in land investment, the most lucrative business at the time. After all, he was in a perfect position to do the job. For outside investors wanting to buy a big piece of property owned by different owners, a local godfather could serve as a special consultant to the project, or he could himself take up the responsibility for buying up and developing land. Acting as a broker, he could easily bring both owners and sellers together, thereby wrapping up deals in a very short time. In the meantime, the flow of investment money into the area opened up a variety of new economic opportunities, and local godfathers would be among the first to learn and take advantage of such openings. Apart from real estate, it is very typical for local godfathers to invest in housing development projects, hotels, and modern shopping centres.

The 'other businesses' of the godfather may not be altogether lawful, however. The kinds of illegal businesses that godfathers take part in are often determined by geographical factors. Of the 25 provinces outside Bangkok identified by the Police Department as areas infested with criminal *chao pho*, five are coastal provinces, four are border provinces, and four are both on the coast and on a border. The number of *chao pho* in these areas far exceeds those found in the rest of the country.[27] Typically, local godfathers in the coastal and border provinces are involved in the business of smuggling firearms, merchandise, or contraband, and in illegal mining or lumbering. Additionally, illegal activities like operating a gambling den or a casino, a brothel, or an underground lottery can be found anywhere provided that a deal can be worked out with responsible local authorities.[28] Even those godfathers who made inroads into respectable fields of endeavour seem reluctant to leave their illegal businesses, for as long as the authorities can be bought off, such enterprises are sure sources of income, and they can always be temporarily terminated if there is a crackdown.

One should not suppose that the *chao pho*'s course is always from criminal to legitimate activity, and not the other way round, since there are also many cases where politicians or their associates or relatives involve themselves in illegal activities, and thus assume the role of *chao pho*.[29] At any rate, local godfathers have found that one sure way of protecting their growing interests is to become directly involved in politics. Instead of merely supporting local politicians at the behest of certain government officials or helping out with candidates they know personally, local godfathers themselves now run for office or deliberately seek to have influence over elected MPs. Undeniably, the democratic process has provided them with a channel through which to rise politically and socially. They can reinforce their economic *itthiphon* with political *itthiphon.* Until 1998, a local godfather wishing to declare himself a candidate for election faced no legal restrictions regarding education, sex, or residential requirement, so long as he was Thai and his father was also a Thai citizen. Furthermore, with the emphasis on connections and money as principal instruments of the election campaigns, a godfather could compete on practically even terms with members of the established elite in Bangkok.[30] In short, electoral politics appears to be a most suitable avenue by which local godfathers or strong men can develop their potential to the full, and a few have even made it to the very top.

Yet, by and large, the *chao pho* try not to associate themselves too openly with any particular party. What they often do is render their services to candidates belonging to different parties, seemingly contenting themselves with a minor but critical role in an election campaign. For example, *Sia* Yae (Somchai Ruekwararak) of Angthong province, who owned construction and lumbering businesses in many provinces, started out by supporting the Social Action Party (Kit Sangkhom, SAP) in 1976. But in the 1979, 1983, and 1986 elections he switched his support to Chart Thai, becoming a member of its executive committee in 1983. However, before the general election of 1988 he resigned from his Chart Thai post, though he continued to support his men in that party. Of six Chart Thai MPs blacklisted as godfathers in 1991 by the Police Department, Udomsak Thangthong was by 1998 with Gen. Chavalit Yongchaiyudh's New Aspiration Party, Piya Angkhinan (*Sia* Paeng) was deputy leader of the Social Action Party (SAP), and Jongchai Thiengtham was a deputy minister in Chuan Leekpai's Democratic Party government.[31]

Kamnan Poh showed similar flexibility. Before 1986, he was known to have helped candidates from different parties. In that year he backed two candidates from the SAP in Election District Two of Chonburi, while in District One he threw his weight behind the candidate from the Chart Prachathipatai (National Democracy) Party. In the election of 1988, *Kamnan* Poh gave his full support to the SAP, claiming that he had been asked to do so by party elders and that furthermore he had friends and relatives running under this party's banner.[32] Indeed, it was an open secret that *Kamnan* Poh had the final say on who was going to run for the SAP in Chonburi province. Even Kukrit Pramoj, a former prime minister and the SAP's founder, had to take a potential candidate for election in Chonburi to see

Kamnan Poh. But in March 1992, with his in-laws and son both running for the Sammakkhi Tham (United Dharma) Party, he switched support to that newly formed organization. With the Samakkhi Tham's demise, and with his sons and relatives now running for the Chart Pattana (National Development) Party, *Kamnan* Poh moved his support to that organization; and by the 1995 election the family had transferred its allegiance to Chart Thai. As for *Kamnan* Poh's own criteria, he stated in a 1986 interview that: 'We are all for our *phuak* [crowd of friends] and not for any *phak* [party]. In rural areas this is how it has to be … I support people, not parties.'[33]

It should therefore come as no surprise that a godfather can occasionally flex political muscle both at national and local levels through individuals he has helped to win election. At the time of the 1988 general elections, *Sia* Yae had this to say about how he acquired such influence:

> All 24 members of the Provincial Assembly are from our team. We have our people in the administrations of Pa Mok, Wisetchaichan, and Muang municipalities. In this general election I have supported candidates in 12 different provinces, namely Singhaburi, Ayutthaya, Phetchaburi, Nakorn Pathom, Nakorn Sawan, Saraburi, Nan, Chaiyaphum, Loei, Nongkai, Lopburi, and Angthong. And several of my people have been elected in the name of different political parties.[34]

In short, as an elected MP or a patron of MPs, a local godfather can now acquire acknowledgment by state power and more easily see to it that his business and power hegemony in the community remains intact. In order to make sure his interests are protected, a local godfather must limit himself to supporting only those candidates who have the potential to win, i.e. they must be at least minimally acceptable to the voters. It is not unknown for *chao pho* to encourage their chances with a bit of sharp practice. *Kamnan* Poh described how he did this:

> Frankly speaking, voter turnout is around 60 per cent, and the reason the count showed 80 per cent was because we rigged the ballot box. The voting day was Sunday, and a lot of women vendors were not available. Not many people turned out, and whenever the opportunity arose, we rigged the ballot box. At the Srinagarinvirote University polling station, which had around a thousand votes or so, only 27.6 per cent showed up – and some of these weren't even on the electoral list. We did not really want

> to get involved at that place; those lecturers, they love to make a fuss out of voting. But how did we rig the ballot box? Well, I can tell you. We had citizen identification cards in our hands, and the officials at the polling place were our own people. They could see that certain voters were not the ones whose names were on the electoral list, but they pretended not to know. Whoever had an ID card could vote, using other voters' names. Who was going to check to see that our ID cards matched the names on the list? Nobody wants to get involved in tampering with ballot boxes; this could mean imprisonment. But this simple method, which nobody knows about, makes district officials happy, for they love to see a high voter turnout. If a large number of people come out to vote, they get some recognition. Sometimes they even win the prize for best electoral turnout. However, we do not do this in many places, only in those where people do not have the time to come and vote do we rig the ballot box. There is no outright fraud.[35]

A godfather becomes politically powerful if he has a substantial number of elected politicians under his control. Probably the most notorious demonstration of such clout occurred in 1988. Here, a group of five MPs from the now defunct Kit Prachakom (Community Action) Party abruptly withdrew their names from a crucial no-confidence motion against Prime Minister Gen. Prem Tinsulanonda that had been sponsored by all the opposition parties, forcing the motion's collapse. Apparently, what happened was that those MPs were under the patronage of *Sia* Leng, who had been asked by a certain general to help block the motion. Once *Sia* Leng intervened, the five MPs went against their party's discipline and withdrew their names.[36] After the dissolution of parliament in 1988, *Sia* Leng took his five MPs to join the Ratsadorn (People's) Party, led by General Tianchai Sirisumphan. But prior to that move – before anyone knew for certain which way these particular politicians would go – one of them had commented that 'We are like professional boxers, with Mr Charoen [*Sia* Leng] as our manager. Whoever and wherever Mr Charoen wants us to fight, we have to oblige.'[37]

THE FUTURE OF THE GODFATHER

Just before the military coup of 1991, it seemed that the social and political influence of local godfathers had reached new heights. Guests who attended *Kamnan* Poh's birthday party that year included not only high-ranking government officials but also leaders of major political parties and some cabinet members. After the military takeover, it appeared for a while that some drastic measures would be launched against the *chao pho*. There was talk about new legislation and other measures to curb their influence. It was even proposed to round them up and detain them on an isolated island. But, apart from a few who fell victim to internecine warfare, the species survived very well. It was reported that, when a team of police commandos raided *Kamnan* Poh's residence, they encountered none of the illegal weapons they had expected to find. Instead they found a big picture of *Kamnan* Poh posing with General Sunthorn Kongsompong, the chairman of the National Peacekeeping Council, with an autograph by the general reading, 'To *Kamnan* Poh with love'.[38] The results of the September 1992 election, following the restoration of democracy, indicated the *chao pho*'s ready adjustment to a new turn of the political wheel.[39]

All the former MPs blacklisted by the Police Department in 1991 as *chao pho* easily won election in September 1992.[40] Indeed, it may be said that in the subsequent period they rose to new heights. The government of Banharn Silpa-archa (1995–1996) gave a new legitimacy to the *chao pho* style, and his successor Gen. Chavalit Yongchaiyudh (1996–1997) appointed as deputy minister of agriculture Udomsak Thangthong (*Sia* Oh), a long-time MP from Prachuap Khiri Khan, who had been on the 1991 police blacklist. Also on the police blacklist had been Police Capt. Chaloem Yoobamrung, a flamboyant MP from Bangkok who, having dissolved his own Muan Chon Party in order to support Chavalit's New Aspiration Party, was rewarded by being made its deputy leader. The Chuan Leekpai government (1997–), though considered relatively clean and favourable to reform, none the less included Vattana Assavahame as deputy minister of the interior.[41] Jongchai Thiengtham (*Sia* Jong), a Suphanburi MP whose name was on the 1991 police blacklist, was made deputy minister of labour and social welfare in the same government. Sonthaya Khunpleum, the eldest son of *Kamnan* Poh, served as deputy minister of industry in the Banharn government and as deputy minister of transport in Chuan's cabinet.

A godfather, so it seems, is an amphibian that can exist both on democratic land and in dictatorial water. Should the democratic process continue, he would rely on the political activities we have described. But should it be interrupted, one can expect him to seek relationships with individual power-holders, as near to the top as possible, in order to protect his economic interests.

Yet, it is possible that changing political realities will affect the *chao pho*'s role. Some, more successful in business than politics, may decide to limit themselves to their more legitimate business ventures. Political success may be dangerous, for it can tempt the ambitious godfather to expand his sphere of influence and eliminate the competition, in the process bringing violent confrontation.[42] And it may even happen that a godfather finds himself under arrest.

Even the mighty *Kamnan* Pho has been exposed to these perils. In late 1993 his right-hand man, 'Kao Pattaya', who reportedly looked after his interests in the booming resort area of Pattaya, was gunned down in broad daylight. It was said that *Kamnan* Pho was really shaken by this loss. Then in 1994 he himself was arrested by Police Maj. Gen. Seri Taemeeyawes, a Thai 'Serpico', together with some minor municipal officials of Pattaya, on charges of corruption and embezzlement in land dealings with Pattaya city (at the time of writing, the case was still pending in court). Perhaps it is understandable that in recent years *Kamnan* Pho (who now graces the office of mayor of Saen Sook municipality in Chonburi) has been attempting to distance himself from overtly dirty politics. This by no means implies that he has relinquished his hold on Chonburi's political life, however.[43]

Godfathers opting to concentrate on legitimate business will attempt to look respectable, presenting themselves more and more as socially responsible businessmen and becoming less openly involved with party politics. In some cases, family members are now in national politics, and they can be relied on to represent their interests.[44] This will be of especial use if the new requirements for electoral candidates to have a higher education and an unblemished reputation are implemented. Here again, *Kamnan* Pho provides vivid illustration of the point. His eldest son, Sonthaya Khunpleum, graduated from Burapha University with a master's degree in Education, was elected to the House of Representatives in March 1992 for the Samakkhi Tham Party and re-elected in September 1992 for the Chart Thai Party. He is currently deputy minister of transport in the Chuan government. *Kamnan* Pho's second son, Wittaya Khunpleum, procured a master's degree in the US, was elected to the House in September 1992 for the Chart Pattana Party, and in 1995 and subsequently for the Chart Thai Party. The third son, Itthiphon Khunpleum, who also returned from the US with a master's degree, has recently announced his intention to enter politics, and everyone expects him to do very well.

Chao pho can also depend to a certain extent on the continued loyalty of the local political machines that they have constructed over the years. As their legitimate businesses grow, some of the *chao pho* may eventually decide to leave their illegal enterprises entirely to others, and very likely this will be even more true in the case of their children. More highly educated and sophisticated, and probably less skilled in intimidation, the children of a godfather are likely to feel that they can compete with business rivals on equal terms, though no doubt their family name will give them a certain advantage.

But this does not mean that the era of the *chao pho* will soon come to an end. On the contrary, the graceful exit by former *chao pho* from criminal enterprise may encourage others to follow their earlier path – beginning with those faithful deputies left to handle illegal businesses. Some of them will gradually emerge as persons with *itthiphon*, who may be influential enough to become local godfathers, and who may some day grow into respectable businessmen-cum-politicians themselves.

CONCLUSION

Since the mid-1970s, thanks to social and economic changes which took place a decade earlier, business people working through political parties have emerged as a new and significant force competing with the military. During this time, provincial and regional businessmen have also risen in economic stature and become part of the new social forces whose growing demands have successfully challenged the legitimacy of the old alliance between the military and its selected business-political clients in the capital. With the reinstatement of electoral politics, political power is no longer concentrated in Bangkok. Yet, while the parliamentary system has presented unprecedented opportunities to the entrepreneurial class, it has at the same time become the best channel for local godfathers to reinforce their personal influence with political power. Provincial godfathers now provide financial and other essential supports to a number of candidates in exchange for favours in the form of economic benefits or protection from law enforcement authorities. They can themselves contest elections, and often are easily victorious. Indeed, as elections in Thailand have become institutionalized, provincial godfathers have extended their influence both politically and socially. With their newly acquired political credentials, they now gain direct access to political power in Bangkok. They no longer need to depend solely on cooperation from local officials, because they themselves have connections with, or even some control over, the superiors of even the highest-ranking of those provincial officials.

It is only natural for bureaucrats in general and the military in particular to be greatly disturbed in principle by this phenomenon. During election campaigns military leaders regularly attack big business and its bad influence (including the *chao pho*) in Thai politics. Claiming that the army too has the responsibility to help develop democracy, the military often points to the fact that political imbalances in favour of affluent business groups who come to power through the practices of bribery and vote-buying will trap Thailand in a vicious cycle of political underdevelopment. But, as the junta of 1991–1992 demonstrated, too often military leaders themselves really aspire to be the godfathers of the godfathers.

Until 1997, civilian governments showed themselves even less eager to tackle the problem, in spite of mounting frustration at the level of corruption and the cost of money politics. After all, most political parties in Thailand are at best regional associations, which differ very little from each other on matters of policy. Moreover, just about every major party consists of a number of small factions, each with its own leader. In order to maintain his status within the party, each faction leader in turn has to rely on the support of certain influential individuals in the provinces. In these circumstances, it seemed likely that only those local godfathers who happened to back the wrong political candidates had any cause for worry.

The economic crisis did much to concentrate politicians' minds on the need for more effective and honest government, however, and the result has been an effort at constitutional and electoral reform that aims particularly at attacking the *chao pho* presence in politics. What success this will bring only time will tell. No doubt it will reinforce the drive towards respectability in politics which we noted earlier as already in train. However, whether it will really reduce the influence of local godfathers is another matter. Given their entrenchment in provincial economic and political life, and their reach into the highest levels of national power, change will not be easy.

NOTES

1. *The Nation*, 8 August 1991.
2. Thus one of the military leaders of the National Peacekeeping Council (NPC) junta remarked that *phu mi itthiphon* ['influential persons', another term for *chao pho*, see below] contributed to the turmoil of the country,

especially those who later sought political power. We think that if nothing is done, the country will suffer' *Khu kang thurakit,* 21–27 October 1991.

3. Acharaporn Kamutphitsamai, '*Nak leng*', in Suwanna Satha-anand and Nuangnoi Boonyate, (eds) *Kam: rong roy kwamkid kwamchua thai* (Bangkok: Chulalongkorn University Press, 1992), p. 229.

4. See Acharaporn Kamutphitsamai, '*Nak leng*', pp. 231–232, for a discussion of the traditional role of *nak leng.*

5. For a discussion of the concepts introduced in this paragraph, see Yoshifumi Tamada, 'Itthiphon and Amnat: An Informal Aspect of Thai Politics', *Tonan Ajia Kenkyu/Southeast Asian Studies* 28 (1991): 455.

6. Sondhi Limthongkul, 'Chao pho: kankamnoet lae damrongyu yang pen rabop', *Samut Sangkomsat* 12 (January-July 1991): 128.

7. Kukrit Pramoj, 'Soi Suanplu', *Sayam rat,* 15 March 1988.

8. Ibid.

9. *Thai rat,* 23 January 1991. For background on *Sia* Leng, see Somrudee Nicrowattanayingyong, 'Thailand's NIC Democracy: A Study of Provincial Election', paper presented to the 43rd Annual Meeting of the Association for Asian Studies, 11–14 April 1991, p. 20 n. 70; also see the contribution of Hewison and Thongyou in this volume.

10. Acharaporn Kamutphitsamai, '*Nak leng*', p. 237.

11. For a discussion of the *pho liang,* see Edward Van Roy, *Economic Systems of Northern Thailand: Structural Change* (Ithaca: Cornell University Press, 1971).

12. While it is true that the first generation of provincial *chao pho* were mostly Sino-Thai, there were some of other origins. A notorious *chao pho* of Saraburi province, for example, was an Afghan (Pathan) who controlled the beef market by monopolizing the import and slaughter of cattle.

13. For a discussion of the characteristics of first-generation *chao pho,* see Sondhi Limthongkul, 'Chao pho', pp. 128–134.

14. Sondhi Limthongkul, 'Chao pho', pp. 134–135.

15. Kukrit Pramoj, 'Soi Suanplu', p. 9.

16. Benedict Anderson, 'Murder and Progress in Modern Siam', *New Left Review* 181 (1990): 49–53; and Tamada, '*Itthiphon* and *Amnat*", pp. 462–464.

17. There is no space here to explore the role of the military in the development of the godfather, but Suriyan Sakthaisong's memoir clearly illustrates such a connection. See Suriyan Sakthaisong, *Senthang mafia* (Bangkok: Matichon Press, 1990).

18. See Rangsan Thanaponphan, *Krabuan kan kamnoed nayobai setthakit kan muang nai prathet thai: bot wikro choeng prawatsat setthakit kan muang 2475–2530* (Bangkok: Social Science Association of Thailand, 1989), pp. 155–178.

19. See Sombat Chantornvong, *Kan muang ruang kan luaktang: suksa chapo koranee kan luaktang tuapai pho. so. 2529* (Bangkok: The Foundation for Democracy and Development Studies, 1987).

20. *Kamnan* Poh explained why he campaigned for Sompong Amornviwat, a prominent businessman, in the election of 1986:'I helped him because I wanted to return his favour. When he was a director of the Srinakhorn Bank, and I wanted to take out a loan to invest because I lacked the cash, I went to him. He helped me.' *Matichon sut sapda*, 25 May 1986.

21. For a discussion of the workings of the *hua khanaen* system, see Chapter 4 in this volume.

22. One of the things the Ministry of the Interior has done to keep provincial officials from falling under the spell of local godfathers is to coin the slogan:'Don't accept any invitation [from a *chao pho*]. Don't accept anything [from a *chao pho*]. Don't consider [a *chao pho*] as a donor.'

23. Tamada, '*Itthiphon* and *Amnat*', p. 459.

24. Thus an interview by Sonthaya Khunpleum, *Kamnan* Poh's son, revealed that 'I am very much like my father in several ways. My father does not know how to say "no". He does not know how to refuse a request put by other people. If personally confronted with a request, he rarely turns it down. Unless it makes absolutely no sense, he will help. He will always give. I am like that myself. My friends tell me so. I am a very considerate person. I don't really know how to say no, for we have to give to those who come to us.' According to his son, for the two years that *Kamnan* Poh was mayor of Sansuk municipality, he spent 20 million baht on charity, going mostly to schools and temples. *Matichon sut sapda,* 18 October 1991.

25. *Thai rat*, 26 July 1988. Another revealing example is the first speech in parliament by Udomsak Thangthong (*Sia* Oh), deputy minister of agriculture in the Chavalit cabinet. Under attack by members of opposition parties during the no-confidence debate of 1997, he stressed the informal network of relationships which exists among Thai politicians, and claimed to have done favours for just about everyone who came to him for help, regardless of the party to which that person belonged.

26. *Matichon*, 7 July 1988.

27. The Division of Research and Development, Police Department, Ministry of the Interior, estimated that there were 97 *chao pho* in border and/or coastal provinces, and 71 elsewhere (*Sayam rat,* 2 November 1991).

28. A list of Bangkok-based and provincial godfathers blacklisted by the Police Department, and the activities they are accused of being involved in, may be found in *Sayam rat,* 2 November 1991. It should be added that Bangkok *chao pho,* unlike their counterparts upcountry, can only exert their influence over very small areas of the city. Such areas are usually home to lower-class people, for whom the *chao pho* can play the role of patron. With local residents on the side of the *chao pho*, the police, even if they want to, find it very difficult to crack down on their illegal activities. During election time, such *chao pho* can also promise a sizable number of votes to the candidates of their choice.

29. It is indeed often quite difficult to say which comes first, the politician or the criminal. On 30 June 1994 police from the Crime Suppression Division

in Bangkok raided a gambling den in Chiang Mai owned by the father of a Chiang Mai MP who also happened to serve as a secretary to the Minister of the Interior. As the house was reportedly rented to somebody else, the father of the MP was not arrested. See *Bangkok Post,* 30 June 1994. After the military coup of February 1991, the Police Department came up with a list of 174 godfathers, which included six former MPs from the Chart Thai Party and a former cabinet member. The former MPs were Piya Angkhinant, alias *Sia* Paeng (Phetchaburi), Boonsong Somjai, alias *Sia* Boh (Prachinburi), Udomsak Thangthong, alias *Sia* Oh (Prachuap Khiri Khan), Sompao Prachuabmoh, alias *Sia* Soh (Prachuap Khiri Khan), Jongchai Thiengtham or *Sia* Jong (Suphanburi), and Thanit Traisuwan or *Sia* Thoh (Trat). The ex-cabinet member accused of underworld activities was Police Captain Chaloem Yoobamrung, the leader of the Muan Chon Party. *Nation,* 8 August 1991.

30. Anderson, 'Murder and Progress', pp. 52–53.

31. The other two, Boonsong Somjai (*Sia* Boh, Prachinburi), and Thanit Traisuwan (*Sia* Thoh, Trat), failed to win re-election in 1996.

32. *Matichon,* 8 June 1988.

33. *Matichon sut sapda,* 25 May 1986. See also the interview given by *Sia* Leng in *Phuchatkan* no. 49 (October 1987).

34. *Thai rat,* 26 July 1988.

35. *Matichon sutsapda,* 25 May 1986.

36. For further details, see Somrudee Nicrowattanayingyong, 'Thailand's NIC Democracy', p. 17.

37. *Sia* Leng later moved his support to the newly formed Khwan Wang Mai (New Aspiration) Party, NAP) under the leadership of former army commander-in-chief (and later prime minister) Gen. Chavalit Yongchaiyudh. Pisal Mulasastsatorn, the secretary-general of the NAP and himself a former permanent under-secretary of the Ministry of the Interior, said of *Sia* Leng: 'Mr Charoen is a good person, with well-established assets. He is a supporter of the NAP as well as of several other political parties. He knows a large number of MPs. I don't know what to call him ... It is difficult to distinguish between a *phu mi itthiphon* and a *phu mi barami* [a charismatic person].' *Matichon,* 22 January 1991.

38. *Matichon,* 31 January 1991.

39. Klaew Thanikul, the alleged No. 1 godfather in Bangkok's underworld, was a member of the executive committee of the Seri Niyom (Liberal) Party and was reportedly thinking of running for office when he was gunned down in April 1991. His son, however, easily won the election and became an MP from Samut Songram province. *Sia* Leng did well as a supporter of the NAP. *Kamnan* Poh placed two sons as MPs in the lower house of parliament.

40. See footnote 28.

41. Vattana, a long-serving MP from Samut Prakan, was not one of the 174 godfathers on the Police Department's 1991 blacklist, but his name has

often been associated with such underworld activities as gambling, drug trafficking, and oil smuggling. In 1994 the US embassy in Bangkok denied him a visa on the ground of suspected involvement in the drugs trade. In late 1997, Vattana broke with the leadership of the Prachakorn Thai Party to lead a group of MPs over to the Chuan side, thereby acquiring his ministerial position.

42. For details of the death of a godfather, apparently as the result of a conflict of business interests, see Anderson, 'Murder and Progress', pp. 58–59.

43. Uthai Phimchaichon, a former speaker of the lower house of parliament, spoke out against *Kamnan* Pho when running as candidate in a Chonburi district in the 1995 elections. In spite of his political experience and high national standing, he lost badly. His political career did not come to an end, for in 1997 he was made president of the prestigious Constituent Assembly, but it seems highly unlikely that he will ever again dare to run for office in Chonburi.

44. Somrudee Nicrowattanayingyong, 'Thailand's NIC Democracy', p. 24, n. 89. It has been rumoured that the well-known godfathers Udomsak Thangthong (*Sia* Oh) and Sompao Prachuabmoh (*Sia* Soh) are preparing to retire from active politics in favour of their offspring; the Democrat Party was said to be particularly interested in persuading Udomsak's son to run under its banner.

FOUR

The Rise of Local Power in Thailand
Provincial Crime, Elections and the Bureaucracy

James Ockey

When the governor of Phichit province ordered the suspension of six local *kamnan*[1] for failure to obey orders in the spring of 1989, he touched off a furore that would reach the highest levels of government. The Democrat Party (DP, Prachatipat), a partner in the governing coalition, gave the governor its full support,[2] and the minister of the interior insisted the governor would not be transferred.[3] Yet his term as governor of Phichit lasted less than two weeks after these declarations. The victory of the *kamnan*, who were reinstated, and the transfer of the governor reflect the changing power relationships between officials and local politicians. A closer examination will help reveal these changes and the influence of local politicians in the national political process.

The governor arrived in Phichit with a reputation for stringency and a record of integrity and confrontation, having served previously as governor of Patthalung, Samut Prakan, and nearby Uttaradit. In Phichit he would work with four members of parliament from two election districts. District Two had been controlled by Prachathipat for two successive elections, with the secretary-general of the party, Sanan Khachonprasat, holding one of the two seats. District One, which included the provincial capital, was split between the Chart Thai (Chart Thai, Thai Nation Party) and the Ratsadorn (Rassadorn) Party.

Sanan was minister of agriculture, and the Ratsadorn Party MP, Phaithun Kaeothong, was deputy minister of industry.

The *kamnan* and *phuyaiban* of Phichit had earlier joined together to form an association to promote unity and cooperation and to prevent outside interference, particularly from corrupt government officials.[4] Many of the members of the Association of *Kamnan* and *Phuyaiban* were involved in the construction industry, including its vice president, who allegedly owned a construction company in partnership with the Ratsadorn Party MP.[5] The president of the association[6] had been the *kamnan* of Hua Dong for the past 10 years. His elder brother had earlier served as *kamnan* for 16 years before resigning to run for parliament where he served consecutive terms in 1975 and 1976. His younger brother was a prominent Bangkok businessman, involved in finance and a shopping mall. The *kamnan* managed the family businesses in Phichit and nearby provinces, which included three rice mills, the whiskey concession[7] for 12 provinces, and a finance company with branches in Phichit, Phitsanulok, Nakhon Sawan, and Bangkok.[8]

Because of his Chinese ancestry and limited education, the president of the Association of *Kamnan* and *Phuyaiban* did not meet the requirements necessary to run for parliament. The *kamnan* did support candidates for parliament, both financially and through his personal ties and influence. It was said that no candidate could be successful in Election District One without his help, and some even alleged that candidates paid him for his support.[9] Certainly his influence as president of the Association of *Kamnan* and *Phuyaiban* and his links to the network of whiskey distributors in the province would make it difficult for a candidate to overcome his opposition.

The confrontation that led to the transfer of the governor was rooted in his efforts to reduce corruption in provincial construction projects, especially in the *Phuyaiban* Development Fund under the control of the *kamnan* and the *phuyaiban* councils. The governor had been successful in reducing corruption in Uttaradit and sought to apply the same procedures in Phichit.[10] One contract, for a bridge spanning the Yom River, was opened for bidding eight times without a proposal acceptable to the governor.[11] Early in the year, the proposals for the new *phuyaiban* development programme budget were submitted to the governor by the *phuyaiban* councils. When he rejected many of them, local politicians increased their resistance to the governor.[12]

On 3 May 1989, the governor suspended six *kamnan* for resisting orders. The following day a group of *kamnan* and *phuyaiban* went to Bangkok with a letter addressed to the minister of the interior. The local politicians met with the members of parliament from Election District One; the Ratsadorn Party member, after 'giving them advice', arranged for the *kamnan* to meet with the deputy minister of interior.[13] Upon enlisting his support, the *kamnan* returned to Phichit.

By 9 May, the Ministry of the Interior had not yet undertaken to move the governor, and the *kamnan* decided to apply public pressure on the governor and the Ministry. A demonstration was organized in front of the provincial government offices. Led by some twenty *kamnan* and *phuyaiban* from Election District One, including the six who had been suspended, an estimated 10,000 demonstrators were assembled to try to force the Ministry of the Interior to move the governor. *Kamnan* and *phuyaiban* served as organizers and representatives for the demonstrators, providing transportation, food, and perhaps other rewards for participants from their own villages.[14] The villagers insisted they would continue their demonstration until their demands were met: to move the governor, restore the six *kamnan* to their positions, and cancel the order suspending the six *kamnan*.[15] After two days of demonstrations, a police officer from the regional police headquarters was sent to Phichit to negotiate with the villagers. He convinced the demonstrators to disperse, promising to present their demands to the Ministry of the Interior for consideration.

Meanwhile, allies of the governor began to organize support. Prachathipat, led in this matter by Secretary-General Sanan, announced its approval of the performance of the governor. Counter-demonstrations in favour of the governor took place in several cities in Election District Two.[16] To end the demonstrations, the Ministry of the Interior promised an investigation into the behaviour of the governor. The investigation was conducted by an inspector-general sent to Phichit from Bangkok. It found the governor blameless, clearing him of dishonesty and commending him for protecting the interests of the government.[17] Perhaps hoping to end the bickering between ministers and MPs from the governing coalition, the minister of the interior announced his support for the governor, declaring that he would not be transferred. The six suspended *kamnan* were restored to their positions, and the governor announced that the controversy had ended.

However, the opponents of the governor continued to manoeuvre for his transfer. With the deputy minister of the interior continuing to agitate at the top, the *kamnan* and their allies set in motion plans to convince the *kamnan*, *phuyaiban*, and their assistants to resign en masse.[18] Leaflets denouncing the governor began to appear. And, after mimeographed resignation letters from some 1,141 *kamnan*, *phuyaiban*, and other *phuyaiban*- and village-level officials were submitted,[19] demonstrations began again. This time the demonstrators vowed they would remain until the governor was transferred.

The governor responded with an investigation into the resignation letters, and with demonstrations by his own supporters. According to the governor, about 80% of the resignation letters were forged without the knowledge of the principals.[20] Some of the *kamnan*, *phuyaiban*, and their assistants were reportedly coerced into signing the letters.[21] The Democrat Party continued to support the governor, and the minister of the interior vowed that he would not be replaced. Large counter-demonstrations began in towns throughout Election District Two and in a few areas of District One.

Although the governor had displayed a good deal of support, particularly within the bureaucracy, he was unable to govern. Ultimately, he resigned: he was moved to Bangkok. How were these *kamnan* and *phuyaiban*, ostensibly the lowest-level government officials – not truly part of the state bureaucracy at all – able to enlist the support of members of parliament, and even a minister from another province, in removing a provincial governor? To answer this question, it is necessary to look at changes in the local and national political levels brought about by economic growth, the rise of provincial gangsters and corrupt politicians, the advent of parliamentary democracy, and the nature of the electoral system.

THE TRANSFORMATION OF THE THAI POLITY

Before the administrative reforms implemented at the turn of the century, local politics in Thailand depended on distance from the centres of power – either Bangkok or the regional lords. Much of rural Thailand was far enough from the centres of power to be little affected by events and edicts issued there. The centre did what it could to gain influence in isolated areas by recognizing the power of existing community leaders and naming them *kamnan*. Having gained their positions through their influence in the community, the *kamnan* used their new posts to develop connections to the centres of power.[22] Positions in the bureaucracy were unsalaried and often hereditary, and bureaucrats were dependent on the localities for resources and influence.

The administrative reforms King Chulalongkorn implemented in the last decade of the nineteenth century aimed at centralizing the bureaucracy and making it dependent on Bangkok rather than on the locality.[23] King Chulalongkorn also sought to 'modernize' and 'professionalize' the bureaucracy along Western lines. Local administrators were placed on salary and subjected to a rotation system in an attempt – of only limited success – to eliminate their personal influence. Since then, the national bureaucracy has expanded and has sought to extend its influence into the remote areas of the countryside, bringing its ideology, its working style, and its expectations with it.[24] With the reforms, local administrators obtained a direct conduit to the top through the hierarchical bureaucracy. Particularly during the first half of the twentieth century, they were in a position to exert considerable control over local notables through both coercion and largesse, based on central government resources. However, the tradition of local power, and of leadership based on local resources, remained in place even as the bureaucracy expanded its reach and power. Since 1986, *kamnan* and *phuyaiban* have been elected rather than appointed, making the position officially dependent on the locality rather than the bureaucracy.[25] Naturally there was a wide variation in the power of the bureaucracy in local areas: in general, however, the growth of independent local power was relatively slow compared to the growth of the bureaucracy during the first half of this century. However, by the 1960s processes had been set in motion that would alter the balance again between the bureaucracy and local power.

Ironically, the balance began to tip noticeably during the dictatorship of Field Marshal Sarit Thanarat (1957–1962), who sought to centralize power through a reassertion of traditional patterns of authority. Sarit, 'as an army officer trained to command and to be followed, ... was naturally inclined to believe in the superiority of the bureaucracy and government over parliament.'[26] He relied on the bureaucracy to carry out his orders and implement his plans for development, even going as far as to eliminate local elections in 1959. However, rather than depending on state enterprises and keeping economic development under the control of the bureaucracy, as his predecessors had, Sarit chose to promote industrial development through private investment. Simultaneously, the government began to invest large amounts of money to build up the infrastructure in the provinces. This allowed local notables, particularly those with good connections to the administration, to develop the financial resources necessary to expand their power and control in the provinces.

Growth, diversification, and the creation of autonomous power centres were the results of the industrial promotion and private investment policies pursued by Sarit and his successors. Gross domestic product grew from 54 billion baht in 1960 to 147.4 billion in 1970, to 658.5 billion in 1980, and 2.1 trillion baht (US$80 billion) by 1990.[27] The average annual growth rate between 1965 and 1980 stood at 7.4%, and for 1980 through 1991 it rose to 7.9%.[28] Most of this growth occurred outside the agricultural sector, which expanded at a rate of 4.9% between 1965 and 1980: growth in the manufacturing sector averaged 10.9%, in industry 9.5%, and in services 8.0%. Rice, as a percentage of the total value of exports, fell from 29.8% in 1960 to 8.8% by 1989.[29] And agriculture, which had accounted for over 50% of GDP in 1950, amounted to just 12% by 1991, while manufacturing, industry, and services had all surpassed agriculture as contributors to the GDP.[30]

The Sarit government's economic planning and its promotion of private enterprise came at a time when the economy was beginning to benefit from the US battle against communism in Southeast Asia. Military aid 'averaged over 1 billion baht (US$40 million) throughout the 1960s. Its aggregate figures amounted to 14.3 billion baht (US$560 million) during 1962–1970.'[31] During this period, military aid amounted to 12% of total earnings from exports.[32] In addition, a large amount of capital entered the country through US soldiers stationed in Thailand and via soldiers in Thailand for rest and recreation (R&R).[33] Meeting the desires of these visitors meant a heavy investment and return in the services sector and led to many opportunities for investment in new businesses.[34]

Much of the aid pouring into Thailand went into the rural economy through the building of military bases, and through the attempts to destroy the Communist Party by enhancing rural infrastructure and by improving the livelihood of villagers. By the time US troops left Thailand in 1976, US military construction costs had amounted to some US$388.3 million, nearly all of it going to the provinces.[35] Beyond these direct costs, the stationing of up to 50,000 US troops (again nearly all in the provinces), the transportation of goods to the bases, and the building of strategic roads all meant more money flowing into the provincial economy. Provincial roads grew from 2,118 to 2,793 km between 1960 and 1965; then, during the peak period of the Vietnam War, road construction projects more than doubled the provincial road system to 5,891 km in 1970, continued at a slightly lower rate of increase to 7,439 km by 1975, and again accelerated to 14,257 km by 1980, to 21,017 in 1985, and 27,595 in 1989.[36]

Increasing rural wealth can be seen in the growth of the provincial banking system during this period. The number of bank branches in the provinces grew from four in 1940 to 32 in 1950 and to 239 in 1960. By 1980 the number of bank branches outside the Bangkok/Thonburi metropolitan area had exceeded 1,000, and by 1988 the total reached nearly 1,500.[37] By 1995, there were over 2,100 bank branches outside Bangkok.[38] Much of the increase was forced by laws designed to promote growth in the provinces,[39] yet economic growth in the provinces continues to lag behind Bangkok. Nevertheless, most rural areas of the country have been integrated into the national economy.

THE RISE OF THE *CHAO PHO*

Among the most profitable businesses that emerged throughout provincial Thailand were many illegal operations, including smuggling, vice, and gambling. These types of enterprise have the advantages of low investment, high returns, and no taxes. By gaining the protection of local officials, the entrepreneurs engaging in these illegal activities prospered; furthermore, those who had close connections with government officials were able to secure lucrative government contracts through the efforts of those officials – in return for a share of the profits. Corruption and criminal activity became important methods of capital accumulation in many provinces. By cooperating with particular individuals, officials helped to concentrate capital, particularly illegal capital, and so bear much of the responsibility for the rise of the *chao pho*.

The gangster image evoked by the English translation of *chao pho* – 'godfather' – is misleading. Rather, *chao pho* tend to exhibit many of the characteristics of the *nak leng*, a traditional Thai leadership figure for whom there has always been much admiration (a 'tough' who is brave, bold and above all loyal to his friends).[40] By adhering to this traditional leadership style, and by being generous to those under his influence, the provincial chao pho can gain considerable legitimacy in his own area. So while the law may view him as a criminal, local voters may see him as a natural choice to represent their interests in Bangkok. And when he offers them money for their vote, this is just a further example of his generosity.[41]

The term *chao pho* has been so widely applied that it is worth identifying several different types. Originally the term was applied to *chao pho* involved in crime, particularly gambling, who were closest to the English-language 'godfather'. The main source of wealth for this type of *chao pho*, at least initially, is criminal activity. A second type of *chao pho* builds a fortune based mainly on corruption. While this involves crime, the business activity itself is legal: only the methods are corrupt. Finally, many cabinet ministers, police officers, or military leaders are now called *chao pho* because of their leadership style. They may or may not be involved in corrupt or criminal activity, but they tend to be decisive, charismatic, and generous.[42] This chapter deals with the first two types, the criminal and the corrupt.

By accumulating wealth, especially through corruption, gambling dens, and the underground lottery, *chao pho* found themselves in a position to associate closely with some of the most important business groups in Thailand. Among the major sectors of business to come into contact with capital-rich *chao pho* was commercial banking, perhaps because many *chao pho* became involved with the *compradore* banks, by which the banking system first penetrated the outlying parts of the country. Until at least the 1960s, many banks in the provinces were supported by local capital: provincial men of wealth arranged with the banks in Bangkok to set up branches, which they headed. The metropolitan bank relied on the local clout of these representatives to attract business and enforce repayments. (Unfortunately, however, little is known concerning the *compradore* bank system.) Later, *chao pho* running the underground lottery began depositing large sums of money in savings accounts, and making withdrawals twice monthly to pay off winners.[43] Sometimes these accounts were large enough to make the *chao pho* important customers and bring them into contact with the executives and owners of the banks. It was apparently in such a way *Sia* Leng, a famous *chao pho* of the Northeast, met Boonchu Rojanasathien of the Bangkok Bank. When Boonchu formed a political party, *Sia* Leng became an important supporter of its electoral efforts in that region. Similarly *Sia* Huat, a reputed *chao pho* from Chonburi, was killed in an ambush while returning from the funeral of a member of a prominent banking family. Although *Sia* Huat reportedly expected an attempt on his life, his relationship with the banking family was close enough to overcome his fears of attack.[44]

Financial relationships between *chao pho* and banks have not been limited to savings accounts fed by the underground lottery, for capital accumulated through other forms of gambling and other criminal activities have also entered the banking system. Moreover, *chao pho* began to invest their capital in legitimate businesses, either to serve as a cover for illegal activities (thus, a timber company provides both a front and the equipment for illegal logging) or to expand their range of activities into legal but lucrative enterprises. Profits could often be enhanced through recourse to threats and violence (real estate deals, for example, where owners of prime land could be coerced into selling at a low price). This move into lawful business had the additional effect of legitimizing the *chao pho* within the business community and giving him property and assets that could be mortgaged and used as collateral for bank loans. This business relationship meant that the continued prosperity of these valuable clients was in the best interests of the powerful banking sector, as both profited from the relationship.

By investing in legitimate businesses, *chao pho* also made contact with business leaders in other sectors of the economy. As Bangkok-based business leaders began to look to the provinces for partners in various industries, it was often the *chao pho* who had the organization and influence necessary to ensure profit. Two of the most important businesses for the *chao pho* have been construction and the distribution of Thai whiskey. Whiskey concessions for different regions are granted on tender, with the winning tender securing the right to produce and distribute domestic whiskey throughout the region. The contractor generally subcontracts the distribution of the whiskey by province, with the province then subdivided into smaller and smaller areas, each subcontracted.[45] Whiskey distribution gives the *chao pho* an organization in the province, jobs for his subordinates, and a source of profit. It also brings him into contact with wealthy business leaders in the region and even national leaders. Like whiskey, construction involves many opportunities for cooperation and subcontracting, and, of course, corruption in securing the contract. It also allows the *chao pho* to employ numerous tough young men while earning large profits.

Economic development was not the only force to generate the local power that would challenge the position of the bureaucracy. The return of elections and parliamentary democracy provided the path to power that had been missing under Sarit's centralized bureaucratic rule. With elections and a parliament, those who were not officials could participate in politics. Although officials have been reluctant to relinquish their power, elected politicians have begun to compete with them, both at the national and the local level.

DEMOCRACY AND VOTE-BUYING

As we have seen in the preceding chapter, the relationship between *chao pho* and government officials was transformed by the emergence of elected government. Elected politicians became another source of protection for the *chao pho*, while the *chao pho* supplied finances and organization for the campaign efforts of the elected politicians. The lack of local-level political party branches[46] meant there was no continuing organization in support of a particular party or platform at the grass-roots level. Consequently, each candidate has had to piece together his own election network in order to ensure victory. This network is made up of those *hua khanaen*, or 'voting chiefs' able to influence the votes of the villagers. Behind the protests in Phichit were the *hua khanaen*, mostly *kamnan* and *phuyaiban*, of the MPs from Election District One. These *hua khanaen* held the key to election victories in the northern half of Phichit; when they demanded the assistance of the MPs from their district, the MPs risked losing the core of their electoral organizations if they failed to respond to the call.

While the *hua khanaen* system has long been a part of local elections, political and economic changes of the last thirty years have expanded its complexity and significance. Until the 1970s, government parties could rely on the bureaucracy to win elections. Only non-government parties were forced to rely on a patchwork system of *hua khanaen*. However, since the 1973 uprising, the absence of a single government party has prevented systematic use of the bureaucracy to maintain control of the election system. Individual ministers continue to use their influence over the members of the bureaucracy to gain votes; however, all parties compete to recruit government officials, military commanders, *chao pho,* factory owners, religious leaders, teachers – in short, anyone who might be able to deliver a block of votes. These recruits, the *hua khanaen,* are then organized into a makeshift hierarchy that extends into every village and every neighbourhood.[47] The individual may be pressured by a teacher to vote for one party, by an employer to vote for another, and by a *chao pho* to vote for yet another. Current campaign methods ensure that the most valuable *hua khanaen* are those involved in crime and corruption.

Regional-level *hua khanaen* and in some areas, provincial-level *hua khanaen,* are at the peak of the *hua khanaen* hierarchy. Regional- and provincial-level *hua khanaen* are the most coveted because of their financial resources, their existing networks of important connections, and their ability to recruit other *hua khanaen* at lower levels of the election network. This recruitment may include the formation of groups or associations such as the Association of *Kamnan* and *Phuyaiban* of Phichit. Regional and provincial *hua khanaen* may have more control over the selection and election of candidates than the parties or the candidates themselves. The *chao pho,* with a network of, for example, underground lottery dealers or whiskey distributors (and not the teacher or factory owner) fills this key role.

Many regional-level *hua khanaen* are themselves members of parliament and thus work for a single political party. This type of *hua khanaen* is often influential in the selection of candidates in his own area and may finance the campaigns of many of those candidates. In return the *hua khanaen* gains influence within the party through his candidates and may obtain a cabinet position. Other regional-level *hua khanaen,* though not MPs, also attach themselves to a single political party, as did *Sia* Yae, a *chao pho* from Angthong, when he was a member of the Chart Thai executive committee. Somchai Khunpluem (*Kamnan* Poh), an admitted one-time operator of the local underground lottery[48] and owner of a number of enterprises, including a trucking fleet, entertainment businesses, and a liquor distributorship, allied himself with the Social Action Party (SAP, Kit Sangkhom) during the 1988 election, resigning from his own position as *kamnan* to campaign for party candidates in Chonburi and adjoining provinces.[49]

Also common is the regional *hua khanaen*, like *Sia* Yae after he left the Chart Thai Party, who supports candidates from several parties in areas under his control.[50] Along with the late *Sia* Yae, the most prominent of these is Charoen Phattanadamronchit (*Sia* Leng) of Khon Kaen.[51] *Sia* Leng controls marketing networks and agricultural processing plants, as well as a stable of race horses, and a variety of other businesses in the Northeast. *Sia* Leng, like *Sia* Yae, denies being a *chao pho* and insists he merely has 'many friends and subordinates who are grateful for my help in the past'.[52] Typically, this type of *hua khanaen* is not interested in political opportunities or prestige for himself, but is seeking protection and privileged access to government resources. By supporting candidates in several parties, he maximizes the chances of getting some of his candidates into a coalition government and into a position where they can protect his interests. There is heavy competition from parties to enlist the support of these *hua khanaen*. Somchai Khunpluem, for example, was visited by representatives of all parties prior to the 1986 election. He supported candidates from more than one party before committing himself to the Social Action Party for the 1988 election.[53] In the 1992 elections, two of Somchai's sons were elected under the Chart Pattana (Chat Phattana, National Development Party) banner of former Prime Minister Chatichai Choonhavan.

As campaign methods have changed over the last 20 years, the importance of corrupt and criminal *hua khanaen* has grown markedly, both at the regional level and at the village level where the *chao pho* may be competing with other types of *hua khanaen* such as teachers and monks. The frequent use of vote-buying and the privatization of intimidation[54] has led politicians to seek the support of criminal groups, and the need for political influence to preserve profits has brought the criminal and the corrupt into cooperation with the politicians. The *chao pho* have experience in violence and illegal activities and the broad-based networks of influence necessary to support their operations. Their ties reach both upwards to government officials and high finance and downwards to the ordinary people. In addition to organizing and financing vote-buying, criminal elements may be able to cooperate with or coerce election officials, police officers, and opposing candidates. Even voters come under the threat of violence to property or person if the wrong candidate is victorious.[55] In the 1996 election, prices reportedly ranged from 100 baht (US$4), paid early in the campaign in the Northeast, to 1,000 baht (US$40), paid to those willing to cast only one vote (of their allotted three), for a candidate in Petchburi.

The dramatic rise of vote-buying that began with the 1969 elections, much of it organized by the *chao pho*, may have been an attempt to compete with the persuasion and intimidation employed by the last of the government-sponsored parties through the bureaucracy. While the bureaucratic hua khanaen sought to coerce votes, private *hua khanaen* sought to entice them with money, holding coercion in reserve to ensure the vote stayed bought. Vote-buying has increased in scope and the price of a vote has increased steadily, with reports of 200 baht (US$8) or more being spent for each vote in some areas by 1988.[56] Vote-buying has been so widespread that despite all the information campaigns, as late as 1996, some 27% of people surveyed in Ratchaburi province believed vote-buying was legal.[57] Surveys carried out by the Ministry of the Interior during the 1988 election reveal that 30.4% of the candidates believed vote-buying to be an effective campaign tactic, and 47.3% of voters admitted that money or distribution of material goods affected their choice of candidates – this in spite of the clear illegality of vote-buying and the official role of the Ministry of the Interior in preventing it![58]

While it is impossible to determine the extent of vote-buying in Thailand, there is abundant evidence that it exists. In the period leading up to the 1986 election in the Northeast, the demand for 20-baht notes was up 110%; for 10-baht notes it was up 80%, for 100-baht notes 50%, and for 500-baht notes (the largest denomination issued) demand was up 20%.[59] The northeastern branch of the Bank of Thailand prepared 4 billion baht worth of 10-, 20-, 50- and 100-baht denominations for use in the 1988 election. During the registration period, the bank disbursed 100,000 baht per day more than usual – this was before campaigning was supposed to begin.[60] Nationwide, some 10 billion baht (about US$400 million) reportedly was spent on vote-buying in the 1988 election.[61] *Sia* Leng, a prominent *hua khanaen*, has been quoted as saying, 'As far as I know, not a single [Northeastern] MP has managed to make their way to the House of Representatives without distributing money or things to solicit people for votes.'[62] A staff member at the headquarters of one political party admitted that the party bought votes, declaring that if only the 'bad' candidates bought votes, the 'good' candidates would never be elected.[63]

In the last few years, resistance to vote-buying has developed, among individuals, among groups organized specifically for this purpose, and even among political parties. In the 1988 election the Palang Darma (Phalang Tham) Party was formed with a platform centred on a pledge not to buy votes. Palang Darma did well in Bangkok, where vote-buying is less effective, winning ten of the thirty-seven seats there, but won only four seats outside Bangkok. In the first election after the coup of 1991 (in March 1992), Palang Darma, led by the popular Chamlong Srimuang, won almost every seat in Bangkok. Following the election, Chamlong was a key leader in the popular uprising that toppled the military regime; however, in the subsequent election in the autumn, his party lost several seats in Bangkok. In this second election since the coup (September 1992), vote-buying, although still reportedly widespread, declined. This diminution was temporary, however. In the 1996 election, the independent monitoring agency PollWatch estimated that over 100 billion baht (US$4 billion) was spent on vote-buying, dramatically higher than the estimated 55 billion (US$2.2 billion) spent on the 1995 election, and a tenfold increase on 1988.[64]

Of course, *chao pho* also resort to intimidation when necessary. The threat of violence is often employed in ensuring that votes that have been bought are delivered as promised. A villager in Chiang Rai reported that in the 1986 election, candidates worked through *hua khanaen* and 'gangsters' to distribute money. 'The village chief gave the money to his assistants and the gangsters who subsequently gave us the money and demanded we vote for certain candidates otherwise we would not get any help.'[65] One former candidate from Phitsanulok claims 'Anyone who breaks this rule [voting as local influential persons demand] will soon find that either their buffaloes or farm machines are stolen. Policemen dare not interfere because they themselves also depend a lot on the influential people.'[66]

Violence has become an integral part of the campaign process. Particularly effective *hua khanaen* from the opposition may be threatened with violence if their efforts are not stopped or shifted to another candidate. When the threat is ignored, *hua khanaen* may be killed. During the 1986 election campaign, with four days to go before voting, police reported that fourteen *hua khanaen* and two 'supporters' had been killed. Others had been attacked but survived. In addition, five 'officials', listed as a teacher, a provincial councillor, two *phuyaiban*, and one assistant *phuyaiban* were killed.[67] During the 1988 election, in Chachoengsao (Paet Riw) province, there were eight deaths believed to be related to the election during the first eight days of June. And the violence does not end with the elections; *hua khanaen* who betray a candidate may be killed to prevent such behaviour in future elections. Successful *hua khanaen* of opponents may also be eliminated.[68]

With vote-buying and violence playing such an important role in elections, *chao pho* have become the key to victory in many provinces. While some *chao pho* are content to support friends or relatives in elections, others have chosen to run themselves, in order to gain direct access to central political power. It is this direct access which frees the *chao pho* from their previous status as clients of soldiers and bureaucrats and gives them power over their former patrons. The parliament and the election process have made it possible for local influential figures to participate in politics at the national level. No longer dependent on the good-will of the local governor, police chief or military commander, these figures can work through members of parliament and the parties, as did the *kamnan* of Phichit when the governor proved resistant.

It is even possible for the most powerful *chao pho* to control MPs and ministers, to have their own family members or supporters appointed, or even to become MPs and cabinet ministers themselves. The *kamnan* of Phichit, as well as *Sia* Leng and others, are now in a position of equality to, and even dominance over, government officials. By pressuring the MPs that depend on them for election, these local notables can force the transfer of government bureaucrats, including even provincial police chiefs and governors. During the Chatichai administration (1988–1991), a powerful provincial businessman-cum-politician, Banharn Silpa-archa, became minister of the interior. This put him in charge of local government, giving him responsibility for the promotion and transfer of all local officials. Such control of government ministries by politicians has helped to ensure the reversal of the relationship between the bureaucracy and local power. From July 1995 to November 1996 Banharn was himself prime minister, and kept the all-important Ministry of the Interior in his own hands. Three other provincial politicians in Banharn's party coveted the position, and the ensuing conflict over control of the Ministry of the Interior contributed to the break-up of the coalition government. Under both the New Aspiration Party-led coalition in 1996 and the

Democrat-led coalition in 1997, provincial politicians headed the Ministry of the Interior.

LOCAL LEADERS IN NATIONAL POLITICS

While it is difficult to determine the importance of *chao pho* on national political or economic policies, in some cases their role is clear. They are able to gain large amounts of money for their cities and provinces, thus affecting the distribution of the budget.[69] When Narong Wongwan, a reputed *chao pho* from the North, was proposed as a candidate for prime minister by the pro-military party in 1992, the US threatened to re-evaluate its relations with Thailand. The US Drug Enforcement Agency claimed Narong was involved in narcotics trafficking. At other times, *chao pho* come to serve as mediators between government officials and the parliament. The military's scuttling in 1988 of a parliamentary motion of non-confidence against Prime Minister Gen. Prem Tinsulandonda was achieved by the defection of five MPs in *Sia* Leng's camp (and their subsequent move to the pro-military Ratsadon party).[70] *Sia* Leng thus ensured the government's continued rule as well as strengthening his ties to the military and his MPs. Such behaviour does not go unrewarded.

Cooperation between *chao pho* and officials, and corruption in local politics are not new. What is new is the dominance of *chao pho* in the relationship. In the past, local elective offices were limited in authority and at times were even eliminated in favour of appointed officials. Revenue was controlled by the central government. Furthermore, only government officials were linked to the national level, and with this power they were able to dominate local politics. It was the bureaucrat who could choose who would benefit from corruption and crime by deciding who would be prosecuted or who would get the contract. Local leaders had little influence over bureaucrats, who derived their power from their positions and their links to Bangkok.

The increase in provincial capital – both private and public – has led to more powerful *chao pho* and more powerful networks of influential individuals under the control of these *chao pho*. New methods of discrediting, pressuring, and otherwise threatening the careers of officials through a position in local politics has allowed the *chao pho*-turned-politician to dominate the relationship. No less important is the ability of politicians to appeal to a political party or a cabinet minister to have uncooperative officials removed: a channel exists outside the bureaucracy that can be manipulated by the politician to transfer recalcitrant bureaucrats. The parliamentary system has created a pathway to national-level politics for *chao pho*, both criminal and corrupt, and has given them the power to gain control over local-level officials. Officials can be moved; *chao pho* cannot.

On the other hand, the *chao pho* emerged during a period of rapid transformation in the countryside. They may have trouble maintaining their positions as economic development and business become routinized. Already the children of the criminal *chao pho* are graduating with MBAs from universities, sometimes overseas universities, and are moving into positions of power in the family enterprises. They bring with them different styles and goals. They, along with their fathers, are finding that land speculation and property development can be far more profitable than crime. The corrupt *chao pho* and their offspring similarly seek legitimacy by identifying themselves as mayors, business tycoons, or cabinet ministers rather than as *chao pho*. These young men, and in some cases young women, are educated, professional, and upper middle class, and often manage to overcome the image of their fathers. In addition, the urban centre – the central state, the media, and the middle classes – continues to attempt to professionalize the bureaucracy and the police force in order to bring 'law' to the countryside. Although their status under the law has so far been of minor relevance to the legitimacy of *chao pho* in the countryside, this may change as they seek to extend their respectability to Bangkok. Criminal activity is then likely to be concealed rather than flaunted. Finally, the military coup of 1991 served as a reminder that parliamentary rule may still be fragile in Thailand, and helped mute criticism of the *chao pho,* whose support has helped sustain parliament. These changes seem to have already lowered the visibility of the godfathers; much of that attention has shifted from their activities to corruption in the bureaucracy (especially the police department), and failure to enforce the law.

The power of these *chao pho* depends, to a certain degree, on their ability to monopolize the local economy and political system. As the economy grew, *chao pho* found themselves in competition with one another – which led to numerous killings – and in competition with other types of entrepreneurs. Many entrepreneurs and other local notables are not involved in crime or corruption, and they may provide alternative leadership. While small business owners, for example, may not be able to influence many votes as individuals, organizations of small business owners or of teachers or of factory owners might be able to compete with *chao pho* for the support of voters and thus of members of parliament. On the other hand, with the economic decline, competition will decrease, at least in the short term, and it is likely that it will be the *chao pho* who will survive. The ability to reassert a monopoly during the current economic crisis may well play a major role in determining the success or failure of *chao pho* to maintain power in any given area. If the first half of the century saw the rise of the bureaucracy, and the second half saw the rise of local power in the guise of *chao pho*, the next few decades may signal the rise of civil society. Like the bureaucracy before them, *chao pho* will resist this change, and will no doubt be successful in some areas and fail in others. Where they fail – if they fail – a further decentralization of power may take place.

NOTES

1. *Kamnan* is usually translated as 'commune leader'. A group of villages (approximately 6–12) makes up a *tambon*, or commune. Each village is led by a *phuyaiban* (village headman). The *kamnan* is elected leader of the commune by the *phuyaiban* from among their number, and serves as both commune leader and head of his own village

2. *Bangkok Post*, 13 May 1989.

3. *Bangkok Post*, 14 May 1989.

4. Interview with the president of the association. He maintained that the association was formed to provide support to a *kamnan* in cases of conflict between a policeman and the *kamnan*.

5. The governor spoke of the involvement of *kamnan* and *phuyaiban* in the construction industry in a number of interviews with the press. *Matichon* 12 May 1989, reported the Ratsadorn MP and deputy minister as owner of a construction company named in the article. As the constitution forbids the granting of government contracts to members of parliament, it is not surprising that the deputy minister denied any involvement in the construction industry.

6. As identified by a provincial official and confirmed by the *kamnan* identified.

7. That is, the right to produce and distribute the locally made brands of whiskey (*lao thai*). The concession to produce whiskey is won through competitive bidding, and often includes the task of building factories that revert to the government. Distribution rights are usually subcontracted.

8. Interview with the president of the Association of *Kamnan* and *Phuyaiban*.

9. Interview with a high-level local official.

10. *Matichon,* 12 May 1989, p. 21 suggests that while governor of Uttaradit, the governor had reduced the provincial construction budget by some 27–30 million baht (about US$1.1 million) in one year by cutting down on corruption.

11. Interview with the Ratsadorn member of parliament from Election District One reported in *Sayam rat,* 14 May 1989.

12. This and much of the information in the following paragraph is acknowledged by the Chart Thai Party member of parliament from Election District One in an interview with *Thai rat,* 11 May 1989. This account substantiates the outlines of the story as told by the governor, though it attributes different motives to each participant.

13. See the statements of the two MPs, the Chart Thai MP in *Thai rat,* 11 May 1989, and the Ratsadorn MP in *Sayam rat,* 14 May 1989.

14. Sometimes demonstrators are paid for their time. As *kamnan* and *phuyaiban,* the organizers are in a position to provide numerous advantages to those who cooperate and, of course, penalties to those who refuse. The governor claimed the demonstration was instigated by the MPs (see *Thai rat,* 11 May 1989), 'dark influences' (*Thai rat,* 13 May 1989), and 'some provincial councillors and banker(s)' (*Matichon,* 12 May 1989), all of whom were connected to the construction industry.

15. *Thai rat,* 11 May 1989, p. 23.

16. The president of the Association of *Kamnan* and *Phuyaiban* believed that *nai amphoe* (district officers) helped organize these demonstrations. Apparently the forces against the governor included some local government officials, as some were later transferred by the governor, allegedly for failing to come to his support. The president of the Association of *Kamnan* and *Phuyaiban* says these transfers led to his participation in the second set of demonstrations against the governor. (This indicates the extent of his concern for his allies in the local bureaucracy.) Interviews with the president of the Association of *Kamnan* and *Phuyaiban,* 23 and 24 June 1989.

17. *Sayam rat,* 12 May 1989.

18. *The Nation,* 10 May 1989.

19. *Thai rat,* 20 May 1989.

20. *Sayam rat,* 12 May 1989.

21. *Thai rat,* 20 May 1989.

22. Tej Bunnag, *The Provincial Administration of Siam 1892–1915* (London: Oxford University Press, 1977), pp. 23–24.

23. Bunnag, *The Provincial Administration of Siam*; Benedict R. O'G. Anderson, 'Studies of the Thai State: The State of Thai Studies', in Eliezer Ayal (ed.), *The Study of Thailand* (Columbus: Ohio University, 1978) pp. 193–233.

24. Fred W. Riggs, *Thailand: The Modernization of a Bureaucratic Polity* (Honolulu: East–West Center, 1966); William J. Siffin, *The Thai Bureaucracy: Institutional Change and Development* (Honolulu: East-West Center, 1966). Note that both these authors, who stress the central role of the bureaucracy in Thai politics, wrote during the 1960s, at the peak of bureaucratic power and before the rise in economic and political power of local leaders became evident.

25. Bunnag, *The Provincial Administration of Siam,* pp. 109–13. Note that this was a means of controlling regional-level notables by enhancing the power of local notables. It was expected that the bureaucracy would then assert itself directly over the *kamnan* and *phuyaiban.*

26. Thak Chaloemtiarana, *Thailand: The Politics of Despotic Paternalism* (Bangkok: Social Science Association of Thailand, 1979), p. 223.

27. *International Financial Statistics Yearbook* (Washington: International Monetary Fund, annual).

28. *World Development Report* (New York: Oxford University Press for the World Bank, annual).

29. Calculated from *International Financial Statistics Yearbook.*

30. *World Development Report, 1993,* table 3.

31. Akira Suehiro, *Capital Accumulation in Thailand, 1855–1985* (Tokyo: Center for East Asian Cultural Studies, 1989), p. 183. For the period 1950–1988, Robert J. Muscat, *Thailand and the United States* (New York: Columbia University, 1990), pp. 328–329, puts total US military assistance at US$2.3 billion. See also R. Sean Randolph, 'Diplomacy and National Interest: Thai-American Security Cooperation in the Vietnam Era' (Ph.D. thesis, Fletcher School, 1978), appendix IX.

32. Akira Suehiro, *Capital Accumulation,*, p. 183.

33. Estimated at US$850 million by 1971. See John L. S. Girling, *Thailand: Society and Politics* (Ithaca, NY: Cornell University Press, 1981), p. 236.

34. The scope of US aid to Thailand is outlined in detail in Muscat, op. cit.

35. Randolph, 'Diplomacy and National Interest', appendix XII. This is divided into construction of US bases (244.6 million), improvement of Thai bases (105.4 million), and miscellaneous construction (38.3 million). The two biggest projects were the Utthaphao air base, costing 99.3 million, and the Sattahip naval base, costing 62.2 million. The remainder was spent in a number of provinces scattered throughout the country.

36. Constance M. Wilson, *Thailand: A Handbook of Historical Statistics* (Boston: G. K. Hall, 1983), p. 172 for statistics through 1975. For the more recent dates, see *Statistical Handbook of Thailand* (Bangkok: Office of the Prime Minister, National Statistical Office, annual). During the same period state highways, most of them in the provinces, grew from 8,761 km in 1960 to 16,814 km in 1989.

37. Figures for 1940–1975 are from Nopalak Rakthum, 'The Development of Branch Banking in Thailand' (MA thesis, Thammasat University, 1983). Figures from 1976–1988 are from the Bank of Thailand Research Division, as reported in January of the following year.

38. *Pocket Thailand in Figures* (Bangkok: Alpha Research Co., 1996), p. 121.

39. The Tambon Development Fund Programme, which gave money to the *tambon* councils, also included provisions to get banks to increase the percentage of loans made to the provinces. In addition, over the last few years the Bank of Thailand has required major banks to build two provincial branches in order to gain approval for any additional branch in the Bangkok/Thonburi metropolitan area.

40. Traditionally the *nak leng* and the *chao pho* were male. The word *chao mae* (godmother) has appeared more recently, but there is as yet insufficient data to generalize about the *chao mae*, still relatively rare, who may act quite differently.

41. See James Ockey, '*Chaopho*: Capital Accumulation and Social Welfare in Thailand', *Crossroads* 8 (1993): 48–77.

42. In this sense, Sarit himself set a prominent example for *chao pho*.

43. Somrudee Nicrowattanayingyong, 'Development Planning, Politics, and Paradox: A Study of Khon Kaen, a Regional City in Northeast Thailand' (Ph.D. thesis, Syracuse University, 1991), Chapter 5.

44. Benedict R. O'G. Anderson, 'Murder and Progress in Modern Siam', *New Left Review*, 181 (May/June 1990): 47–48.

45. At the top, the whiskey industry is largely controlled by two very rich Sino-Thai families who have long been heavily involved in politics. Note the similarity of the present liquor concession system to the organization of the tax farms of a century ago.

46. The exception is the Democrat Party, which has branches organized in a number of rural areas. However, these branches are usually tied to individuals more closely than to the party, and their main purpose has been to influence intra-party elections. See Chai-anan Samudavanija, *Kanluaktang phak kanmuang, ratthasapha, lae khana thahan* (Bangkok: Bannakit Trading, 1981), pp. 174–189.

47. There are a number of advantages to the parties in relying on these ad hoc organizations rather than branches. First, since they exist only during elections, they are much cheaper. In fact, they are largely self-supporting, with the candidate and the corrupt *chao pho* often paying for the organization. Second, they can be organized and mobilized quite rapidly to contest an election. And third, they cannot be dissolved by military coups. Existing political parties have been dissolved by every coup group except that of 1991.

48. *Bangkok Post*, 29 June 1988; *Prachachat thurakit*, 20 April 1988, p. 31. Somchai says that he quit the underground lottery racket after it was discovered that the national lottery had been fixed. The *Prachachat thurakit*

article quotes him as saying 'Speaking of the *nak leng* I can take charge of them ... In the eastern region, I can have my orders carried out within one hour.' He denies being a *chao pho.*

49. *Bangkok Post,* 29 June 1988; *Dao Sayam,* 2 July 1988. See also the interview with Somchai in *Matichon sutsapda,* 30 April 1989.

50. In the 1988 election, which occurred less than a year before his death, *Sia* Yae supported candidates from the Chart Thai, Social Action, Democrat, Ruam Thai and Palang Darma (Phalang Tham) parties. By early June (the election was held on 24 July) *Sia* Yae had already spent 5 million baht (US$200,000) concentrating his efforts on Loei, Angthong, Singburi, and Chaiyaphum provinces. See *Bangkok Post,* 8 June 1988.

51. Politics in Khon Kaen and the role of *Sia* Leng in the politics of that province, are covered in detail in Somrudee, 'Development Planning', ch. five. See also *Khao phiset,* 23 April 1990; *Thai rat,* 10 May 1987; *The Nation,* 8 June 1988; *Matichon sutsapda,* 3 May 1987; *Phuchatkan,* October 1987, pp. 154–157; and *Lak thai,* 14 July 1988.

52. *Bangkok Post,* 8 June 1988.

53. *Matichon sutsapda,* 25 May 1986. *Sia* Leng was approached by almost every major party before the 1988 election, including the Social Action, Ratsadorn, Prachakorn Thai, Puang Chon Chao Thai, and Seriniyom parties. He supported candidates from several parties but worked particularly closely with the Ratsadorn Party, which assigned him responsibility for thirteen provinces in the Northeast. See *The Nation,* 6 June 1988, and *Sayam rat sapda wichan,* 24 July 1988.

54. Anderson, 'Murder and Progress', pp. 33–48.

55. Interview with a provincial police chief.

56. Kramon Thongthammachat, Sombun Suksamran, and Pricha Hongkrailoet, *Kanluaktang phak kanmuang lae sathienphap khong ratthaban* (Bangkok: Chulalongkon University, 1988), p. 73, reported that 10–200 baht a vote was being paid in a by-election in Buriram. The average seems to be between 50–100 baht a vote (US$2–4). An article in *Suannakhot,* 6 July 1988, discussed the inflation of the value of a vote from 10 baht to 100 baht in Nakhon Nayok.

57. *Bangkok Post,* 4 November 1996.

58. Krasuang Mahatthai, Krom kanpokkrong, kong kanluaktang, *Raingan wichai kanluaktang samachik sapha phuthaen Ratsadornpho. so. 2531* [Research Report of the Election of Members of the House of Representatives, 1988] (Bangkok, n.d.), pp. 44–45. More than one response was allowed in the poll. Other answers of interest from the candidates include: donations for public works projects, 19.9%; distributing goods, 17.7%; and betting, 14.1%.

59. *Bangkok Post,* 24 July 1986.

60. *Bangkok Post,* 30 June 1988.

61. *Bangkok Post,* 23 August 1988; 18 April 1989.

62. *The Nation,* 11 June 1988.

63. Interview, January 1988. Prachan Rakphong, *Kansueksa kanhasiang nai kanluaktang 27 karakadakhom 2529 changwat Lampang* (Bangkok: Samakhom Sangkhomsat haeng prathet Thai, 1986), p. 120, described a candidate in the Lampung provincial elections of 1986 who claimed he objected to vote-buying but was later forced to buy votes to compete with the opposition. There are increasing attempts to fight vote-buying in all areas of the country.

64. *Krungthep thurakit,* 17 November 1996.

65. *Bangkok Post,* 3 July 1988.

66. *Bangkok Post,* 8 July 1988. In a censure debate in parliament, one MP claimed that for a policeman to be appointed inspector, he must pay 3 million baht (US$120,000); for superintendent, 5 million baht; for commander, 7 million baht; and for police director-general, 50 million baht (US$2 million). See *Bangkok Post,* 19 and 20 July 1990. As a journalist pointed out in an interview, this kind of spending on positions in the police department could only be maintained if criminals were supplying the capital. See also the comments of Police Colonel Seri Temiyawet in Phasuk Phongphaichit and Sungsidh Phiriyarangsan (eds), *Rat, thun, chao pho thongthin kap sangkhom thai* (Bangkok: Chulalongkon University, 1992), pp. 145–149.

67. *Sayam rat,* 24 July 1986. At least one more *hua khanaen,* along with his wife, was killed between the time of the report and the election on July 27. See *Thai rat,* 26 July 1986.

68. In Chonburi, for example, a number of *hua khanaen* loyal to Uthai Phimchaichon were killed. See *Bangkok Post,* 8 September and 11 October 1988.

69. See, for example, the interview with *Kamnan* Poh shortly after he became mayor in *Matichon sutsapda,* 30 April 1989.

70. See *Khao Phiset,* 23 April 1990; *Thai rat,* 10 May 1987; *Sayam rat sapda wichan,* 24 July 1988; and Sombat's chapter in this volume.

FIVE

MARKET SOCIETY AND THE ORIGINS OF THE NEW THAI POLITICS

*Michael J. Montesano**

The emergence of a new Thai politics in the late 1980s and early 1990s was nowhere so apparent as in the provinces. Among the many striking features of this provincial political change, scholars have attached particular importance to two. The first is the role of formal business organizations.[1] The second is the importance of men of influence whose power rests principally on provincial bases rather than on access to the national government. Discussions of these influential provincials have placed disproportionate emphasis on the violence-prone, gangster-like subset dubbed, since the 1980s, *chao pho* or 'godfathers'.[2]

As a whole, scholarship treating business organizations and influential provincials has pursued two basic objectives. First and most fundamentally, it has sought simply to describe the operation of these

* The support of the Fulbright-Hays Program of the United States Department of Education, of the Social Science Research Council, of the Chulalongkorn University Social Research Institute, and of the Department of History and the Southeast Asia Program of Cornell University made possible the work on which this essay draws. Special thanks are due to Dr James Ockey, Professor David Wyatt, the late Dr Jennifer Cushman, and Ms Yuphin Chancharoensin. Professor Sherman Cochran, Dr Susan Matt, Dr Caroline Hau, Dr Eva-Lotta Hedman, and Dr Michael Malley offered detailed comments on earlier drafts of this essay.

increasingly institutionalized presences in the Thai political arena. Second, it has essayed an assessment of their potential to advance or retard the cause of 'democracy' in Thailand. Pursuit of the first of these goals has called for detailed examination of particular events, inevitably rather recent, in local and national politics. And prosecution of the second has tended to lead to broad macro-historical generalization. Each of these approaches has, given its objectives, helped to clarify the nature of the political change in provincial Thailand.

But both the objectives motivating most studies of business organizations and provincial notables and the approaches drafted to serve them have worked to truncate understanding of that political change. For if they have served to illuminate the function played by business organizations and provincial notables in recent decades and to clarify the position of these incipient institutions in the macro-historical structure of Thai politics, they have devoted only cursory attention to their origins in the social history of the last half-century. We have, as a result, considerable knowledge about the political role of and apparent demand for business organizations and provincial notables, but we know next to nothing of their supply.

The business organizations and influential provincials that have assumed such political significance in provincial Thailand acquired their basic characteristics from a particular socio-historical milieu. A specific wave of Chinese immigration to Siam resulted in a new variant in the social life of the kingdom. In the innumerable market centres where the immigrant settled, prestige came from commercial success, wealth, social mobility, and dedication to the community. Conformity to standards set in other segments of Thai society counted for little. Through its influence on business organizations and influential provincials, the culture of these market centres has had a profound and continuing impact on the course of Thai political life.

This essay attempts to give some idea of the importance of this social variant by examining the careers of two figures, one Surin Tothapthiang, the most famous leader of a Thai provincial chamber of commerce, and the other Suchon Champhunot, a long-time member of parliament heavily involved in money-politics. It devotes only minimal attention to specific events in the political realm, focusing instead on the how the backgrounds of Surin, Suchon, and others like them have shaped the outlook or 'style' with which they approach politics. This biographical approach underlines the need for studies of Southeast Asian politics to devote attention not only to 'theories of origins' for the supply of institutions,[3] but also to the origins of the individuals who give those institutions life.

SURIN TOTHAPTHIANG

As founding president of the Trang Chamber of Commerce and tireless promoter of his native province's potential as a destination for tourists, Surin Tothapthiang elaborately and effectively identified himself with the province of Trang, in Southern Thailand. His own fame brought to the Trang Chamber of Commerce a reputation for being one of Thailand's 'best' provincial chambers. Similarly, Surin came in popular perception to exemplify the new importance of business organizations on the Thai political landscape.

The Trang with which Surin is most accurately identified is that of the quarters surrounding the municipal market in the first decades after the Second World War. This was the era in which recently arrived Teochiu Chinese displaced the Hokkien, Cantonese, and Hakka who had previously occupied this neighbourhood. The majority of these Teochiu were China-born, part of the great wave of immigration to Siam in the decade and a half following the First World War.[4] As they spread out across provincial Siam they decisively altered the character of the *talat,* or marketplaces, in which they settled.[5] The presence of women among them enabled the establishment of Chinese-speaking households and slowed the pace of assimilation that had characterized earlier waves of immigrants.[6] And, clustered in markets like that of Trang, critical masses of such households made possible the emergence of a new variant of Chinese immigrant society in Thailand.

In the three or four decades to the mid-1970s, this market society incubated the traits and practices that have more recently become central to Thai politics. The majority of the kingdom's Chinese in this era regarded frequent contact with the Thai governmental elite as neither necessary nor desirable. And the market society of the time structured their lives around values and status systems that owed nothing to such contact. Inward-looking, peopled above all by self-employed traders and shopkeepers, this society spanned Thailand. It afforded both great opportunity for social mobility to the commercially ambitious and access to extensive commercial and social networks through which such successful merchants could move.[7]

Among the Teochiu immigrants who settled in Trang and helped build such a society there was Tou Nguan Tiang. He arrived in Trang shortly before the Second World War and started out as a small-scale fish trader.[8] Able eventually to establish his own dry-goods store in a shophouse behind the market,[9] Tou Nguan Tiang typified by the early 1960s the class of successful Teochiu retail and wholesale merchants who prospered in the Trang market and in many others like it. In addition to a thriving business, he had ten children and a representative in Bangkok to help him secure stock.

Close personal and business ties among local merchants characterized the market society of which Tou Nguan Tiang had become a prominent member. Commerce and community were mutually reinforcing pursuits. It was, in fact, the insolvency of a friend and fellow merchant for whom he had served as guarantor which brought a sudden end to Tou Nguan Tiang's prosperity in 1965. He died a broken man three years later. In the intervening time his two oldest sons, Sutham and Surin Tothapthiang,[10] left school to support their family and repay their father's debts. Having worked for a time as a clerk in a rice mill in the northern province of Uttaradit, Sutham became a travelling salesman for a seasoning-powder firm several months before his father's death.

While Sutham's decision to go to work for someone else represented a departure from his family's previous means of earning a livelihood, it demonstrated at the same time important continuities with his father's activities. Tou Nguan Tiang's reliance on a network of suppliers and his formal relationship with an agent in Bangkok had reflected his integration into a marketing system that extended well beyond Trang or even Southern Thailand. Truly national in scope and built by members of the same immigrant wave that had brought Tou Nguan Tiang from China, this system linked Teochiu merchants into a network comprised of rice millers, grocers, and fishmongers alike. It was among the members of this network that Sutham Tothapthiang now moved.

In the meantime, Surin had begun making wheat noodles for sale, selling eggs and duck meat, and buying rice by the sack for delivery in 10 kg and 20 kg lots to retail customers in Trang. He had, in essence, resumed just those sorts of activities that his father and his fellow immigrants had undertaken in the years directly following their arrival in Siam.

Sutham's contacts in Central, Northern and Northeastern Thailand, coupled with Surin's increasing knowledge of the intricacies of the rice trade in chronically rice-deficient Southern Thailand, soon made it possible for the brothers to enter a new line of business. By 1970, Surin was able to open a small store in Trang from which he sold rice and seasoning powder on both retail and wholesale bases.[11] This business grew, and the Tothapthiang brothers became wholesale suppliers of rice to merchants in provinces across the lower South as far as the Malaysian border, long home to a highly profitable commerce in smuggled paddy. The Tothapthiang brothers' success in the rice trade lifted the family's fortunes higher than they had been even in the years of their father's greatest success.

With capital to invest, in 1975 Sutham and Surin joined in founding the Kwang Phaisan Company with their sister and brother-in-law and a number of merchants based in the Song Wat quarter of Bangkok.[12] Song Wat was the centre of the national foodstuff and dry-goods distribution networks; Tou Nguan Tiang and the other Teochiu dry-goods merchants of Trang had long done business with the merchants there. Sutham and Surin Tothapthiang could therefore view their new business associates more as peers than as patrons.

Among other trading activities, the Kwang Phaisan Company launched a new brand of canned fish on the Thai market. By 1979, its sales, above all in the provinces, justified the family's decision to lease a fish cannery in Trang and to incorporate the Kwang Phaisan Food Products Company. During the 1980s, Sutham Tothapthiang remained as active as ever in the family's businesses, but he avoided publicity. Surin was to be the public face and leader of the Tothapthiang empire.[13]

As Surin served more and more as the visible principal in the Tothapthiang family's growing group of firms, so also did the group's renown increase. From the early 1980s it began extensively to advertise its 'Smiling Fish' (*pla yim*) brand canned fish on Channel 7, the national colour television network owned by the Royal Thai Army and operated by the Bangkok Broadcasting and Television Company.[14] More than any other, this step accounts for Surin Tothapthiang's current fame and importance. It also represented his family's initial contact with patrons of truly national power and influence.

The Tothapthiang family's decision to advertise on Channel 7 linked it for the first time with economic interests outside the Chinese market society within which it had previously operated. It took the family into the main course of Thailand's post-1945 national political economy, dominated by a number of large financial conglomerates with close links to the Thai military. In the 30 years from the conclusion of the Second World War, the scope and nature of such conglomerates' undertakings necessitated military patronage and protection. Success and often even survival in business required that the financial conglomerates' Chinese principals establish personal connections with members of the Thai governmental elite.

Bangkok Broadcasting and Television and its concession to operate the Army's Channel 7 resulted from just this sort of connection. Established in 1967 by a group that included Chuan Rattanarak and General Praphat Charusathien's wife *khun ying* Sawai,[15] it became one of the most important components of the Rattanarak family's business empire. Centred on the Bank of Ayutthaya, this financial conglomerate's astonishingly rapid growth from river transport into banking, insurance, cement production, and numerous other activities during the 1960s and early 1970s owed much to the active assistance of General Praphat, who with Marshal Thanom Kittikachorn ruled Thailand between 1963 and 1973.[16] The conglomerate was an exemplar of Thai capitalism in the 1945–1975 period, just as its patron General Praphat epitomized the military-bureaucratic sponsors on which the major Sino-Thai business empires depended in those decades.

Along with such families as the Sophonphanich and the Techaphaibun, the Rattanarak family symbolized the nature of business–politics relations at the highest level during the era of close links between leading Chinese bankers and top Thai military figures between the late 1940s and the 1970s.[17] Those were decades during which Tou Nguan Tiang and merchants like him pursued their own, considerably smaller fortunes within Chinese market society and without any need for connections with senior Thai bureaucrats, whether military or civilian. Similarly, businessmen of Surin Tothapthiang's generation could also do without such connections, not so much because they did not aspire to participate in business at the national level but rather because, by the late 1970s and early 1980s, bureaucratic patronage had become less of a *sine qua non* in business at that level. In moving out of market society, this generation faced a very different set of circumstances from those that had confronted Chuan Rattanarak.

Responsibility for managing Channel 7 alternated between two of Sawai Charusathian's nephews, Chatchua Kannasut and Lieutenant

Colonel Chaichan Thianpraphat.[18] The former, a progressive professional manager who also served as deputy chairman of the board of the Rattanarak family's Ayutthaya Life Assurance Company, became an important investor in a number of firms in the Tothapthiang group. Tothapthiang firms in which Chatchua held equity included the Trang Cannery Company, a manufacturer of aluminium cans; the Trang Sure Company, a producer of *surimi* and frozen sea-food products; the Kraitawan Company, a maker of ready-to-eat noodles; and the Trang Kwang Phaisan Company, which owned the most prestigious hotel in Trang, theThammarin Hotel.[19] At the same time, the Tothapthiang family's Constant Advertising Company produced and owned the popular night-time television programme *Si Thum Square* which appeared on Channel 7.[20]

Chatchua Kannasut's relations with Surin Tothapthiang and his family became close and personal, going well beyond a mutually profitable toleration between patron and client. They also constituted the Tothapthiang family's only channel of access to the resources of the Rattanarak empire. Direct Rattanarak or military investment in Tothapthiang firms was non-existent or at best insignificant. Surin and his family's enterprises lay, then, on the periphery of this great commercial and financial empire; contact with its centre was indirect and mediated, infrequent and of no discernible importance.

As part of its policy of giving the private sector a voice in the formulation of economic policy through the medium of formal business organizations, the government of Prem Tinsulanonda decided during the mid-1980s to promote the establishment of provincial chambers of commerce.[21] It was, then, in response to a directive from Bangkok that he should organize a chamber in Trang that the provincial commercial officer brought together a group of local businessmen to discuss that possibility. Given the growing fame and apparent success of the business group over which Surin presided, it was natural that the commercial officer should include him among those he contacted.[22]

This invitation was not Surin's first involvement with the government's effort to increase private sector participation in Thai public life. He had earlier attended the National Institute of Development Administration training course for provincial businessmen, which emphasized not only improved business practices but also the potential benefits chambers of commerce could bring to the provincial private sector.[23]

In 1986, a president was selected from among the seven founding members of the Trang Chamber of Commerce, men who had been willing to cooperate with the provincial commercial officer in his efforts to comply with the instructions that he had received from Bangkok. Surin's extensive business and media contacts outside the province and the national reputation of his Smiling Fish brand canned fish made him the logical choice.

The members of the Trang Chamber of Commerce, numbering over 250 by 1992, elected Surin to second and third terms as their president.[24] Under his leadership, its activities included lobbying the government for more effective transportation links between Trang and Bangkok, and promoting various local festivals as a way to highlight the province's potential as a tourist destination.[25] These goals reflected a general and somewhat vague sense of priorities more than a scheme targeted at the promotion of various sectors or interests. Southern Thailand enjoyed a boom in tourism from the second half of the 1980s, and Trang merchants felt left out. Likewise, there was a perception that the train service to the province was not as convenient as it might be. Efforts to tackle such problems in a coordinated fashion represented a departure for Trang, as did the notion that the business sector could speak with one officially sanctioned voice. Still, the continued extreme centralization of government in Thailand imposed real limits on the ability of provincial chambers of commerce like that in Trang to address many of the issues of greatest economic importance.

Surin Tothapthiang's national fame came to exceed his real commercial or political importance. Leadership of the Trang Provincial Chamber of Commerce complemented and paralleled his earlier contact with Channel 7. It provided greater exposure for him and his family's businesses. Extensive coverage of events organized by the Trang Provincial Chamber of Commerce on Channel 7 contributed more than any other factor to the development of Surin's prominence as chamber of commerce president and an outstanding provincial businessman.[26] Even as his national reputation grew, however, Surin demonstrated his continued connection to the local market society in which his father first thrived and then failed. He worked hard to enter the leadership ranks of one of Trang's oldest Chinese voluntary organizations, the uniquely respected Association for the Promotion of Education.[27]

In expanding the scope of its operations beyond the provincial Chinese market society in which first Tou Nguan Tiang and later his two elder sons prospered, the Tothapthiang family found in Chatchua Kannasut a bridge to the national commercial and political elite. In affording Surin Tothapthiang access to television, Chatchua made available to the family's firms the resources of one of Thailand's greatest business empires of the post-war era. And, however different the environments in which Tou Nguan Tiang and Chuan Rattanarak operated, Surin Tothapthiang's links to the Rattanarak empire made possible his emergence as a representative of one aspect of Thailand's new politics.

In taking an active role in the officially promoted Trang Provincial Chamber of Commerce, Surin Tothapthiang made use of a second causeway to commercial prominence at the national level. Although he was neither one of Thailand's most important businessmen in financial or economic terms nor an influential figure in the area of parliamentary politics or economic policy, Surin nevertheless came to embody the provincial variant of the prominence accorded to organized business since the 1980s. No single event marked so starkly the important role officially granted to organized business in the Thai political order as Prime Minister Chuan Leekpai's visit to the People's Republic of China in August 1993.[28] Chuan travelled with a delegation of more than 100 Thai businessmen whose inclusion on the trip reflected both official and business interest in the enhancement of commercial links between Thailand and the People's Republic. This group included such leading figures as Chartri Sophonphanich of the Bangkok Bank, Thanin Chirawanon of Charoen Phokphand (CP), Sutthikiat Chirathiwat of the Central Department Store group, Chokchai Aksaranan of the Federation of Thai Industries, and many others of similar prominence. Representing the Trang Chamber of Commerce was its president, Surin Tothapthiang.

SUCHON CHAMPHUNOT

Surin Tothapthiang's presence among the business leaders who accompanied Chuan to China reflected the prominence of one variety of the new national politics in Thailand. The importance of another, the influential provincial variety, was evident in the appearance of Suchon Champhunot, long-time member of parliament from the lower Northern province of Phitsanulok, among exclusive company of a very different sort: those politicians accused by the junta that ruled Thailand from February 1991 to March 1992 of being 'unusually rich'.

In the days immediately following the putsch that overthrew the elected government of Prime Minister Chatichai Choonhavan in February 1991, the self-styled 'National Peace-Keeping Council' (NPC) created an 'Assets Investigation Committee'.[29] To aid this body in executing its mandate to investigate the provenance of the wealth of various members of Chatichai's government, the NPC moved quickly to order the Bank of Thailand to freeze the assets of 22 former cabinet ministers and deputy ministers. Among those affected were many of the leading figures in contemporary Thai politics.[30] Those under investigation included virtually every politician who had overseen major government projects initiated or put out to bid during General Chatichai's premiership.

The new Thai money-politics had risen to a high watermark during the two and a half years of Chatichai's leadership. Influential provincial businessmen dominated the cabinet; their aggressive approach to the opportunities for personal enrichment presented by their ministerial posts[31] accounted for the initial public support for the putsch and justified the NPC's creation of the Assets Examination Committee. Having served as deputy minister of finance for the duration of Chatichai's premiership, Suchon Champhunot could not have been surprised to find his name among those whom the committee decided to investigate for corruption.

Suchon Champhunot was not born in Phitsanulok. When in 1942 the 28-year-old China-born Teochiu rice-trader Tang Chung Yuai moved his family north from Bang Munnak, Phichit province, his oldest son Tang Ui Chiao was already four or five years old. Tang Chung Yuai came to Phitsanulok to join with a number of friends in the operation of one of the city's two major rice mills. Lying just south of the main municipal market on the banks of the Nan River, the mill had become the property of a professional gambler who, uninterested in or incapable of running it himself, had let it to this group of Chinese.[32] Their arrival in Phitsanulok reflected a first breaking out of the petty-commercial beach-head that they, like hundreds of thousands of their fellow immigrants of the inter-war period, had established in provincial Thailand during the 1930s. In moving from Phichit to Phitsanulok, too, they followed commercial channels developed in the rice trade in this period, when upcountry mills began to play more of a role in the Thai rice trade, and the traders who dealt with all the mills in a given region knitted towns such as Bang Munnak into the wider network of national market society.

Unable after a few years to renew their lease, Tang Chung Yuai and his colleagues made clear their faith in post-war Phitsanulok's commercial promise by building their own rice mill on a site just to the south of the one that they had previously operated. Tang Chung Yuai served as its manager.[33] In 1956, this concern was registered as a limited company with 40 shareholders, including Chinese merchants resident both in Phitsanulok and in Bang Munnak, Nakhon Sawan, Lampang, and Bangkok. Capital as well as rice flowed along the channels that held the market society of post-war Thailand together. And, while he and his immediate family held fewer than 10 per cent of the total shares, Tang Chung Yuai nevertheless served as managing director of the new company.[34] While formally just *primus inter pares* among the principals in the mill, he clearly had the skill and ambition to become the driving force behind its expanding operations.

Tang Chung Yuai had by the mid-1950s emerged not only as the most prominent rice miller in Phitsanulok but also as one of its leading merchants and as a mainstay of its Chinese community. Involved in the ice business as well as the rice trade, he was among the founders of the newly registered all-speech-group Phitsanulok Chinese Association in 1947.[35] The size and composition of the Chinese community of Phitsanulok in this post-war period reflected the many arrivals of the preceding 15 to 20 years. Many Chinese who, like Tang Chung Yuai and his associates, had only come to the city relatively recently were nevertheless active and accepted members of local market society. Tang Chung Yuai served a term as chairman of the Phitsanulok Chinese Association in the early 1950s and held the same position again for three consecutive terms in the early 1960s.[36]

The attainment of such a formal position of leadership, above all for an extended tenure, reflected very high status in the informal hierarchy fundamental to the market society of the era. Commercial success and the wealth that it usually brought, participation in Chinese organizations and work for the good of the community, and acquaintance with and respect from a wide circle of people all contributed to one's position in this hierarchy.[37] None of these accruements was, of course, entirely unrelated to any of the others. And, while the gradations of rank might have been imperceptibly fine, they were no less real or consequential for that reason. For example, comparison of the positions occupied in the late 1950s or early 1960s by Tou Nguan Tiang in Trang and by Tang Chung Yuai in Phitsanulok reveals a stark contrast. While Tou Nguan Tiang had certainly achieved commercial success and a position of respect in local market society, he never became the sort of figure whose influence and leadership would lead others to describe him as *kwangkhwang*, a term describing a person with 'a wide circle of friends and acquaintances'[38] and implying, in post-1945 market society, extensive and useful connections. Tang Chung Yuai, however, was just such a figure. In part, of course, the transition from trading rice to milling rice made when he moved his family from Bang Munnak to Phitsanulok carried him into a commercial environment qualitatively different from that of even the most successful provincial shopkeeper. As we have noted above, however, Tou Nguan Tiang himself was by this time no longer a local pedlar without well-established, regular links to Bangkok commercial interests.

Unlike some other provincial businessmen in this era, Tang Chung Yuai required little bureaucratic patronage in his activities. He held no concessions granted by the government. He moved, rather, within an ever-widening network of contacts in local, regional, and national market society; and it is in this context that the new line of business that he undertook from the early 1960s can best be understood.

In 1961, the Bangkok Bank opened a branch in Phitsanulok. It was the fourth commercial bank branch to open there, following the Thai Farmers' Bank (1950), the Agricultural Bank (1954), and the Bangkok Bank of Commerce (1959).[39] While managed by trained professionals sent out from its headquarters, newly established branches of the Bangkok Bank also ordinarily engaged well-known local figures to serve as compradores (*khomprado*) in this period. The central purpose of the compradore system was to compensate for bank branches' inability to assess the creditworthiness of prospective borrowers in unfamiliar settings. The compradore would typically 'introduce' customers to the bank, personally guarantee loans made to them, and in return receive a percentage of the interest paid to the bank on such loans.[40]

It is important to be clear about the social positions occupied by compradores such as those employed by the Bangkok Bank in the three decades after the Second World War. They served to link the bank to the rank and file of Chinese market society, both in Bangkok and in the provinces. They played no role in mediating between the Thai bureaucracy and Chinese merchants. Rather, they served as the means through which the great banking tycoons of Bangkok, operating at the pinnacle of Chinese business and thus forced into frequent contact with Thai bureaucrats, dealt with the vast majority of those Chinese merchants for whom bureaucratic contact was not necessary. From the bank's perspective, the most important qualifications required of a compradore included wealth, respect in the community, and a wide circle of acquaintances.[41] Such prominence as Tang Chung Yuai had achieved in his first 19 years in Phitsanulok made him an ideal choice to serve as compradore for the Bangkok Bank's new branch there.

During his decade as a bank compradore, Tang Chung Yuai remained active in the rice business. By the second half of the 1960s he needed to spend less time at the bank, for he had begun to share his duties there with his oldest son.[42] After Tang Ui Chiao completed his elementary education at the Chinese Sin Min School in Phitsanulok, Tang Chung Yuai had sent him to the Si Racha branch of the prestigious Assumption College.[43] Not merely his growing means but also clearly his broadening horizons led Tang Chung Yuai to make such a choice for his oldest son. At a school like Assumption, Tang Ui Chiao would rub shoulders with the sons of families prominent in social realms very different from the Chinese market society in which his father had made his fortune.

Tang Ui Chiao left Assumption Si Racha for Thammasat University, where both his education and his exposure to a broader elite continued apace. In 1957, the same year that he graduated from Thammasat's Faculty of Commerce and Accountancy, 20-year-old Tang Ui Chiao legally changed his name to Suchon Champhunot.[44] From Thammasat, Suchon moved to a job at the headquarters of the Bangkok Bank. While his academic preparation would have made a professional career with the Bangkok Bank a logical choice, Suchon stayed there only a year or two before returning to Phitsanulok.[45] His time in the bank's headquarters served above all to familiarize him with its business and its personnel.

In addition to sharing his father's responsibilities as bank compradore, Suchon Champhunot soon began to play significant commercial, social, and political roles in Phitsanulok in his own right. He worked as managing partner of one of the rice mills controlled by his family, served as chairman of the Sin Min School Alumni Association, and was a member of the Phitsanulok municipal council.[46] In 1969, running as an independent, he won election to one of the province's three seats in the national parliament.[47]

Within weeks of his election to parliament, Suchon joined several dozen other independent members in the formation of an allegedly 'neutral group'.[48] In fact, however, this bloc was the creation of Senator Prasit Kanchanawat, a Bangkok Bank executive and strong backer of General Praphat Charusathien in the struggle for control of the military government's own electoral vehicle, the United Thai People's Party (UTPP).[49] The most important Chinese capitalist in post-1945 Thailand, Chin Sophonphanich, had brought his close friend and business associate Prasit into the Bangkok Bank soon after becoming its managing director in 1952. Together with Bunchu Rojanasathien, the two of them had saved the bank from the difficulties then facing it, and Prasit had remained one of Chin's most trusted *consiglieri*.[50] General Praphat himself became chairman of the Bangkok Bank in 1957 in one of the paradigmatic relationships between Thai military bureaucrat and Chinese finance capitalist of the post-war decades.[51] And now Chinese banker Prasit came to the assistance of Thai soldier Praphat in the latter's struggle for influence within the military clique that dominated Thai politics. The resources on which Prasit could draw in this effort included provincial members of parliament, among them a Bangkok Bank compradore from Phitsanulok.

These events prefigured the developments of the 1980s, when influential provincial businessmen would come to dominate the Thai parliament. In this earlier case, not only did General Praphat need to rely on Prasit for the assembly of an entourage of supporters, but electoral forms also required Prasit to reach beyond his own personal and financial resources in assembling this entourage. He needed, that is, to secure the cooperation of individuals with enough local resources and influence to win election to parliament.

Soon registering as the Liberal Party (*Phak Itsara*),[52] the group into which Suchon had integrated himself continued, under Prasit Kanchanawat's direction, to serve its original purpose of lending support to Interior Minister General Praphat in parliament. By the time of the dissolution of that parliament in late 1971, the UTPP had largely absorbed the Liberals,[53] and Suchon Champhunot ended his first parliamentary term as a member of the UTPP.[54]

In these same years Suchon had begun two major commercial projects in Phitsanulok. One was the city's first modern hotel, the Amarin Nakhon, on a prime government-owned site opposite the Bangkok Bank branch.[55] The other was a complex of shophouses surrounding a large, air-conditioned movie theatre, the Phitsanulok Rama. Suchon built this complex on the site of the rice mill that had first drawn Tang Chung Yuai to Phitsanulok in 1942.[56] To complete the project, he secured mortgage finance from the Bangkok Bank.[57] The visibility, modernity, and sheer scale of both the Amarin Nakhon Hotel and the Phitsanulok Rama complex reinforced Suchon's own prominence in Phitsanulok. His high status was only confirmed by the decision of the Ministry of the Interior, still controlled by General Praphat, to appoint him the city's mayor in December 1972.[58]

Neither at this early stage in his career in business and politics nor later on did Suchon's income seem to have depended to any significant extent on such illegal local economic activities as are often taken to typify the *chao pho*.[59] At the very least, his personal wealth has not appeared wildly disproportionate to the scope and scale of his many licit and open undertakings. Nevertheless, both his roots in provincial market society and his career in electoral politics have marked him as an influential provincial in Thai public life since the late 1960s.

Following the overthrow of Thanom and Praphat in October 1973, the shrewd Prasit Kanchanawat displayed fine form as a political survivor. He founded and led the Social Nationalist Party, which won 16 seats in the parliamentary elections of January 1975.[60] Representing Chachoengsao province, Prasit became speaker of the parliament.[61] In Phitsanulok, newly divided into two electoral districts, Social Nationalist candidate Suchon Champhunot finished third in the contest for the two seats in the first district.[62] By the elections of April 1976, however, Suchon was able to win more votes than any other candidate in the province.[63] While the Social Nationalists took only eight seats in the new parliament, their leader Prasit Kanchanawat served first as minister of justice and then as deputy prime minister. Thirty-nine year old Suchon Champhunot became a deputy government spokesman.[64]

Still active in a wide range of business activities in Phitsanulok, Suchon Champhunot sat out the 1979 national elections, as did

Bangkok Bank vice-chairman Prasit Kanchanawat.[65] In 1983 and 1986, recruited into the party by Police General Pramarn Adireksan, Suchon won election to parliament as a Chart Thai candidate.[66] It was in these elections that his political style showed the traits often associated with the *chao pho* most evidently. In each trip to the polls, Suchon and Prachakorn Thai candidate Yingphan Manasikan ran very close to each other.[67] Rather than reflecting intense rivalry between politicians belonging to different parties, however, their similar levels of electoral support reflected close cooperation in campaigning.

Helped by the organizational efforts of Suchon's younger brother Wiramet, the long-time chairman of the Phitsanulok Provincial Council, Suchon and Yingphan mobilized an extensive network of shared canvassers (*hua khanaen*).[68] As in the increasingly wide areas of provincial Thailand where vote-buying efforts directed and financed by influential provincials have determined electoral outcomes, money-politics dominated the First Electoral District of Phitsanulok. The cross-party partnership forged between Suchon and Yingphan proved an efficient arrangement for ensuring the capture of two of the three seats now at stake there. No less than reliance on a network of canvassers (*hua khanaen*) and on large sums of money, the emergence of this arrangement reflected the fundamental characteristics of the parliamentary behaviour of Thai influential provincials. Party loyalty has been weak and ideology almost insignificant in the areas over which this variant of the new Thai politics holds sway. Instead, personal, financial, and electoral ties among candidates have proved the most important basis of political organization.[69]

In 1988, when the Chart Thai Party under the leadership of General Chatichai won more seats in parliament than any of its rivals, Suchon's electoral partnership with Yingphan brought success once again.[70] By now a deputy leader of Chart Thai, Suchon became deputy minister of finance.[71] His appointment reflected not only his seniority in the party but also the operations of a spoils system that has allowed many influential provincial businessmen to enter the cabinet.[72]

Suchon's educational background and work experience with Thailand's most powerful bank related directly to the responsibilities he shouldered at the Ministry of Finance.[73] Many cabinet ministers from provincial Thailand may owe their positions above all to success achieved far from Bangkok, but that does not mean they are country bumpkins unprepared for the positions which their influence has won for them. They have proved themselves in the commercially and socially competitive setting of market society, in which relatively well-educated people have been no rarity. And through their involvement in national politics they have come into regular contact with a wide variety of sophisticated and accomplished people whose examples further shape their already considerable drive and talent.

The NPC's Assets Investigation Committee cleared Suchon, like Banharn but unlike Pramarn, of the charge that he had taken advantage of his ministerial position to engage in corruption.[74] And when the master-mind of the NPC, General Suchinda Kraprayoon, became prime minister after the March 1992 election, he included Suchon in his short-lived cabinet.[75] In the September 1992 elections Suchon ran under the banner of General Chatichai's new Chart Pattana Party and took his seat as a member of the parliamentary opposition to Prime Minister Chuan Leekpai's government.[76] He also began to devote his time and energy to the development of a resort in Phromphiram District of Phitsanulok.[77]

CONCLUSION

The comprehensive history of the mid-twentieth-century market society created by the last great wave of Chinese immigration to Siam and of its impact on the commerce and the society of Thailand remains to be written. In the meantime, we must make do with more focused inquiries into the social history of modern Thailand and market society's place in it. Surin's and Suchon's careers attest to important continuities in Thailand's political, social, and institutional features, but they also show that we cannot think in terms of a single, unchanging past. The Chinese element in organized business and in the conduct of influential provincials includes little that would prove recognizable to the Sinologist. Nor does it mirror the role played by the Chinese traders who helped King Taksin use international commerce to rebuild Siam after the fall of Ayutthaya in 1767.[78] It shows no continuity with the important assistance extended to the Siamese state in its competition with British interests in peninsular Siam by the wealthy Chinese families who served King Chulalongkorn (1868–1910).[79] Nor does it descend from the criminally active Chinese secret societies of nineteenth-century Siam.[80] Analyses drawing parallels between Thai society of the last two decades and that of the late nineteenth century – or even earlier – obscure the impact on contemporary Thai politics of socio-historical developments specific to the mid-twentieth century. Today's influential provincials demonstrate continuity above all with those *kwangkhwang* figures who enjoyed the highest status in the market society of the three or four decades to the mid-1970s.

It is to this historically specific environment, where success in commerce and work on behalf of the community rather than prowess in crime brought respect and prestige to these *sia* (tycoons),[81] that one does best to look for the antecedents of Thailand's new politics. This observation in no way denies either the overwhelming ambition or the willingness to resort to fiercely competitive business practices of the men who rose to the top of market society. It simply seeks to offer a more precise understanding of the milieu which gave rise to today's influential provincials and leaders of organized business.

Men such as Surin Tothapthiang and Suchon Champhunot have stood with one foot firmly rooted in what remains of the market society from which they emerged and with the other resolutely planted on the stage of contemporary national affairs. But to what extent are Surin and Suchon representative of the leaders of business organizations and of influential provincial politicians? Certainly, each demonstrates atypical elements. Suchon seems to have derived the lion's share of his income from basically legitimate undertakings. Surin's path to success in business ran by way of his father's failure. Neither of these men relied on monopolistic or monopsonistic concessions from the state. And it goes without saying that many individuals combine leadership of business organizations with renown as influential provincials and even fully fledged *chao pho*. These roles are not always as mutually exclusive as in the cases of Surin and Suchon. Still, despite such potential deviations from hypothetical norms, Surin and Suchon have shared with countless comparable figures their deep roots in market society. Analyses of contemporary Thai politics that stress the official aims and formal structure of business organizations and emphasize the gangsterism and vote-buying of *chao pho* risk obscuring these origins.

In leaving the origins of men like Surin Tothapthiang and Suchon Champhunot in the shadows, we forfeit insight into the world-view and patterns of conduct, learned in market society, that they bring to national affairs. It is not just that a scattered few such men have moved into the mainstream of Thai politics. Rather, through a variety of channels, many of the leading figures of Thailand's national political class have, as a group, emerged from Chinese market society.[82] Fluid, competitive, wide open to those who refused to see obstacles to their ambition, that society gave these men their first experience of public life, of politics in its broadest, most literal, and least formal sense. It taught them early lessons about the many uses of wealth and the value of a wide circle of connections. It conditioned them to attend carefully to their status in the *talat* and among people of their own kind but not at all to the standards of the wider society. The appearance of men trained in these norms of market society on the national political scene has reshaped the public life of the kingdom.

The two careers examined here suggest a number of additional conclusions about the role of Chinese market society as a source of the most dynamic segment of contemporary Thailand's national elite. Rapid economic growth, parliamentary rule, and Thai citizenship[83] opened the way for the transformation of many of market society's leaders into 'Thai' leaders. Connections to Bangkok also proved important. In Surin Tothapthiang's relationship with Channel 7 and in Suchon Champhunot's ties to the Bangkok Bank we find, however, a very particular form of such connections.

Both Surin and Suchon positioned themselves on the fringes of economic empires that trace their origins to the heyday of Thai military-bureaucratic sponsorship of Chinese financial conglomerates.The positions that Surin Tothapthiang and Suchon Champhunot staked out account for many of the successes recorded in this essay. For neither Surin nor Suchon functioned merely as a dependent provincial client of Bangkok interests. Each of them was, rather, able to 'localize' his relationship with these interests, to make it serve his own purposes in the provincial setting in which he operated.[84] Now, however, economic links between Bangkok and provincial Thailand are changing fast, in part through the activities of men like those considered here. And, as figures from market society integrate themselves into the mainstream of national life and appear among its leading elements, market society has itself lost much of its formerly distinctive traits. Indeed, by the mid-1980s the idea of market society may already have become anachronistic. That society may in the end have groomed but a single generation of the

Thai political elite. Its members have, however, already reshaped the political order. And genuine progress towards greater openness and broader participation must take the pass to which their influence brought Thai politics as its point of departure.

NOTES

1. Anek Laothamatas, 'Business and Politics in Thailand: New Patterns of Influence', *Asian Survey* 28 (1988): 451–470, and Anek Laothamatas, *Business Associations and the New Political Economy of Thailand: From Bureaucratic Polity to Liberal Corporatism* (Boulder, Col.: Westview Press, 1992) are the most influential works arguing for the importance of these organizations.

2. For perhaps the best treatment of these latter figures, *see* James S. Ockey, 'Business Leaders, Gangsters, and the Middle Class: Societal Groups and Civilian Rule in Thailand' (Ph.D. thesis, Cornell University, 1992) and James Ockey, '*Chaopho*: Capital Accumulation and Social Welfare in Thailand', *Crossroads* 8 (1993): 48–77.

3. See Robert H. Bates, 'Contra Contractarianism: Some Reflections on the New Institutionalism', *Politics & Society* 16 (1988): 387–401, 393, and Richard F. Doner, 'Limits of State Strength: Toward an Institutionalist View of Economic Development', *World Politics* 44 (1992): 398–431, 430–431, and 'Approaches to the Politics of Growth in Southeast Asia', *Journal of Asian Studies* 50 (1991): 818–849, 835–836.

4. G. William Skinner, *Chinese Society in Thailand: An Analytical History* (Ithaca, NY: Cornell University Press, 1957), pp. 172–178.

5. Note that, like its English equivalent 'market', the Thai word *talat* has a range of meanings from the literally concrete (or wooden) to the abstract. First, it may denote complexes of stalls manned by vendors during fixed periods of each day or week. Second, it may refer to clusters of shops in rural areas or to the commercial quarters of towns. Each of the latter is typically arrayed around a *talat* in the first meaning of the term. Finally, in its most abstract sense, *talat* is used to refer, for example, to 'the land market' (*talat thi din*), to 'the labour market' (*talat raeng ngan*), and even to 'the capital market' (*talat thun*). In its use of the term 'market society', this essay draws on the second of the denotations of *talat*.

6. See Kenneth Perry Landon, *Siam in Transition: A Brief Survey of Cultural Trends in the Five Years since the Revolution of 1932* (Shanghai: Kelly & Walsh, 1939), p. 87, and G. William Skinner, 'Change and Persistence in Chinese Culture Overseas: A Comparison of Thailand and Java', reprinted from *Journal of the South Seas Society* 16 (1960): 86–100, in John T. McAlister (ed.), *Southeast Asia: The Politics of National Integration* (New York: Random House, 1973), pp. 399–415, 409.

7. Detailed studies tracing the development and analysing the various aspects of Chinese market society in a variety of Thai locales during the decades between the 1930s and the 1970s include Chester F. Galaska,

'Continuity and Change in Dalat Plu: A Chinese Middle Class Business Community in Thailand' (Ph.D. thesis, Syracuse University, 1969); Stephen F. Tobias, 'Chinese Religion in a Thai Market Town' (Ph.D. thesis, University of Chicago, 1973); Maria Cristina Blanc Szanton, 'People in Movement: Mobility and Leadership in a Central Thai Town' (Ph.D. thesis, Columbia University, 1982); and Pornchai Trakulwaranont, 'Wang Thong: A Study of History, Civic Identity, and Ethnicity in a Thai Market Town' (M.A. thesis, University of Kent, 1987).

8. Unless otherwise noted, the early history of the Tothapthiang family in Trang is drawn from interviews with Sawat Tothapthiang on 18 December 1992 and Surin Tothapthiang on 22 December 1992, both in Trang, and from Suphatra Suphap, 'Surin Tothapthiang: chao pho pla krapong phan lan', in *Arunsawat* 5, 56 (November 1992): 32–37. Basic biographical data on the family of Tou Nguan Tiang are available in Commercial Registration File (hereafter CRF) Bo.O.Cho.To.Ngo. 133 (Tothapthiang Company, Ltd), Trang Provincial Commercial Office.

9. His Tou Nguan Ki Store appeared among the entries for Trang in Krom kansonthet, Krasuang setthakan, *Phanit songkhro 2500–2501* (Bangkok, 1957), section 6, p. 56.

10. Sutham was born in 1945 and Surin in 1949; CRF Bo.O.Cho.To.Ngo. 133 (Tothapthiang Company, Ltd).

11. In 1973, this firm was registered as Sin Thai (Trang) Limited Partnership. Surin, as managing partner, held a 400,000-baht share. Two younger siblings held shares of 300,000 baht each; CRF Ho.So.Cho.To.Ro. 262 (Sin Thai (Trang) Limited Partnership), Trang Provincial Commercial Office.

12. CRF Bo.Cho. 1082/2518 (Kwang Phaisan Company, Ltd), Commercial Registration Department, Ministry of Commerce, Bangkok.

13. Interview with Surin Tothapthiang, 22 December 1992, Trang; also, CRF Bo.O.Cho.To.Ro. 11 (Kwang Phaisan Food Products Company, Ltd), Trang Provincial Commercial Office. The firm's registered capital was 2 million baht, initially paid in to the level of 25 per cent. By 1992, its registered and fully paid capital amounted to 50 million baht.

14. Interview with Surin and Bonsai Group, *200 setthi phuthon* (Bangkok: Creative Publishing, 1991), p. 279. Duncan McCargo, 'The Buds of May', *Index on Censorship* 22, 4 (April 1993): 3–8, 4, reviews the ownership and management of Thailand's broadcast media. Channel 7's signal reached much of provincial Thailand long before those of any of its rivals; see the profile of Chatchua Kannasut in *Thai rat*, 27 October 1989. As it afforded access to the markets in which the Tothapthiangs expected their canned fish to sell best, this range played a role in their original decision to advertise on Channel 7 (interview with Salin Tothapthiang, 29 December 1992, Trang).

15. CRF Bo.Cho. 575/2510 (Bangkok Broadcasting and Television Company, Ltd), Commercial Registration Department, Ministry of Commerce, Bangkok.

16. Suehiro Akira, *Capital Accumulation in Thailand, 1855–1985* (Tokyo: Centre for East Asian Cultural Studies, 1989), pp. 259–260, 290–291. Further data on Chuan Rattanarak and his involvement with Channel 7 appear in *The Nation*, 5 and 9 August 1993.

17. See, for example, Fred W. Riggs, *Thailand: The Modernization of a Bureaucratic Polity* (Honolulu: East–West Center Press, 1966), pp. 243–310; Kevin Hewison, *Bankers and Bureaucrats: Capital and the Role of the State in Thailand* (New Haven: Yale University Southeast Asia Studies, 1989), pp. 174–205; and Suehiro Akira, *Capital Accumulation in Thailand*, pp. 245–265.

18. Lieutenant Colonel Chaichan died in 1980; biographical data are available in two cremation volumes: *Anuson nai ngan phrarachathanphloengsop phan tho Chaichan Thianpraphat* (Bangkok, 1981) and *Phim pen thiraluk nai ngan phraratchathanphloengsop phan tho Chaichan Thianpraphat* (Bangkok, 1981). Profiles of Chatchua Kannasut appeared in *Deli niu* on 4 January 1982 and in *Thai rat* on 1 June 1986, 9 March 1987, 25 August 1988, 27 October 1989, 6 March 1990, 30 December 1990, 11 October 1991, and 25 November 1991.

19. CRF Bo.O.Cho.To.Ngo. 60 (Trang Cannery Company, Ltd), CRF Bo.O. Cho.To.Ngo. 85 (Trang Sure Company, Ltd), and CRF Bo.O.Cho.To.Ngo. 55 (Trang Kwang Phaisan Company, Ltd), all in Trang Provincial Commercial Office; and CRF Bo.Cho. 7571/2531 (Kraitawan Company, Ltd), Commercial Registration Department, Ministry of Commerce, Bangkok. Suphatra, 'Surin Tothapthiang', p. 36, offers a more complete list of the firms in the Tothapthiang group. Description of the activities of Trang Sure Company comes from interview with Salin Tothapthiang.

20. Suphatra, 'Surin Tothapthiang', p. 36. Also, interview with Salin.

21. Anek Laothamatas, *Business Associations*, pp. 58–65.

22. Unless otherwise noted, details concerning the establishment of the Trang Chamber of Commerce come from interviews with Sophon Uasithongkun and Somphon Chianwichai. The Trang Chamber of Commerce was registered with the Division of Trade Institutions, Department of Internal Trade, Ministry of Commerce, in March 1985. Official registration records list Surin, Sophon, Somphon, and four other local businessmen as its founders (Division of Trade Institutions data). Thai chamber of commerce data indicate that the Trang Chamber of Commerce received official permission to operate in February 1986.

23. Anek Laothamatas, *Business Associations*, pp. 59–62.

24. Suphatra, 'Surin Tothapthiang', p. 35. For membership total, 1992 Trang Chamber of Commerce roster.

25. Suphatra, 'Surin Thothapthiang', p. 36; also interviews with Sophon (22 December 1992 in Trang) and Somphon (23 December 1992 in Trang), both of whom stressed that the promotion of tourism was a first step towards attracting commercial and industrial investment to Trang.

26. Bonsai Group, *200 setthi phutton*, p. 279.

27. That is, *Samakhom bamrung kansuksa Trang*; see 'Report of the Board Meeting of 23 July 1992', registration file on Association for the Promotion of Education, Trang Provincial Clerk's Office. It is clear that, to the degree that Surin succeeds in this effort, he will be able to cloud the memory of his family's earlier failure in business and therefore also in Trang market society.

28. All data in this paragraph come from *The Nation*, 18 August 1993. Note that Prime Minister Chuan (1992–1995 and 1997–) is himself a Trang native, though a product of its Hokkien–Cantonese stream.

29. The creation, activities, and ultimate purposes of this committee are treated in great detail in *Khao phiset*, 10 March 1991, pp. 18–21 and 2 February 1992, pp. 12–16; *Matichon sutsapda*, 10 March 1991, pp. 10–13; *Bangkok Post*, 1 March 1992. The following account comes from these sources.

30. The list included Police General Pramarn Adireksarn, Banharn Silpa-archa, and Sano Thianthong of the Chart Thai Party; Samak Sundaravej of Prachakorn Thai; Major General Sanan Khachonprasat of the Democrat Party; Police Captain Chaloem Yoobamrung of the Muan Chon Party; Montri Pongpanich of the Social Action Party; and Narong Wongwan of the Solidarity Party. Complete rosters of the those former ministers initially named as targets for investigation appear in the 10 March 1991 articles cited just above.

31. See Ockey, 'Business Leaders, Gangsters, and the Middle Class', pp. 229, 404–407; Scott Christensen, 'Thailand after the Coup', *Journal of Democracy* 2 (1991): 94–106, esp. pp. 99 ff.

32. Author's interviews with Suthep Sukkasem, 28 May 1993, Wang Thong; Sakchai Champhunot (Tang Chung Yuai), 27 July 1993, Phitsanulok; and Suchon Champhunot, 10 August 1993, Phitsanulok.

33. Interviews with Suthep Sukkasem and Sakchai Champhunot. For Tang Chung Yuai as manager, *see* Krom kansonthet, Krasuang setthakan, *Phanitsongkhro 2500–2501* (Bangkok, 1957), section 6, p. 169.

34. CRF Bo.Cho.Pho.Lo. 45 (Charoenphanit Rice Mill Company, Ltd), Phitsanulok Provincial Commercial Office. By 1974 members of Tang Chung Yuai's immediate family held all the shares in this company.

35. CRF Bo.Cho.Pho.Lo. 46 (Thai Siwarat Ice Company, Ltd) and CRF Ho.So.No.Pho.Lo. 34 (Kiang Ngiap Rice Mill General Partnership), both in Phitsanulok Provincial Commercial Office; and file To. 279/2490 (Phitsanulok Chinese Association), Office of the National Cultural Commission, Division of Private Sector Relations.

36. *Peng-shi-luo Fu Huaqiao Xiehui Huiyan Tongxun Lu Benhui Huodong Tupian* (Phitsanulok: Chinese Association, 1985), no pagination. This volume is dedicated to Tang Chung Yuai in recognition of his role as a leader of the Association of Phitsanulok for nearly four decades. The author is indebted to Dr Julian Wheatley for his generous assistance with these Chinese language materials.

37. See the studies by Galaska, Tobias, Szanton, and Trakunwaranon cited in note 7 above.

38. *New Model Thai-English Dictionary: Library Edition* (Samrong, Samut Prakan: So Sethaputra Press, 1965), pp. 72–73.

39. National Archives (Thailand) Ko.Kho. 0301.4.1, box 1, folder 2.

40. See *Nai okat sadetphraratchadamnoen phraratchathanphloengsop nai Chin Sophonphanit po. cho., po. mo.* (Bangkok, 1988), pp. 126–128, for a relatively frank explanation of the 'compradore system' in Thai banking. It must be kept in mind that relationships between compradores and banks varied considerably from bank to bank and place to place.

41. Ibid., p. 127; for the last term, this source uses *kwangkhwang*.

42. Interviews with Sakchai and Suchon; also, interview with long-time Bangkok Bank officer and current assistant branch manager Mongkhon Sonsri, Phitsanulok, 23 June 1993.

43. Interviews with Sakchai and Suchon. For Suchon's educational background, see also *Tamnan ratthaban Thai* (special issue of *Matichon*, 1989), p. 112, and Chatchai Yenbamrung and Thamrongsak Phetloetanan (eds) *Banthuk kanmuang Thai* (Bangkok: Prachum Chang, 1987), p. 760.

44. Copies of the official documentation are found in CRF Ho.So.No. Pho.Lo. 34 (Kiang Ngiap Rice Mill General Partnership). Tang Chung Yuai took the name Sakchai Champhunot in 1967; see CRF Bo.Cho.Pho.Lo. 45 (Charoenphanit Rice Mill Company, Ltd).

45. Interview with Suchon; *Tamnan ratthaban Thai*, p. 113.

46. CRF Ho.So.No.Pho.Lo. 80 (Setthaphanit Phatthana Rice Mill General Partnership), Phitsanulok Provincial Commercial Office; file To. 135/2504 (Sin Min Alumni Association), Office of the National Cultural Commission, Division of Private Sector Relations; and interview with Suchon.

47. Kanok Wongtrangan, *Khu mu kanmuang Thai: 2475–2525* (Bangkok: Faculty of Political Science, Chulalongkorn University, 1983), p. 428.

48. *Bangkok Post*, 27 February 1969.

49. On Prasit's political manoeuvring in early March 1969, see *Bangkok Post*, 1 and 7 March 1969; also, David Morell and Chai-anan Samudavanija, *Political Conflict in Thailand: Reform, Reaction, Revolution* (Cambridge, Mass.: Oelgeschlager, Gunn, & Hain, 1981), pp. 110, 134.

50. *Nai okat sadetphraratchadamnoen phraratchathanphloengsop nai Chin Sophonphanit*, pp. 146–147. Further biographical information on Prasit Kanchanawat (Khou Tong Mong) is available in *Phunam thurakit* 3, 26 (February 1989): 15–64, and in Kasian Tejapira, 'Commodifying Marxism: The Formation of Modern Thai Radical Culture, 1927–1958' (Ph.D. thesis, Cornell University, 1992), pp. 495 ff.

51. Bangkok Bank, *How It Happened: A History of the Bangkok Bank* (Bangkok: Thai Watana Panich, 1981), p. 159.

52. See *Bangkok Post*, 19 March 1969, where it is noted that Suchon was to serve as assistant treasurer of the new party.

53. Morell and Chai-anan, *Political Conflict in Thailand*, pp. 110 and 134. On the dissolution of parliament in 1971, see David K. Wyatt, *Thailand: A Short History* (London: Yale University Press, 1984), p. 298.

54. Interview with Suchon.

55. Interview with Suchon; CRF Bo.Cho.Pho.Lo. 99 (Amarin Nakhon Hotel Company, Ltd), Phitsanulok Provincial Commercial Office; and data from Royal Property Office [*samnakngan ratchaphatsadu*], Phitsanulok.

56. Interview with Suchon; CRF Bo.Cho.Pho.Lo. 105 (Phitsanulok Commercial Center Company, Ltd), Phitsanulok Provincial Commercial Office; and background files [*sarabop*] for deeds 1106 (issued 1 March 1971) and 1140 (issued 27 August 1958), Phitsanulok Provincial Land Office.

57. Deed 1106, Phitsanulok Provincial Land Office.

58. Interview with Suchon; *Prawat thetsaban lae muang Phatthaya: thiraluk khrop rop 50 pi thetsaban* (Bangkok: Rongphim suanthongthin, Krom kanpokkhrong, 1987), p. 660; and, on Praphat, *Tamnan ratthaban thai*, p. 91. Suchon served as mayor of Phitsanulok until November 1974.

59. As examples of such activities, Ockey lists 'gambling, smuggling, illegal mining or logging, protection rackets, [and] extortion' in 'Business Leaders, Gangsters, and the Middle Class', p. 99.

60. That is, *Phak sangkhom chatniyom*; Kanok, *Ku mu kanmuang Thai*, p. 509; Morell and Chai-anan, *Political Conflict in Thailand*, pp. 110, 113.

61. Kanok, *Ku mu kanmuang Thai*, pp. 370, 436.

62. Chatchai and Thamrongsak, *Banthuk kanmuang Thai*, p. 752.

63. Ibid., p. 759.

64. Morell and Chai-anan, *Political Conflict in Thailand*, p. 265; *Tamnan ratthaban thai*, pp. 95–96: Chatchai and Thamrongsak, *Banthuk kanmuang thai*, p. 754; 'Who's Who in the Suchinda Cabinet', *The Nation*, 18 April 1992.

65. Kong kanluaktang, Krom kanpokkhrong, *Rainganwichai kanluaktang samachik sapha phuthaen ratsadon pho. so. 2522* (Bangkok: Krom kanpokkhrong, 1980), pp. 483–484; *Thai nikon*, 2 April 1979. In the event, 1976 was Prasit's last campaign for parliament.

66. Interview with Suchon; Chatchai and Thamrongsak, *Banthuk kanmuang thai*, p. 758.

67. The remainder of this paragraph is based on Chatchai and Thamrongsak, *Banthuk kanmuang thai*, pp. 754–756, and *Khao phiset*, 3 September 1989, pp. 59, 92.

68. S Ockey, 'Business Leaders, Gangsters, and the Middle Class', pp. 150–190, and in this volume.

69. Ockey, 'Business Leaders, Gangsters and the Middle Class', pp. 244–260. Such ties are important above all as the basis for building *intra*-party factions. Nevertheless, the case of Suchon and Yingphan is by no means unique as an instance of similar *inter*-party cooperation.

70. Kong kanluaktang, Krom kanpokkhrong, *Rainganwichai kanluaktang sapha phuthaen ratsadon pho. so. 2531* (Bangkok: Krom kanpokkhrong, 1989), p. 181; *Tamnan ratthaban thai,* p. 62.

71. *Tamnan ratthaban thai,* p. 112.

72. See Ockey, 'Business Leaders, Gangsters, and the Middle Class', pp. 269–283.

73. Suchon served first under Pramuan Suphawasu and later under Banharn Silpa-archa. *Khao phiset,* 2 February 1992, p. 13.

74. *Bangkok Post,* 5 December 1991. Suchon demonstrated to the satisfaction of the Assets Investigation Committee that his income of 42 million baht ('mostly from land sales, his salary, and other sources'), his acquisition of 32 million baht of other property, and his expenses of 9 million baht during the period of Chatichai's premiership were not 'unusual'. See further *Bangkok Post,* 1 March 1992; *The Nation,* 18 April 1992; and *The Nation,* 15 September 1992.

75. *The Nation,* 18 April 1992.

76. *The Nation,* 15 September 1992.

77. Interview with Suchon.

78. See Sarasin Viraphol, *Tribute and Profit: Sino-Siamese Trade, 1652–1853* (Cambridge, Mass.: Harvard East Asian Monographs, 1977), pp. 163, 171.

79. See Jennifer W. Cushman, *Family and State: The Formation of a Sino-Thai Tin-Mining Dynasty, 1797–1932* (Singapore: Oxford University Press, 1991).

80. Ockey, '*Chaopho*: Capital Accumulation and Social Welfare in Thailand', pp. 51–53, takes this as the most noteworthy Chinese antecedent of the *chao pho.*

81. Ibid., p. 51, offers 'tycoon', a term with no connotation of criminality, as a rough translation for *sia.* See also the discussion of *chao sua* in Chapter 2 of this volume (Ed.).

82. Of course, this political voyage has had an *exact* parallel in the social realm. Considerations of space and subject make it impossible to treat that parallel social voyage here. It must, however, be noted that the sons and daughters of provincial Chinese did not go unrepresented among those members of the educated 'middle class' who took to the streets of Bangkok in May 1992. Market society, then, played a role in the emergence of yet another type of new, though not yet consistently influential, force on the Thai political scene, one not treated at all in this essay.

83. Ockey, 'Business Leaders, Gangsters, and the Middle Class', argues at length for the importance of parliamentary rule in most of the period since 1977 as an enabling factor in the emergence of 'new' political actors of various sorts; see, especially, Chapters 2, 5, and 6. For background on the question of nationality status, see Skinner, *Chinese Society in Thailand,* pp. 374–378.

84. On 'localization', see Oliver W. Wolters, *History, Culture, and Region in Southeast Asian Perspectives* (Singapore: Institute for Southeast Asian Studies, 1982).

SIX

THE LOCAL DYNAMICS OF THE 'NEW POLITICAL ECONOMY'

A District Business Association and Its Role in Electoral Politics

*Daniel Arghiros**

For many years following the mid-1960s publication of Fred Riggs' seminal study, the Thai polity was conceptualized as a 'bureaucratic polity', a state dominated by the bureaucracy.[1] In the early 1990s Anek Laothamatas added to the growing body of critiques of this model, arguing that it had outlived its usefulness because business interests now hold the centre ground. Anek's argument is that from the late 1980s extra-bureaucratic forces, such as chambers of commerce and business, trade, and employers' associations, have

* This essay is based on field research undertaken between 1989–1990 and 1995–1997, augmented by two briefer visits in December 1993 and in mid-1998. Research permission was kindly granted by the National Research Council of Thailand. The main fieldwork was supported by the UK University Grants Committee, Evans Fellowship Fund, the Emslie Horniman Anthropological Scholarship Fund, Mervin Jaspan Field Research Awards, and the Radcliffe-Brown Memorial Fund for Social Anthropological Research. The most recent period was aided by a research fellowship from the Economic and Social Research Council (UK) and two British Academy Research Awards. Research between 1995 and 1997 was funded by a small award from the Faculty of Social Sciences, University of Hull. All places and individual names, except those of national politicians, are pseudonyms.

played a pre-eminent role in policy formation, creating what he called 'the new political economy'.[2] Although the most influential interest groups in this new order are all Bangkok-based, some provincial business associations have also become effective sources of pressure. Like their Bangkok counterparts, they have begun to lobby provincial and central government over policy and the development of regional infrastructure.[3] As provincial business associations are relatively recent phenomena, very little qualitative research has so far been done on them. We know little of their local origins, of how they operate, or of how they wield influence *vis-à-vis* the bureaucracy, other businesses, and labour. We also know very little about their aspirations and to what extent we should view them as representatives of a new force of liberal civil society.

Lacking a qualitative perspective on provincial business associations, we also have no way of knowing whether such institutions are common at the more localized level of the district (*amphoe*).[4] An absence of studies makes it difficult to establish whether such groups are widespread, and whether those that do exist act to counterbalance bureaucrats at the district level in influencing local decision-making and policy. In other words, to use Anek's term, does the 'new political economy' exist at the district level, or has there been change only at provincial and national levels? This chapter presents evidence that at least in one Central Thai district of Ayutthaya province, which we shall call Klang, some ingredients of this 'new political economy' are in evidence. For the first time in the history of the district, local entrepreneurs have organized themselves into an association, and this association not only has a strong corporate identity but also carries enough weight to lobby the district and provincial administrations successfully when the need arises. These entrepreneurs, owners of mechanized brickyards, have formed the Brick Manufacturers' Association (BMA), and it is this organization that forms the focus of this chapter.

But to assess only the capacity of these new local extra-bureaucratic forces to influence bureaucratic decision-making is to miss much that is significant about them. The importance of groups like the BMA lies not only in their potential as lobbying groups, for much of their significance lies in their broader social and political activities. Petitioning the bureaucracy is just one of the activities undertaken by the Association: it also provides members with credit, protection, and a strong social identity. And one of the BMA's most significant activities, particularly in view of the themes of the other contributions to this volume, is its involvement in electoral politics. Members have repeatedly supported each other's attempts to win administrative and political office at the subdistrict and provincial levels. Indeed, the BMA's involvement in electoral politics indicates a shift in the balance of power between the bureaucracy and organized business at the district level.

A major incentive driving individual businessmen to fight expensive campaigns for local office is that office gives the holder access to district and provincial administrators and opportunities to establish mutually helpful relations. The BMA as a group is motivated by the same concern: members understand that more office-holding members means more lobbying power. Since its inception the BMA has supported members' election campaigns, for it has recognized that it must fill its ranks with office-holders if it is to carry enough weight to lobby bureaucrats. This fact also reveals the extent to which local power and influence are still concentrated in the state administration. The district-level political economy is thus not 'new' in Anek's sense so much as it is a hybrid between the old system and the new. The once-sharp socio-economic markings that divided lowland rice-growing districts such as Klang into villagers, bureaucrats, and Sino-Thai merchants are now being muddied by the substantial and abiding presence of local industrialists.

The discussion of Klang's experience will begin by sketching the background of its brick industry, and then will describe the features and activities of the BMA. Next, the association's role in electoral politics will be taken up, illustrated by case studies of members' election campaigns at the subdistrict and provincial levels. It concludes with an examination of the changing status of the BMA through to the late 1990s, after the onset of the Thai economic crisis.

THE BRICK INDUSTRY IN KLANG

In 1990, approximately 700 mechanized brick manufacturing enterprises were scattered throughout Thailand, directly employing over 20,000 people.[5] Brickmaking has long been practised in the Central Region, but appears to have become firmly established in the early nineteenth century with the influx of some 30,000 ethnic Mon – traditionally skilled brick makers – who fled Burmese persecution.[6] Comparatively, the district-wide industry in Klang is only a very recent, though rapid, development. In the early 1970s it was concentrated in one subdistrict and was entirely home-based and non-mechanized. The industry is now well established and is entirely dependent on indigenous capital. It is an example of the growth of labour-intensive forms of industrial commodity production within a wider economy of capital-intensive and factory-based production, or, as Cook has put it, of 'industrialization within industrialization'.[7] Economic growth has boosted the construction industry, which in turn has generated demand for bricks. The Klang brick industry supplies merchants and building contractors in Bangkok and the provinces of the Central Region, particularly around the Eastern seaboard.

Brick production in Klang takes two forms, 'non-mechanized' and 'mechanized'. What differentiates these production methods is not the use of machinery *per se* but the method of forming bricks. In non-mechanized brickyards (*rong it mu, rong it mon*), bricks are moulded by hand. Machines are sometimes used to mix brick-earth, but not for other stages of production. Mechanized brickyards (*rong it khruang*) use diesel or electrically powered machines, technically called extruders, to form bricks. Other machinery is also often used to handle the extruders' greater output. Some non-mechanized brickyards use only household labour and can thus be considered petty commodity producers. Many, however, use a mix of household and hired labour, or only hired labour and are petty capitalist enterprises.[8] All mechanized brickyards, on the other hand, are necessarily petty capitalist or capitalist. At the very least 10 people are required to generate and handle the output of a single extruder, which can be up to 15,000 bricks a day, and no single household can supply this number of labourers. Mechanized brickyards employ between 15 and 120 workers, but the average number of employees is around 40. In this chapter I am concerned solely with mechanized brickyards. Owners of non-mechanized brickyards have not organized themselves in any form.

Brick-earth is obtained from Klang rice-fields and is generally bought from contractors, most of whom also own mechanized brickyards. To fire bricks almost all brickyards in the district use rice husks; these are purchased from local middlemen, who obtain them from Ayutthaya rice mills. The capital needs of an enterprise range from 10,000 baht (approximately US$400), for the most basic non-mechanized brickyard, to more than a million baht for a mechanized one. Start-up capital is obtained by taking out a loan, selling landholdings or reinvesting capital obtained from other enterprises, for example petty trading or poultry rearing. Significantly, of 16 mechanized brickyard owners I interviewed, none claimed to have obtained their initial capital from agricultural production. This is not surprising: in this district rice cultivation is barely profitable, with few areas obtaining more than one harvest a year. Instead, loans are taken from banks, private moneylenders, and kinfolk. Both mechanized and non-mechanized enterprises fire their bricks on the premises in kilns built entirely of unfired bricks; these require only a roof as shelter and little capital expenditure. Fired bricks are collected by wholesalers, independent middlemen or, if they have the means, are transported to clients by the enterprise owners.

The number of mechanized and non-mechanized brickyards in Klang has increased rapidly in recent years. There is no record of the number of non-mechanized brickyards, because most of these are untaxed, but the number of registered mechanized brickyards in the district increased from 32 to 55 in one year (1989–1990).[9] This industry provides employment for a significant proportion of the local land-poor and landless population. Of 165 households I surveyed from two subdistricts in Klang district, more than a third (60) have at least one member employed in the industry, and almost a quarter of the workforce (101 of 408 people) find employment in brickyards. The relative importance of mechanized brickyards in terms of employment is indicated by the fact that they employed 84 per cent of these workers.[10] No labour unions exist in the brick-making industry; in mechanized brickyards labour is on a daily wage basis, and a piecework wage is paid in non-mechanized brickyards. There is a general shortage of local workers in Klang, a situation that is by no means particular to this area.[11] Both mechanized and non-mechanized brickyards employ migrant workers to make up shortfalls.

Entrepreneurs come to own mechanized brickyards in one of two ways: either they graduate from non-mechanized production, or they are 'instant' investors in mechanized production. Of 16 owners of mechanized brickyards I interviewed, five graduated from ownership of non-mechanized works, and the others were 'instant' investors. Of the five, three had expanded from household-based production, and two had owned non-mechanized capitalist enterprises. All but two mechanized brickyard owners are from the locality: most entrepreneurs are representative of outwardly oriented 'rich' villagers[12] who are part of a small capitalist class increasingly evident in Thai rural communities.[13] Several owners run other enterprises alongside brick manufacturing; a number supply landfill for construction sites and brick-earth to the industry, for example.

Insofar as the majority of these entrepreneurs are rural rather than urban based, it is perhaps not surprising that the majority are of Thai rather than Sino-Thai ethnic descent: only a quarter of the owners interviewed were Sino-Thai (4 of 16). Another two owners had previously worked for Sino-Thai businessmen and claimed that the experience had been formative for their entrepreneurial development. Of those enterprise owners I interviewed, 11 were members of the Brick Manufacturers' Association. The ethnic composition of the Association itself is predominantly Thai: only four of the 37 members active in 1995 were of Sino-Thai descent.

THE BRICK MANUFACTURERS' ASSOCIATION

In 1987, as new mechanized brickyards sprang up in response to a surge in demand in the construction industry, conflict arose between owners as they competed for markets and labour. The largest producer requested a fellow entrepreneur, whom he had introduced to brickmaking, to convene a meeting of all owners of mechanized brickyards. The former, whom I call Bay, was at the time a village headman (*phuyaiban*) and felt that his friend – an extremely wealthy *kamnan*, Damrong – would carry more influence in any effort to organize producers. Quite apart from owning the second largest brickyard in Klang, Damrong was an important political figure in the district, if not the province. He was chairman of the district's Association of *Kamnan* and Village Heads; he had been a provincial councillor in the days when *kamnan* were permitted to hold that office concurrently; and he has large landholdings. There was, however, no obvious way in which acting as co-ordinator of an industry association could advance his own interests except through supporting conditions for the industry generally. Acting on Bay's prompting, *Kamnan* Damrong called together owners of mechanized brickyards with an eye to diffusing tension.

This first informal gathering led to the formation of the Brick Manufacturers' Association, and since then meetings have been held monthly. They are generally held in a reserved room of air-conditioned restaurants, or, more rarely, at members' homes. The venue is rotated in order to reduce the likelihood of robbery, since members handle large sums of money at meetings. In an early gathering Damrong and Bay were elected chairman and vice-chairman respectively, and a third man, a village head, was elected secretary. A poll has not been taken since this occasion and the present incumbents seem to occupy these positions more or less permanently.

Shortly before each meeting, a letter is sent to members with details of the venue; agendas are drawn up for meetings, and minutes are taken. Although representatives of all the district's mechanized brickyards are eligible to attend meetings, since all are nominal members, in December 1990 only 24 were regularly represented. By December 1993 this number had increased to 31. Active members tend to be owners of larger brickyards, and the fact that more owners do not become members is probably explained by the heavy demands made by membership: much time is spent meeting social obligations, both to members and in the name of the Association; and members are constantly required to contribute to funds for both social and industry-related causes. In the paragraphs below I shall focus on the ways in which members co-operate, how the Association serves the needs of members, and finally the potential the BMA has had for extending its role.

Before the BMA was established, owners of mechanized brickyards did not socialize, and relations between them were said to be marked by mutual distrust and competition. The BMA, in contrast, is a forum where owners' relations have to some extent 'become overlaid with social content that carries strong expectations of trust and abstention from opportunism'.[14] The regular, semi-formal interaction resulting from its meetings has laid the foundation for more personal and binding relations. Members are honour-bound to attend events hosted by co-members (weddings, ordinations, new house parties, and funerals) and are consequently involved in a complex network of gift-exchange (*chuai ngan*). Members use kin terms fictively to address one another – the chairman is addressed as *lung*, paternal uncle, while other established members call each other *phi*, elder sibling. The Association gives the impression of being an extremely cohesive group, one characterized by intimate and supportive relations. Members frequently told me that 'there is unity between us' (*mi khwam samakhi kan*); the vice-chairman went so far as to assert that members were bound together by 'secure and intimate affection' (*khwam rak thi naen, thi sanit*). Several members themselves identified 'friendship' and 'socializing' as the key benefits ensuing from membership.

The BMA has symbolized its identity in a uniform that members were asked to wear whenever they appear together in the name of the Association. Towards the end of 1990 a great deal of meeting time was spent defining the features of this uniform – its colour, the fabric, the cut, and the design of a badge. The badge is orange, supposedly brick-coloured, and bears a logo portraying two hands clasped in a handshake set above a machine-produced brick (two holes through the brick indicate that the brick is extruder-produced and not hand-produced). The Association's name is embroidered around the circumference of the badge. The style and fabric of the uniform suggest that members wished to identify themselves as government servants: the design is identical to that of bureaucrats, and the fabric is of a similar shade to those worn by Ministry of Health officials.

Much collective BMA action is devoted to creating and disseminating a public image of the Association as a cohesive and philanthropic organization. It seems that, at least in the view of the leadership, the Association's influence is intimately linked with its reputation. Members spoke of the Association as gaining 'fame' (*chu siang*) by its collective patronage of high-profile events. Such activity was represented by members as 'helping society' (*chuai sangkhom*). At *kathin*, which marks the end of the Buddhist Lent, outsider ritual patrons donate goods and money to temples. The Association, as a unit, was the patron of a *kathin* rite in one temple in 1990, and made sizeable contributions to others. Members were also patrons of *kathin* rites in an individual capacity – where they were so, however, they would also collect funds from fellow members and present these as BMA contributions.[15] After the vice-chairman hosted a housewarming, attended by 1,000 guests, the BMA chairman announced to members that the Association 'is in a position of respect' (*mi na mi ta*). Members were repeatedly encouraged to attend important parties as a group; that is, to 'display' (*ok na ok ta*) the Association.

The main recipients of the BMA's generosity are members of the local bureaucracy. During the research period the BMA repeatedly contributed to collections made by representatives of the district office, for which it received recognition in the monthly local office-holders' meetings. Instances I observed in 1990 include the donation of leaving gifts to two outgoing district officials, a sizeable contribution to the district office's *kathin* collection, and the presentation to the district police station of an electric grass trimmer (a Fly-Mo). A photograph of the presentation of this gift appeared in *Thai rat*, one of Thailand's most popular daily newspapers. As a matter of course, the BMA invites all district office and police personnel to its annual New Year party. In contrast to all other guests, these state representatives do not make financial contributions to the hosts. Members appeared to resent but accept this situation, for, in the chairman's words, these are 'people with (officially sanctioned) power' (*phu mi amnat*).

The Association gives members direct and indirect economic assistance in at least four ways:

- it provides members with information,
- it grants loans,
- it facilitates co-operation between individual members, and
- it acts on their behalf in specific contexts.[17]

Before the Association was established, it was rare for producers to share information about the selling price of bricks and the cost of inputs. Merchants were thus able to play producers off against one another to their own advantage. Insofar as members share relevant information, they are able to set generally agreed prices. The BMA also provides funds from one of two sources for members to borrow. The first scheme, in place since the early days of the Association, is a rotating credit society (*len chae*): each participant contributes a fixed amount of money each month and bids to borrow the total sum (normally around 200,000 baht). The member who proposes paying the highest rate of interest receives the money. The second source of funds was set up in 1991 and comprises a lump sum deposited in a bank account. Members are each required to deposit 1,000 baht for every extruder owned and can borrow up to ten times the amount they invested initially. Members surveyed claimed that the *len chae* fund was not significant in terms of their initial investment, but that it was useful for funding the purchase of extra machinery or solving cash-flow problems.

Members co-operate outside meetings, and sometimes in ways that were previously sources of competition. For example, to counter local shortages of labour, some owners regularly recruit Northeastern villagers: when owners acquired more workers than were needed, they sent them on to the brickyards of fellow BMA members.

The BMA represents members' interests to state representatives at the district and provincial levels. The chairman organizes 'protection' from district police on behalf of members. Lorries laden over a certain weight are prohibited from using national highways and local roads. Local police use this as an excuse to obtain money from drivers on a regular basis. The BMA pays the police a monthly sum to exempt the trucks of members, and of those with whom they do business. The Association also represents mechanized brickyards to those who legally make demands on their profits. In the late 1980s the leadership won for the mechanized industry as a whole significant concessions from provincial tax authorities in that for several years, brickyards paid less tax than similarly sized enterprises in other branches of industry.

The BMA has adopted a greater lobbying role as mechanized brickyards have taken on the characteristics of larger industries. In late 1990 there were signs that it was preparing itself for such a role. A group of BMA representatives attended a seminar at the provincial seat that introduced the national insurance scheme to business people. It subsequently reported back to members. A little later it sent representatives to a district office lecture in which provincial officials introduced value-added tax to local office-holders and business people. The Association hired caterers to provide food for those attending the lecture.

Lastly, it is important to note that some members have wished to use the Association to strengthen their position against that of labourers. One member went so far as to claim that a primary goal of the Association was to take away workers' freedom of movement in the industry. Finding and holding on to a sufficient number of workers was a constant concern to brickyard owners. In one of the meetings I attended, the vice-chairman asked members not to take on workers who had left other brickyards as a result of disputes with their employers. On a separate occasion the chairman asked members not to accept workers who left other brickyards voluntarily.

We have seen that the Association, with its uniform and its collective donations to state representatives and temple communities, consciously cultivates the image of being a unified business group. The economic ways in which it services members' needs are, for the present at least, fairly circumscribed. The Association represents members to the police and has at least once acted on members' behalf to tax authorities. While the BMA has demonstrated a capacity and ability effectively to protect members' interests, when it was tested in the late 1990s it failed to rise to the challenge.

It is to be expected that, given the fact that members compete for markets and labour, relations within the Association are also marked by conflict and a lack of co-operation. Despite the impression that personal relations are entirely convivial, rivalry between some members is intense. I was initially puzzled by the contradictory messages given to me in the course of interviews with several BMA members: interviewees would first extol the unity which existed within the Association but then proceed to condemn other members and their business practices. Co-members were accused of producing shoddy bricks, and thereby spoiling the market for others, of under-cutting selling prices, of treating their labourers badly, of supplying adulterated brick-earth if they were dealers, and so on. Male owners tended to represent themselves as larger and better producers than their fellow Association members. It could be said that the BMA uniform acts like a boundary-marking symbol that hides differences within the group while presenting the appearance of unity to the outside.[18]

Perhaps more fundamentally, the Association has not been able entirely to transcend the conflicts arising from the fact that members are rival producers. It has only partially solved the problems it was established to address: success in setting prices and eliminating competition for labour have been limited. Members still undercut one another by selling below the generally agreed price. No mechanisms exist to enable the leadership to force other members to sell at a set price: members who are known to be undercutting others can only be upbraided in meetings. Similarly, no mechanisms exist to ensure that members follow the requests of the leadership concerning the control of labour. Furthermore, not all employers were equally keen to pursue those strategies that were suggested. When the leadership asked members not to take on workers coming from other brickyards because of a dispute with their employer, I overheard one member say in an undertone that workers should be permitted to work wherever they wanted.[19] Lastly, members privately complained that 'poaching' of workers persisted. It is likely that the practice is less prevalent between core members, because they may feel a measure of obligation towards one another.

Thus, there are limits to the ability of the BMA to set common standards within the brickmaking industry: there are no mechanisms for enforcing rules, and beneath a facade of good relations, interpersonal and business conflicts exist. The BMA has not been able entirely to quell the competition and conflict between members which is an inevitable corollary of the fact that they compete for markets and labour.

THE BMA IN ELECTORAL POLITICS

One of the ways in which the leadership seeks to increase the local influence and standing of the Association is by supporting members who contest elections for subdistrict and provincial political office. This represents another way in which the Association attempts to cultivate a powerful voice for the industry. It would be misleading, however, to claim that all members support the electoral campaigns of other members: business and interpersonal conflict and the strength of pre-existing, cross-cutting ties limit co-operation. Individually, BMA members seek office for a combination of reasons that may relate to both prestige and economic interest. Office holding at the subdistrict level may facilitate the expansion of the individual's enterprise by providing greater access to labourers or by attracting business partners. It may also enable brickyard-owning *kamnan* to use their dominant position in the subdistrict council to propose development projects, for example road improvements, from which they will benefit.

By the end of 1990, six BMA members held political office, three as *kamnan* and three as headmen. Two *kamnan* and one headman had obtained office during the previous two years and had done so with the explicit support of the Association. In late 1990, a further member submitted his candidacy for the local government position of provincial councillor but failed to secure the post by a narrow margin. In order to describe the ways in which members assist one another and the limits to co-operation, I will sketch out two of these cases: the first recounts one member's successful bid to become a *kamnan*; the second concerns the unsuccessful attempt of another to become one of the two representatives from Klang district to the provincial council.[20] Three points are common to both cases. First, neither of the candidates submitted their candidacy as representatives of the BMA. Association members did not select a candidate from amongst their ranks, and then collectively finance the individual's campaign. Rather, the members who were candidates appeared to decide to compete for office independently of the Association, and only subsequently sought its support. Second, just as members were not BMA representatives as such, their campaigns did not hinge around the support the BMA could give them. In both cases, the assistance sought from BMA members was just one vote-procuring strategy. Third, in both cases members did not all rally behind the member candidate despite appeals by the Association chairman. The BMA could not compel members to act in solidarity, mainly, it seems, because relationships forged outside the Association were given priority over those entailed by membership.

The BMA's Role in Subdistrict Elections

Han is a BMA member. He is a Sino-Thai native and former resident of a Klang commune called Ban Thung, which comprises five administrative village units. He owns a sizeable mechanized brickyard in a neighbouring subdistrict. As he approached retirement age, the incumbent *kamnan* of Ban Thung commune asked Han to campaign to replace him in the subsequent poll. In terms of residence, socio-economic status, and ethnicity, Han was an 'outsider' to Ban Thung, and was recognized as such. He had, however, some 40 residents among his employees and kept active links with a handful of consanguines from Villages Three and Four, and with affines from Village Five, from where his wife comes. Han did not stand unopposed but faced fierce opposition from the incumbent headman of Village Three, Headman Nakun. The main features of Han's campaign as it was related to his standing as a brickyard operator and BMA member can be summarized as follows.[21]

Han received a declaration of support from the chairman of the BMA at a meeting shortly before polling. Approximately 40 people, including the wife of the district chief of police, were present at the vice-chairman's mansion when the chairman declared to members, 'If you have any means to help Boss Han, then help him.' He reminded members that several of them employed Ban Thung residents, and that they could be influenced to vote for Han. Another member reinforced the chairman's appeal and added that 'prosperity (*khwam charoen*) is brought to any subdistrict over which a brickyard owner presides', thereby presenting intervention on Han's behalf as a service to villagers.[22]

The BMA chairman was instrumental in helping Han when his campaign ran into trouble at an early stage. A headman of one Ban Thung village who had promised to give Han his villagers' votes resigned. It now appeared inevitable that votes in this village would be divided if a poll to elect a new headman were held. Han feared that Headman Nakun would impose his own candidate, or that even if this did not occur, the defeated candidate would voluntarily ally himself with Nakun, taking his relatives' votes with him. The BMA chairman used his contacts at the provincial hall to stop the headman's letter of resignation from reaching the provincial governor. Han himself organized a cavalcade of villagers to petition for the headman's reinstatement at the district office. The headman remained in office and subsequently used his influence to encourage villagers to vote for Han.

Aside from Ban Thung headmen, brickyard owners who employed Ban Thung residents were perceived to control bloc votes. Consequently, the opposing candidates sought their support. Ban Thung residents were mainly employed in one of four brickyards and co-workers tended to reside in discrete neighbourhoods. Around 30 Village Two residents worked for Sukhum, an elderly BMA member disposed towards Han; the BMA vice-chairman employed around 30 workers from Village Three; Ray, not an active BMA member, employed about 20 people also from Village Three. Han himself, as indicated above, employed around 40 residents: 30 or so from Village Five and about 10 from Village Three.[23] All of these brickyards are some distance from Ban Thung, so that in order to vote, employees would either have to stay at home or be ferried to the polling station on election day.

Although the BMA member named Sukhum promised Han his support, it turned out to be ineffective. Han perceived that Sukhum's workers, because they were kin of his opponent, were more strongly in favour of Headman Nakun than himself. Consequently, he asked Sukhum to 'buy' his workers' identity cards in advance of polling to prevent them from voting. Apparently, after asking his employees to bring their identity cards to work, Sukhum received a threatening unsigned letter – probably from Headman Nakun himself. His subsequent attempt to influence his employees was half-hearted: they did not give up their identity cards, nor, on polling day, did they meet the vehicle sent, as was usual, to take them to the brickyard. In all likelihood they cast their vote for Nakun.

Han also asked the vice-chairman for his Ban Thung workers' votes, offering to transport them to and from the brickyard on polling day. Although the vice-chairman's response was non-committal, Han seemed to assume that he would receive his support. However, he did not, as he discovered to his dismay on the eve of polling when it emerged that the vice-chairman was at Headman Nakun's campaign headquarters. Personal antagonism born of a business conflict, a complex obligation,[24] and his own employees' allegiance appear to have influenced the vice-chairman's decision. Rather than support Han's campaign, he actively assisted Headman Nakun's.

Han was also unable to obtain the support of Ray, with whom his elder brother was in conflict. It seems that a smouldering disagreement, as well as the fact that many of Ray's employees were kindred of Headman Nakun, led him to oppose Han. Indeed, Ray was one of Headman Nakun's vote brokers (*hua khanaen*).

A small number of votes came from other brickyard owners sympathetic to Han. After the election the BMA chairman told me he had 'given' Han the votes of two of his workers, both of whom came from Village Three. Although they had already been approached by Headman Nakun, the BMA chairman gave them both 100 baht and persuaded them to vote for Han. He commented to me that he 'could have forced (*bip bangkhap*) them [to vote without payment] but that would not be good'. The BMA secretary, on the other hand, claimed to have 'forced' two of his five Village Three employees to vote for Han. The other three workers were without identity cards and thus did not have voting rights.

The above case shows that the chairman's appeal to BMA members to assist Han was not altogether successful. It would be a misrepresentation to say that Han's success was due to the unanimous support of a group sharing his class interests. One BMA member was unable to make his support effective, another opposed Han for a combination of reasons, and a third, who was not an active BMA member, also actively opposed him for a number of reasons. However, this does not negate the fact that the BMA leader did ask members collectively to assist a fellow-member to gain office, nor that he himself was active in this respect.

Han proceeded to win the election. His success seemed largely due to a highly efficient vote-buying campaign, the support he received from the former *kamnan*, and legitimating strategies in which he invested heavily. His campaign was also fundamentally foolproof: he made arrangements whereby he obtained a running total of ballot results as votes were cast. As he told me, if the margin between himself and Nakun were to prove narrow, he would use every means possible to obtain the extra votes. Thus, the support Han received from the BMA was significant but far from pivotal. Finally, I think it is important to note that the fact that Han used illegal means to obtain office does not mean that he necessarily proceeded to abuse office by using public funds for private gain. To my knowledge, since gaining office, *Kamnan* Han has not attempted to recoup his campaign expenditure by exploiting his position illegally. This is not so surprising when one realizes that the sums he could make from graft are relatively small in comparison to his income from brick manufacture. The reader, especially one familiar with the general record of local office-holders, may consider that I am being extremely naïve in asserting this. However, I would suggest that Han aspired towards cultivating a reputation as an exemplary 'developer-*kamnan*', in the image of the incumbent BMA chairman.

The BMA's Role in Provincial Elections

The provincial council is a representative institution whose members, except the provincial governor, are elected every five years. Although officially empowered to pass bylaws, councils tend to be ineffective in terms of government, and generally appear more concerned with serving the interests of individual members than with matters of policy.[25]

Chit is a BMA member and owns a mechanized brickyard employing some 30 migrant workers. He also owns a coach that he leases out. Like Han, he submitted his candidacy independently of the BMA and sought its support only subsequently. Chit made a determined effort to curry favour with the BMA: he twice gave members free use of his coach and driver, once for the BMA annual weekend holiday, once to take members to a party celebrating the ordination of the son of an important Chonburi brick merchant. He first announced his candidacy and appealed for support on his coach during the weekend holiday, and he was requested by the Chairman to repeat his request at the Association meeting prior to polling. On this latter occasion the chairman spoke in Chit's support and reminded members of the services he had rendered.

Chit's chief opponents were two Sino-Thai merchants-cum-building contractors based in the district town. As brothers-in-law and business partners, they campaigned jointly. One, Sanit, was an incumbent provincial councillor; the other, Sawat, had been a policeman and now owned a construction company and the only building supplies store in the district.

A fellow BMA member, who had previously masterminded the vice-chairman's successful campaign to become a *kamnan*, supplied Chit with advice and a fleet of tipper lorries which Chit used to donate road surfacing to village roads. The chief benefit of this strategy was that it enabled him to obligate the electorate directly, without the need to pass through headmen and *kamnan*. The BMA chairman was said to have contributed 100,000 baht to Chit's campaign funds, which one informant put at between 700,000 and 800,000 baht. It seems likely that BMA members with whom Chit enjoyed close relations attempted to influence their workers in similar ways to those used by brickyard owners in Han's campaign. The chairman used his influence within his own subdistrict on behalf of Chit, and in doing so came into bitter conflict with the abbot of one of the temples there, whose allegiance lay with Sanit and Sawat.[26]

The assistance Chit received from BMA members was, however, but one small part of a complex and broad strategy. Chit also sought the support of individual *kamnan*, headmen, and temple abbots – the latter, by offering every temple in the district *kathin* contributions of 20,000 baht. He enjoyed close links with the heads of the district's primary education and health services who, he claimed, would exert their influence on subdistrict subordinates. Lastly, he bought votes on a large scale.

Not all BMA members gave Chit their support. Moreover, the leadership appeared to have lent theirs almost by default: they harboured great resentment for Sanit and Sawat. These two candidates had attempted to canvass in the subdistricts of the chairman and vice-chairman without first seeking their permission, and had approached headmen within these subdistricts with whom the *kamnan* were at odds. In so doing the candidates had not acknowledged their authority and had given offence. Several members, including '*Kamnan* Han' and the Association secretary, enjoyed closer and deeper links with Sanit and Sawat than with Chit.[27] The chairman unsuccessfully attempted to dissuade such members from supporting Sanit and Sawat. At the last BMA meeting before polling I overheard the chairman trying vigorously to convince *Kamnan* Han to retract his support for 'the opposition'. The chairman had already failed to persuade the Association secretary to do so and I was aware of at least one other member who tacitly supported Sawat and Sanit while outwardly following the chairman's line. Thus, the BMA could not enforce unity among members.

Whereas before polling, Chit had been an unknown candidate – one informant spoke of him as having 'come darkly' – his campaign was such that in the days leading up the polls it seemed highly likely that he would oust Sanit. In the event, however, Chit was beaten by a small margin. This brief sketch of his campaign demonstrates that the assistance he received from fellow brickyard operators was, though significant, only one of several strands in his effort.

THE BMA IN PERSPECTIVE

It should be evident that an examination of electoral politics in Klang would be incomplete if the BMA and its members were excluded. Members have provided co-member candidates with electioneering support. This has included:

- giving advice on campaign strategy,
- providing transport on polling day,
- 'giving' the votes of employees,
- influencing villagers in the 'territory' over which the member holds office or operates,
- petitioning district and provincial officials, and
- contributing to electioneering funds.

Whether they are office-holders or not, BMA members are sought as *hua khanaen* in subdistrict, provincial, and general elections. Candidates see workers in the brick industry as comprising a captive electorate, and employers are perceived to exert some control over their employees' voting behaviour. Employees are likely to vote in accordance with the wishes of their employers to a degree, since to reject openly their 'advice' might be to invite dismissal. However, as was demonstrated by the failed attempt of Sukhum to influence his workers in the first case study, any leverage is weak where the majority of employees have loyalties at odds with those of their employer, and where the employer is not prepared to risk alienating the entire workforce. Moreover, the employer/employee relationship is not so strong that the former will expect the latter to vote for a candidate of his choosing without payment: votes must still be paid for. It is likely that this observation can be generalized to other rural areas in Thailand where similar relations of production obtain.[28]

When considering the pattern of leadership within the Association, it is important to ask whether we are dealing with an entourage of a *chao pho*-type figure, or with an interest group of independent individuals of roughly equal economic and political standing. Despite the fact that the BMA chairman tends to dominate meetings, behaves with largesse fitting of a patron, and tends to have the casting vote where decisions are split, it would be a mistake to say that the Association is simply his entourage. The group is comprised of individuals of comparable economic, though not political, status; some members are as wealthy as the chairman and the vice-chairman. A further indication that the BMA is not the entourage of the chairman comes from the fact that members other than the chairman often act as representatives of the Association at public events or private parties. Moreover, the Association is not a façade for representing the chairman's particularistic interests: none of the Association's actions that I observed or heard about could be said to have been in the direct and sole interest of the chairman. Any moves concerned and benefited the mechanized industry as a whole, or, more specifically, members' enterprises. Nor does the chairman control other members with clientelist ties. That this is so should be clear from the fact that members did not act according to the chairman's wishes in both elections.

To a degree, an office-holding BMA member will be expected to protect the interests of co-members in relation to the area over which he has jurisdiction. For instance, shortly after *Kamnan* Han assumed office, villagers of Ban Thung and a contiguous subdistrict proposed raising a levy on brickyard and tipper lorries using local roads. This was in an effort to gain compensation for the destruction they wrought. *Kamnan* Han undermined this move by persuading those proposing the scheme that it would not be viable. Had he not done so independently, he would probably have been subject to pressure from fellow BMA members, whose operations would have been affected. He did not appear to have acted primarily to serve his own economic interests: his lorry did not use any but the shortest stretch of the road over which villagers wished to impose a toll.

It is likely that other BMA members could obtain office if they wished to. Certainly, several members have the prerequisite knowledge, economic wherewithal, and personal contacts necessary to campaign successfully at the subdistrict and perhaps also at the provincial levels. Two members with whom I spoke volunteered strategies they would use should they contest the 1990 provincial council or election. One told me he would buy votes, employ 'toughs' (*nak leng*) to 'intimidate' (*khum khu*) voters, and buy the support of the necessary officials.[29] The other said he would sponsor merit-making at all of the district's temples in rotation. Probably more owners of large brickyards do not seek office because of the perceived costs of incumbency. These two owners stated they did not want to become provincial councillors because incumbency would take them away from their enterprises in terms of time and energy and because office would necessarily involve them in corrupt practices. According to these informants, one could not belong to the council without participating in illegal practices – rigged bidding for construction contracts, for example.

It might be tempting to view the electoral battle between the BMA and the two merchant-contractors as a manifestation of Anek's 'new political economy'. Merchant-contractors like Sanit and Sawat are often in symbiotic relationships with bureaucrats, collaborating to fix provincial development grants to their mutual benefit. One could interpret BMA opposition to Sanit and Sawat as an attempt to displace this arrangement. But, although this would neatly fit the theory and there is some supporting evidence for it, this interpretation does not stand up to scrutiny.

The BMA leadership and other members did periodically complain about the incumbent councillor's abuse of provincial development grants, and about the poor quality of the construction projects he executed. The chief destination of these funds is road improvement and construction, and it can be argued that shoddy work on such projects increases costs to industrialists. This is particularly true of the brick industry: brickyards close to good roads fetch higher gate prices for their bricks than those that are difficult to reach. And certainly, Chit based his appeal to the BMA on an anti-corruption ticket: in his campaign letter he pledged to 'oversee the work of the administration and the use of grants to ensure efficient and honest practices', and he promised not to be a contractor.

However, this does not mean that conflict between the two 'camps' derives from systemic conflicts of interest. The economic interests of BMA members and the merchant-contractors are not as clearly opposed as they at first appear. Members do not belong to one economic camp, and their interests are diverse. They not only make bricks but also run trade, and supply landfill and brick-earth. Although if Chit had won office he would have increased the lobbying capacity of the BMA, there is no obvious way in which he would have promoted the organization's interests against those of the merchant-contractors. And finally, the BMA's commitment to the rule of law and to technocratic administration is highly selective. When it suits members, they do not hesitate to use illegal methods to fight elections, as we have seen.

A more plausible explanation for the conflict is that the BMA leadership was without a hidden agenda and simply desired a political presence at the provincial level, and that some members were subsequently personally affronted by the campaign strategies of the other candidates. However, a general desire for more transparent use of development funds may none the less have informed their position.

THE BMA TO THE LATE 1990S

In the first half of the 1990s, demand for bricks from the construction industry continued to increase and was met by an ever-increasing number of new brickyards. However, buoyant demand did not automatically translate into greater profits, because sustained national economic growth made labour shortages even more severe than they were at the beginning of the decade. Most brick producers experienced persistent worker shortfalls and consequent rising wages reduced their profit margins. In 1995 more than three-quarters of the operational enterprises where I had first conducted inverviews in 1990 were producing at half of their capacity solely as a result of their inability to find workers (three of the 16 enterprises initially surveyed had folded). In this same period, wages had almost doubled while brick prices had risen by no more than 25–30 per cent.

The BMA's membership has continued to grow at a modest rate. Between 1993 and 1996 it attracted six new producers, giving it an active core of 37 members. One marked change since 1990 is that core members started to diversify their economic activities away from brickmaking, partly in response to labour shortages. Two core members discontinued brick production altogether, but they remained active members. They thus retained access to the BMA rotating credit fund and ensured that their economic activities remained 'protected' from unreasonable demands by state officials.

According to members, the economic influence of the BMA peaked in 1992, when it was most able to influence brick-pricing. Since then its capacity to set prices has steadily diminished because of the proliferation of mechanized brickyards. The Association's influence on the market for extruded bricks is now negligible, but nevertheless it still operates as a mouthpiece for producers' interests. For example, in an attempt to solve members' labour shortages, it petitioned the provincial government in early 1996 to permit the district's mechanized brickmaking industry to employ about 500 illegal Burmese immigrants. Many other business groups throughout the country had also lobbied provincial and national administrations to secure the employment of such immigrants, and shortly afterwards it was legalized. However, beyond occasional interventions such as this, the Association has not promoted the industry in any systematic way. Some younger members have privately expressed frustration at the chairman's lack of ambition for the group. These would-be 'Young Turks' do not, however, consider launching any independent projects, out of deference for the status of the chairman. The respectful behaviour that informs much of Thai social life, particularly in the bureaucracy, still colours social relations within the BMA and thus effectively constrains the group's capacity to evolve and develop. Social solidarity remains one of the key values of the group, and at the New Year party held in January 1996 members wore the uniforms that they had spent so much time designing in 1990.

The Brick Manufacturers' Association has retained its pre-eminent social and political position in Klang society. Since 1990 a number of industries funded by Bangkok and international capital have set up in the locality, and these have displaced brickyards as the district's largest employers. However, because the owners and managers of these factories remain outsiders and do not hold positions of local office, they have little social or political influence in local communities. Alongside the Sino-Thai merchant-contractors from the market town who won the 1990 provincial council election, brickyard owners remain the most influential capitalists at the district level. The following event illustrates the continuing importance of BMA members rather well. During the monsoon season of 1995, when swollen rivers threatened low-lying regions of Central Thailand, protesters in a province adjacent to Klang began to destroy a barricade that was the district's sole protection against rapid and widespread inundation. The only resistance and representation offered by the district's residents came from six BMA members. As events unfolded, members telephoned each other and rallied at the site of the conflict: the five office-holding members brought villagers with them in a show of force. When negotiations began, national and provincial politicians represented the interests of the protesters, and an ad hoc group of BMA members represented Klang district. Ayutthaya government officials, and indeed politicians, were conspicuous by their absence.

Through the mid-1990s the BMA still saw the need to increase the number of local office-holders, *kamnan* and village heads, within its ranks. One prominent member was elected a village head in 1994. In early 1998 the Association secretary, also a village head, received co-members' support in his bid to become the group's fourth *kamnan*. However, owing to determined opposition from local villagers, his bid was unsuccessful.

The Association has continued to promote its political profile at the provincial level, albeit sometimes by default and somewhat reluctantly. When in late 1995 Chit competed for a seat on the Ayutthaya provincial council for the second time running, he again had the backing of core members of the BMA. Since his first campaign Chit had sold his brickyard, yet he remained a regular participant at meetings. He now manages and part-owns a transport company comprising 50 coaches. Once again Chit submitted his candidacy autonomously of the Association; indeed the leadership initially tried to dissuade him from standing, as they perceived his chances of success to be slim and the costs of competing high. While he claimed he wanted to be a councillor in order to 'develop' the district, his closest associates concluded that he was motivated by a desire for status and honour (*kiat*) – and, specifically, to better his standing in his circle of family and friends. At the BMA meeting prior to polling, the chairman made an earnest and powerful appeal on Chit's behalf. He recalled how close Chit had been to success five years previously, and told members that Chit had pledged not to work as a construction contractor; nor would he use the position to claw back money. A number of Association members subsequently gave Chit their active support and, on a few occasions, groups of around 20 members canvassed with him. Among villagers he was known as 'the BMA candidate'. Because in 1995 proportionately few locals worked in brickyards, BMA support did not give Chit large numbers of workers' votes: rather, BMA members – and particularly office-holding ones – were useful because they remained locally influential people and were thus effective vote brokers. As in 1990, not all members supported Chit: the prior social and economic ties of some members to the incumbent councillors overrode loyalty towards a co-BMA member. Of those who did support Chit, some members wanted to wrest control of the district's council seats from the two incumbents because, in the previous five years, they had managed to control all lines of patronage from MPs and access to all major projects that emanated from the provincial council.

If anything, in 1995 canvassing was more intense and competition was fiercer than it had been five years earlier: one indication of this is that votes doubled their 1990 price. Again, candidates competed by making donations to community institutions and infrastructure, hiring the support of canvassers and, in the last stages of campaigning, outright vote-buying. Much to the disappointment of some BMA members, the incumbent councillors defeated Chit, once again by a slim margin. He has declared that he will stand again in the year 2000.

The financial crisis that hit Thailand in mid-1997 threatened the very existence of the BMA. The construction industry was amongst the first to be hit. Building projects were suspended and demand for bricks plummeted, as did the price: the brickmaking industry was devastated with startling rapidity. By late 1998 few mechanized brickyards in Klang still operated as going concerns; those that had managed to survive their debts produced mainly to use up stockpiles of raw materials and to prevent machinery seizing up. The fragility of the BMA became apparent in the face of this crisis. As their businesses collapsed, a third of members defaulted on their repayments to the Association's rotating credit scheme. By defaulting they excluded themselves from the Association. Remaining members who had lost out financially were thrown into conflict with a leadership that was reluctant to take punitive action against those unable to pay back loans. It is ironic that the scheme that had previously bound the BMA now became the primary force hastening its collapse. The scope of activities undertaken by the Association narrowed to the monthly meeting, as their severely reduced circumstances meant that few members were able to afford either the time or money to meet any more onerous obligations of membership. The Association was on the verge of collapse when the chairman's wife established a new cycle of the rotating credit scheme, using family capital to make the first payment, and thus expressing confidence in the Association's continuity. Eager to take advantage of any new opportunities to raise capital, members had a direct incentive to continue to attend meetings.

However, the post-1997 BMA is but a shadow of its former self. The Association's new frugal consumption habits are a somewhat poignant illustration of this. At its meeting of August 1998 I was struck by the fact that members ate a somewhat spartan meal rather than partaking of a feast, as was previously the custom: in better times successive dishes of delicacies were ordered, and rice only appeared as a final supplement. Post-crisis, however, members self-consciously ordered cheap staple dishes and consumed rice simultaneously, much as one eats at home. As one member said, without exaggeration: 'Let's order cheap food. We're all poor, we can't afford it'. Under the circumstances, meetings have ceased to be a forum for voicing industry interests and the BMA has failed entirely to represent the needs of members in their time of need. Despite, for example, one member's appeal to the leadership to initiate research into the plight of the industry in the district, and to make representations to provincial authorities, the Association has remained inactive.

But even in these straitened circumstances, the BMA remains a political force in the district, with an agenda to increase its political profile. At the meeting mentioned above, the chairman announced the candidacy of yet another member who was making a bid to elevate his office from village head to *kamnan.* The chairman appealed to members to aid the candidate, and at an earlier meeting, asked members who still employed residents from this subdistrict to exert their influence over them. On the day of the election the candidate – who was successful – was surrounded by BMA members who had come to offer their support. Since this election, almost a quarter of the district's *kamnan* have also been members of the BMA (4 of 17).

The Association has demonstrated that it is not an ephemeral social group, although the extreme circumstances of the collapse of the industry almost led to its dissolution and showed just how fragile it is. But, despite its longevity, it has not made any systematic attempts to carve a weightier role for itself in the past few years. Its membership has grown, but only modestly. It has continued to promote the industry's interests, but only in fairly limited ways and unevenly. Yet it has retained its pre-eminent social and political position in the district despite the fact that the industry has been supplanted as the major source of employment for locals. This is partly explained by the fact that members are still keen to increase the number of office-holders in their ranks. One can interpret this preoccupation as a desire to build up the 'critical mass' of the Association. In turn, this critical mass protects members from being subject to excessive demands for financial 'contributions' by local state representatives; it helps members avoid strict enforcement of laws that impinge on their businesses; and it increases the chances that the state will listen to any formal appeals the Association makes on behalf of the industry. When studying groups such as the BMA, we cannot ignore the investment they make to establish their political presence, for to a large extent, this is what enables them to act as economic interest groups. Groups such as the Brick Manufacturers' Association are thus just as much political aggregations as they are business associations.

The BMA's systematic attempts to fill its ranks with local office-holders and politicians also indicate that the balance of power between bureaucratic authority and civil society at the local level has not greatly changed. Business associations representing larger entrepreneurs at higher levels of government have tended not to involve themselves actively in electoral politics, preferring instead to depend on their economic clout to enable them to deal directly with bureaucrats.[30]

But, if we are to generalize from the case of these petty industrialists, it seems that district-level groups cannot afford this luxury. To have their needs heard it is necessary for such groups to gain standing in the eyes of the bureaucracy — and the means to this end is the acquisition of local office. To the extent, then, that groups such as the BMA find it necessary to fill their ranks with office-holders and politicians, Anek's 'new political economy' has failed to emerge at the district level. However, while acknowledging the prior state of affairs, we should be aware that the very process whereby such groups gain renown and status itself constitutes a change in the distribution of power between the state and civil society. The accumulation of formal status positions within such groups represents the arrival of business-based civil society in the provinces. The rise of groups such as the BMA does lead to the dilution of state hegemony, but largely in the restricted sphere of local economic policy-making. However, we must appreciate that this 'new political economy' comes at a cost. The rise of groups like the BMA is often at the expense of the partial disenfranchisement of the majority: as this essay illustrates, entrepreneurs collectively and individually convert their economic power into political power by buying votes, dispensing patronage, and manipulating their workers. The majority of the population lack comparable access to capital and are excluded from meaningful political participation by these strategies. Villagers do not view positively the fact that the results of local elections are sometimes decided as much by the explicit support of a group of elite outsiders, some of whom are their employers, as they are by their own choices in the voting booth. Prior to the Thai financial crisis, we could have anticipated the continued expansion of provincial business, and perhaps more scenarios such as this. We could have expected that formal and informal groups such as the BMA would proliferate at the district level, further diluting local state power, and creating even greater differentiation of power-holders. However, with Thailand's economic stagnation of the late 1990s, the future is less certain.

NOTES

1. Fred Riggs, *Thailand: The Modernization of a Bureaucratic Polity* (Honolulu: East–West Center Press, 1966).

2. Anek Laothamatas, *Business Associations and the New Political Economy of Thailand: From Bureaucratic Polity to Liberal Corporatism* (Singapore: Institute of Southeast Asian Studies, 1992)

3. Anek, *Business Associations,* pp. 94–102.

4. At least one formal group has been noted: Eiji Murashima, in 'Local Elections and Leadership in Thailand: a Case Study of Nakhon Sawan Province', *The Developing Economies* 25 (1987): 382, makes passing reference to a pig-raisers' association. Ananya Buchongkul describes an informal grouping of large-scale poultry farmers in Chachoengsao province in 'From Chaonaa to Khonngaang: The Growing Divide in a Central Thai Village' (Ph.D. thesis, University of London, 1985), pp. 286–288. And in *Business Associations,* p. 59, Anek notes that most founders of chambers of commerce had formerly led trade association or informal business groups, some of which presumably would have been located outside the provincial seat.

5. Stephen Joseph *et al.*, 'A Study of Brick Production in Thailand', *TDRI Quarterly Review* 5 (1990): 11.

6. B. J. Terwiel, *Through Travellers' Eyes: An Approach to Early Nineteenth Century Thai History* (Bangkok: Editions Duang Kamon, 1989), p. 110.

7. Scott Cook, 'Peasant Economy, Rural Industry, and Capitalist Development in the Oaxaca Valley, Mexico', *Journal of Peasant Studies* 12 (1984): 4–40.

8. The exact point at which petty commodity producers become petty capitalist producers is debatable: Scott Cook and L. Binford have suggested, in *Obliging Need: Rural Petty Industry in Mexican Capitalism* (Austin: University of Texas Press, 1990), p. 236, that the transition occurs when more than half the value of an enterprise's output is generated by wage labourers.

9. Non-mechanized brickyards are not taxed unless their income exceeds 6,000 baht a month because they are classified as cottage industry. Tax avoidance is likely to make the figures regarding mechanized brickyards err on the conservative side.

10. These data derive from a household survey I conducted between September and November 1990.

11. Joseph *et al.*, in 'A Study of Brick Production in Thailand', have observed that Southern Thai brickyard owners are constrained by labour shortages and are compelled to hire migrants from the Northeast. Similarly, Naruemol Bunjongjit and Xavier Oudin, in *Small-Scale Industries and Institutional Framework in Thailand* (Paris: Organization for Economic Co-operation and Development, 1992) note, in their study of Bangkok and urban-based provincial small-scale enterprises, that the owners' main problem was finding sufficient employees. Rapid economic growth has given rise to shortages, despite growth rates in the size of the labour force (p. 37).

12. To use a category employed by Stephen Holland in 'Development and Differentiation in Rural Thailand: A Case Study from the Central Region' (Ph.D. thesis, University of Oxford, 1990), p. 101.

13. See Andrew Turton, 'Local Powers and Rural Differentiation', in Gillian Hart, Andrew Turton, Benjamin White (eds), *Agrarian Transformations: Local Processes and the State in Southeast Asia* (Berkeley: University of California Press, 1989), p. 81.

14. M. Granovetter, 'Economic Action and Social Structure: the Problem of Embeddedness', *American Journal of Sociology* 91 (1985): 481–510.

15. For an insightful analysis of the legitimating power of royal *kathin*, see Christine E. Gray, 'Hegemonic Images: Language and Silence in the Royal Thai Polity', *Man* 26 (1991): 43–65. Ananya (*From Chaonaa to Khonngaan*, pp. 287–288) describes large-scale poultry farmers acting as ritual patrons on an individual basis and in Daniel Arghiros, 'Rural Transformation and Local Politics in a Central Thai District' (Ph.D. thesis. University of Hull, 1993, pp. 166–169) I detail the ways in which politicians use *kathin* in election campaigns.

16. A point also made by Yoshifumi Tamada, '*Itthiphon* and *Amnat*: An Informal Aspect of Thai Politics', *Tonan Ajia Kenkyu* 28 (1991): 459.

17. In several ways, the BMA resembles the Bangkok-based Chinese business associations described by G. William Skinner in the 1950s (*Leadership and Power in the Chinese Community of Thailand* [Ithaca: Cornell University Press, 1958], pp. 25, 177–179). These associations of firms in the same line co-operated to limit competition, set price levels, and provide economically useful services.

18. See Anthony P. Cohen in *The Symbolic Construction of Community* (Chichester/London: Ellis Horwood/Tavistock, 1985)

19. This speaker, incidentally, used strong incentives to keep hold of his workforce. He used 'psychology' (*chitwitthaya*) and 'benevolence' (*phrakhun*), as he put it: every year he gave his workers items of value in the context of a brickyard merit-making ceremony. In 1990 he gave large wooden wardrobes, which, he said, would be a constant reminder to his workers and their families of the benefits that employment in his brickyard brought.

20. In brief, the circumstances of two of the other four office-holders mentioned are as follows. The vice-chairman became *kamnan* with the help of the Association in 1988 when, reportedly, the chairman contributed campaign funds, and members canvassed on his behalf and provided transport on polling day. In 1990, with explicit advice from fellow members, another BMA associate became a headman: he simply bought the votes of as many electors as would accept his money, while his competitors were not prepared to follow suit. He was the first headman candidate in this subdistrict to use vote-buying as a campaign strategy. His actions gave rise to a good deal of resentment, particularly when it emerged that he was more interested in running his brickyard than in affairs of office. By December 1993 another three BMA members had obtained the office of headman, bringing the total number of office-holding members up to nine.

21. Han first had to obtain office as headman of one of the composite villages in the subdistrict in order to be eligible to stand as *kamnan*. Details of what this entailed are not presented here. It is worth noting, however, that a group of 11 BMA members turned up to congratulate Han after the poll, and to partake of a celebratory meal given at the temple hall.

22. If, as is locally the case, one understands 'prosperity' to signify the presence of urban infrastructure and services, then this assertion carries an element of truth. According to the district civil engineer, the chairman and vice-chairman had their requests for provincial development funds approved each and every year while other subdistricts, whose *kamnan* were less influential, were passed over. Not only were these brickyard-owning *kamnan* able to introduce prosperity in the form of subdistrict administrative centres, all-weather roads, water tanks and so on, but in doing so they were able to demonstrate themselves as exemplary *kamnan* – that is, commune heads who brought 'development' and 'prosperity'.

23. In polling, a total of just over 1,150 votes were cast.

24. Apparently the vice-chairman felt that Han had 'poached' some of his workers. He was also said to resent Han for not supporting him against a villager, a resident near Han's brickyard, in a dispute over a cow run down by his son. Lastly, the vice-chairman was said to have obligated himself heavily to an MP, to the extent that when approached by him, he could not but agree to help Nakun. The obligation was entailed when the MP brought his co-member of the Social Action Party, the then minister of communications, Montri Pongpanich, to the chairman's housewarming in March 1990. Montri's celebrity status gave the event renown throughout the province, and reflected glory on to the vice-chairman.

25. For an example, see Eiji Murashima, 'Local Elections and Leadership in Thailand: A Case Study of Nakhon Sawan Province', *The Developing Economies* 25 (1987): 363–385, p. 384. For the (in)effectiveness of provincial councils, see Likhit Diravegin, *Thai Politics: Selected Aspects of Development and Change* (Bangkok: Tri-Sciences Publishing House, 1985), p. 438.

26. I knew of two other cases in which religious leaders came into open conflict with secular leaders over support for Sawat. Sawat had cultivated a network of supporters in the form of religious leaders. As sole supplier of construction materials in the district, he extended generous and often interest-free credit to many of the district's 37 temples. Abbots and temple committees wishing to enhance the appearance and thereby reputation of their temples were thus in a relation of dependence with Sawat. He translated this dependence into votes.

27. Han had received moral and some material support from Sanit and Sawat during his campaign to become *kamnan*. Han had also been a longstanding neighbour of Sanit in the market town, where in addition to his rural brickyard, he owns a house. All three, of course, are Sino-Thai. I am unaware of the nature of the relationship between the BMA secretary and Sanit and Sawat.

28. Buchongkul, in 'From Chaonaa to Khonngaan', p. 381, suggests that the wage labour relationship was a source of political support for big Chachoengsao poultry farmers, who were seen by some employees as 'an alternative source of patronage'. However, Ananya does not reveal whether or not votes were paid for in elections.

29. This member went on to become a *kamnan* in August 1998, as mentioned below.

30. Anek, *Business Associations*, pp. 116–117.

SEVEN

The Entrepreneurs of Khorat

*Yoko Ueda**

Nakhon Ratchasima City (Thetsaban Muang Nakhon Ratchasima) – popularly known as Khorat, by which more manageable title we will call it – is Thailand's second largest urban centre.[1] Yet compared to the capital city it is a dwarf. In 1991 the northeastern municipality claimed 202,503 inhabitants; Bangkok's counted 5,620,591, without taking into account the capital's extensive conurbation.[2] Given this discrepancy, and the extreme concentration of economic power and activity that it reflects, we need to ask whether the recent flowering of Thai entrepreneurship has not been peculiar to Bangkok and the five surrounding provinces that form its immediate economic domain.[3] Indeed, are national-level observations about business development relevant at all to the rest of the country?

The Setting

Khorat is a particularly useful focus to examine this question because, aside from its status as the second city, it is located well outside the

* This contribution is a revised and updated version of the author's 'Research Note: Characteristics of Local Entrepreneurs in Nakhon Ratchasima City', published in *Tonan Ajia Kenkyu* [Southeast Asian Studies] (Kyoto), Vol. 30, No. 3, December 1992. The editor is grateful to that journal for granting permission to include the article in this collection. For this discussion placed in a broader local context, see Yoko Ueda, *Local Economy and Entrerpeneurship in Thailand: A Case Study of Nakhon Ratchasima* (Kyoto: Kyoto University Press, 1995).

Table 7.1: Variation in value of economic activities in Nakhon Ratchasima province, the Northeast and Thailand (by sector at current market prices)

SECTOR	1975	1980	1985	1990
Nakhon Ratchasima (Gross Provincial Product – GPP)				
Agriculture	45.0	42.5	28.4	25.2
Mining and Quarrying	0.8	1.5	1.1	0.9
Manufacturing	11.4	8.9	8.8	9.5
Construction	4.1	6.4	9.0	9.5
Electricity and Water Supply	1.1	1.0	2.1	2.1
Transport and Communic'n	3.4	3.2	4.4	5.6
Wholesale and Retail Trade	18.2	20.9	17.5	18.1
Banking, Insur. + Real Estate	1.9	3.0	2.3	3.7
Ownership of Dwellings	1.8	1.2	5.6	4.7
Public Admin. and Defence	5.7	6.2	7.6	6.9
Services	6.6	5.3	13.3	13.7
GPP	100.0	100.0	100.0	100.0
(Millions of Baht)	7,186	14,987	22,096	38,883
The Northeast (Gross Provincial Product – GRP)				
Agriculture	48.8	43.2	28.4	27.0
Mining and Quarrying	0.6	0.6	0.5	0.4
Manufacturing	7.1	6.9	6.7	8.3
Construction	5.0	5.3	8.1	7.9
Electricity and Water Supply	0.5	0.5	1.3	1.4
Transport and Communic'n	4.0	5.6	4.2	3.9
Wholesale and Retail Trade	19.8	21.8	21.2	21.6
Banking, Insur. + Real Estate	1.5	2.3	1.9	2.7
Ownership of Dwellings	2.0	1.5	6.6	5.4
Public Admin. and Defence	4.6	5.7	7.4	7.1
Services	6.1	6.6	13.6	14.3
GPP	100.0	100.0	100.0	100.0
(Millions of Baht)	51,279	102,841	147,326	254,113

Table 7.1: Variation in value of economic activities in Nakhon Ratchasima province, the Northeast and Thailand (by sector at current market prices)

SECTOR	1975	1980	1985	1990
Thailand (Gross Domestic Product –GDP)				
Agriculture	31.5	25.4	14.9	12.8
Mining and Quarrying	1.4	2.1	2.5	1.6
Manufacturing	18.1	19.6	21.9	27.3
Construction	4.3	5.8	5.1	6.1
Electricity and Water Supply	1.1	0.9	2.4	2.2
Transport and Communic'n	6.3	6.6	7.4	7.2
Wholesale and Retail Trade	18.3	18.8	18.3	17.3
Banking, Insur. + Real Estate	4.9	6.1	3.3	5.6
Ownership of Dwellings	1.5	1.1	4.2	3.0
Public Admin. and Defence	4.1	4.1	4.6	3.5
Services	8.7	9.4	14.5	13.4
GDP	100.0	100.0	100.0	100.0
(Millions of Baht)	298,895	684,909	1,056,496	2,182,100

Source: National Economic and Social Development Board (hereafter NESDB), data from Regional and Provincial Products series for 1986 and 1994.

area of Bangkok's primary economic influence. Located 256 km from the capital, it is the principal city of the Northeastern region, the poorest and least developed part of the country. The town has its own entrepreneurial tradition, for it commands the Saraburi–Khorat Pass that was long the main point of access between the northeastern plateau and the central plain. It thus became the main node of commerce between the Northeast and the rest of Siam. Already in the time of the kingdom of Ayutthaya (1351–1767) it was one of Siam's main trading centres, handling especially the collection and shipment of forest products from the Northeast and what is now Laos.

The first major break in Khorat's isolation came with the opening of a railroad from Bangkok in 1900. With this, the Northeast began to participate significantly in the rice trade, which had become the staple of the national economy since the opening of Siam's economy to the international market following the Bowring Treaty (1855). Khorat became the centre for rice shipments from the Northeast, which provided nearly 20 per cent of total Thai rice exports by 1935.[4]

Agriculture has remained the region's overwhelming activity, with cassava joining rice as the staple crop in the 1970s. Together, these two products accounted for more than 70 per cent of Nakhon Ratchasima province's planted area in 1990/91 and more than 60 per cent of the value of its crop production.[5] Agriculture has retained a far greater significance for Khorat and the Northeast than for the country as a whole, as can be seen from Table 7.1. Moreover, Khorat's manufacturing sector is overwhelmingly concerned with the processing of its two agricultural staples, as Table 7.2 shows.

Table 7.2: Factories in the manufacturing sector of Nakhon Ratchasima province, 1989

Type of Manufacturing	No. of Factories		Registered Capital (Million Baht)		No. of Employees	
Rice Milling	4,559	(*73.3*)	714	(*6.1*)	6,595	(*14.2*)
Cassava Processing	769	(*12.4*)	3,927	(*33.4*)	8,906	(*19.1*)
Others	894	(*14.4*)	7,124	(*60.6*)	31,035	(*66.7*)
Total	6,222	(*100.0*)	11,765	(*100.0*)	46,536	(*100.0*)

Source: Samnakngan Utsahakam Changwat Nakhon Ratchasima [n.d.].

Hence, although the agricultural sector declined from 46 per cent of Nakhon Ratchasima province's gross product in 1976 to 26.5 per cent in 1989,[6] its importance is still overwhelming. The opening of the rail line brought a shift to production for export but not a move away from agriculture.

Economic development in Khorat and the Northeast was affected by two further historical moments which, though they did not have the profound impact of the rail line's connection of the region with the world market, made a distinct contribution to its accumulation of capital and entrepreneurial opportunity. One was the Vietnam War (1960–1975). Even before that, Thailand's Cold War alliance with the United States and the Northeast's strategic location with regard to Indochina had a marked impact on the town's fortunes, most notably with the construction of Friendship Highway, which in 1958 brought the first good road link between Khorat and the capital via Saraburi. With the war, five US air-bases came to the Northeast, bringing a considerable injection of money and employment possibilities. One of these, fully operative between 1965 and 1975, was located at Khorat town. Moreover, the exigencies of the war and the counter-insurgency effort in the Northeast meant that the region acquired 'one of the best transportation systems in Asia'.[7] The result was that the regional economy experienced something of a boom: inequality in terms of household income between the Northeast and the whole kingdom decreased from 1962 to 1975, and that between the Northeast and Bangkok from 1962 to 1981.[8]

The second spur to Khorat's development was provided by the premiership of General Chatichai Choonhavan, who had been an elected member of parliament for Nakhon Ratchasima province since 1975 and became prime minister in August 1988. Although Chatichai's administration was ended by a coup in February 1991, he exerted himself as patron of the province while in power. In his last cabinet (from December 1990) six of the 15 members of parliament for Nakhon Ratchasima province held ministerial positions. One became deputy minister of communications (an office that wielded considerable power in deciding nation-wide transportation projects); another two were appointed deputy education ministers. Khorat became the beneficiary of several large projects, such as the Thailand Agricultural and Industrial Exposition 1992 (EXPO) and the Suranaree Technology University (STU), which was to be the first university outside Bangkok to specialize in modern technological instruction. It was planned to widen the Friendship Highway, and this provided further incentives for business investment and expansion.

True, not all these programmes had originated with the Chatichai regime, and some were more clearly connected with family interests than concern for regional development; both the EXPO and STU projects were postponed after Chatichai's overthrow.[9] Nevertheless, the ferment of those years gave a considerable fillip to entrepreneurship in Khorat. A number of local businessmen made plans to expand their investments. The Suranaree Industrial Zone (SIZ), opened outside Khorat city in 1989, was probably the largest single development. This privately operated industrial zone was brought about with the cooperation of a local entrepreneur and members of parliament for Nakhon Ratchasima province, including Chatichai. The EXPO plan, combined with augmented investment in the SIZ from Bangkok and abroad, induced several local businessmen to invest in the construction of new high-class hotels in Khorat, although work on some of these was stopped by the overthrow of Chatichai's government. Two big, modern department stores – each owned by a different local family – were opened in Khorat in 1991, attracting a good deal of public interest. One of these families planned to construct a 23-storey building complex, which was expected to be the largest in the Northeast when completed.[10] Other local businessmen rushed to implement investments during Chatichai's term of office, with the result that several new enterprises emerged in Khorat. One result of all this was a sharp increase in land prices around Khorat and the major roads and project sites, as people from Bangkok as well as locals sought to take advantage of the new opportunities and infrastructure.[11]

This ferment was also the product of the boom that Thailand as a whole experienced at this time. In national comparison Nakhon Ratchasima province's growth rate, though very respectable, was not particularly high, and the level it did achieve was partly a result of a high growth rate in the agricultural sector (see Table 7.3 overleaf). Nakhon Ratchasima province's share in GDP decreased from 2.4 per cent in 1975 to 1.8 per cent in 1990. This was accompanied by a marked increase in the GDP share of Bangkok and later of the provinces surrounding the capital, a tendency which was strengthened when Thailand experienced two-digit economic growth in 1988 and 1990 (see Table 7.4 overleaf).

Whereas in the kingdom's GDP the reduction in the agricultural sector since 1975 coincided with an increase in manufacturing's share, in Nakhon Ratchasima province, as in the Northeast as a whole, a decline in the relative importance of agriculture was accompanied by an increase in the share of services, construction, and ownership of dwellings (see Table 7.1). In other words, Khorat – and the Northeast generally – has not shared in the manufacturing growth which has accounted for much of the country's increased wealth and, in spite of strong agricultural performance, its already modest share in that wealth is slipping. Under these circumstances, can we see a real change and a more than evanescent ferment among its entrepreneurs?

Table 7.3: Economic growth rate in Thailand, the Northeast and Nakhon Ratchasima province, 1975–1989 (percent, based on constant 1972 prices)

Year	Thailand (GDP)	The North-east (GRP)	Nakhon Ratchasima (GPP) (average)	(agric. sector)
1975*	6.8	17.0	29.8	(*52.1*)
1976	8.7	1.6	7.5	(*10.6*)
1977	7.2	-2.7	-0.7	(*-4.2*)
1978	10.1	14.8	14.5	(*17.6*)
1979	6.1	6.1	0.1	(*-3.0*)
1980	5.8	7.4	10.5	(*11.2*)
1981*	8.7	10.6	18.3	(*-8.5*)
1982	4.1	7.0	6.0	(*5.9*)
1983	7.3	8.8	8.8	(*13.0*)
1984	7.1	7.3	7.7	(*1.9*)
1985	3.5	4.7	-0.6	(*3.0*)
1986	4.9	1.5	1.7	(*-9.9*)
1987	9.5	2.7	0.6	(*-9.8*)
1988	13.2	11.9	10.4	(*18.6*)
1989	12.0	8.1	9.0	(*9.2*)

* **Note**: Data seems aberrant as data series for 1975–1979 and 1981–1989 exclude 1974 and 1980.

Source: NESDB, 1986 and 1991.

SOCIAL CHARACTERISTICS OF THE ENTREPRENEURS

To answer this question I have relied mainly on interviews with local businessmen which I conducted in Khorat from February 1991 to February 1992, in addition to some published materials (including local newspapers). Influential businessmen were selected on the basis of their experience in leading associations such as the Nakhon Ratchasima Chamber of Commerce, the Nakhon Ratchasima branch of the Federation of Thai Industry, and several Chinese associations. Businessmen who had served on the provincial council or the municipal council of Amphoe Muang Nakhon Ratchasima were also included, as were those indicated as important by the local press. Finally, 67 businessmen were chosen with the help of the executive head of the

Table 7.4: Share in GDP, population and per-capita GDP in Nakhon Ratchasima province, the Northeast, Bangkok and Thailand, 1975–1990

Year	Nakhon Ratchasima	Northeast	Bangkok Metropolis	Bangkok & Vicinity*	Whole Kingdom
GDP (%)					
1975	2.4	17.2	29.3	36.8	100.0
1980	2.2	15.0	34.8	42.4	100.0
1985	2.1	13.9	35.9	46.2	100.0
1990	1.8	11.6	39.4	52.2	100.0
Population (%)					
1975	4.1	35.1	9.9	14.1	100.0
1980	4.2	35.2	10.4	14.8	100.0
1985	4.2	34.9	10.8	15.5	100.0
1990	4.1	34.5	11.0	16.0	100.0
Per capita GPP, GRP and GDP (baht)					
1975	4,244	3,527	21,309	18,827	7,221
1980	7,642	6,257	48,930	42,155	14,660
1985	10,282	8,193	68,322	61,228	20,483
1990	16,717	13,152	139,642	127,099	38,908

* **Note**: Comprises Bangkok Metropolis, Samut Prakan, Pathumthani, Samut Sakhon, Nonthaburi and Nakhon Pathom.

Source: NESDB, 1986 and 1994.

Chamber of Commerce, Mr Khomkrit Soetnuansaeng, to whom I am grateful for suggesting several important names which had not figured on my list. Of these, 46 were analysed for purposes of this essay.[12] Only one refused, but enough information on him was available from published materials to allow his inclusion in the overall statistics. Interviews varied greatly in length; some businessmen were kind enough to make time for two or three sessions.

All of the 46 interviewees were male; the oldest was 82 and the youngest 27. Classified by age, the 41–45 age group was the largest; the average age being 49.8 years, more than 40 per cent having been born after the Second World War. This indicates that influential businessmen in Khorat are relatively young, contrary to the stereotypical notion of old-fashioned gerontocratic local Chinese running the economies of Thailand's outlying provinces.

In Table 7.5, the interviewees are classified by occupation. This confirms our earlier observation about the unimportance of manufacturing in Khorat. Only three entrepreneurs were engaged in *modern* manufacturing – that is, industry which can develop a series of high-value and exportable new products in response to changes in the world market – which requires a high technological standard. Of these three, two operate factories producing vehicle parts, some of which are for export. The third runs a tapioca-processing factory and, with the technical cooperation of a German company, plans to branch out into related processing and equipment-manufacturing activities. No businessman is involved in the textile industry, though the Thai

Table 7.5: Occupations of interviewees

Manufacturing		**4**
• Rice miller	1	
• Kenaf processor	1	
• Factory operator: tapioca processing	1	
• Factory operator: production of automobile parts	1	
Manufacturing-cum-Commerce		**4**
• Maker and seller of food products	3	
• Maker and seller of furniture	1	
Construction-cum-Commerce		**4**
• Construction contractor and shopkeeper of constr'n materials	4	
Commerce		**14**
• Shopkeeper: gold shop	3	
• Shopkeeper: general shop	2	
• Shopkeeper: household electrical appliances shop	2	
• Shopkeeper: construction materials shop	2	
• Operator of department store	2	
• Shopkeeper: photography shop	1	
• Shopkeeper: automobile parts shop	1	
• Automobile dealer	1	

Table 7.5: Occupations of interviewees

Service		**11**
• Travel agency	2	
• Operator of bus company	2	
• Hotel operator	2	
• Cinema operator	1	
• Operator of transportation company	1	
• Real estate agent	1	
• Operator of law office	1	
• Newspaper editor	1	
Other		**1**
• Repairman and seller of secondhand construction vehicles	1	
Unclassifiable		**8**
1: Operator of bus assembly factory and bus company, and automobile dealer		
2: Operator of industrial zone and factory of constr.-vehicle parts		
3: Operator of ice factory, hotel and agency of office automation machinery, and real estate agent		
4: Operator of match factory and hotel		
5: Operator of tapioca-processing factory and transportation company, and automobile dealer		
6: Operator of gas station, transport'n company, and bus station		
7: Shopkeeper selling automobile parts and operator of computer parts factory		
8: Operator of passenger transit company and hotel, and real estate agent		
Total		**46**

Notes: (1) Interviewees are classified based on the occupations which I judged to be their largest source of income.

(2) The eight persons grouped as 'unclassifiable' were involved in so many businesses that I was unable to judge which one was crucial for them. Joint operations with other businessmen are included.

government has given this a high priority in its industrialization drive. Weakness in *modern* manufacturing means that Khorat lacks exportable industrial products, and this in turn means that Khorat businessmen can contribute little to the present Thai economic development drive.

Table 7.6: Ethnicity and dialect groups of interviewees

Ethnicity and dialect group	Number		Percentage	
Chinese or of Chinese descent		41		89.1
Teochiu	34		73.9	
Hakka	4		8.7	
Hainanese	2		4.3	
Cantonese	1		2.2	
Thai		4		8.7
Unknown		1		2.2
Total		**46**		**100.0**

THE IMPORTANCE OF BEING CHINESE

The survey confirms for Khorat the findings of other researchers emphasizing the importance of Chinese immigrants and their descendants for Thailand's economic development.[13] Nearly 90 per cent of the group of most influential businesspeople are of Chinese descent; as generally in Thailand, the overwhelming majority are of the Teochiu speech group (see Table 7.6 above). However, it seems that Chinese cultural consciousness is decreasing, largely because of generational change. Only three of the 41 ethnic Chinese were born in China; second-generation immigrants form by far the largest group (68.3 per cent), and over a quarter are third generation (see Table 7.7 opposite).

All of the 41 entrepreneurs of Chinese descent spoke Thai fluently, although three spoke it with a Chinese accent and said that their ability in reading and writing was far better in Chinese than in Thai. There were only six individuals who were at home in both Chinese and Thai; about two-thirds of the sample stated that their first language was Thai and that their Chinese was poor. Those of the third generation gave knowledge of English a higher priority than Chinese.

Table 7.7: Generation of Chinese immigrants and Chinese descendants

Generation	Born in	Number	Percentage	Average age (years)
First	China	2	4.9	69.5
Second	China	1	2.4	68.0
Second	Thailand	27	65.9	50.1
Third	Thailand	11	26.8	42.3
Total		41	100.0	49.4

Note: Generation of Chinese people is defined as follows. *First generation*: an individual born in China of a China-born father who never resided in Thailand. *Second generation*: an individual born in China or in Thailand of a China-born father who immigrated to and resided in Thailand. *Third generation*: an individual born in Thailand of a second-generation father.

Knowledgeable senior members of the group confirmed the decline in the importance of Chinese connections, arguing that although Chinese speech groups had affected business behaviour in the past, they now had little relevance.[14] Moreover, as we shall see below, Chinese associations are of diminishing importance in the local business world. None the less, it should be noted that Khorat's Sino-Thai business leaders have not entirely lost their links with a Chinese identity. This is evidenced by the fact that three-quarters of them have studied the Chinese language in one way or another.

The central role of the Chinese in Khorat's business world has had another result, which may help to explain Khorat's failure to evolve *modern* manufacturing enterprises. No doubt the main factor in its non-industrialization is its distance from the capital, but another element is its lack of continuity of entrepreneurial activity over several generations, especially when combined with the bringing of relevant skills and ideas from elsewhere. Although until very recently Sino-Thai have been stereotyped as shopkeepers without an interest in manufacturing investment, we can often trace the roots of local industry in Thailand to modest beginnings by local Chinese a generation or two ago. Thus, research I conducted in Ratchaburi province showed that the local textile industry had its origin in small-scale manufacture started by Hakka Chinese who had worked in Chinese-run textile factories in Bangkok and moved to the province in the late 1930s.[15]

Table 7.8: Attendance of Chinese school by Chinese immigrants and Chinese descendants

Attendance		Number		Percentage
Attended Chinese school* or studied Chinese		31		75.6
Less than 1 year	3		7.3	
1 - 3 years	7		17.1	
4 - 6 years	7		17. 1	
More than 10 years	1		2.4	
Attended but unknown how long	3		7.3	
Did not attend but studied Chinese†	10		24.4	
Never attended Chinese school nor studied Chinese		9		22.0
Unknown		1		2.4
Total		**41**		**100.0**

Notes: (*) Includes three individuals who attended a school in China.

(†) Includes one individual who never attended school but learned Chinese because he was born in China and resided there until he was about 20 years old.

In Khorat's case, Chinese migrants from the capital in the 1930s engaged in commerce and not in manufacturing.[16] Moreover, they were soon forced to leave. In September 1941, a royal decree named

Table 7.9: Birth place of Chinese immigrants and Chinese descendants

Birth Place		Number		Percentage
Thailand		38		92.7
Khorat City	13		31.7	
Nakhon Ratchasima prov. (except for Khorat)	6		14.6	
Central (except for Bangkok)	7		17.1	
Bangkok	6		14.6	
Northeast (except for NR province)	5		12.2	
North	1		2.4	
China: Kwangtung Province		3		7.3
Total		**41**		**100.0**

the Amphoe Muang Nakhon Ratchasima, together with two other *amphoe*, as a prohibited area. The ban, which lasted until 1945, meant that people who did not possess Thai nationality could not live there. As a result, the non-naturalized Chinese population departed for Bangkok, Chiang Mai, and other parts of the country. They had to sell or lost nearly all they had, and the disruption to economic activity was such that the Khorat area suffered 'economic paralysis and acute food shortages.'[17] Very few of those who were forced to flee returned after the war,[18] and the result is that only a small number of ethnic Chinese families have been in Khorat for more than one generation (see Tables 7.9 and 7.10).

Less than one-third of all the Sino-Thai businessmen in the sample were born locally. Most came to Khorat from a variety of places elsewhere in Thailand. The families of only two entrepreneurs had lived in Khorat city for three generations, and the families of 11 had been

Table 7.10: Birth place of Chinese immigrants and Chinese descendants, analysed by generation

Generation	Born in		Number
First	China		2
Second	China		1
Second	Thailand		27
Khorat City		6	
NR Province		5	
Central		6	
Bangkok		5	
Northeast		4	
North		1	
Third Generation	Thailand		11
Khorat City		7	
NR Province		1	
Central		1	
Bangkok		1	
Northeast		1	
Total			**41**

there for two.[19] So far few Khorat business families have sought opportunities in *modern* manufacturing. This might be attributed to the discontinuity of its Chinese community, for the wartime eviction of Chinese families from Khorat effectively crushed whatever inclination they might have had to engage in such enterprises and ensured that the Khorat economy lacked locally developed manufacturing with significant industrial possibilities.

Table 7.11: Self-made Men – Chinese immigrants and Chinese descendant

Type	Number	Percent
Self-made from Scratch	3	7.3
Self-made	20	48.8
Partly Self-made	4	9.8
Not Self-made	13	31.7
Unknown	1	2.4
Total	**41**	**100.0**

CAPITAL RESOURCES AND SOCIAL MOBILITY

It is useful to begin a discussion of Khorat's entrepreneurial development by applying Skinner's four-fold classification of how Chinese business leaders in Thailand got their start.[20] *'Self-made from scratch' men* are those who had nearly nothing to fall back on when they started to work in Thailand; their success was due solely to their hard work and good judgement. *'Self-made' men* had someone to support them, such as parents or brothers, but they were not born rich and received only basic education. At the start of their careers, some of these worked helping their fathers, and others were given a small amount of capital by their parents to start modest enterprises of their own. *'Partly self-made' men* succeeded to businesses that their fathers had established, and used these as a launching-pad for enlargement and diversification. *'Not self-made' men* are those who literally owe almost everything to their fathers in operating their businesses. Thus, the father of one 'not self-made' man in our group built a factory for his son when the latter finished a graduate course in the United States, and another bought a hotel and let his son manage it on graduation from university.

Table 7.12: Self-made Men – Chinese immigrants and Chinese descendant, analysed by generation

Generation		Number
First Generation		2
Self-made from Scratch	2	
Second Generation: Born in China		1
Self-made from Scratch	1	
Second Generation: Born in Thailand		27
Self-made	18	
Partly Self-made	2	
Not Self-made	6	
Unknown	1	
Third Generation		11
Self-made	2	
Partly Self-made	2	
Not Self-made	7	
Total		**41**

Tables 7.11 and 7.12 show Skinner's classification applied to Khorat. As we can see, nearly half of the businessmen of Chinese descent are self-made men. The fourfold classification correlates closely with generation. All of those born in China are 'self-made from scratch',

Table 7.13: School career of Chinese immigrants and Chinese descendants

School career	No.	Percentage
No formal schooling or less than 4 years of schooling	3	7.3
4 years of primary school	12	29.3
More than 4 years of primary school	1	2.4
Middle School but did not graduate or less than 12 years of schooling	4	9.8
Middle School graduates or 12 years of schooling	8	19.5
College or university graduates or more than 12 years of schooling	9	22.0
Master's course graduates in the United States	3	7.3
Unknown	1	2.4
Total	**41**	**100.0**

as are about two-thirds of the second generation, born in Thailand; while nearly two-thirds of the third generation are 'not self-made'. The upward shift between first and third generations is also visible in their school careers (see Tables 7.13 and 7.14).

Table 7.14: School career of Chinese immigrants and Chinese descendants, analysed by generation

Generation		Number
First generation (born in China)		2
No formal schooling	1	
4 years of primary school	1	
Second generation (born in China)		1
Less than 4 years of schooling	1	
Second generation (born in Thailand)		27
No formal schooling	1	
4 years of primary school	10	
More than 4 years of primary school	1	
Middle School but did not graduate or less than 12 years of schooling	4	
Middle School graduates or 12 years of schooling	4	
College or university graduates or more than 12 years of schooling	6	
Unknown	1	
Third generation (born in Thailand)		11
4 years of primary school	1	
Middle School graduates or 12 years of schooling	4	
College or university graduates or more than 12 years of schooling	3	
Master's Course Graduates in the United States	3	
Total		**41**

Those we have categorized as 'self-made men' received only primary or at best middle school education. None of the 'self-made' men graduated from college or university, although one individual enrolled after he became wealthy enough to pay for tertiary education himself. The breakdown by generation shows that length of education is closely connected with generation. All of the first-generation and those second-generation Chinese born in China had only four years or less of formal schooling. Roughly 40 per cent of second-generation individuals born in Thailand had no education or only four years' primary education, while more than 20 per cent of them received tertiary education (more than 12 years of schooling). Among third-generation Chinese, the share who received tertiary education rises to about 55 per cent. In addition, half of them obtained a master's degree in the United States. Only one third-generation individual had not gone beyond primary school education.

Available data on father's employment allow comparisons only between the second generation born in Thailand and the third generation (see Table 7.15 overleaf). In both generations, those whose fathers were merchants account for roughly half of the total number. Most of these were small-scale general shop operators and middlemen dealing in agricultural products. It is interesting to note that nearly one-fifth of the second-generation Sino-Thai fathers were farmers; this has no counterpart in the third generation.

Picking out the most successful and influential ten businessmen among those interviewed, we find that eight are 'self-made men' (of whom seven are second-generation Chinese born in Thailand and the other an individual whom I could not interview and whose ethnicity I could not ascertain), one is a 'self-made from scratch' first-generation Chinese, and the last a 'partly self-made' third-generation Sino-Thai. Therefore, Khorat's top businessmen are predominantly 'self-made' second-generation Chinese born in Thailand. The dominance of this category can be explained by the halting of new immigration to Thailand after 1949 and the subsequent lapse of a generation. Moreover, since the average age of second-generation Chinese is nearly eight years higher than third-generation Chinese in the group (see Table 7.7), the former have had more time to establish their leading role.

METHODS OF CAPITAL ACCUMULATION

Here, I would like to concentrate on how the key group of 'self-made' second-generation Sino-Thai, especially those whom I consider to be among the top ten Khorat businessmen, started and extended their businesses. Many of them were born of poor Chinese immigrant fathers; they had helped since childhood in their father's shop or other business, and usually started making money as employees or salaried workers (*luk chang*). When they sought employment outside

Table 7.15: Father's occupation

Ethnicity and generation of interviewees	Father's occupation	Number	
Chinese – First generation (born in China)			2
	Unknown	2	
Chinese – Second generation (born in China)			1
	Merchant	1	
Chinese – Second generation (born in Thailand)			27
	Merchant	13	
	Farmer	5	
	Company Employee	2	
	Laundry Worker	1	
	Tailor and Dressmaker	1	
	Maker and Seller of Food Products	1	
	Photography Shop	1	
	Hotel Operator	1	
	Unknown	2	
Chinese – Third generation (born in Thailand)			11
	Merchant	5	
	Factory Operator	1	
	Cinema Operator	1	
	Hotel Operator	1	
	Maker and Seller of Food Products	1	
	Automobile Dealer	1	
	Subcontractor in Construction	1	
Thai			4
	Government Employee	2	
	Company Operator	1	
	Newspaper Dealer	1	
Unknown			1
	Merchant	1	
Total			46

the family, connections combined with ethnicity seemed to count for something. Once they had accumulated enough experience, they set up small-scale businesses of their own, usually with a small amount of capital that they had saved or obtained from their immediate family.[21]

Before the banking system became well established in Khorat, the *chae*, or rotating credit society, was the most common way for local businessmen to raise additional capital; it is still important for those who have not yet established sufficient financial credibility to borrow from banks.[22] Discussing the system, a senior Khorat business leader emphasized that Chinese merchants took care to select as members of their *chae* trustworthy acquaintances with whom they expected to do business satisfactorily. Apparently, business credibility and not membership in the same dialect group or other Chinese association was what counted. Interest charges were at most 4 per cent a month, which was not considered a heavy burden by those who made use of this credit source.[23] In effect, the *chae* constituted a mutual dependence system among Chinese merchants; it was crucial for those who wanted to make use of it to establish a good reputation and business credibility in local Chinese community.

Occasionally, Chinese merchants engaged illegally in the business of discounting post-dated cheques (*plian chek*).[24] In the past, the discounting of post-dated cheques was one of the methods Chinese used to obtain short-term loans and to raise capital for their businesses.[25] Post-dated cheques have been discounted both in the organized financial market – that is, by commercial banks and finance companies – and in the informal market. This came about because the monetary authorities imposed an interest ceiling on loans in the organized financial market, which reduced the amount lent. This resulted in 'credit rationing', and in order to meet the excess demand for credit, post-dated cheques that commercial banks and finance companies would not discount, were put in the hands of Chinese businessmen who may not have had licences to engage in finance. In the unorganized market, Chinese merchants usually determined the discount rate by the creditworthiness of the drawers and drawees, as well as the market interest-rate level. Probably, a high discounting rate was imposed on those businessmen who had not established a reputation in local Chinese society.

My research in Khorat revealed that there were many local Chinese merchants who in the past had been engaged in the discounting of post-dated cheques as a sideline. According to Ratprathip Kiratiurai, a businessman of long experience in the Khorat financial world, local merchants had come to use post-dated cheques widely by about 1960, due to the increase in trade between Bangkok and Khorat. At that time he and his father began to discount such cheques drawn on merchants of Khorat by businessmen of Bangkok. Until 1972 they were able to run this business without being subjected to any legal restrictions. In that year, however, the government began to regulate the activities of non-bank financial institutions, and those who desired to undertake such businesses were required to obtain permission from the Ministry of Finance. Ratprathip and his father managed to obtain this, and set up a finance company in 1972; it was the only one in the Northeast at that time, and the 49th to be established in Thailand.[26]

At the end of the 1970s Sunthon Phumhothong, another Chinese merchant, established a company in Khorat dedicated to the discounting of post-dated cheques. According to him, by the mid–1980s there were 27 such companies run by Chinese merchants in the Northeast. His company was registered at the Ministry of Commerce as a *len chae* company – that is, a firm which arranges rotating credit schemes. Chinese merchants arranging a *chae* might use post-dated cheques discounted by this type of company for the purpose.

In 1983, a run involving 44 finance companies of Thailand threatened the solvency of the finance business in the Northeast. *Chae* faced financial difficulties in 1984, and the number of dishonoured post-dated cheques increased, especially those drawn in arranging *chae*.[27] According to Sunthon, all of the Northeast's 27 finance companies went down; his own was taken over by a Bangkok-based finance and securities company affiliated to the Thai Farmers Bank, whose Khorat branch it became.

It appears, therefore, that Chinese merchants formed the backbone of an indigenous financial industry that existed in the provinces several decades ago. The post-dated cheque business gave Chinese merchants a competitive edge over commercial banks, for they could avoid the strict regulations which hampered commercial banks in dealing with small borrowers. Moreover, small loans involved disproportionately high administrative costs for the banks, which were therefore not too interested in them. On the other hand, informal financial agents that were free from legal regulations could adjust interest rates to match the borrower's creditworthiness. Chinese merchants had a competitive advantage, as their local relations meant that they could inform themselves much more efficiently than branch offices of Bangkok banks about the credit status of other local Chinese businessmen. As a whole, their businesses were based on personal relationships within local Chinese society; they arranged the discounting of post-dated cheques in order to cut down fellow businessmen's transactions costs associated with processing loan contracts and to help them raise capital. Ultimately, they helped to increase the efficiency of Chinese business transactions and to redress a resource allocation distorted by economic regulation.[28]

Another very common method used to raise the capital necessary to finance business is joint investment among local entrepreneurs. As with the *chae* and the discounting of post-dated cheques, this means that entrepreneurs must involve themselves actively in the local business world and seek to maintain good relations with its members. The importance of interpersonal trust and credit for Sino-Thai businessmen should not be underestimated. To illustrate this, let me recount the misfortune – the details have been slightly changed – of one of the interviewees, X, a senior business leader of Khorat. Now retired, he had held responsible positions in local Chinese associations, as do several of his family members today. His family is much respected for their success in commercial and service undertakings. Seeking diversification, the family decided to enter the manufacturing sector. Gaining the acquaintance of an engineer and plant manager, whom we will call Y, the family agreed on a joint undertaking and set up a factory. Unfortunately, X's family had no knowledge of production, and their company incurred heavy losses. In the resulting confrontation between X's family and Y, the latter suggested they dissolve the enterprise. X refused this decisively; he and his family believed their name would be damaged if they abandoned the factory. Although the project had burdened them with terrible debts, they feared that the damage to their reputation in the business community would outweigh the economic relief they could obtain by giving it up.

Because of the importance of ascertaining business reliability and establishing trust among potential associates, arenas where members of the business community can communicate informally are very important. In the next section we will consider the several kinds of association which link Khorat businessmen and help to cement relationships among them.

LINKS BETWEEN LOCAL ENTREPRENEURS

We shall first consider the Chinese associations, which are the oldest groups to provide this service. The Teochiu, the largest dialect group in Khorat, do not have a local *samakhom* (society) of their own. However, the Munithi Lak Siang Siang Tung, a nation-wide charitable foundation organized originally by Teochiu in Siracha (Chonburi province) established itself in Khorat in 1957, and this has since served as a kind of club for the Teochiu population. In addition, the Samakhom Haka Nakhon Ratchasima was set up in 1949 to strengthen solidarity among Khorat's Hakka Chinese; it is a particularly large association, having more than 700 members.

Chinese immigrants and their descendants also have societies for those who bear the same family name. One of these is the Samakhom Tia Charoen Nakhon Ratchasima, which was set up for those who bear the name of Tia. Most of the group's 200 or so members are Teochiu, but Hakka also take part in it. The association has existed for a long time, but it only registered formally as a society in 1989, when it began to operate a finance company. Such a company, run by and for the benefit of people with the same family name, suggests the importance of social ties for business dealings among the local Chinese. Nowadays, however, it is something of an anomaly; more usually, Chinese societies focus on charitable work and do not play a direct part in business matters. As we have noted earlier, business credibility rather than shared Chinese social membership has been the key for acquiring access to capital.

Indirectly, however, Chinese associations may play a significant role in capital accumulation. As Barton observed for South Vietnam, 'voluntary associations within the Chinese community provided merchants with another outlet for demonstrating their wealth and building their reputations'.[29] Chinese merchants place great importance on creditworthiness; associations based on such non-economic criteria as dialect groups, surnames, and native places offer opportunities not only to get acquainted and exchange information, but also to establish a reputation for financial solidity through monetary contributions to the society's activities. In other words, Chinese associations provide a means by which businessmen can display their creditworthiness.

The benefits of links based on Chinese attributes are, however, offset by the limitations that the Chinese community imposes on local entrepreneurs. This is particularly the case in a relatively small business community, such as that of Khorat. The situation is not too different from that described for local *zaibatsu* (*chiho zaibatsu*) in pre-war Japan, who had to devote much of their time to local community service, representation, and arbitration.[30] The Chinese associations, in Khorat as elsewhere, are very much oriented to the local community rather than region- or nation-wide links; and of course they do not include non-Chinese, who may still be peripheral to business but whose connections are increasingly important for larger undertakings.

Local Chinese societies are thus becoming less significant for business circles; in their place have come trade associations and charitable/social groups whose focus is nation-wide. The Chamber of Commerce and the Rotary Club have won the wide participation of the younger Khorat businessmen, most of whom are second- or third-generation Chinese. The principal members of the Chinese societies, most of them first- or second-generation Chinese, are now elderly; a number of second- and third-generation Chinese have not sought membership in them, even though their fathers belonged. The president of the Teochiu Chinese charitable foundation, which previously was the leading arbiter in the Khorat business world, noted that it had handed over this role to the Nakhon Ratchasima Chamber of Commerce.[31] I expect that the Chinese associations will fade away by the time social leadership passes to third-generation businessmen, who do not identify themselves strongly as Chinese.

The best organized of the new type of association is the Nakhon Ratchasima Chamber of Commerce, established in 1980. By October 1991 it included about 900 members for the whole province; its leadership includes Hakka and Hainanese as well as Teochiu. Its leading members have united to set up several important projects. Two that have attracted a good deal of public attention centre on hotel management, and it is noteworthy that both involve Bangkok-based businessmen as investors.[32] The fact that the Chamber of Commerce is a nation-wide network has enabled local businessmen to form better connections with business circles in the capital, a matter of increasing importance.

Finally, although we have stressed the importance of association membership for making business connections, we should consider the importance of marital ties for cementing relations between local entrepreneurs. Skinner's survey of Bangkok entrepreneurs found that intermarriage among important families enhanced their position in the business world.[33] Hewison too stressed the importance of family ties among leaders of big financial business groups for linking themselves to each other, to other business leaders, the bureaucracy, and the military – in short, to other sources of power.[34] Both of these authors make reference to the Bangkok business elite; in Khorat's case, it is perhaps only natural that there is intermarriage among the eminent families of its small business population. It is not clear that these marriage ties have been particularly directed towards business advantage; at least, there are no cases where this seems evident. Nor were there notable marriage links between local and Bangkok-based businessmen, or with members of the central bureaucracy or military. What seems to count in establishing and cementing relationships is a local reputation for reliability on the part of the individual entrepreneur.

ETHNIC THAI ENTREPRENEURS

Among my 46 interviewees, only four were Thai businessmen. Although this is too small a number to be statistically meaningful, it is interesting to see how they were successful in a local business world that is dominated by Sino-Thai entrepreneurs.

Two interviewees managed manufacturing-cum-commercial enterprises (one a maker and seller of food products, another of furniture, see Table 7.5). Of the other two, one was an operator of a travel agency and the other a newspaper publisher. None of them was ranked among the most influential and successful ten businessmen of Khorat. If the fourfold classification in Table 7.11 is applied, three of them were partly self-made and the last wholly self-made. This reflects the fact that prominent Thai entrepreneurs come from well-to-do families, relative to Sino-Thai entrepreneurs. They are better educated than their Sino-Thai counterparts; two finished tertiary education and the other two secondary education.

The three partly self-made businessmen owed much to their fathers and/or families in starting their business or receiving higher education. Sunthon Chanrangsi, the newspaper publisher, was in his mid–40s and was born in Khorat. He came to the business by succeeding to his father's newspaper dealership; his newspaper enjoyed the second largest circulation among all provincial newspapers in Thailand. Wichian Bunnak, nearly 60, the operator of the travel agency, was of noble birth – his grandfather had the conferred title of *Chao Phraya* and was a governor in southern Thailand. The family was rather rich, and Wichian's father managed a company in Bangkok. After graduating from college, Wichian worked for a German automobile distributor in Bangkok; he moved to Khorat when he was granted the right to operate a sales agency for German automobiles there. Later, he abandoned the car dealership to concentrate on his travel agency. The third partly self-made businessman was Prasut Minpraphan, a 57-year-old maker and seller of processed meat products. Born in an outer *amphoe* of Nakhon Ratchasima province, he was adopted by an official of the Ministry of the Interior. He studied agricultural technology at a university in the Philippines, which led to his entering the food-processing business.

The last ethnic Thai businessman, entirely self-made, was Wirasak Phromdi, a maker and seller of furniture in his mid–40s. He was born in an outer *amphoe* of Ubon Ratchathani province, where his father was a school teacher. When Wirasak graduated from a vocational school in Khorat, he began to work as a carpenter in the nearby US military base. After the withdrawal of the US army, he changed his occupation several times, but was eventually able to turn his experience in furniture-selling to use by establishing a furniture factory and outlet in the early 1980s. He started this business without partners, and his initial capital consisted of his own savings and a bank loan; so far it has been a success.

Compared to Chinese entrepreneurs, who enjoy a well-developed local information network and occasionally dedicate themselves to business associations, Thai entrepreneurs are less integrated into local business circles. None of these four Thai businessmen was involved in any outstanding joint ventures with local entrepreneurs. Although two of them (Wichian and Wirasak) belonged to the Chamber of Commerce, they had never been leading members of it. Although Sunthon, the newspaper publisher, was once a member of the Chamber of Commerce, he withdrew because of dissatisfaction with its management.

However, this does not mean that Thai entrepreneurs have no business connections on which they can rely. Wichian, the operator of the travel agency, was planning a joint venture to build a first-class hotel on his land in Khorat with a foreign hotel enterprise. Sunthon promoted the circulation of his newspaper in such eastern provinces as Chonburi through cooperation with a newspaper company in the Eastern region. Although it is difficult to draw conclusions from only these four samples, they do seem to have been independent of local Chinese society and the efforts of Chinese entrepreneurs to build up creditworthiness in order to drive transaction costs down. Instead, Thai entrepreneurs seemed to seek relationships with business circles in Bangkok and/or other provinces, through their own activities and their families' connections.

Two of the four Thai entrepreneurs have had experience in local politics. Sunthon was a member of the municipal council of Amphoe Muan Nakhon Ratchasima for five years (1980–1985), and Prasut was a member of the council of Nakhon Ratchasima province for eight years (1975–1983). However, after a local political machine was established in Khorat by an influential businessman in 1985, their political careers ended. For this reason they did not join the circle of politically ambitious businessmen (dominated by Chinese entrepreneurs) which I shall describe later.

THE IMPORTANCE OF NON-LOCAL CONNECTIONS

We have mentioned the importance of joint investments by local businessmen as a way of raising capital. Such cooperation is now frequent between local and Bangkok-based entrepreneurs. The latter have increasing importance in projects involving sophisticated know-how or technology and large amounts of capital. Cooperation with Bangkok-based business for the purpose of tapping technology and expertise is important regardless of the size and kind of business. Thus, automobile and electric appliance dealers are given guidance in repair technology by head offices located in Bangkok, which in turn are backed by foreign companies. If they are unable to effect the repair, specialists are called in from Bangkok or the goods are sent to the capital for repair. Some factories entrust the repair of their machinery to the firm that installed it, usually based in Bangkok.

At the same time, Khorat businessmen have made investments in Bangkok, especially in enterprises such as real estate, financing, and export. In particular, they have found an outlet for their capital in the construction boom that Bangkok experienced in the late 1980s and early 1990s. This, of course, has been a mere drop in the ocean of Bangkok's capital inflow; it has directed investment away from local possibilities, which Khorat may eventually recoup if the entrepreneurs place some of their Bangkok-derived profits locally.

A deluge of direct foreign investment was one of the driving forces behind Thailand's boom, especially after 1988. However, Khorat enjoyed almost no foreign investment until about 1990, when foreign companies began to operate in the Suranaree Industrial Zone (SIZ), a privately developed industrial estate which opened in the previous year. After that, the inflow of foreign capital, mainly from Japan and Taiwan, became a steady stream. Almost all the foreign companies that have invested in and around Khorat are located in the SIZ. As in the country as a whole, direct foreign investment established few if any close links with local small and medium-sized industries. Khorat provided foreign investors with scarcely any of the materials, parts, and machines necessary for production; these came from other regions or abroad, and the foreign companies' products were exported.

Among the entrepreneurs I interviewed in Khorat, only one made use of cooperation with a foreign company to acquire the advanced technical knowledge necessary to enter a new manufacturing business, although this is a pattern common to the industrialization process in Thailand.[35] Another, however, was able to take advantage of experience abroad to acquire technical knowledge himself; he has also employed foreign engineers in his enterprise, which may be the technologically most advanced automotive parts factory in Thailand. Both these entrepreneurs are exceptional in Khorat's context, but the fact that they exist is significant in itself.

Thai companies have recently begun to invest in foreign countries, particularly with regard to Indochina. In April 1992 Thailand was reported to stand first, in terms of numbers of projects, on the list of approved foreign investment in Cambodia.[36] Given Khorat's location and historical role as a gateway to Indochina, we might expect interest in this by local entrepreneurs. Some Khorat businessmen did indeed express an interest in investing there in the future, but the only one who had concrete plans for foreign investment intended to undertake a joint venture in Malaysia.[37] The economic horizons of Khorat businessmen are still limited compared to those in more developed parts of the country; nevertheless they have greatly expanded in terms of their past.

POLITICIANS AND BUSINESS

The horizons of local entrepreneurs have also expanded in another way: they have become more deeply involved with politics and politicians. At one level this is perhaps self-evident, for both local businessmen and Khorat representatives in parliament have a common interest in promoting local enterprise. If a businessman establishes a close business relationship with an influential Bangkok political figure, he can expect something in return, such as an increase in public investment in Khorat, which will work to his benefit. At the same time, members of parliament from Khorat expect some form of support from local businessmen. This mutual patronage was highly evident during the Chatichai regime. As we have seen, Chatichai Choonhavan brought several large projects to Khorat, which were enthusiastically received by a local business community convinced they would boost the city's economy, and in return Khorat businessmen increased their support for the politicians involved.

The Suranaree Industrial Zone (SIZ) is an example of such intervention by powerful Bangkok-based politicians in Khorat's economy. This industrial estate, which opened in 1989, was begun by the local entrepreneur Aphisak Phiriyaphongsak, who – according to his own account – was advised by Chatichai to purchase a piece of land for this purpose. The estate was developed with the aid of Chatichai, Chatichai's nephew Korn Thapparangsi, who had represented Nakhon Ratchasima province in parliament since 1983, and another influential member of the Chart Thai party.[38] By 1991 it covered an area of 5,000 *rai* and had 25 factories operating. As we noted earlier, the zone drew investment from Bangkok and abroad; its production was highly export-oriented, and it had few relations – other than Aphisak himself – with local entrepreneurship.

Those Khorat entrepreneurs involved in large business projects find it crucial to recruit politicians with connections in the central government. Aphisak claimed that the idea for an industrial estate had originated with him, but that he had only been able to realize it with Chatichai's patronage. Another example of the importance of political support is the Royal Princess Khorat project, one of several current endeavours to build a new first-class hotel in Khorat. As of 1991, its registered capital was 120 million baht.[39] Half of this was held by an affiliate of the Dusit Thani Group, Thailand's leading hotel-franchising company; the other half was divided between local businessmen (with 40 per cent) and the former deputy minister of communications, Suwat Liptapallop (10 per cent).[40] The Dusit Thani Group had of course its own well-developed Bangkok political connections; none the less, the business participants evidently found it prudent to include Suwat, as a power broker with important sources of support in both the central government and local circles.

Let us consider for a moment the background of Suwat Liptapallop, for political strongmen are of considerable importance to provincial business. He is somewhat unusual in that he was not born in the town which became his power base, and that he came into politics from a business background. Of Chinese descent, Suwat was born in Ratchaburi province, where his parents were traders in a floating market. When they moved to Bangkok, they came to be involved in the trucking of construction materials, and their enterprise developed into a construction company. Suwat's father was close to General Arthit Kamlang-ek, and during that general's term as commander-in-chief of the army, in the early 1980s, his company was said to have won many military construction contracts. Much of his work was in Khorat, and the firm's involvement in building roads and hospitals there gave the family considerable local influence. Suwat eventually assumed leadership of the construction business, and he also went into politics. As a member of General Arthit's Puang Chon Chao Thai Party, he ran for parliament in 1988 in the same Khorat election district as Chatichai Choonhavan, whom he defeated by a wide margin. As prime minister, Chatichai appointed him deputy minister of communications in the cabinets of August and December 1990. After Chatichai was removed in the February 1991 coup d'état, Suwat was one of 20 members of the National Legislative Assembly appointed by the National Peacekeeping Council. For the general election of March 1992, he and Gen. Arthit defected to the Samakkhi Tham Party, favoured by the currently dominated military faction. Several months later, following the collapse of the military regime, Suwat joined Chatichai's new party, the Chart Pattana (National Development Party). As of that year, his company secured an important part of the contract for widening the Friendship Highway.[41]

We can see from this the importance of personal links with Bangkok political patrons for the provincial big businessman, particularly if – as in the construction business – public contracts are involved. It also reveals the extent to which Bangkok leaders find it useful to cultivate provincial strongmen who have a solid political as well as economic base.

BUSINESSMEN IN POLITICS

Stereotypically, businessmen of Chinese extraction found it wiser to leave politics to the Thai, relying for protection and influence on their personal and financial relationships with those in power. In recent years, however, businessmen have made themselves felt directly in politics, not only in the capital but in provincial centres.[42] Khorat is no exception: as Table 7.16 shows, about 30 per cent of my interviewees had run themselves or their children in local elections.

This involvement seems to have begun in about 1974, when some politically minded local entrepreneurs under the leadership of Banyong Lotharaprasoet formed the Klum Mit Pracha, a political club, to support candidates for seats on the municipal council of Amphoe Muang Nakhon Ratchasima.[43] This was during Thailand's turbulent 1973–1976 democracy, which no doubt affected the businessmen's awakening interest in electoral politics. However, according to Banyong, the club had no connections with any central political parties, and it was not very successful in its electoral campaigns.

Table 7.16: Experience in local elections

Experience*		Number	Percentage
Ran in local election in person		10	21.7
Elected†	7		
Not elected	3		
Children ran in local election		4	8.7
Elected	3		
Not elected	1		
Have never run in local election, either in person, or through a child		32	69.6
Total		46	100.0

Notes: (*) Those who have run in elections for the municipal council of Amphoe Muang NR and the provincial council of NR province included.

(†) One individual who was returned once, but lost a subsequent election, is included.

It was in the 1980s that local businessmen really began to make themselves felt in Khorat politics.[44] A leading spirit in this involvement was Wichai Choetchai, one of Khorat's most successful businessmen and an exemplar of the profitable linkage between business and politics. In 1985 he took the leadership in forming a political club called the Klum Prasan Mit (Friends Unite Group), in order to support candidates in the local elections. The club, which absorbed the following of Banyong's grouping in 1990, made business success a major element in attracting members and votes. In the elections for the Amphoe Muang Nakhon Ratchasima council held in September of that year, it put forward 18 candidates, some of them from entrepreneurial backgrounds, including Wichai's son. All of them won seats. A month later, in elections for the provincial council, several candidates running for Prasan Mit, including another of Wichai's sons, gained seats. Their business success and their ability to purchase support were no doubt important elements in their victories, for vote-buying was an increasing element in the politics of the area.

Another reason for the success of the Prasan Mit was that its core group was bound to Wichai by business and social as well as political connections. Bunyong, whose following was absorbed into Wichai's club, remained active in local politics and was linked to Wichai by marriage ties. One of his sons was returned in the 1990 city elections, with the support of Prasan Mit. Two other Prasan Mit leaders were Wichai's associates in a transport company, begun in 1985, which had a government railroad concession between Bangkok and the Northeast. Their sons, like Wichai's, ran in the 1990 city elections.[45]

Although Prasan Mit began as a purely local machine, connections with local and central political strongmen were also an important factor in its success. Wichai seems to have been an important backer of Suwat Liptapallop's rise in politics, and one of his close associates in the transport company and the Prasaan Mit, Arun Tangphanit, ran for parliament in 1988 as a candidate of the Puang Chon Chao Thai Party, General Arthit's vehicle, which was locally Suwat's machine. Arun was no stranger to politics, having earlier served about two years as mayor of Khorat.

Wichai himself was widely known as a sponsor of Chatichai Choonhavan, who honoured him with a seat in the upper house of the Thai parliament, reportedly in recompense for financial support in the national election of 1988. After Chatichai's government was overthrown by military leaders in the February 1991 coup, Wichai is said to have distanced himself from Chatichai's Chart Thai and sought links with the Samakkhi Tham Party, sponsored by the dominant military faction. However, once the military had been overthrown and Chatichai had established the Chart Pattana Party as his vehicle for the September 1992 elections, Wichai resumed his role as a Chatichai supporter. Meanwhile, he was grooming his son, who was gaining political experience as a member of the Khorat provincial council, to assume a role in central politics. Reportedly, his son's candidacy was sought by three parties – Samakkhi Tham, Chart Thai, and Social Action – in the March 1992 general elections, but Wichai could not decide under which banner to run him at that most uncertain point in Thai politics.[46]

Other businessmen have also attempted to assert themselves in politics. The Nakhon Ratchasima Chamber of Commerce backed two of its leading members who were running in the municipal election of 1990, but they were soundly beaten by Wichai's group. In effect, the Chamber of Commerce and the Prasan Mit represent different factions in Khorat's political leadership; the divisions are based on personal loyalties rather than principles.[47] Another of Wichai's close business and political associates, Wirat Tanchindaprathip, seems to have served as a solicitor of votes (*hua kanaen*) for several political parties. In 1988, he established a local society, Chomrom Mit 31 (Friendly Get-Together '31). According to him, this was a club of some 200 members that promoted friendly relations between various Khorat leading groups – businessmen, politicians, government officials, and so on. Chomrom Mit '31 held a meeting every month, and a guest speaker was invited to address it. Guest speakers ranged from high military officials to influential politicians such as Suwat. Although this local society was not an explicit political club like Klum Prasan Mit, which played a decisive role in local elections, it could be regarded as Wirat's forum for political activities.

Next I would like to focus on the question of why entrepreneurs are so eager to launch into local politics. Pertinent to this point is the problem of political intervention in the economy. If entrepreneurs have the latitude to carry out their business activities within the sphere of a (completely) free market, their entry into politics will be motivated by reasons other than economic ones, such as a desire for fame. This is because they can maximize their economic utility only within the economic sphere as long as (and to the degree that) the principles of the free market are upheld. However, if politicians interfere in economic matters, entrepreneurs cannot necessarily attain utility maximization through purely economic activities. Businessmen who aspire to economic success, in other words, may not be able to find a way to do so other than by joining hands with politicians or by launching into politics themselves.

As is frequently noted, many big business groups in Thailand have established close relations with influential figures in the government, a relationship originally caused by racially based political intervention into the economy, which forced Chinese businessmen to seek political patronage. Thus Skinner wrote of the second Phibun era (1948–1957) that government intervention into business sectors under the Thai-ificaton programmes 'have forced economic cooperation at the highest levels between Chinese leaders and Thai government officials'.[48] Chinese entrepreneurs were forced to make contact with Thai politicians in order to protect their businesses against discriminatory economic legislation and popular prejudice. The basic motive at this time was not a desire for economic gain, but the need for political protection: *fear*, not *greed*, to put it in blunt terms.

However, racial tension in Thailand today has dissipated to such an extent that Chinese entrepreneurs no longer feel the need for protection from racially motivated political intervention. Their cooperation with politicians must therefore be explained in other terms. It is fair to say that Chinese businessmen today seek political patronage for economic utility: to gain favours for their own businesses or to influence the legislative process, economic legislation understandably being a source of great concern for businessmen. Entrepreneurs in the provinces understand very well that political patrons can be a great help in attaining business success. Many of them become politicians themselves, with the ultimate aim of making contact with members of the central political circles of Bangkok.

CONCLUDING REMARKS

From the above we can see that Khorat's economy has experienced a number of significant changes which are similar to the transformations occurring in the Thai economy as a whole. Although business in Khorat is still largely a matter of commerce and is dominated to an overwhelming extent by individuals of Chinese descent, radical changes have taken place within the local business community with regard to political involvement and cultural values. Younger entrepreneurs now look to non-Chinese associations that have national and international linkages, rather than to local Chinese groupings. There is a close involvement between entrepreneurs and politicians at both the local and the national levels. Prominent businessmen are participating directly in political activities; they not only establish individual relations with political patrons, but they are organizing collectively to procure conditions more favourable to entrepreneurial activities.

The involvement of local entrepreneurs in politics can be seen as essentially a rent-seeking activity, in which entrepreneurs spend scarce resources (capital, time, and energy) competing for government favours. Until 1997 there were a large number of opportunities for rent-seeking, and these attracted Thai entrepreneurs at many levels. Under the circumstances of the time, it was rational for provincial businessmen to turn to politics as a way of maximizing returns on investment. However, this undoubtedly had the effect of retarding Khorat's economic development, in that it drew local entrepreneurs' attention away from building a productive and competitive capitalist base.

Since the 1997 crash, there has been an abrupt contraction of investment in the provinces. The depressed state of the national economy has added to the burden of provincial businessmen, who had already borrowed well above their limits. The economic crisis and subsequent credit crunch are undoubtedly having a major effect on both provincial business development and provincial entrepreneurs' behaviour. Perhaps this will simply discourage business, or it may help to rationalize and thus eventually to stimulate provincial economies; only time will tell.

The economic crisis has made the Thai economy's structural problems all too clear. If it is addressed effectively, it could result in a healthier economy than Thailand possessed prior to the crash. If Thailand successfully follows the IMF's recommendations, healthier provincial economies should result. The privatization and deregulation urged by the IMF would limit the scope for rent-seeking activities, and free competition should then replace them as the most effective means of pursuing profit. If such international organizations as APEC and AFTA, which are supposed to promote free trade among their member countries, would likewise urge the Thai government to further liberalize the economy, that would also help the cause of rationalizing provincial business activity.

However, all this assumes a relatively benign course to the crisis. The most immediate question is whether or not the Thai government can address the economic situation. Can it deal with the financial aspects, such as the credit crunch and non-performing credit, and will this serve to get the Thai economy on its feet again? The future of the provincial economies depends critically on this, and it illustrates how the role of the national government has become of increasing importance to provincial economic development.

NOTES

1. 'Khorat' generally indicates the town of Nakhon Ratchasima proper, corresponding more or less to the area that was enclosed by a fort of the Ayutthaya period, and to the administrative district of Nakhon Ratchasima municipality today. However, it may also be used to indicate a broader area, of which Nakhon Ratchasima municipality is only one part.

2. *Statistical Yearbook Thailand 1992* (Thailand: National Statistical Office, n.d.). Officially, the second largest municipality (*thetsaban*) was Nonthaburi (population 264,201), but this is effectively part of Greater Bangkok.

3. Samut Prakan, Pathumthani, Samut Sakhon, Nonthaburi and Nakhon Pathom.

4. James C. Ingram, *Economic Change in Thailand 1850–1970* (Stanford: Stanford University Press, 1971), p. 47.

5. Samnakngan Kaset Changwat Nakhon Ratchasima, statistics for the crop year 1990/91. Nakhon Ratchasima province developed as a cassava-producing centre with the emergence of Thai participation in tapioca production for export; during the 1980s it provided from 19 to 27 per cent of all Thailand's cassava production (Thailand: Centre for Agricultural Statistics, *Agricultural Statistics of Thailand, Crop Year 1982/83, 1984/85, 1987/88*).

6. *Phalittaphan phak lae changwat chabap 2521, 2528, 2529* (Thailand, Office of the National Economic and Social Development Board (hereafter NESDB); *Gross Regional and Provincial Products, Preliminary Series 1981–89.*

7. Barbara Leitch LePoer, *Thailand: A Country Study* (Washington: Library of Congress, 1989), p. 72.

8. Yukio Ikemoto, *Income Distribution in Thailand: Its Changes, Causes, and Structure* (Tokyo: Institute of Developing Economies, 1991), pp. 57–65.

9. The STU and the widening of Friendship Highway were initiated under the government of Gen. Prem Tinsulanonda, though Chatichai took credit for pushing their implementation (*Khorat rai wan yuk khao isan*, 2

October 1991; *Prachachat thurakit*, 12–14 December 1991). The interests of Suwat Liptapallop, deputy minister of communications in the last Chatichai cabinet, seemed to be particularly reflected in the Friendship Highway project, because a construction company which he ran with his family in Bangkok obtained a contract for part of it (Thonkon, 'Suwat Liptapallop: adit ratthamontri chuai wakan krasuang khamanakhom' *Maha lap*, 25 June 1991: 38–39, 46, 61). For a discussion of the highly informal manner of project handling under the Chatichai government, which gave great freedom to ministers and enhanced pork-barrel politics, see Paul Handley, 'Thailand Aims to Clean Up Project Procedures: Call to Wise Men', *Far Eastern Economic Review*, 9 January 1992: 47–48; *Asian Wall Street Journal*, 13 July 1992.

10. One family member stated that they conceived the idea of the building in 1988, when the local investment climate seemed particularly favourable *(Loet tham thurakit,* Nakhon Ratchasima, 5–20 December 1991).

11. According to Sunthon Citamnuaiwatthana, a committee member of the Nakhon Ratchasima Chamber of Commerce of 1989, the price of land near the STU and the site of EXPO rose four- to ten-fold during that year alone (interview, 1989). See also *Raingan pracham pi 2532* (Nakhon Ratchasima: Ho kankha changwat Nakhon Ratchasima, 1990), p. 93. Land around the SIZ also experienced a sharp price increase in the same period.

12. Those of the original 67 who were not included were dropped for various reasons: some declined to be interviewed, the whereabouts of others was unknown, and some turned out not to have been as important as had originally been thought.

13. Krirkkiat Phipatseritham and Yoshihara Kunio, *Business Groups in Thailand* (Singapore: Institute of Southeast Asian Studies, 1983); G. William Skinner, *Leadership and Power in the Chinese Community of Thailand* (Ithaca: Cornell University Press, 1958); Akira Suehiro, *Capital Accumulation in Thailand 1855–1985* (Tokyo: Centre for East Asian Cultural Studies, 1989).

14. Interviews, Wirat Tanchindaprathip and Charin Thanyaset.

15. Yoko Ueda, 'Bankoku no keizai seicho to Bankoku kinko ni okeru shihonka keisei' [The Economic Growth of Bangkok and the Formation of Capitalists in Bangkok's Outlying Areas], *Southeast Asian Studies* 28 (1990): 55–82.

16. Ingram (*Economic Change*, p. 117) noted that Khorat had long been a silk-weaving centre, but that after the railway was opened, the production of silk began to decline in the Northeast. Brown traces the decline of Thailand's sericulture industry to imports of silk products from Asian countries in the early twentieth century, and investigates the failure of a sericulture programme which was set up with the cooperation of Japanese officials in *monthon* Khorat at the beginning of the century. Ian Brown, *The Elite and the Economy in Siam c. 1890–1920* (Singapore: Oxford University Press, 1988), pp. 157–164, 166. There are at present several factories producing raw silk or silk cloth in the rural areas surrounding Khorat. However, according to my survey of the White Mulberry Research Centre at

Khorat, these enterprises, which began to operate several years ago, have no continuity with the older silk industry.

17. G. William Skinner, *Chinese Society in Thailand: An Analytical History* (Ithaca: Cornell University Press, 1957), p. 275. For details, see ibid, pp. 270–272, 274–275; and Thavi Therawongseri, *Sathanaphap thang kotmai khong chao cin nai prathet thai* (Bangkok: Samnak Phim Odian Store, 1973), pp. 121–123.

18. Interview, Choethin Saeliw. At 82, he was the oldest business leader in the group I analysed; as a young man he experienced the evacuation, was rusticated to a nearby *amphoe* town, and was one of the few evacuees to return to Khorat.

19. The grandfathers of the two individuals whose families have lived in Khorat for three generations had operated gold shops in Bangkok, and transferred their businesses to Khorat, the first arriving there in the early 1920s. The next longest-resident were three two-generation families that settled in the early 1930s. One came from Bangkok, where he had worked for a Chinese-run photography shop, and went into the same business for himself. Another, from Nakhon Pathom Province, came from a fruit-growing family and went into business by establishing an ice factory in Khorat in the 1950s. The last engaged in various jobs in Khorat until his family managed to open a store.

20. Skinner, *Leadership and Power*, pp. 43–45.

21. This accords with the results of Rozental's study of urban credit in the latter half of the 1960s; see Alek. A. Rozental, *Finance and Development in Thailand* (New York: Praeger Publishers, 1970), pp. 260–262. His survey found that 88 per cent of the initial capital used to start the businesses of those entrepreneurs included in his sample was their own.

22. Wichian Suphasiraprapha, who is a second-generation Hakka Chinese and one of the top ten businessmen, noted that in the 1970s he and his brother had set up a *chae* to raise 70,000 to 80,000 baht to open a shop *Sengli hoe* (supplement to *Loet tham thurakit,* Nakhon Ratchasima, 1991). Phaisan Manasin, another leading Khorat businessman, stated that after opening his department store in 1976, he met his operating costs on several occasions by setting up a *chae* (*Phuchatkan rai sapda,* 25–31 May 1992).

23. Interview, Charin Thanyaset. Rozental (*Finance and Development,* pp. 261, 266–267, 270), discusses this system; he noted that such rotating credit societies played a larger role in raising capital for ongoing business operations than in setting up new enterprises. Nearly 30 per cent of the firms he studied relied on rotating credit societies, although the amount of money derived from this source amounted to less than 5 per cent of their operating capital.

24. With the spread of commercial banking in Thailand, post-dated cheques have been used among businessmen as a means of making payments in trading. The use of post-dated cheques became widespread throughout the

country after 1954, when legislation criminalizing the use of bad cheques was passed and post-dated cheques began to gain the confidence of merchants. Paul Sithi-Amnuai ed., *Finance and Banking in Thailand: A Study of the Commercial System, 1888–1963* (Bangkok: Thai Watana Panich, 1964), pp. 131–134; Alek A. Rozental, 'Branch Banking in Thailand', *The Journal of Developing Areas* 3 (1968): 37–50, 42–43.

25. Interview, Wirat Tanchindaprathip.

26. After Ratprathip began to operate a finance company, he tried to develop this into a local bank. However, this ambition was frustrated by the monetary authorities' refusal since the mid–1960s to grant permission for any new commercial banks. In 1980, he finally decided to sell most of his finance company shares to a friend who operated another such company in Bangkok. At present his former firm operates as a branch of a Bangkok-based finance company established by the merger of six finance companies after the run in 1984. Ratprathip himself has concentrated on real estate.

27. The International Bank for Reconstruction and Development, *World Development Report 1989* (New York: Oxford University Press, 1989), p. 72; Thailand, Bank of Thailand Northeastern Regional Branch, *Raingan setthakit lae kan ngoen phak tawanokchiangnua pi 2527* (Khon Kaen: Bank of Thailand Northeastern Regional Branch), pp. 1–2.

28. For indigenous financial businesses in the provinces, see Yoko Ueda, 'The Development of Commercial Banking and Financial Businesses in the Provinces of Thailand', *Southeast Asian Studies* 31 (1994): 385–411.

29. Clifton A. Barton, 'Trust and Credit: Some Observations Regarding Business Strategies of Overseas Chinese Traders in South Vietnam', in Linda Y. C. Lim and L. A. Peter Gosling (eds), *The Chinese in Southeast Asia*, 1 (Singapore: Maruzen Asia, 1983), p. 57.

30. Hidemasa Morikawa, *Chiho zaibatsu* (Tokyo: Nihon Keizai Shinbunsha, 1985), pp. 252–253, 283.

31. Interview. The Hakka society's president, a first-generation Chinese, also noted the diminishing importance of his association in local society.

32. One is a project to modernize an old hotel; the other is a joint venture between local businessmen and a well-known Bangkok-based hotel chain to establish a first-class hotel. In the latter project, the president of the Nakhon Ratchasima Chamber of Commerce has taken the lead in organizing local business participation.

33. Skinner, *Leadership and Power*, p. 183.

34. Kevin J. Hewison, 'The Financial Bourgeoisie in Thailand', *Journal of Contemporary Asia*, 11 (1981): 395–412.

35. This businessman sought technical cooperation from a German company when he planned to start production of a higher value-added product than he had previously manufactured.

36. Murray Hiebert, 'Baht Imperialism: Thai Investors Pour into Cambodia', *Far Eastern Economic Review,* 25 June 1992, pp. 46–47.

37. Amon Wongsurawat had an ice factory and, through a Thai company which produced ice-making machines (of which he was a shareholder), he made the acquaintance of a Malaysian businessman who had approached the company seeking an associate with ice-making experience who would help to set up factories in Malaysia producing ice-cubes for the Malaysian and Singapore markets. The Malaysian partner's experience was in real estate, so the technological expertise was to come from Khorat.

38. Interview, Aphisak Phiriyaphongsak.

39. However, the company was reported to be preparing to increase this to 550 million baht. See *Khorat rai wan yuk khao isan,* 17 December 1990.

40. *Bangkok Post,* 17 May 1991.

41. *The Nation* , 21 March 1991. Thonkon, 'Suwat Liptapallop', *Bangkok Post,* 8 February 1992; *Khorat rai wan yuk khao isan,* 17 December 1990.

42. For a discussion of this in another area, see Eiji Murashima, 'Local Elections and Leadership in Thailand: A Case Study of Nakhon Sawan Province', *The Developing Economies* 15 (1987): 363–385.

43. Interview, Banyong Lotharaprasoet. He is a second-generation Teochiu Chinese born in Khorat, who is said to have made a fortune from a petrol station which he set up on the newly opened Friendship Highway in the late 1950s. He and his family subsequently established several transport businesses.

44. Interview, Sunthon Chanrangsi, editor of the *Khorat rai wan yuk khao isan.* (This newspaper changed its name to *Khorat rai wan yuk khao thai* in 1992.)

45. It is worth noting that politically ambitious businessmen like Wichai and Banyong have not run in local elections in person, but instead have let their children stand as candidates. This might be influenced by the fact that Thai electoral law stipulates that if a candidate is of Thai nationality but his father was an alien, he/she must have completed higher secondary education or its equivalent, or must have studied at a tertiary educational institution in Thailand and obtained the equivalent of a bachelor's degree. Banyong is a second-generation Chinese, and he finished only primary education. Wichai's lineage is unknown, but he also had only primary education, so if his father was a first-generation Chinese he would have faced the same problem. Thus second-generation Chinese businessmen of humble origins may be prevented from playing a direct role in electoral politics.

46. Wichai's political activities received much press attention in that period, testifying to their importance; see among others, *Matichon sut sapda,* 30 September 1990, pp. 21–22; *The Nation,* 21 March 1991; *Bangkok Post,* 8 February 1992; *Khorat rai wan yuk khao isan,* 27 October 1991; *Khorat rai wan yuk khao thai,* 11 and 16 January and 2 February 1992; *Loet tham thurakit,* 5–

20 October and 5–20 December 1991; *Prachachat thurakit* 15–18 December 1991; *Phuchatkan rai sapda*, 20–26 July 1992.

47. Wichai also established the Federation of Thai Industry in Khorat, but this was poorly organized and, as far as I know, it has hardly functioned in its task of uniting local manufacturers.

48. Skinner, *Leadership and Power*, pp. 186–187.

EIGHT

DEVELOPING PROVINCIAL CAPITALISM
A Profile of the Economic and Political Roles of a New Generation in Khon Kaen, Thailand

*Kevin Hewison and Maniemai Thongyou**

For three decades Thailand saw dynamic economic growth, reaching exceptional rates during the period of the elected Prime Minister Chatichai Choonhavan (1988–1991). This performance brought great structural change to the economy, and saw the significance of manufacturing and the service sector increase, while agriculture declined in relative terms. This remarkable performance was produced by, and itself further fostered, a vigorous capitalism.

---

* This paper draws on issues raised in Kevin Hewison, 'Of Regimes, State and Pluralities: Thai Politics Enters the 1990s', in Kevin Hewison, Richard Robison and Garry Rodan (eds), *Southeast Asia in the 1990s* (Sydney: Allen & Unwin, 1993), pp. 159–189; and on data in Kevin Hewison and Maniemai Thongyou, *The New Generation of Provincial Business People in Northeastern Thailand* (Perth: Murdoch University Asia Research Centre, Working Paper No. 16, 1993). The research was completed in 1993. The 1997 economic crisis has had an effect on business in Khon Kaen but no new survey could be conducted.

The support provided by the Asia Research Centre and the Research and Development Institute, Khon Kaen University is acknowledged. The work of research assistants Waranan Bunnag and Jutthathit Kraipiraphan and the time given by each of the respondents was also greatly appreciated.

Although capitalist development has been thorough-going and widespread, relatively little is known about the rapid changes that have taken place outside the greater Bangkok area. While there has recently been an increased interest in the historical development of the economy in provincial areas, there is still relatively little information available regarding the nature of provincial and regional development, the character of local business groups, their development trajectories or their political activity.[1] This essay, surveying a small group of 20 young business people operating in Khon Kaen in northeastern Thailand, provides a profile of business groups in that city, specifically the new generation of business people; to begin the investigation of the provincial and national political and economic significance of such groups; and to contribute some preliminary insights into the contemporary processes of capitalist development in Thailand.

Rapid provincial economic development is not a phenomenon confined to Thailand; the Philippines, for example, has seen a marked provincial entrepreneurialism, and the quite staggering economic growth in southern China is throwing up significant provincial business groups.[2] Given that there has been some comparative analysis of national-level business groups in the Asian region,[3] this small study may provide some relevant data at the sub-national level.

The methodology used was relatively simple, involving a questionnaire administered to the group, although the selection of the interviewees was not so straightforward. The researchers chose the initial and core set of interviewees based on their affiliation with a development-minded group of entrepreneurs, who were wont to refer to themselves as the 'Young Turks' of business in Khon Kaen. This base was chosen because the researchers had contacts with many of them, thus easing the often difficult process of establishing confidence; moreover, they seemed particularly relevant to the goal of exploring emerging differences between business generations. Initial discussions with this group sought to identify the most important businesses and business families or groups in Khon Kaen, with the aim of expanding the number of potential interviewees. From a list of about 35, it was possible to complete comprehensive interviews with 20 over the period of the study. All the interviewees were from the young generation, since a principal aim of the study was to develop an understanding of local business through discussions with this young cohort. Clearly, the sample is not random, but consultations with the interviewees and persons knowledgeable about business in Khon Kaen suggest that it included a wide cross-section of the major business interests. However, as will be noted below, the sample is skewed away from manufacturing industry.

Interviewing took place over a seven-month period, being interrupted by the political turbulence of 1992, which overtook both the interviewees and the interviewers.[4] The time expended on each interview varied, according to the willingness of each interviewee to allocate time, from 30 minutes to over an hour. The results of the survey form the basis of the information presented in this essay, following a brief introduction to the relationships between business and politics in provincial areas.

BUSINESS AND POLITICS IN THE PROVINCES

Fred Riggs characterized Thailand as a 'bureaucratic polity', a concept which included a theorization of the relationship between business and government. In summary, he saw business as having little influence over government, arguing that the political elite 'is not politically responsible to the business community, [and] there is no reason to think that it would want to adopt or enforce any general rules protecting the business interests of the businessmen'.[5] For Riggs, writing in the early 1960s, business and politics was essentially carried out in Bangkok, with the provinces being relatively unimportant. With the significant exceptions of tin and rubber in the South and timber in the North, this was probably an accurate picture. There was, moreover, a general assumption that business in the provinces, and the relationship between provincial business and government, was like Bangkok only smaller and more backward.

This perspective on business consolidated an intellectual position which imagined Thailand's society as loosely structured; politics was seen to revolve around a politicized elite which presided over the vast apolitical mass. Hierarchy and status were important factors in binding the mass to the elite through a vast network of patron–client relations. The political elite was dominated by civil and military bureaucrats, who took a predatory attitude towards business, which was composed of people of Chinese origin who often were not integrated into the ruling political structure. Business was very much in the position of a client in its relations with state officials.

Virtually no informed contemporary author would want to argue that business is so totally subordinate to government as this model implies. Instead, Anek Laothamatas has shown that business has become a significant political player through interest-based lobbying. He noted that in 1987 there were more than 200 Bangkok-based trade associations and chambers of commerce, and that there had been a rapid expansion of provincial chambers. In 1979 there had been only four of the latter, but by 1987 there were 72, one in each province. The formation of many of these chambers has been at government initiative, although there is a stated determination to enhance their independence.[6]

In recent years a formal mechanism of business–government relations has also been established in the form of the Joint Public-Private Consultative Committee (JPPCC). This body was formed in 1981, after years of attempts to formalize the relationship between the bureaucracy, government, and business. The JPPCC, whose role has been emphasized by Krayudht Dhiratayakinant, included the prime minister, the ministers responsible for economic matters, and representatives of banking, industry, and commerce associations, and was provided with a secretariat within the National Economic and Social Development Board.[7] Similar provincial committees were also encouraged, with the financial support of a US aid project.[8]

The emphasis on private interest lobbies by Anek and Kraiyudht represents an essentially instrumentalist approach to capital–state relations, characteristic of pluralist and corporatist theory. The perspective is useful and such relations are indeed important, but structural constraints and imperatives upon state officials should not be overlooked.[9] For example, the fact that the economy is now unambiguously capitalist means that state officials must be more and more cognisant of the general interests of capital, for these interests are increasingly those of the fiscal agencies of the state.

Less formal, but arguably as significant, is the changing relationship between business people and state officials, especially but not exclusively in the provinces. Contrary to the predatory relationship of bureaucrats to business implied by the bureaucratic polity model, business and government have long had a symbiotic relationship, each drawing on the strengths of the other.[10] As social and economic transformation has taken place, and especially as electoral politics developed in the 1980s and 1990s, the role of 'money politics' has become increasingly significant. Much press and increasing academic attention has thus been given to the phenomenon of 'godfathers' or 'dark influences' (*chao pho* or *itthiphon muet*).[11] It is all too easy to focus on this small and infamous group, important and puissant as it is, while ignoring the more thoroughgoing changes affecting provincial business. Not all business people are *chao pho*, and it needs to be remembered that the transformations that have increased the power of the *chao pho* have also created a significant provincial business class. In what follows, it is only possible to outline some aspects of these relationships, in providing a context for Khon Kaen.

Provincial business groups have developed at a crucial economic conjuncture. No discussion of Thailand's exceptional economic growth until 1997 is required here, except to note that regional GDP growth has also been rapid, and that agricultural diversification over the last three to four decades enhanced the scope for considerable surplus extraction in the countryside. This has meant increased opportunities for the accumulation of wealth in provincial towns and cities. Anderson has noted the swift expansion of provincial business and has commented that these entrepreneurs have developed lifestyles which are 'competitive with those of locally stationed state officials' and that they have 'put down strong local roots, social as well as commercial', in contrast to officials, who are regularly transferred, and who rarely develop such ties. Many, and especially the local *chao pho*, have become immensely wealthy, with no area of economic activity outside their influence.[12]

Politically, rural areas have become increasingly significant. In part, this has had to do with the expansion of the rural economy and of the state apparatus, making the roles of those at the nexus of relations between the local and national levels increasingly complex and significant.[13] Arguably more consequential, however, has been the development of electoral politics, for money has become the single most important factor in electoral success.[14] This began in the 1970s, when Kukrit Pramoj's elected government placed greater emphasis on local-level funding, which many villagers saw as a benefit provided by elected politicians. Later policies on decentralization and local development funding tended to reinforce this perspective, and also showed the benefits which might flow to local contractors from local-level development policies. Of course, money, business, and politics had long been linked at the national level, but there was a coincidence of this with the emergence of electoral politics at the local and provincial level. The expansion of parliamentary representation has meant that rural areas have become crucial bases for virtually all political parties. The tremendous impact of money politics on parties and electors has meant that business is entrenched in the political system – in parties, as political funders, and as candidates and elected members of parliament.[15]

The data aggregated in Table 8.1 clearly indicate that people with a business background are now, as Somkiat says, 'the most important group in the Thai electoral system, at both the national and local levels'.[16] While provincial and municipal councils are not particularly powerful or prestigious, and are often controlled by governors and

Table 8.1: Business people and electoral politics

Occupation	National Parliament (Sept. 1992) %	Provincial Council (Oct. 1990) %	Municipal Council (Sept. 1990) %
Trade/business	45.5	61.6	61.6
Official	11.1	3.0	10.0
Lawyer	10.3	5.9	n.a.*
Politician	19.7	n.a.*	n.a.*
Farmer	2.8	19.8	6.1
Labourer	2.7	8.5	9.3
Other	7.8	1.2	13.0
Total number	360	2,046	1,842

*__Note__: These categories not listed.

Source: National data are from Khana kammakan tittam lae sotsong dulae kan luaktang samachik sapha phutaen ratsadon, *kan luaktang samachik sapha phutaen ratsadon* (Bangkok: Khana thamngan fai wichakan, 1992), p. 117; while the provincial and municipal data are from Somkiat Wanthana, 'Nak thurakit thongthin kap prachathippatai thai'. Paper presented to the 3rd Annual Conference of the Center for Political Economy, Chulalongkorn University, 18–19 November 1992, pp. 4–6.

district officers, they are increasingly seen as an arena of legitimate political activity.

The pattern of seeking financial support from business has meant that the *chao pho* are finding their positions and wealth legitimized, even when gained through illegal activities. This is happening through their support of legal parties and the linking of representative politics and democracy. Arguably more significant than money, the *chao pho* and business people provide the organization and networks required for electoral politics. For example, the underground lottery, played in every village, requires an extensive local network, while local traders and agents enter villages on a regular basis. These networks were 'offered' to aspiring politicians, bestowing increased influence on the local business people controlling these networks.[17]

The Northeast region provides a good example of these links. The region has the largest number of potential voters in the country, and is therefore important to any political party wishing to form a government. This is undoubtedly why army commander General Chavalit Yongchaiyudh emphasized the economic and social development of the region (the Green Northeast Project) when establishing his party political base there in the late 1980s. Both *chao pho* and business people were courted by Chavalit's New Aspiration Party (NAP, Phak Khwan Wang Mai). The combination of these political and economic conjunctures means that the *chao pho* are often all-powerful in the provinces. Thus, when Khon Kaen's Charoen Phattanadamronchit (*Sia* Leng) was shot by rivals, some criticized the then military supreme commander for visiting him in hospital. However, the Supreme Command Headquarters responded that the visit was justified as *Sia* Leng had assisted the army's Green Isan Project. Other businessmen-politicians have been elected to parliament or had their puppets elected.[18]

It is thus clear that business people have carved out a more significant and public political role for themselves. Prior to examining these issues in relationship to the group surveyed, we should look briefly at the context in which they operate.

The Northeast and Khon Kaen

The Northeast has been considered the poorest and least developed region of the country. Ethnic difference, remoteness from Bangkok, and poverty have been its best-known attributes. Historically, the region's significance was as a buffer between the Siamese kingdom and, first, the Cambodian, Vietnamese and Lao kingdoms, and later French colonialism. Even so, the Northeast remained isolated from Bangkok, and it was only in the 1960s, with the rise of a communist insurgency in the region, that the government felt impelled to expand economic development and central control. The state's development and counter-insurgency efforts saw, for example, the rapid development of the road network, directed at ending the isolation of villages from central government officials, while upland cropping and logging were promoted to reduce the base areas of the communists. In addition, the use of bases by the US military brought a new edge to the regional economy and to the security issue.[19]

The decline of the insurgency after 1980 did not reduce the political significance of the Northeast, as the rise of electoral politics meant that votes were important, and in this the region offered great promise. The Northeast is the most populous region of the country, with 21 million people (about one-third of the nation's total population), of whom about 6 per cent were officially recorded as living in municipal areas. The population is dominated ethnically by lowland Lao, although there is a remarkable diversity of ethnic groups. In the southern provinces of the Northeast there are large numbers of Khmer, and a rich variety of smaller ethnic groups may be found scattered throughout the hill areas, while Vietnamese are found in towns along the Mekong River. Urban areas include Siamese (Central Thai), Chinese or Sino-Thai, Khmer and Lao.

Even though the political spotlight has increasingly fallen on the Northeast, the region has remained in the economic shadows, even when national growth rates have been exceptionally high. While absolute poverty has been reduced, wealth disparities have widened, with rural income growth rates being lower than in urban areas. This pattern is illustrated by a comparison of the population and productivity across the regions (see Table 8.2). In 1993, in per capita terms, GDP in the Northeast was less than one-third of the national figure and less than one-tenth the figure for Bangkok.[20] In most provinces a similar pattern of disparity exists between the provincial capitals and rural areas.[21] Northeastern Thailand continues to rely heavily on agricultural production, which accounts for about one-third of the region's Gross Regional Product (GRP). Manufacturing, the most productive sector in national terms, accounts for only about 13–14

Table 8.2: Regional productivity, 1993

Region	% of Population	% of GDP
Bangkok	16.2	55.3
Central	16.9	16.7
Northeast	34.3	10.6
North	18.9	9.1
South	13.7	8.2

Source: Thailand Development Research Institute, *Thailand Economic Information Kit* (Bangkok: TDRI, 1995)

per cent, and much of this consists of the processing of agricultural commodities.[22]

There were, however, some important changes taking place in the business sector in the 1990s. For example, Thailand's trade with Laos, Cambodia and Vietnam increased substantially. This was facilitated by the improvement of transportation links, including the completion of the Mekong River Bridge in 1994.[23] It was clear to even the casual observer that major regional centres like Nakhon Ratchasima, Ubon Ratchathani, Khon Kaen and Udon Thani, saw considerable growth in the early and mid 1990s, with new hotels being constructed in each of these cities, and shopping centres being built and expanded. This is confirmed in data from the Bank of Thailand, which shows growth of 6.4 per cent in 1991 and 5.7 per cent in 1992, with the non-agricultural sector growing at rates in excess of 7 per cent.[24] While much of this expansion could be attributed to Thailand's own dynamics, there was undoubtedly economic growth related to trade with Indochina. Indeed, the government emphasized the region's pivotal position as the gateway to Indochina.[25] It remains clear, however, that without further state efforts to decentralize development, income and wealth disparities between Bangkok and the Northeast will remain a problem.

Khon Kaen province is located 450 km to the northeast of Bangkok, and had a total provincial population of 1.69 million (49.9 per cent female) in 1991, making it the fifth largest in the country; it has a population density of about 156 persons/sq km.[26] The Gross Provincial Product of Khon Kaen was estimated at 22 billion baht in 1988 (the most recent figures available), or about 12 per cent of the total for the whole of the Northeast, with 20 per cent from agriculture and more than 18 per cent from industry. Per capita income was estimated to be 13,507 baht. Growth accelerated in subsequent years, especially during the period of the Chatichai government (1988–1991), which coincided with a big jump in both domestic and foreign investment.

Table 8.3 indicates this rise in economic growth, and also the importance of industry to it, a pattern matching that for the rest of the country. The expansion and establishment of factories in Khon Kaen have been rapid, as the growth figures suggest, with 264 factories being set up between 1987 and 1991, and a further 143 being expanded. (In 1991 there were 4,505 factories registered in the province, although 79 per cent of these were rice mills.)

Table 8.3: Growth Rates in Khon Kaen, 1984–1992 (%)

Sector	Average 1984–88	1987	1988	1989	1990*	1991*	1992*
Overall growth	4.0	8.0	11.6	9.7	7.0	6.7	6.9
Agriculture	1.4	-3.8	13.4	7.4	3.8	3.5	3.7
Industry	8.4	11.6	22.0	16.7	9.0	8.0	10.0
Trade	2.6	4.2	7.5	9.7	4.5	3.0	3.2
Services	5.2	11.4	7.0	8.1	5.5	5.5	5.7

*__Note__: 1990–1992 rates are estimates.

Source: Research Section, Northeastern Branch, Bank of Thailand, 'Khruangchi phawa setthakit lae longthun thi samkhan khong changwat khon kaen', undated briefing paper.

This rapid growth has also seen the city expanding, with the area under construction having doubled each year from 1988 to 1993. This has been partly fuelled by Khon Kaen's status as a financial and trade centre for the region, with 45 branches of 14 commercial banks operating, together with an office of the Industrial Finance Corporation of Thailand. In 1991 loans by commercial banks centred on the commercial trade sector, with 33 per cent of loans going to this area, compared to 23 per cent to industry and just 11 per cent to agriculture. Industrial development was officially recognized in the

7th National Development Plan (1992–1996), which acknowledged Khon Kaen as an industrial centre for the Northeast.

The rise of representative politics has seen the electoral spotlight fall on Khon Kaen as a particularly populous province of the Northeast. Because it has a large population of eligible voters, it is seen as a crucial province for national political parties aspiring to ministerial seats in Bangkok. It has also been a centre for a more populist style of political activity, as the obvious poverty of many farmers has lent itself to promises of a better future and pork-barrelling campaigns.[27]

A PROFILE OF KHON KAEN'S YOUNG BUSINESS PEOPLE

As noted above, the small group interviewed in this study was chosen because they portray the new generation of provincial business, perhaps challenging the status quo. It was felt that their political actions, ideology, and business activities might indicate significant divergences from those of their parents' generation, and could show the future of provincial business. The personal attributes of these people have been discussed in detail elsewhere, so are merely summarized here.[28]

Of the 20 persons interviewed, 16 (80%) were males and four (20%) females; they ranged in age from 26 to 52 years, with an average of 37 years. Only six of the respondents remained single, and two were divorced. The majority of the group matured during the politically turbulent decade of the 1970s, and many were undoubtedly influenced by the events of 1973 and 1976.[29]

They show a slightly different cultural pattern from the widely noted one of overwhelmingly Chinese or Sino-Thai dominance. Somkiat has noted that 90 per cent of a sample of the 206 economically most powerful provincial business people were second-generation Chinese.[30] As is widely reported in the academic literature, Thailand's business people are overwhelmingly Chinese or Sino-Thai. However, the 20 younger-generation interviewees in this study, while almost all from ethnically Chinese or Sino-Thai families, appear more 'Thai' than their parents and more 'local' in their personal and business orientation. All the interviewees were born in Thailand, 70 per cent of them in the Northeast. Only one respondent's spouse was not born in Thailand, whereas for the parents' generation, 30–40 per cent were born outside Thailand, mostly in China, and 30 per cent of marriages involved immigrant Chinese. For the new generation, family association with Khon Kaen is long, averaging 42 years in 1992–1993. Today, the new generation is often identified as 'local', and the respondents tend to view themselves in this way also.

This move away from identifiably Chinese attributes is also clear when language is considered. The Thai language is now predominant, both within the family and for business purposes. The Central Thai taught in schools is now the most common commercial language, used by all respondents. Spoken Chinese was used by 65%, but only 30% claimed to be literate in Chinese, ranking it below English. Even at home these people are likely to use Thai (80%) rather than Chinese, the latter tending to be reserved for use with elderly parents. By contrast, the parent's generation was far less familiar with Thai and the northeastern dialect, and far more likely to use a Chinese language (up to 70%). It is not possible to draw firm conclusions regarding 'Chinese-ness' from a small survey. However, this study suggests that Ueda's comment, based on a survey of business leaders in Korat, that 'it seems that their consciousness of being Chinese is decreasing', also holds true for the business people of Khon Kaen.[31]

Education has also played a significant role in this process of 'Thai-ification'. The new generation is overwhelmingly Thai-educated and very well educated by any measure. The results of the survey show that only one of the new generation has had a Chinese education, whereas this was more common for their parents. While formal education was not an important attribute for the older generation, they apparently saw that it was crucial for their children, believing that successful people in modern Thailand require education. None of the younger generation has had less than nine years of formal schooling, and 60 per cent of respondents have a university qualification, as do about 42 per cent of their spouses. Not one of the older generation held a university degree or diploma (compared to 12.5 per cent of Northeastern business people reported by Somkiat).[32] The great importance attributed to education is applied to all children of the respondents' generation, with women more likely to have a university education than men (66 as opposed to 51 per cent respectively). The respondents had studied in a range of locations, with 65 per cent receiving education outside the Northeast, mainly in Bangkok. Education has tended to 'nationalize' and 'internationalize' the outlook of these people, which is clearly important for the world of modern business. Also important are the contacts made through higher education, which are often used later in business.

THE YOUNG GENERATION'S BUSINESS ACTIVITIES

The respondents are overwhelmingly the children of traders and merchants. Thus they are from business families and are not embarking on any new economic path, as their parents or grandparents might have done. While the kinds of activity may not be the same as their parents', they are clearly drawing on their family's business experience. They have also concentrated their activities in the Northeast, their home region.

In terms of the kinds of business entered by the respondents and their families, the range was remarkably wide, with 39 family businesses being reported, and 53 claimed by the respondents themselves, incorporating 41 different business activities, mainly in the trade and service sectors (see Table 8.4). Significantly, very few of these businesses are in manufacturing.[33] A notable exception was an agricultural machinery factory: not only is this one of the largest industrial plants in

Table 8.4: Business activities of respondents and families

	Respondents		Families	
Business	**No.**	**%**	**No.**	**%**
Wholesale & retail trade	12	22.6	17	43.6
Vehicle & machinery parts & sales	8	14.8	6	15.4
Construction & constr. materials	4	7.5	3	7.7
Timber milling & export	1	1.9	3	7.7
Hotels & restaurants	5	9.4	3	7.7
Entertainment	10	18.9	1	2.6
Transport & fuels	4	7.5	1	2.6
Rice milling	0	0.0	2	5.1
Medical services	0	0.0	3	7.7
Land and housing	2	3.8	0	0.0
Manufacturing	3	5.7	0	0.0
Other	4	7.5	0	0.0

Note: Multiple responses were possible.

Khon Kaen, with 1,600 employees, but it was established and is owned and managed by one of the few women in the surveyed group. Interestingly, it operates almost entirely as an import-substituting industry, manufacturing products of good quality at affordable prices, and suitable for the local population.

When asked why it was that most investments were outside the manufacturing and productive sector, a common initial response referred to the ease of making a profit in the service and entertainment area. However, it was also noted that commercial banks assessed provincial enterprise as being a greater risk than Bangkok businesses, and demanded more collateral and higher interest rates. This has been confirmed by Thailand's Board of Trade, which has argued that more government incentives must be provided if decentralization is to be successful.[34] It was also claimed that the banks often pushed business people to the service area, where short-term profits were usually expected to be better than other sectors. In addition, provincial business people bemoaned their lack of adequate information and access to technology to allow them to move into higher value-added areas.

SOCIAL ROLES

Many years ago Skinner pointed out the importance of social and community activities in linking Chinese business people together in vast networks.[35] These roles are seen as necessary for important and wealthy people, being both the mark of membership in a dominant class and an important element in maintaining class solidarity. The new generation continues to place significance on these roles, for 85 per cent of respondents reported that they or their families took major social or community positions. But it is noticeable that they apparently place less importance on Chinese groups and emphasize business and industry associations, as indicated in Table 8.5, with a fuller list presented in Appendix 1. This appears to confirm other information on the increasing significance of these associations.[36]

The respondents and their families held at least 45 committee-level or higher offices in these associations, indicating that these people are identified as holding high social positions. Interestingly, in the Chinese associations most offices were held by members of the parents' generation. It remains to be seen whether the new generation will take over these positions, but their significance certainly appears to be declining relative to that of business, industry and service associations.

Table 8.5: Reported association memberships

Association	No. of Members
Business & industry	23
Community service	18
Chinese	10
Social/charities	8
Other	5

Note: Multiple responses were possible.

While it is true that many of these business and industry associations have been fostered by the state, it is also clear that in many provinces they have been able to develop a degree of autonomy. Khon Kaen is no exception; while the various associations and chambers are prohibited by their charters and various laws from engaging in 'political activity', there is no doubt that they now have considerable political influence. The various associations are capable of taking up issues of concern to members with both provincial and national policy-makers, often with a degree of success. For example, following the first-ever cabinet meeting held in the Northeast in 1989, the Khon Kaen and Udon Thani Chambers of Commerce criticized the government, demanding more support for private enterprise and a reduction in bureaucratic 'red tape'.[37]

One of the reasons for the influence of such groups is that they have come to be seen as a legitimate forum for business people to lobby on economic policy. In Khon Kaen, the local Chamber of Commerce had an individual membership of 459 at the end of 1992, taking in a wide range of business activities.[38] Just the size of this organization and the breadth of its membership in a major provincial centre mean that it must be influential, both amongst its members and with officials and politicians. Indeed, in most social and economic activities sponsored by the government, provincial authorities will routinely consult with the chamber.

POLITICAL ROLES

Respondents were generally not so willing to speak of their political activities, for 60 per cent claimed no *personal* political role or interest, while about half declared that their *family* took no political roles. Of those 13 who did claim political involvement – defined as having participated in elections (by standing or actively supporting a candidate) or having taken positions in political parties or the various city and town councils – eight expressed interest in politics at the local or community level and five at the national level. (Appendix 2 provides a more detailed listing.)

Based on other research results, it might have been expected that there would be a greater political involvement from this group of economically influential persons. For example, Somkiat notes that in the data he had for provincial business people, about 12 per cent had been MPs, while a further 8 per cent had been provincial or municipal council members. In addition, Somrudee's report suggests that locally influential persons had expressed a willingness for their family to become involved in local politics.[39] Given that the survey occurred in a turbulent period, there may well have been a degree of under-reporting. However, it is worth noting that a purely instrumental search for political involvement may under-estimate the real political power of provincial business people. When the combined economic and social roles of Khon Kaen business people are considered, it would seem that the members of the group are in close contact with one another and with other decision-makers in the city on virtually a daily basis, and that they have a very cohesive network of influence. It is clear that they have good political contacts at the local level. Nationally, while not all are involved, connections can also be made reasonably easily. When in late 1992 a Khon Kaen MP became a minister, this was seen to bring great benefit to the town and its business community, especially in facilitating national-level contacts. In addition, the centrality of economic development to national and provincial government policy means that the interests of business are seldom ignored by government, whether at the local, provincial, or national level.

In fact, the expansion of local involvement in political activity appears to be in line with the recent government desire to open channels of communication with the population. For example, at a seminar on Problems in Business–State Relations in the Isan Region held in Nakhon Ratchasima on 9 January 1993, then minister without portfolio Savit Bhotiwihok stated that the Chuan Leekpai government intended to bring the private sector into official provincial development committees, by inviting representatives from commercial banks and the chambers of commerce. He further urged that provincial business people not wait to have the ear of influential ministers, but should make their problems known to local MPs, the provincial Joint Public-Private Consultative Committee, and their chambers of commerce. At the same seminar Peerapol Triyakasem, a Bangkok-based Indochina investment adviser who was close to former Prime Minister Chatichai Choonhavan, exhorted provincial business people to support democratic government, as it was the political wave of the future for business. He further urged them to cut their links to the military. 'National security', he said, 'comes from having the citizenry behind the state'. Indeed, provincial business people are being encouraged, by activists and Bangkok-based business people as well, to expand their political roles.

INFLUENCE AND POWER IN KHON KAEN

The respondents were also asked to identify the people or groups they considered to be of most political and economic significance in Khon Kaen.[40] It was anticipated that this would indicate something about their perceptions of power and might also identify groups for further research. Interestingly, when speaking of significance in the economic sphere, a long list of some 76 different groups and individuals was generated; but only 12 of these were listed by more than two of the interviewees, and three of these emerged as clearly dominant (see Table 8.6). Of the top five groups listed in this table, four were involved in this survey through the new generation or their close relatives.

Table 8.6: Perceptions of economic significance in Khon Kaen

Person/Group	Businesses and positions	No.	%
Vinyu Kuwanan	Kowyoo-ha Group and president, Khon Kaen Chamber of Commerce	16	21.1
Charoen Phattanadamrongchit	Charoen Group and well known businessman (*Sia* Leng)	14	18.4
Fairy Plaza	Department stores	10	13.2
Raja Group	Manufacturers of agric. machinery	5	6.6
Kaen Inn Hotel	Hotel	3	3.9
Others	Various	28	36.8

The two major economic powers are nationally significant players. Vinyu Kuwanan has extensive business interests, mainly in the Northeast, but spread throughout Thailand. These businesses include vehicle distribution and sales, agricultural trading and marketing, insurance, hotels and travel. Charoen Phattanadamrongchit's business interests are in agricultural trading, marketing and export, agricultural credit, hotels, construction, and alcohol sales. He is known to be involved in many other highly profitable, *chao pho*-type ventures in the Northeast.[41]

The list of politically influential persons was far shorter, with only seven being mentioned. Of these, only three were mentioned by more than one respondent (see Table 8.7). Not one of the interviewees mentioned any government officials in the politically influential group, all of whose members are wealthy business people or current or former MPs.

Table 8.7: Politically influential persons

Person/Group	Position	No.	%
Suwit Khunkitti	MP and then minister of justice	15	40.5
Charoen Phattanadamrongchit	Businessman	9	24.3
Adison Piengket	MP	9	24.3
Vinyu Kuwanan	Businessman and president, Khon Kaen Chamber of Commerce	1	2.7
Former MPs	—	2	5.4
New Aspiration Party	Political party with focus on Northeast	1	2.7

Only two persons appear on both lists – Vinyu and Charoen. Vinyu's political involvement is reasonably open, as he is known to give support to certain parties, but he is not particularly well known outside the local area. If Vinyu maintains a reasonably low profile, this is certainly not the case for Charoen, who is well known for his *chao pho* style and political influence. He is courted by political parties and candidates, and tends to support these on the basis of his assessment of the individuals involved and his own interest, rather than a particular party or ideological position. While operating in quite different ways, both Vinyu and Charoen are significant political players;

they possess the networks which political parties need to draw on and they have large amounts of money to assist parties and candidates.

It is significant that the only reference to a government official was in the economic list, where the provincial governor was mentioned by only one respondent, as was the manager of the northeastern branch of the national bank. This is not what would have been expected by the researchers, as the governor has traditionally been considered to be all-powerful. However, as far as the business people interviewed were concerned, officials are no longer considered to have great political clout.

An explanation for this can be derived from Somkiat's discussion. He notes that certain kinds of provincial business demand an especially close relationship with 'the centres of power'. His view, supported by Sombat, is that businesses involved in the extraction of natural resources (timber, gems, minerals), building and engineering contracting, and those acting as alcohol sales agents must have close relations with officials.[42] The business groups surveyed in Khon Kaen indicated relatively few enterprises in these areas. If this were to hold true for a larger sample it might suggest that, as business develops, it moves away from activities that depend on relationships with state officials and the issue of licences. It would imply a movement towards involvement in electoral politics rather than a reliance on personal relationships with influential officials. The latter still occur, but are no longer so crucial to the success or failure of business.

From this small sample it appears that the new generation is more likely to engage *directly* in politics rather than to operate in the manner of the *chao pho*. With the balance of power in provincial politics apparently shifting away from officials such as the governor and district officers, there are increased opportunities for business people to enter politics at the local and national level. While the *chao pho* tended to operate as influential persons, often behind the scenes, paying off and buying support, the new generation seems to prefer to have family members involved or to support acceptable and local candidates and, increasingly, parties. This changing balance may well reflect the development of provincial economies, with illegal activities being reduced and the business opportunities requiring the support of officials assuming less significance. Political activity will need to respond to this regularization of the economic sphere. However, given the significance of money politics, it is unlikely that the *chao pho* will become political dinosaurs in the near future.

The political outcome is by no means certain, and will depend very much on the further development of representative political institutions. After the May 1992 uprising against military involvement in politics, it appeared that the interests of provincial business people were in further establishing popular representation. The provinces were to be crucial to this process, assisting the creation of a better electoral system, expanding the role of elected representatives, and developing methods for grassroots participation. However, subsequent elections have indicated that the growing significance of money politics in the electoral process is limiting representation and leading to a financially unsustainable form of parliamentary rule. This relies heavily on the involvement of local business people, who appear to favour buying votes and politicians over securing popular agreement through the democratic process. This threatens to widen even further the political divide between rural villagers and urban middle-class voters. The 1997 constitution was meant to ameliorate this, but it will not be until the 2000 election that this reform becomes effective.

NOTES

1. For the historical development of the provincial economy, see Plai-oh Chananon, *Phokha kap phatthanakan rabop thunniyom nai phak nua pho. so. 2464–2523* (Bangkok: Chulalongkorn University Social Research Institute, n.d.); and Jennifer W. Cushman, *Family and State. The Formation of a Sino-Thai Tin-Mining Dynasty* (Singapore: Oxford University Press, 1991). Studies of recent developments, in addition to those collected in this publication, include Niran Thongban, *200 setthi muang thai (phumiphak)* (Bangkok: Bonsai Group, n.d.); Jonathan Leightner, 'On the Periphery of Phenomenal Growth: Lampang, Thailand in 1981, 1991, and in the Future', *Journal of Southeast Asian Business* 8 (1992): 47–58; Somkiat Wanthana, 'Nak thurakit thongthin kap prachathippatai thai', paper presented to the 3rd Annual Conference of the Center for Political Economy, Chulalongkorn University, 18–19 November 1992; Yoko Ueda, 'The Entrepreneurs of Khorat', this volume; Somrudee Nicrowattanayingyong, 'Local Businessmen and Political Contest outside Bangkok', paper presented to the Fifth International Conference on Thai Studies, London, July 1993; and Somrudee, 'Thailand's NIC Democracy: Studying from General Elections', *Pacific Affairs* 66 (1993): 167–218.

2. On the Philippines, see Rosanne Rutten, 'Provincial Entrepreneurs in Philippine Crafts', *Philippine Studies* 40 (1992): 497. For China, see William Mellor, 'A Border Bonanza', *Asia Inc.* (November 1993): 38–47.

3. See J. A. C. Mackie, 'Overseas Chinese Entrepreneurship', *Asian-Pacific Economic Literature* 6 (1992): 41–64.

4. The research began prior to the bloody events of May 1992, when pro-democracy demonstrators forced out a military-dominated regime. Many have argued that the revolt represented the triumph of a 'middle class' which was itself born of the expansion of business. As these events also spread to provincial centres, it drew attention to the role of local business in the developing economy and representative political system. See Somkiat, 'Nak thurakit thongthin', pp. 1–2.

5. Fred W. Riggs, *Thailand: The Modernization of a Bureaucratic Polity* (Honolulu: East–West Center Press, 1966), p. 252; emphasis in the original. Critiques of the long-popular, but now increasingly inappropriate bureaucratic polity model may be found in Kevin Hewison, *Power and Politics in Thailand: Essays in Political Economy* (Manila: Journal of Contemporary Asia Publishers, 1989), Ch. 2; Kevin Hewison, *Bankers and Bureaucrats. Capital and the Role of the State in Thailand* (New Haven: Yale Center for International and Area Studies, Yale University Southeast Asian Monograph No. 34, 1989), pp. 7–13; and Yoshifumi Tamada, '*Itthiphon* and *Amnat*: An Informal Aspect of Thai Politics', *Tonan Ajia Kenkyu* 28 (1991): 455–457. For the view which accepts the model but sees it as not 'fitting' con-temporary realities, see Anek Laothamatas, *Business Associations and the New Political Economy of Thailand. From Bureaucratic Polity to Liberal Corporatism* (Singapore: Institute of Southeast Asian Studies, and Boulder. Col.: Westview Press, 1992), Ch. 1.

6. Anek Laothamatas, 'Business and Politics in Thailand: New Patterns of Influence', *Asian Survey* 28 (1988): 456–459. For a more detailed discussion see Anek, *Business Associations.*

7. Kraiyudht Dhiratayakinant, 'Role of the Private Sector in the Thai Economy: Now and in the Future', in Suchart Prasith-rathsint (ed.) *Thailand on the Move: Stumbling Blocks and Breakthroughs* (Bangkok: Thai University Research Association, 1990), p. 117.

8. Anek, 'Business and Politics in Thailand', p. 460.

9. For a critique of neo-pluralist approaches, see Kevin Hewison, 'Liberal Corporatism and the Return of Pluralism in Thai Political Studies', *Asian Studies Review,* 16 (1992): 261–265. For more on structuralism related to Thailand, see Hewison, *Power and Politics in Thailand,* Ch. 2.

10. Tamada, '*Itthiphon* and *Amnat*', p. 456, refers to a symbiotic relationship, specifically rejecting the patron–client construction.

11. *Chao pho* are important local business people whose leverage is based on both their businesses and their control of not-so-legal enterprises involving prostitution, gaming, murder, drugs, logging, land encroachment, weapons trade, smuggling, and protection rackets. Both Turton and Anderson note the increased political significance of these persons in recent decades, but neither says much about their role in business – see Andrew Turton,

'Limits of Ideological Domination and the Formation of Social Consciousness', in Andrew Turton and Shigeharu Tanabe (eds), *History and Peasant Consciousness in South East Asia* (Osaka: National Museum of Ethnology, 1984), pp. 56–59; and Benedict Anderson, 'Murder and Progress in Modern Siam', *New Left Review*, 181 (1990): 33–48. The significance of such groups has been examined in Pasuk Phongpaichit and Sungsidh Piriyarangsan (eds), *Rat, thun, chao pho thongthin kap sangkhom thai* (Bangkok: Political Economy Center, Chulalongkorn University, 1992).

12. Anderson, 'Murder and Progress', pp. 39–40. See also Rodney Tasker, 'Time for a Cosy Chat', *Far Eastern Economic Review* [hereafter *FEER*], 18 April 1991: 25–26.

13. On the impact for villages, see R. A. Hall, 'Middlemen in the Politics of Rural Thailand: A Study of Articulation and Cleavage', *Modern Asian Studies* 14 (1980): 441–464.

14. Khana kammakan tittam lae sotsong dulae kan luaktang samachik sapha phutaen ratsadon, *Kan luaktang samachik sapha phutaen ratsadon* (Bangkok: Khana thamngan fai wichakan, 1992), pp. 114–118; and Somrudee, 'Thailand's NIC Democracy'.

15. Khana kammakan tittam, *Kan luaktang*, pp. 114–118. During the 1988 election, one commercial bank estimated that 'money-dumping' would exceed 3,000 million baht – see *The Nation*, 6 June 1988.

16. Somkiat, 'Nak thurakit thongthin', p. 6.

17. Somrudee, cited in Sombat Chantornvong, 'Botbat khong chao pho thongthin nai setthakit lae kanmuang thai: khoseno sangket buangdon', in Pasuk and Sangsit (eds), *Rat, thun, chao pho*, p. 119. The political role of local traders may well have been strengthened by the fact that many have been seen as responsive to village and local needs. Charles Keyes noted this receptiveness 25 years ago – cited in Hall, 'Middlemen', p. 461.

18. Prakarn Saen-Ubol, 'The Strange Political Conversion of *Sia* Leng', *The Nation*, 16 July 1995. *Sia* Leng, who felt that Chavalit's party had not taken sufficient heed of his views, shifted his support to the Nam Thai Party in the 1995 elections. Nam Thai thereupon won all three Khon Kaen seats. *Sia* is a Chinese derived term signifying wealth and power.

19. See Ueda, this volume, and Prachoom Chomchai, *The United States, the Mekong Committee and Thailand* (Bangkok: Institute of Asian Studies, Chulalongkorn University, 1994).

20. Thailand Development Research Institute, *Thailand Economic Information Kit* (Bangkok: TDRI, 1995).

21. Somrudee, 'Local Businessmen', p. 1.

22. Rachen Chinthayarangsan, 'Kankrachai utsahakam bai su tang changwat', *Warasan phattana borihansat* 31 (1991): 32.

23. David Stifel, 'Vietnam's Reform Process: Implications for Thailand', *TDRI Quarterly Review* 7 (1992): 7. The Mekong River Bridge stimulated economic and infrastructural activity in both Laos and Thailand – see Somkiat Osotsapha, 'Important Economic Issues Between Thailand and Vietnam: Policy and Planning Considerations', and Somkiat Osotsapha and Pranit Chotkrittiwet, 'Khomun setthakit chin lae vietnam', papers for the Seminar on Trade and Investment Opportunities in China and Vietnam, Research and Development Institute, Khon Kaen University, 6 January 1993.

24. Data supplied by the Northeastern Branch of the Bank of Thailand in Khon Kaen.

25. *The Nation*, 8 May 1993.

26. Data in this section are drawn from materials supplied by the Research Section of the Bank of Thailand's Northeastern Branch, including: 'Khruangchi phawa setthakit lae longthun thi samkhan khong changwat khonkaen' (Khon Kaen, undated briefing paper); 'Khomun phunthan changwat khonkaen' (Khon Kaen, June 1991); and 'Raingan setthakit lae kanngoen phak tawanok chiengnu'a pi 2534' (Khon Kaen, September 1992).

27. Somrudee, 'Local Businessmen'; and Somrudee, 'Thailand's NIC Democracy'.

28. See Hewison and Maniemai, *The New Generation.*

29. Somkiat, 'Nak thurakit thongthin', p. 2, also mentions the significance of these events for businessmen and the middle class.

30. Ibid.,, p. 26. He bases his paper on data presented in Niran's study.

31. Ueda, this volume.

32. Somkiat, 'Nak thurakit thongthin', pp. 26–27.

33. Given that Khon Kaen is increasingly recognized as an industrial centre, the small number of respondents reporting an interest in manufacturing suggests that further investigations are necessary. Note, however, that a study in Nakhon Ratchasima produced similar results – see Ueda, this volume

34. *The Nation*, 8 May 1993.

35. G. William Skinner, *Leadership and Power in the Chinese Community of Thailand* (Ithaca: Cornell University Press, 1958).

36. Somkiat, 'Nak thurakit thongthin', p. 27, also mentions that about 40 per cent of big provincial business people in the sample he had were members of chambers of commerce. On Nakhon Ratchasima see Ueda, this volume. For a national perspective see Anek's 'Business and Politics in Thailand'; and his *Business Associations.*

37. *Bangkok Post Weekly Review,* 24 November 1989. Ueda, in this volume, notes the political role of the Nakhon Ratchasima Chamber of Commerce.

38. Membership information supplied by the Khon Kaen Chamber of Commerce.

39. Somkiat, 'Nak thurakit thongthin', p. 27; and Somrudee, 'Local Businessmen', p. 14.

40. There has been some debate over the correct term for 'power' in Thai with, for example, Tamada (pp. 455–466) noting the difference between the words and meanings of *itthiphon* and *amnat*. Attempting to recognize this, the questionnaire utilized the term '*thi mi khwam samkhan thisut*' ('having greatest significance or importance') when referring to politics (*'kan muang'*) and business-trade-investment activities (*'thurakit kan kha kan longthun'*).

41. For some comments on Charoen, based on interviews, see Somrudee, 'Local Businessmen', pp. 10–11. Further information can be obtained from Niran, *200 setthi muang thia*, pp. 208–209.

42. Somkiat, 'Nak thurakit thongthin', p. 27; and Sombat, this volume.

APPENDIX 1

Social Association Memberships

(Respondent and Family)

Business and Industry (23)

Chamber of Commerce (8)
Women's Professional Business Group (4)
EBM3 – Alumni of a business management training course (3)
Tourism and Travel Groups (2)
Khon Kaen Branch of Industry Association (2)
Khon Kaen Industrial Council (1)
Small Industry Development Project (1)
Fish Sauce Association of Thailand (1)
Khon Kaen 1991 Business Group (1)

Jaycees/Lions/Rotary (18)

Rotary (8)
Jaycees (6)
Lions (4)

Chinese Associations (10)

Tia-An (Teochiu) Association (3)
Kak-Sung Association (2)
Chao-Ieng Association (1)
Chinese Music Association (1)
Prue-chi Relations Club (1)
Hua Kiew School Alumni Association (1)
Khon Kaen Samakki Utid Foundation (1)

Social and Charitable Associations (8)

Zonta Club (6)
Red Cross (1)
Poor School Children's Fund (1)

Other (5)

Honorary Judge (2)
School Parents' Club (1)
Thammasat University Alumni Association (1)
Pentanque Club (1)

APPENDIX 2

Political Activities

(Respondent and Family)

Local or Community Politics (8)

Membership or former membership of the Municipal Council (*Sapha Tetsaban*) (4)
Supported candidates for election to Municipal Council or unsuccessfully ran as a candidate (2)
Brother is municipality mayor in another province (1)
Member of Provincial Council (*Sapha Changwat*) (1)

National Politics (5)

Support for a member of the family who is an elected MP and a minister (2)
Committee member of the Khon Kaen Branch of the Democrat Party (1)
Support for some or all Khon Kaen candidates for the National Parliament (2)

NINE

BEYOND BANGKOK
The Provincial Middle Class in the 1992 Protests

James P. LoGerfo

Of all the dramatic images to emerge from Thailand's movement for democracy in 1992 – the hunger strikes, the mass demonstrations, the lethal military crackdown, the King's intervention – the one that captured the attention of journalists and academics was that of the white-collar Bangkok professional arriving at Ratchadamnoen Avenue in his BMW to join the democratic struggle, one fist raised in protest, the other clutching that quintessential symbol of prosperity, the mobile phone. Media reporting and scholarly analysis of the May democracy movement have focused on the prominent role played by the Bangkok middle class. The Thai newspapers gave the demonstrators such names as the 'mobile-phone mob' and the 'yoghurt mob'; Thai academics published books like *The Mobile Phone Mob: The Middle Class, Businessmen, and the Development of Democracy*, and *The Middle Class on the Current of Democracy*.[1]

This concentration on the Bangkok middle class has obscured one of the most significant aspects of the May uprising: the emergence of protests in at least 30 provinces both in support of and in opposition to the premiership of General Suchinda Kraprayoon and the constitution promulgated by the military junta. To an extent unprecedented in modern Thai history, those living outside of Bangkok were involved in the contest over the nature of the nation's political regime. This chapter describes the upcountry[2] protest movements, places them in the context of the growth of a middle class with an interest in clean politics and the rise of a network of local and national NGOs, and assesses the role of provincial business people and business organizations in their inception.

This study of the provincial protest movements will describe the upcountry campaigns broadly, making three points:

1. that Bangkok was not alone in experiencing large-scale demonstrations against the military junta but that extensive protest action occurred in provinces throughout the country;
2. that middle-class academics and professionals, along with activist groups and local politicians, led these upcountry movements; and
3. that this middle-class opposition grew out of an interest-based preference for clean politics, anger at Suchinda's violation of his promise not to assume the premiership, and a principled desire for a more democratic system.

Next, results of field research conducted in Nakhon Si Thammarat, Patthalung, and Songkhla in the South, Buriram and Sisaket in the Northeast, and Chiang Mai in the North will be presented. Examination of the protest movements in these provinces yielded five significant findings:

1. Civil society organizations and social networks were vital to the establishment of local movement leadership structures. Of special importance were the branch organizations of the Union for Civil Liberties and the networks created by PollWatch in January–March 1992. Meanwhile, provincial business people and their associations, to the extent that they participated in the movements at all, generally contented themselves with providing support from behind rather than assuming visible leadership.
2. The professional middle class provided the vast majority of the provincial movement leadership. Academics, teachers, lawyers, doctors, and NGO workers played an indispensable role in forming and leading protest movements around the country.
3. Institutes of higher learning, and universities in particular, contributed essential resources to many upcountry campaigns. All three provinces outside Bangkok that hosted a university had protest movements, which centred on those institutions. Teachers' colleges also played a significant role.
4. While provinces of every description experienced protest actions, especially during the second wave of demonstrations from May

17–21, there was at least a rough correlation between a province's level of socio-economic development and the timing, size, and number of protest actions there.

5. While in some provinces we might have expected a high degree of economic dependence on tourism or the affiliation of local MPs to opposition parties to facilitate mobilization, many provinces with the opposite conditions none the less produced strong democracy movements.

The provincial protest movements were important for several reasons. In the uncertain political atmosphere in the months following the May 1992 uprising, a time when there was a real possibility of military action against the newly installed civilian government, any would-be coup-makers had to add to the costs of seizing power in Bangkok the probable need to suppress widespread provincial protest as well. More generally, the movements reveal the political potential created by several decades of rapid economic growth and the more recent emergence of an activist NGO community. Class structure and civil society in the provinces are much more complex now than they were two or three decades ago, and these changes have contributed to the growth of a possible constituency for democracy outside Bangkok.

This chapter will begin by analysing the political regime preferences of the Thai middle class over time, with an eye towards understanding the conditions under which it has supported either dictatorship or democracy. It will then sketch out the events leading up to the outbreak of the protest movements, and detail the emergence of the upcountry campaigns. Next, the results of field research on the protest movements in six provinces will be presented, and the implications discussed. The chapter will conclude by looking at the direction of Thai politics in the seven years after 1992, to see how this may have affected the provincial middle class's political role.

THE POLITICAL REGIME PREFERENCES OF THE THAI MIDDLE CLASS

The Thai middle class is understood here to consist of professionals such as lawyers, teachers, and journalists; middle managers; small and medium capitalists; low- and mid-level government officials; clerks; salespeople; and service workers. Defined negatively, the middle class excludes manual labour, agricultural producers, senior executives, high-ranking civil servants, and large capitalists.[3] The middle class is engaged in mental rather than physical work, at a level generally requiring at least a secondary education and often years of specialized training. In contrast to the upper class, individual members of the middle class do not wield enough power to influence significantly the outcome of policy decisions or political events, and their decisions to withhold or invest capital have no real impact on the national economy. On the other hand, they are sufficiently important to the existing order that their preferences cannot be ignored. Despite the heterogeneity of the middle class, the broad similarities among its segments are significant enough for it to be considered a class 'in itself', even if its diversity might make it difficult for it to act as a class 'for itself'. In terms of it providing a social base for democracy, the provincial movements of 1992 showed that the growth of the professional strata was of primary importance.

Because the middle class in Thailand has historically been ambivalent towards democracy, its vanguard position in the upcountry protests requires explanation. If we review the many regime changes of the last three decades, we find four main factors explaining middle-class support for a particular regime type:

- effectiveness of the government,
- level of political corruption,
- perceptions of threats from below and without, and
- severity of state repression.

Weak or ineffective governments and excessive corruption have turned the middle class against both democratic and authoritarian regimes; the perception of significant threats from the lower classes or the external environment have helped turn the middle class against democratic regimes; and extreme state repression has alienated the middle class from authoritarian rule. What the middle class has shown itself to favour is effective and transparent governance in a context of political stability and relatively limited state controls.

The demonstrations of 6–15 October 1973 against the 'trio of tyrants' Thanom, Praphat, and Narong marked the first time in Thai history that a mass movement emerged to contest the nature of the political regime.[4] The students who led that struggle were the children of the middle and upper class, and the movement received support across the spectrum of the Bangkok populace. Middle-class opposition to the authoritarian Thanom–Praphat regime arose largely from the gross corruption and nepotism of that military government, its ineffectual management of the 1973 rice crisis, and its heavy-handed attempts to shut down the nascent movement for a permanent constitution.

But the same urban middle class whose participation was crucial to the success of October 1973 would three years later welcome the return of dictatorship under Prime Minister Thanin Kraiwichian.[5] Workers and small farmers, supported by increasingly radicalized student activists, took advantage of the more open political environment that prevailed after the fall of Thanom and Praphat to agitate for higher wages and commodity prices, protective legislation, and land reform. The right responded with a campaign of intimidation, violence, and assassination. Even as the middle class was more and more disturbed by growing domestic instability, revolutionary victories in Vietnam, Cambodia, and Laos in 1975, together with the US withdrawal from the region, intensified Thai fears of invasion from abroad and communist insurgency from within. Meanwhile, the democratic regime produced a rapid succession of weak coalition governments unable to mollify the lower classes or rein in the reactionary right. In October 1976 the middle class embraced the restoration of authoritarian rule as an answer to the looming threats from the lower classes and the Indochinese communist armies.

However, the cure proved worse than the disease. Prime Minister Thanin proved to be too repressive even for the military coup group that had installed him. The middle class, along with nearly every other significant group in Thailand, greeted with relief the October 1977 coup that ousted the sternly anti-communist Thanin government and began a gradual process of democratization. During the 1970s, then, the middle class rejected both free-for-all democracy and corrupt or extreme authoritarianism.

The 1977 coup ushered in a long period of stable semi-democratic rule that would last until the military seized power in February 1991. Over the course of the 1980s the collapse of the Thai communist insurgency, the relative quiescence of the lower classes, the end of the Cold War, and improving relations with Indochina lowered the middle class's perception of threat and increased quality of governance as a major factor determining middle-class regime preferences. The decline in internal and external threats coincided with another important political trend: the increasing role of business people and business associations in politics at all levels.[6] But the expanding political involvement of big businessmen brought on twin crises of corruption and legitimacy that reached a peak under the Chatichai government.[7] The leaders of the business-based machine parties – such as Social Action Party (SAP, Kit Sangkhom), Prachakorn Thai, Ekkaparb (Solidarity), and Chatichai's Chart Thai (Chat Thai, Thai Nation Party) – which dominated politics in the 1980s, focused not on building mass support through ideological appeals but on using control over the state apparatus for personal gain as well as for access to public resources for distribution to political supporters. In doing so they increasingly encroached on areas traditionally belonging to the military and the civil service, angering the armed forces.[8]

At the same time, widespread vote-buying in the 1988 elections which brought Chatichai to power undermined the claims of his government to be the legitimate representative of the people. As cabinet ministers used public office to recoup campaigning expenses and enrich themselves and their clients, academics and journalists attacked their corruption and even declared that military authoritarianism would be preferable to rule by businessmen-criminals.[9] Middle-class critics of Chatichai-style democracy effectively formed a coup coalition with the armed forces.

Deteriorating civil-military relations gave the military a motive to seize power, and the corruption of the Chatichai government provided the excuse.[10] On 23 February 1991, a group of senior officers calling themselves the National Peacekeeping Council (NPC) detained Prime Minister Chatichai, declared the constitution null and void, and installed a provisional government in what was Thailand's eighth successful coup since 1932. Initially there was little popular resistance to the NPC. Many among the Bangkok middle class tacitly approved of the military take-over because of their disgust with Chatichai's 'buffet cabinet'.[11] But middle-class acquiescence began changing to opposition in the autumn of 1991 when the military junta revealed its intention to perpetuate its grip on power through the draft constitution. The middle class erupted in a frenzy of protest in May 1992 when its worst fears came true as General Suchinda was named prime minister and the government coalition parties refused to amend the junta-sponsored charter.

The middle class thus supported transitions to democracy in 1973, 1977, and 1992, but welcomed the impositions of authoritarianism in 1976 and 1991. Clearly, its political regime preferences have been deeply ambivalent. However, the middle class has displayed one consistent pattern since at least the mid-1980s: it supports 'clean' politics, meaning a politics in which electoral outcomes and policy decisions are determined by the merits of competing choices rather than the amount of cash spent on buying votes and offering bribes. When the Chatichai government's corruption seemed to pose a choice between either democracy or clean politics, the middle class chose the latter.

The first manifestation of this penchant for clean politics was the election of Major-General Chamlong Srimuang as governor of Bangkok province in 1985.[12] In both private life and public office Chamlong conducted himself according to the highest moral principles. Palang Darma (Phalang Tham), the political party he founded for his followers to contest the 1988 parliamentary elections, required its members to obey four rules of unprecedented strictness: do not buy votes, do not compete for position, do not speak impolitely, and do not cheat. When Chamlong ran for re-election as governor in 1990, Bangkok voters returned him to office with a huge majority.[13] While most of Palang Darma's seats in parliament came from Bangkok, some of its MPs came from upcountry – almost invariably from Election District One, which included the provincial capital and therefore the largest local concentration of the middle class.

The political fortunes of Chamlong and the Palang Darma declined after May 1992, but this was due to the fortunes of political warfare rather a loss of middle-class interest in clean politics. It is significant that the party that benefited the most from Palang Darma's fall from popular grace was the Democrat Party (DP, Prachatipat), Bangkok's traditional favourite. The Democrats have had a long reputation for administrative integrity and opposition to the military. By the mid-1990s, heavily patronage-based parties like Chart Thai, New Aspiration, and Social Action had yet to make political inroads into the capital. This was evidenced by the fact that in the four parliamentary elections held between 1992 and 1996, none of the candidates fielded by these parties in Bangkok won a single victory. The middle class might have withdrawn its support for Chamlong and Palang Darma, but its preference for clean politics remained.

The second 'clean politician' to win the heart of the middle class was Anand Panyarachun. Although appointed to the premiership by the NPC, Anand turned out to be no creature of the military. Not only was his administration independent from the junta on many issues, but it was also highly productive, passing nearly 200 laws by March 1992.[14] Anand made 'transparency' the watchword for his administration, and set out to dismantle through deregulation and privatization some of the many bureaucratic mechanisms that distorted the economy and created opportunities for corruption. His government restructured the tax system by introducing a value-added tax, liberalized the trade and financial systems, began privatizing Thai Airways, and reviewed infrastructure projects approved by the Chatichai cabinet.[15]

Anand won tremendous middle-class respect for his performance as prime minister. Columnist Sopon Onkgara stated that 'the Anand administration, it can be said, is the best government we have had since 1932'.[16] Although Anand stepped from the private sector to the premiership through military appointment rather than victory in parliamentary elections, his government enjoyed broad middle-class acceptance.[17] In contrast, though Chatichai was an elected prime minister, his cabinet's rampant corruption incurred the wrath of academics, journalists, students, and NGO leaders. For the middle class, clean and effective administration is apparently more important than the process by which a government comes to power.[18]

A third indication of the middle-class preference for clean politics was its dominance within the PollWatch organization established by Prime Minister Anand to prevent vote-buying, educate the public about democratic principles, and monitor the campaigning and balloting processes for the elections of March and September 1992. Table 9.1 presents data on the occupational background of the 30,594 PollWatch volunteers who oversaw the 22 March 1992 parliamentary elections. If one includes as members of the middle class college students (on the grounds that they will likely serve in middle-class positions after graduation), civil servants, teachers and professors, lawyers, doctors and nurses, and NGO workers, a full 64 per cent of the PollWatch corps came from middle-class occupations. While students and farmers formed over half the total number of PollWatch volunteers, they tended to serve on the ground at the village level, and middle-class professionals like teachers, academics, and lawyers tended to dominate the leadership through the provincial PollWatch co-ordinating committees.[19] The staff at the PollWatch offices in Bangkok,

Table 9.1: Occupational background of PollWatch volunteers, 22 March 1992 elections

Profession	No.	%
University student	13,594	45.5
Civil servant	2,744	9.0
Teacher/professor	1,746	5.8
State enterprise employee	1,057	3.5
Private sector employee	2,150	7.0
Lawyer	912	3.0
Doctor/nurse	24	0.1
Farmer	5,855	17.1
NGO worker	193	0.6
Other	2,604	8.5
Total	**30,594**	**100.0**

Source: Khana kammakan tittam lae sotsongdulae kanluaktang samachik sapha phuthaen ratsadon [PollWatch], *Kanluaktang samachik sapha phuthaen ratsadon, 22 minakhom 2535* (Bangkok: Yello kanphim chamkat, 1992), p. 172.

Trang, Chiang Mai, and Ubon Ratchathani for the September polls consisted almost entirely of the same middle-class groups that led the upcountry protests: lawyers, doctors, academics, students, and NGO workers.[20] These middle-class stalwarts were acting to ensure that Thailand's largely rural electorate would choose only 'good' politicians who did not buy votes.[21]

The enchantment of the middle class with clean politics comes from at least four sources:

- a desire for 'good government',
- an understanding that ideally democratic politics should be clean,
- an interest in a merit-based society, and
- a need for a level playing field.

The former two sources are normative, and the latter two are based on economic interest. Made up as it is partly by small business owners or salaried professionals with often substantial incomes, the middle class pays taxes and wants the government to spend its money properly:

taxation creates a demand for good representation. Concentrated in urban areas, the middle class expects the government to provide it with adequate infrastructure and municipal services, along with educational opportunities for its children, and to do so without blatant corruption.[22]

Second, many members of the middle class carry an image of the democratic ideal based on the political systems of advanced capitalist democracies. In this model the following four conditions pertain:

- politicians should win votes by offering clear policy choices rather than cash and a bottle of fish sauce;
- candidates should seek political office to implement their policy proposals rather than raid the national treasury for the benefit of their backers and themselves;
- the parties to which they belong should represent identifiable ideologies; and
- politicians should make their careers in a single party rather than jumping from one to another depending on their calculation of probable electoral outcomes.[23]

While political practice in the industrialized democratic states may well fall short of this standard, many educated Thais none the less would like the politics of their own country to adhere more closely to the ideal. Their exposure to international ideological currents, either through direct experience overseas or through the dissemination of information domestically about political systems in developed capitalist states, has led them to accept a definition of democracy that excludes the patronage-based politics commonly practised in Thailand.

Third, the upward mobility of the middle class depends in large part upon personal ability. Both within the professional middle class and in the business community, there is an increasing number of individuals for whom the old patron–client system is either irrelevant or obstructive to their material progress. Those in knowledge-based professions see that their own career advancement requires not just good connections but talent as well. Success in a growing number of Thailand's economic sectors is not determined by special relationships with strategically placed state officials or powerful politicians. Two examples are consumer goods production and retail sales, in which profit margins depend on satisfying (or even creating) consumer tastes, not upon personally obtained political favours.[24]

Fourth, it is also possible that the rapid expansion of the private sector means that the number of businesses vastly exceeds the amount of available patrons. Annual business starts have soared over the last two decades: 31,447 new corporations were registered with the Ministry of Commerce in 1992, the year of the May crisis, which is almost three times the number of firms registered a decade before (11,535) and nearly seven times that of 1972 (4,735).[25] Given such a substantial private sector, there are likely to be many more businesses that could benefit from patronage than there are patrons to go around, leading the large numbers of firms left out of the network of privilege to demand a 'level playing field' on which to compete fairly. The middle class and elements of private enterprise thus have a direct and compelling interest in a political economy in which all players start from an equal footing and the meritorious receive the rewards.

The middle-class distaste for vote-buying politicians from rural areas who use public office to provide their supporters with special business opportunities and extort payoffs from private sector contractors for personal gain makes sense when seen in the light of its desire for clean politics. In the eyes of the middle class, Chamlong and Anand stood for a meritocratic system free from backroom deals and under-the-table payoffs, and PollWatch was an organization that would deny the Chatichai-style politicians access to parliamentary office and public resources.

Middle-class opposition to Suchinda was a part of this 'clean politics, level playing field' syndrome. Numerous actions by prominent NPC officers suggested there was little real difference between them and the civilian politicos they had just overthrown. Leading junta members appeared to engage in the same kind of rent-seeking behaviour for which they had so sternly condemned their predecessors. For example, NPC generals refused to renegotiate a massive telecommunications contract signed on terms disadvantageous to the Thai state by a Chatichai minister whom the NPC's Assets Investigation Committee had placed under scrutiny for corruption, raising concern about an illicit quid-pro-quo between the generals and the private sector concessionaire.[26]

As another example, the air force under Air Chief Marshal Kaset Rochananin pushed hard for several major weapons acquisitions, two of which – totalling 14 billion baht – were rejected by the Anand government.[27] Arms deals have long been a source of supplemental income for the senior officers who sign the dotted line,[28] and ACM Kaset was facing a heavy financial burden, namely the formation of a new political party.

This was the Samakkhi Tham Party, established in October 1991, and its formation was a second signal to the middle class that the NPC represented a continuation of the money-driven politics that had flourished under Chatichai. Political observers considered it to be the Trojan horse by which the NPC would smuggle its interests into parliament after the elections promised by the junta for March 1992. It was constructed of the same material that had built the previous governmental coalition – rural network politicians seeking public office for private enrichment.[29] The head of Samakkhi Tham, Narong Wongwan, was known as 'the godfather of the North' and had been denied a visa by the US government on suspicion that he was involved in the heroin trade.

Middle-class fears concerning the true nature of NPC rule were confirmed following the March 1992 elections. At that point, moral outrage at Suchinda's lack of sincerity, the fear of rampant corruption, and the principled belief of some in the inherent value of democracy created a volatile mixture in middle-class temper that was to explode in the May crisis.

PROMISES MADE TO BE BROKEN: SETTING THE STAGE FOR MAY 1992

General Suchinda himself prepared the conditions for the major political upheaval of May 1992. Although the Bangkok middle class had been quietly pleased by the military ouster of the Chatichai government, and was thoroughly impressed by the efficiency of the NPC's Prime Minister Anand, it was alarmed by the implications of the junta's effort to introduce a new constitution. The proposed charter contained many undemocratic clauses, apparently aimed at preserving the military's political control.[30] As political parties and activist organizations launched protests, and opposition to the draft constitution grew, General Suchinda summoned the media to Army Hall and proclaimed, 'I can reaffirm here that both [*sic.*] General Suchinda and ACM Kaset will not be prime minister after the promulgation of the constitution.'[31] But sometimes, promises are made to be broken.

The elections of 22 March 1992, held under the new constitution, occurred amidst massive vote-buying and gave the pro-military parties a parliamentary majority with 195 seats against 165 for the democratic opposition.[32] Five parties formed a coalition – Samakkhi Tham, Chart Thai, Social Action, Prachakorn Thai, and Muan Chon – and began wrangling over the distribution of ministerial portfolios. As the head of Samakkhi Tham, the largest party in parliament, Narong Wongwan naturally claimed the premiership for himself, until the uproar over his alleged narcotics trafficking led him to withdraw from the bidding.[33] In the end the coalition offered the premiership to General Suchinda. On 7 April 1992, in a tearful speech announcing his submission to the higher claims of patriotic duty, Suchinda resigned from the military and accepted the post.

Given the fact that leaders of the Chart Thai and Social Action parties had been particular targets of the junta's initial anti-corruption drive, it might seem strange that they appeared as pro-military parties in the election and, as core members with Samakkhi Tham of the governing coalition, offered the premiership to Suchinda.[34] However, the general needed their votes, and they wanted renewed access to state resources; so a deal was struck. Suchinda repaid his debt for their political support by allowing into his cabinet six Chart Thai and Social Action MPs who had previously been accused of being 'unusually wealthy'.[35]

Protest against General Suchinda's appointment began immediately in Bangkok. On the same day, a thousand students rallied at Thammasat University to call for his resignation, and the leaders of student, labour, and activist groups, along with representatives from the New Aspiration, Democrat, Palang Darma, and Solidarity parties, gathered to denounce General Suchinda for going back on his word and to insist that he step down.[36] On 8 April, sub-lieutenant Chalad Worachat launched a hunger strike in front of parliament against Suchinda's premiership. The democracy movement which quickly emerged had two demands: that Suchinda resign; and that parliament amend the constitution to reverse the measures introduced to ensure conservative bureaucratic/military control.[37]

The political temperature rose in Bangkok as Suchinda refused to leave office and the government parties resisted amending the constitution. Then, on 4 May, Palang Darma leader Major-General Chamlong Srimuang made a dramatic declaration that he would fast until either he died or Suchinda resigned, an act which mobilized massive support behind the burgeoning democracy movement.[38]

THE EMERGENCE OF UPCOUNTRY PROTESTS

The day after Chamlong's proclamation, an anti-Suchinda demonstration occurred in Chiang Mai, and protests soon broke out in 29 other provinces in every region of the country. There were two waves of continuous large-scale protests in Bangkok, first from 4–10 and then from 17–21 May, and the upcountry demonstrations essentially followed this pattern.[39]

Protest actions[40] outside Bangkok took place between 5 and 10 May in Chiang Mai, Chiang Rai, Khon Kaen, Nakhon Ratchasima, Buriram, Sisaket, Nakhon Si Thammarat, Songkhla, Satun, and Phuket provinces.[41] In Chiang Mai, Khon Kaen, and Songkhla, all provinces with universities, the campus served as a focus of opposition, and students and professors provided political leadership throughout the May events. Lawyers and Palang Darma Party members played a key role in launching the first demonstrations in Nakhon Ratchasima and Nakhon Si Thammarat.

Movement leaders in Bangkok agreed to a truce on 9 May, when house speaker Dr Arthit Urairat announced that all political parties had agreed to amend the constitution. Activists upcountry followed the lead of their Bangkok counterparts and remained basically quiet while they waited to see if the governing parties would keep their word. To sustain momentum and raise awareness about the issues, movement organizations in Chiang Mai, Sisaket, and Songkhla provinces, and probably elsewhere as well, maintained information centres in public places that listed their demands, explained the constitutional and political principles at stake, and recounted the course of the protest campaign to date in Bangkok and around the country.[42] But as the government coalition partners began denying that they had made any such promise, the democratic opposition started preparations for major protests on 17 May to pressure them into passing the desired amendments.

At the same time, the state apparatus was not idle. On 15 May, under orders of the Ministry of the Interior, local officials mobilized villagers for rallies in support of General Suchinda and the new constitution. Newspaper reports claimed that over 150,000 people in 27 provinces turned out for these carefully managed demonstrations (see Table 9.2). The extent to which the pro-Suchinda demonstrations everywhere followed the same format suggests a certain lack of spontaneity. All such gatherings took place at the provincial office, and

Table 9.2: State-sponsored pro-Suchinda rallies, 15 May 1992

Region/province	**No. of demonstators**	**Region/province**	**No. of demonstators**
Central Region		***Northern Region***	
Ang Thong	2,000	Kamphaeng Phet	7,000
Ayutthaya	1,000	Lampang	3,000
Chonburi	300	Nakhon Sawan	3,000
Lopburi	10,000	Nan	2,000
Uthai Thani	300	Phayao	2,000
Total	*13,600*	Phetchabun	1,000
		Phichit	200
Northeast Region		Phitsanulok	20,000
Buriram	20,000	Phrae	3,000
Kalasin	5,000	Sukhothai	10,000
Khon Kaen	20,000	Utaradit	10,000
Mahasarakham	700	*Total*	*61,200*
Nakhon Ratchasima	4,000		
Nong Khai	5,000		
Sakon Nakhon	4,000	***Southern Region***	
Sisaket	3,000	Patthalung	8,000
Yasothon	7,000	Songkhla	1,200
Total	*68,700*	*Total*	*9,200*
Nationwide total	***152,700***		

Source: *Matichon*, 17 May 1992.

the provincial governor and senior provincial bureaucrats were present to greet the arriving villagers. The rallies in each province invariably began with the provision of drinking water and sometimes food to the crowd, followed by speeches attacking the anti-Suchinda protestors in Bangkok along with the opposition political parties, and ended with the presentation of a letter to the provincial governor supporting Suchinda as prime minister.

However, events on 15 May occasionally spun out of official control. Among the 20,000 villagers who reportedly showed up for Suchinda at the Phitsanulok provincial government headquarters were about 50 anti-Suchinda protestors. In Patthalung, the 8,000 villagers assembled at the provincial office became angry when civil servants tried to hand them banners with slogans supporting PM Suchinda, and they shouted down a border patrol police officer who tried to turn them against the demonstrators in Bangkok. Then a provincial councillor mounted the stage and declared that the people of Patthalung wanted a prime minister who was an elected MP and wanted the constitution amended, to which the crowd responded with applause and cheers. At the urging of villager Nipat Ritthidet, a thousand people re-assembled at the nearby football field for an anti-government demonstration.[43] The provinces were becoming a political battleground between forces in favour of and opposed to Suchinda's premiership and the military-sponsored constitution.

On 17 May, when it was clear that the government coalition had no intention of making the promised changes to the charter, the democracy movement once again took to the field both in and outside Bangkok. Protests occurred in Chanthaburi and Lopburi in the Central region, Chiang Mai in the North, Buriram, Khon Kaen, Nakhon Ratchasima, Sisaket, and Udon Thani in the Northeast, and Phuket, Songkhla, and Surat Thani in the South. By far the largest demonstrations on 17 May occurred in the three southern provinces, with about 5,000 people present at each site.[44]

The military began its crackdown on the night of 17 May. While the violence unleashed in Bangkok shrank the size of the protests there, it inflamed anti-government passions in the provinces. Together with resentment of the misrepresentation of events in the state-controlled broadcast media, this brought huge numbers of people into the upcountry streets. From 18 to 21 May, no less than 50 protest actions occurred in 25 provinces all around the country. The southern region continued to see the most political activity. The peak of the protests in the South occurred on 20 May, when about 80,000 southerners appeared at rallies: 30,000 in Nakhon Si Thammarat, 10,000 in Patthalung, 30,000 in Songkhla, and 10,000 in Trang. The number of protestors in the South alone equalled the size of the crowd in Bangkok that night at Ramkhamhaeng University (the new centre of protest in the capital after the military had secured Ratchadamnoen Avenue), which was estimated at 80,000. Total turnout in the provinces on 20 May reached nearly 190,000 participants.[45]

Table 9.3: Protest actions outside Bangkok province, 5–21 May 1992

Region/province	No. of protest actions	Total participants at all actions	Average no. of participants/ actions
Central			
Ang Thong	1	n.a.	n.a.
Chanthaburi	3	850	283
Kanchanaburi	1	200	200
Lopburi	1	n.a.	n.a.
Nakhon Pathom	1	1,000	1,000
Phetburi	2	5,000	2,500
Rayong	2	100	50
Saraburi	1	10,000	10,000
Uthai Thani	1	100	100
Total	***13***	***17,250***	***1,327 (average)***
North			
Chiang Mai	15	67,000†	4,786
Chiang Rai	1	n.a.	n.a.
Nakhon Sawan	1	10,000	10,000
Phichit	1	300	300
Phitsanulok	1	50	50
Total	***19***	***77,350***	***4,550 (average)***
Northeast			
Buriram	6	7,000	1,750
Khon Kaen	11	43,000	4,300
Mahasarakham	1	20,000	20,000
Nakhon Ratchasima	5	50,000	12,500
Roi Et	1	1,000	1,000
Sisaket	5*	12,500	3,125
Surin	4	12,300	3,075

Table 9.3: Protest actions outside Bangkok province, 5–21 May 1992

Region/province	No. of protest actions	Total participants at all actions	Average no. of participants/ actions
Ubon Ratchathani	2	10,000	10,000
Udon Thani	1	200	200
Total	*36*	*144,930*	*10,229 (average)*
South			
Nakhon Si Thammarat	10	110,000†	13,750
Pattani	1	200	200
Patthalung	4	21,000†	5,250
Phuket	2	11,000	5,500
Satun	3	n.a.	n.a.
Songkhla	11	90,000	10,000
Surat Thani	4	13,000	4,333
Trang	4	19,000	4,750
Total	*42*	*246,200*	*8,523 (average)*
National total	**110**	**503,730**	**5,660 (average)**

Note: Where no estimates were available for the number of participants in a protest action, and there was no way to make a reasonable guess based on the published account of the event, I did not include that protest action in the calculation of the average number of participants per demonstration. (*) Figure adjusted upward based on interviews with local protest leaders. (†) Figure adjusted downwards based on interviews with local protest leaders.

Sources: *Matichon*, 6–22 May 1992; *Bangkok Post*, 6–16 May 1992; *Khana kammakan.*

Tables 9.3 and 9.4 present data on the upcountry protest actions.[46] Table 9.3 includes the sum total of participants involved in all actions in each province. Some of the figures are probably exaggerated: for instance, while *Matichon* reported 70–80,000 participants at the demonstration in Nakhon Si Thammarat on 20 May, local protest leaders I interviewed stated that at no point did the rallies there exceed 30–40,000. In cases where the crowd size estimates of *Matichon* and local leaders I interviewed differed, I used the lower figure. *Matichon* under-reported the number of protest actions in Sisaket (and quite possibly elsewhere), listing only two incidents when local people cited at least four actions.[47] The numbers reported in Table 9.3 should thus be considered indicative rather than definitive.

The figures in the column labelled 'total participants at all actions' reflect the magnitude of overall protest for each province, and not necessarily the number of individuals taking part in the local movement, since some people turned out for more than one action. Adding up the number of demonstrators at each of the four rallies held in Nakhon Ratchasima, for example, yields a total of 50,000 participants, but in all likelihood many of the same people showed up for the four demonstrations there. What these numbers do reflect is the magnitude of overall protest for each province. Looking at the average number of participants per action provides a more accurate picture of the size of a 'typical' action in a given province. Either way, what Table 9.3 shows is the extraordinary strength of the opposition in the South to Suchinda's premiership and the NPC constitution, both in absolute terms as well as relative to the other regions. Table 9.4 reveals the regional distribution of the protests, which makes clear the breadth of protest in the South and the Northeast. Protest actions occurred in half of all the southern provinces.

Newspaper reports named teachers, university students and faculty members, lawyers, doctors, nurses, opposition political party members, provincial councillors, and local and national democracy organizations as the provincial protest leaders.[48] Interviews with journalists, business leaders, and political activists in six provinces – Songkhla, Pattha-

Table 9.4: Protest actions by region

Region	No. provinces in region	No. provinces with protests	% provinces with protests
Central	25	9	36
North	16	5	31
Northeast	17	9	53
South	14	8	57

Sources: *Matichon*, 6–22 May 1992; *Bangkok Post*, 6–16 May 1992; *Khana kammakan.*

lung, Nakhon Si Thammarat, Buriram, Sisaket, and Chiang Mai – named the same kinds of people as the leaders of the local protest movements. Most categories of people who were claimed to be provincial protest leaders both by *Matichon* newspaper reports and by knowledgeable local figures were members of the middle class. Newspaper accounts of the class composition of the participants were less specific. Because of the sheer numbers involved, it is safe to assume that at the large rallies of 10,000 and upwards, those in attendance represented a range of social classes; indeed, interviews with activists in the six provinces confirmed this multi-class character. Provincial middle-class activists provided a crucial intermediary function, linking upcountry Thais to the movement in Bangkok as well as in other provinces by maintaining phone and fax contact with protest leaders elsewhere, and communicating that information to the local population through 'democracy walls', leaflets, word of mouth, and other means.

THE PROTEST MOVEMENTS IN SIX PROVINCES

By now three points should be clear concerning the May 1992 disturbances:

1. there was extensive protest action taken against Suchinda's premiership and the NPC constitution in many provinces throughout Thailand;
2. this upcountry movement was led by middle-class academics and professionals along with activist groups and local politicians; and
3. middle-class opposition grew out of interest-based preference for clean politics, anger at Suchinda's violation of his own word, and desire for a more democratic system.

Within the provincial middle class, however, professionals such as teachers, professors, lawyers, and doctors were much more important than business people in leading and participating in the May democracy movement. Field research in Patthalung, Nakhon Si Thammarat, and Songkhla provinces in the South, Buriram and Sisaket in the Northeast, and Chiang Mai in the North revealed a division of labour within the middle class in which teachers, lawyers, journalists, and local politicians led the protest actions while business people largely limited their participation to the provision of support from behind the scenes.

In conducting this field research, I made a list of six mostly social and economic factors which I assumed would be associated with a propensity to protest for democracy:

1. the number of students at institutes of higher learning, defining an 'institute of higher learning' as one that requires entrants to hold at least a high school diploma;
2. the level of urbanization;
3. per capita income;
4. the size of the middle class;
5. the party origin of MPs elected in March 1992; and
6. the degree of dependence on tourism.

The logic behind the choice of these factors is as follows: I selected the number of students at institutes of higher learning because Thai students have been a major force agitating for democracy and social justice since at least the 1950s. The mass democracy movement of 1973 is the most prominent example, but students have participated in or led many smaller campaigns for reform; hence a large number of students in a given province would make it more likely for a democracy movement to emerge.

Per capita income, the level of urbanization, and the size of the provincial middle class are all ways of measuring provincial socio-economic development. Per capita income is a single number that implies many characteristics associated with 'development' such as levels of literacy and education, socio-economic complexity, and industrialization. The statistical relationship between democracy and wealth is irrefutable.[49] This is not to suggest that poor people are incapable of launching a political movement such as a campaign for democracy, or that other factors such as the level of pre-existing social networks and freedom from dominant-class hegemony are not also important, but the point remains that wealthier people are generally better placed to take political action than are the poor.[50] Although similar per capita incomes across provinces may disguise very different patterns of income distribution, there should still be a rough correlation between levels of per capita income and the number of people with sufficient resources to participate in politics.

I picked urbanization because the democracy movement in 1991–1992 (as well as in 1973) was almost entirely based in cities. Whenever newspapers reported a demonstration for democracy in 1973 or 1991–1992 taking place outside Bangkok (which was always the centre of protest), the location was invariably a town, not a village. Indeed, protests in nearly every province occurred exclusively in the provincial capital[51] which led me to hypothesize that a province's level of urbanization might affect its ability to produce its own protest movement.

Given the highly visible role played by the middle class in the 1991–1992 movement, the size of a province's middle class was a natural factor to choose.[52] In fact, in both Bangkok and the provinces, participants came from a range of social backgrounds. Slum-dwellers and working-class members also turned out for the Bangkok protests in large numbers, and without strong lower-class participation the movement might well have failed. An analysis of those injured or killed during the violence on 17–21 May shows that those on the frontlines were generally young working-class males.[53] As in 1973, after the shooting started it was the working class more than the middle class that stayed out in the streets and stood up to the armed forces. It was this working-class resistance, along with the strength of the provincial protest movement, which brought the King into the fray and led to the collapse of the Suchinda government. None the less, middle-class dominance of the leadership of the provincial movements suggested that the size of a province's middle class affected the chances for the emergence of a democracy movement there. The size of a provincial middle class might not make a big difference to the strength of a campaign that already exists, but it might influence the possibility that such a movement would emerge in the first place.

I postulated that the party affiliations of a province's MPs could affect the likelihood that a movement would arise there. This might seem doubtful, since party membership has meant little in Thai politics, and party platforms have typically been vague and virtually indistinguishable from one another. The basic building-block of Thai political parties has been the faction, organized around region, personality, kinship, business ties, shared election-canvassing networks, or the exchange of material benefits for support. The archetypal Thai political party is assembled from the top down on the basis of personality rather than ideology, and has neither organization nor mass membership nor assets. Because party labels carry few ideological implications, and do not even appear on the ballot, politicians can and do change parties frequently, based on offers of cash and their assessment of a party's prospects to form part of the government.[54] However, the March 1992 elections did offer voters a clear choice between conflicting political principles. Parties were divided into those campaigning for a more democratic constitution and a prime minister that had been elected to parliament, and those that had not opposed the NPC's constitution and were willing to support a 'neutral' non-parliamentarian as premier.[55] I therefore hypothesized that the higher the share of a province's MPs who belonged to a party favouring a more democratic constitution, the more probable it was that the province would produce a protest movement in May.

Finally, it seemed likely that a provincial economy's degree of dependence on tourism could shape the prospects for the rise of a local democracy movement. Tourism had become Thailand's most importance source of foreign exchange in the 1980s. Its benefits were distributed unevenly, with most of the tourists and revenue being attracted to Bangkok and Phattaya in the Central region, Chiang Mai in the North, and Phuket in the South. Thais in heavily touristed areas might be more aware of international standards of democracy and concerned for Thailand's image abroad. News of demonstrations would also drive away the tourists, and bring concern for an orderly resolution to the crisis.[56]

I chose for in-depth study six provinces that (a) represented several regions, (b) had experienced at least several protest actions, and (c) varied among themselves in terms of the above six factors. These were Patthalung, Nakhon Si Thammarat, and Songkhla in the South, Buriram and Sisaket in the Northeast, and Chiang Mai in the North. I travelled to each of these provinces and interviewed members of the executive committee of the provincial chamber of commerce, leaders of the local protest movement, and in most cases journalists reporting on provincial news. Tables 9.5 and 9.6 overleaf present the results of this exercise.

Beginning with the number of students at institutes of higher learning, the six provinces fall into three clusters, with Patthalung and Sisaket having virtually none, Buriram and Nakhon Si Thammarat in the middle with a couple of thousand each, and Songkhla and Chiang Mai at the upper end with roughly 20,000 tertiary students each. This three-cluster pattern holds true for the indicators of socio-economic development – gross provincial product per capita, level of urbanization, and size of the middle class. With respect to the

Table 9.5: Selected characteristics of Patthalung, Nakhon Si Thammarat and Songkhla provinces

Characteristic	Patthalung	Nakhon Si Thammarat	Songkhla
No. of students in higher education institutes (1990)[1]	0	3,232	17,475
Gross Provincial Product per capita (1991)[2]	16,228	20,926	31,093
Share of population in urban areas (1992)[3]	8.3%	7.0%	19.8%
Size of middle class (1990)[4]	28,995 (11.7%)	106,224 (14.7%)	136,477 (24.1%)
Share of MPs from parties opposed to Suchinda, March '92	100%	100%	86%
Share of opposition MPs from Election District 1	100%	100%	67%
Importance of tourism to provincial economy*	none	minor	substantial (Hat Yai)
Role of businessmen in protest leadership*	minor	minor	moderate
Role of businessmen in protest participation*	minor	minor	moderate
Number of protest actions[5]	4	10	11
Protest size range[5]	1,000–10,000	1,000–30,000	150–30,000

***Note**: On a scale of none, minor, moderate, or substantial – author's estimate based on interviews.

Sources: (1) *Report on Educational Statistics by Province, 1990,* Office of the Permanent Secretary, Ministry of Education.

(2) *Gross Regional and Provincial Products, 1981–91,* National Statistics Office. Figures in baht.

(3) *Statistical Yearbook Thailand, 1993.* National Statistics Office

(4) *1990 Population and Housing Census, Provincial Reports,* National Statistics Office. The 'middle class' here consists of professional, technical, and related workers; administrative, executive, managerial workers and government officials, etc.; clerical and related workers; sales workers; and service workers. The percentage figure in parentheses is the share of the middle class in the province's total workforce.

(5) *Matichon,* 6–22 May 1992; *Bangkok Post,* 6–16 May 1992; *Khana kammakan;* and interviews with local activists and business leaders.

Table 9.6: Selected characteristics of Buriram, Sisaket and Chiang Mai provinces

Characteristic	Buriram	Sisaket	Chiang Mai
No. of students in higher education institutes (1990)[1]	1,448	291	24,638
Gross Provincial Product per capita (1991)[2]	13,091	11,460	36,976
Share of population in urban areas (1992)[3]	4.1%	2.9%	11.3%
Size of middle class (1990)[4]	59,062 (7.3%)	46,607 (5.9%)	185,295 (22.4%)
Share of MPs from parties opposed to Suchinda, March '92	11%	44%	33%
Share of opposition MPs from Election District 1	33%	67%	67%
Importance of tourism to provincial economy*	minor	none	substantial (Chiang Mai city)
Role of businessmen in protest leadership*	none	none	none
Role of businessmen in protest participation*	minor	minor	minor
Number of protest actions[5]	6	5	15
Protest size range[5]	500–10,000	10–1,000	3–40,000

***Note**: On a scale of none, minor, moderate, or substantial – author's estimate based on interviews.

Sources: (1) *Report on Educational Statistics by Province, 1990*, Office of the Permanent Secretary, Ministry of Education.
(2) *Gross Regional and Provincial Products, 1981–91*, National Statistics Office. Figures in baht.
(3) *Statistical Yearbook Thailand, 1993.* National Statistics Office
(4) *1990 Population and Housing Census, Provincial Reports*, National Statistics Office. The 'middle class' is composed as in Table 9.5.
(5) *Matichon*, 6–22 May 1992; *Bangkok Post*, 6–16 May 1992; *Khana kammakan;* and interviews with local activists and business leaders.

proportion of MPs from parties opposed to Suchinda, Buriram had the lowest share, Chiang Mai and Sisaket were in the middle, and Songkhla, Patthalung and Nakhon Si Thammarat had the highest percentages.[57] Finally, tourism was of more than minor importance only to the economies of Hat Yai and Chiang Mai cities.

What this comparison shows is that no single one of the six factors that might be associated with the emergence of a local democracy movement was shared by all of these provinces. Recurring protests broke out in provinces with many university students and with no university students; with relatively high and relatively low per capita incomes; with relatively high and relatively low levels of urbanization; with proportionately large and proportionately small middle classes, with MPs from parties that supported Suchinda's government and those from parties that opposed it, and with significant and insignificant tourist industries. Common to all provinces, and of overwhelming importance in building the local protest movements, was a pre-existing network of politically aware individuals who would form the core of the movement leadership in May 1992.

Activists in all six provinces mentioned at least one of two organizations as sources for local leadership: PollWatch and the Union for Civil Liberties. PollWatch was a nationwide organization formed in January 1992 with an explicitly political mission which brought together local activists in every province into networks that in many cases also provided the leadership for the protest movement in May. PollWatch reinforced 'strong ties' among activists with long-established relationships, and created bridging 'weak ties' between networks of individuals who had not had much previous contact; in both cases, the ties facilitated the formation of local movement coordinating groups.[58] Protest leaders in Songkhla, Patthalung, Buriram, and Sisaket all reported that members of the local PollWatch committee in March helped lead the demonstrations in May, and often went on to form the membership of the local PollWatch committee for the year's second round of parliamentary elections in September.[59]

The Union for Civil Liberties (UCL), as an organization with branches nationwide and a membership committed to the protection and extension of democratic rights, also contributed resources and leadership to the May protest movement. In some provinces, such as Sisaket and Songkhla, UCL committee members served in the local PollWatch organization in early 1992, then went on to launch democracy movements a few months later.[60] In addition, many non-governmental organizations (NGOs) local to each province participated both in the March PollWatch effort and in the May protests. A key moment in the evolution of Thailand's NGO movement had been the founding in 1985 of the National NGO Coordinating Committee on Rural Development (NGO-CORD) along with five associated regional NGO-CORDs. This forged a national network which facilitated the emergence of provincial protest movements in May 1992.[61]

Provincial universities were yet another source of movement personnel and resources. As institutions that concentrated large numbers of highly educated, politically aware, and well-informed individuals, it is not surprising that the important universities in Songkhla, Chiang Mai, and Khon Kaen provinces all saw their students and faculties play active roles in the May protest movements.[62]

The ideal-typical process by which provincial protest movements emerged might be described as follows: activists associated with branches of the Union for Civil Liberties and local NGOs, already embedded in interpersonal and organizational networks and predisposed to oppose the extension of NPC power through Suchinda's premiership,[63] came together with members of the provincial middle class like teachers and lawyers in early 1992 to carry out PollWatch election-monitoring responsibilities. The PollWatch volunteers then witnessed the victorious coalition of scandal-ridden, vote-buying political parties form a government and name a military junta leader as Thailand's nineteenth prime minister. As protests grew against Suchinda's premiership in Bangkok, the expanded network of activists created by PollWatch began organizing demonstrations in their own provinces, drawing on the resources of local and national NGOs, high schools, teachers' colleges, and universities to mobilize support for the movement.[64]

While leadership came from middle-class professionals and NGO workers, movement participants represented a broad range of social categories – labourers, farmers, students, white-collar workers, and small and medium-sized business people. Following Bangkok, protest actions occurred in two waves, the first from 4 to 10 May, and the second from 17 to 21 May. As in the capital, the movement ended after local activists received news about the royal audience the King held on the night of 20 May with Major-General Chamlong Srimuang and General Suchinda Kraprayoon. Although actual events in Songkhla, Patthalung, Nakhon Si Thammarat, Buriram, Sisaket, and Chiang Mai varied somewhat in terms of timing, size, duration, and number of protest actions, and the backgrounds of movement participants and leaders, the information provided by activists in all six provinces about the emergence of their protest movements and the identities of those involved coincides closely enough to this ideal-typical sequence to justify its construction.

Provincial business people played only a minor role in the protest movement, preferring to provide material assistance from behind rather than lead the demonstrations up-front. *Matichon* reports on provincial protest actions throughout the country rarely named business people as local protest leaders.[65] Business people in Patthalung, Nakhon Si Thammarat, Buriram, Sisaket, and Chiang Mai conformed to this pattern. In these five provinces, they played only a minor role as leaders or participants in the local democracy movements. To the extent that business people in these provinces did become involved, they largely limited participation to donating food, water, and money to the protestors, or closing factories early to allow their workers to attend the demonstrations. Business associations played no role whatsoever in any of these provinces.

However, business people in Hat Yai city in Songkhla province publicly displayed their opposition to Suchinda's premiership and openly participated in and led the protests there.[66] The reason for their uncharacteristically overt political involvement is undoubtedly the importance of tourism to the Hat Yai economy.[67] About 800,000 tourists a year visit Songkhla province, and most of them spend their time and money in Hat Yai; 80 percent of them are Malaysians. Tourism and trade are the foundations of Hat Yai's visible prosperity. The military's use of violence against the unarmed demonstrators in Bangkok on the night of 17 May virtually emptied out Hat Yai's hotels (and brothels) as the visitors already there promptly returned home to Malaysia and those intending to come quickly cancelled their plans. It was after 18 May that local businesspeople began taking part directly in the protest actions by giving speeches at rallies and hanging banners condemning Suchinda from their establishments.

Hat Yai was also the only place in which the heads of business associations, in violation of the law which forbids registered bodies from political involvement, protested in the names of their organizations rather than in their status as individuals. The three business associations so involved were the Songkhla Chamber of Commerce, the Songkhla–Hat Yai Hotel Association, and the Songkhla Tour Agency Association. Two of these three associations are directly related to the tourism industry, and the repression unleashed in Bangkok had

had a sharp impact on the profits of their members. There are other local groups in Hat Yai representing industries unrelated to tourism, such as the Songkhla Rubber Merchants' Association, but those interviewed did not mention officers of such bodies as having played a similarly open role.

The six provinces varied not just in terms of the role played by business people and their associations; they also differed in the timing, size, and number of protests. To explain these disparities we must look more closely at the social and economic characteristics of each province. In general, protest emerged earliest in large, wealthy provinces with institutes of higher education and substantial middle classes. There were more protest actions in these provinces, and the scale of the protests was generally larger.

While the largest and wealthiest provinces produced the biggest movements overall in terms of number and size of protests, this link between degree of socio-economic development and the timing and magnitude of provincial movements appeared to weaken during the second wave of actions (17–21 May). Patthalung is an example of a small, relatively poor province that none the less witnessed several days of major demonstrations. On 18 and 19 May, 10,000 people turned out. How did these protests begin? Who organized them? How were leaders able to mobilize mass support?

Social networks and the process of diffusion played an important role in the emergence of protest in Patthalung. Activists and politicians from that province began not by launching their own campaign in early May, but by travelling to adjacent Songkhla province and attending meetings held by the democracy movement there. No opposition activity occurred in Patthalung itself during the first wave of protest, but after their return the Patthalung activists began planning their own demonstration with the assistance of a protest leader from Songkhla.[68]

The movement's leadership in Patthalung consisted of members of parliament, provincial councillors, teachers, and lawyers. On 18 May (a Monday) Patthalung teachers called on local schools to close; three did. The teachers held a rally at a public field, then moved their protest to the provincial administration building in order to join a demonstration led by local politicians there.[69] While the teachers had used their influence to close schools and thus free up students (and themselves) for protest, the politicians drew on their own networks of associates, party members, and clients. Like many southerners, the people of Patthalung tended to identify with the Democrat Party; this was in opposition in May 1992, so political party loyalties predisposed them to oppose the Suchinda government.[70] Furthermore, given the local population's history of deep resentment towards the armed forces for the brutality of the anti-insurgency campaign, the lethal military crackdown in Bangkok rekindled old hatreds and made it easy for protest leaders to amass a crowd.[71]

Diffusion processes may have facilitated the formation of movements in other provinces. For example, although there were no protest actions in Mahasarakham province during 5–10 May, activists from Mahasarakham (as well as Kalasin) travelled to neighbouring Khon Kaen and gave speeches at a demonstration there on 10 May. On 20 May, during the second wave of protests, a 20,000-strong demonstration occurred in Mahasarakham itself.[72] While I do not know whether those who spoke at the Khon Kaen rally on 10 May were directly involved in launching the Mahasarakham protest, it is certainly the case that the extensive opposition activity in Khon Kaen provided an example for the people of Mahasarakham to follow.

The experience of the provincial protest movements suggests five conclusions.

1. Civil society organizations and social networks were vital to the establishment of leadership structures for local movements. Of special importance were the branch organizations of the Union for Civil Liberties and the networks created by PollWatch in January–March 1992.
2. The professional middle class provided the vast majority of the provincial movement leadership. Academics, teachers, lawyers, doctors, and NGO workers played an indispensable role in forming and leading protest movements around the country.
3. Institutes of higher learning, and universities in particular, contributed essential resources to many upcountry campaigns. Where universities existed, they formed the core of the local campaign for democracy; and teachers' colleges also played a significant role.
4. While provinces of every description experienced protest actions, especially during the 17–21 May second wave of demonstrations, there was a rough correlation between a province's level of socioeconomic development and the timing, size, and number of protest actions there.

5. While in some provinces a high degree of economic dependence on tourism or the affiliation of local MPs to opposition parties might have facilitated mobilization, many provinces with negligible tourist industries or a high proportion of government MPs none the less produced strong democracy movements.

The question left unanswered is why there were protests in some provinces but not in others. There are at least four possible explanations. First, activists in smaller provinces might have focused on working with a growing movement in a larger nearby province rather than using their limited resources to try to create a movement back home. For example, representatives of various organizations in Kalasin travelled to adjacent Khon Kaen province and gave speeches there at a demonstration on 10 May.[73] I found no evidence of protest activity in Kalasin, and it may be that local activists preferred to take part in the thriving movement in Khon Kaen.

Second, the level of repression may have varied across provinces, depending on the personal and political loyalties of local officials. Thus in one smaller northern provincial capital, some activists handed out leaflets and tried to mobilize a demonstration.[74] The police ordered them to stop, and that was the end of their movement. On the other hand, Chiang Mai University administrators were in contact with the lieutenant-general commanding the Third Army Region, headquartered in Chiang Mai; he was not a member of the NPC faction and told them that the protest campaign could continue without fear of army repression. Chiang Mai movement leaders also had a good relationship with the local police, who promised to inform them in advance if an order to suppress the demonstrations came in.[75]

Third, those wanting to initiate protest action in certain provinces might have been isolated from one another, or subject to countervailing pressures that inhibited them from instigating a movement. Individuals are embedded in a variety of networks, and some important ones may oppose movement participation. In other words, the social context of would-be activists might not have been conducive to movement formation and growth.

Fourth, it might be more than coincidence that no protest actions were reported in the provinces of prominent politicians in the government coalition such as Narong Wongwan (Samakkhi Tham Party leader, Phrae province), Montri Pongpanich (Social Action Party head, Ayutthaya province), or Banharn Silpa-archa (Chart Thai Party secretary-general, from Suphanburi province). In Suphanburi, all five MPs belonged to Chart Thai, one of the core parties in the government coalition. Banharn Silpa-archa, representing Suphanburi Election District One, received more votes than any other parliamentary candidate in Thailand, and one of his District One running-mates, Bunua Prasoetsuwan, ranked second.[76] An MP for Suphanburi for two decades, Banharn was past master of diverting state resources to his constituency.[77] He was named transport and communications minister in the Suchinda cabinet, a post that gave him tremendous opportunities for delivering infrastructure to Suphanburi (and possibly enriching himself along the way). Given these circumstances, potential movement leaders in Suphanburi may have thought they could not mobilize support for anti-government demonstrations; and similar considerations may have discouraged activists in other provinces controlled by powerful pro-government politicians.

Generally speaking, however, the party affiliation of a province's MPs did not seem to prevent the emergence of a local democracy movement. For example, only one of Buriram's nine MPs was from an opposition party, yet local activists managed to launch a number of protest actions, including demonstrations that drew crowds of up to 3,000 (in a province whose capital had a population of just under 30,000 in 1992).[78] In Nakhon Ratchasima, only five out of 15 MPs were from opposition parties, and every MP from District One, the site of all protest in the province, belonged to a government party. None the less, numerous protest actions occurred in Nakhon Ratchasima, and the demonstration held there on 20 May attracted an estimated 40,000 participants.[79]

POLITICAL AND SOCIAL FOUNDATIONS OF THE PROVINCIAL DEMOCRACY MOVEMENTS

Never before have Thais outside Bangkok taken part in the struggle for democracy on such a scale. The only comparable mass movement occurred in October 1973, when student-led popular protests against dictatorship succeeded in ousting the hated military triumvirate of Thanom, Praphat, and Narong. As in 1992, the unrest was not confined to Bangkok, but the upcountry protests of October 1973 were led and attended almost exclusively by students. At universities, teachers' colleges, technical institutes, agricultural colleges, commerce colleges, and high schools in 22 provinces around the country, students staged demonstrations for the release of prominent democracy activists and the promulgation of a new constitution.[80] Save for one incident, students were reported to be responsible for initiating, leading, and participating in protests outside the capital.[81]

There are two basic reasons why participation in the 1992 provincial protests was so much wider than that of 1972: first, the informal networks and formal organizations that formed the core of the 1992 provincial movement leadership scarcely existed in 1973; and second, the provincial middle class of 1973 was much smaller in both relative and absolute terms in 1973 than it was in 1992. In October 1972 there was as yet no Union for Civil Liberties, no network of development-oriented NGOs, and no PollWatch. Provincial civil society was rudimentary at best. Possibly the only network of extra-bureaucratic organizations with any level of political and social awareness in existence then was the National Student Centre of Thailand.[82] To be sure, by 1973 business associations were already brought together into peak organizations under the Thai Bankers' Association, the Federation of Thai Industries, and the Thai Chamber of Commerce, and these formed another network with political potential, but business people at that time operated in close collusion with high-ranking state officials and were not involved in the 1973 democracy movement.

The proliferation of provincial networks of organizations and activists between 1973 and 1992 responded to the tremendous growth in the middle class in the 1970s and 1980s. Table 9.7 overleaf shows the dramatic increase in the relative and absolute size of the middle class that occurred both at the national level and in the six case study provinces between 1970 and 1990.

Table 9.8 overleaf presents data specifically on the rapid growth of the professions over those two decades. Because the teachers, academics, lawyers, journalists, and doctors who spearheaded the 1992 provincial protest movement are all included under this category, we can see how the expansion of the professions helped build the social foundations for the democratic struggle that emerged in the provinces in 1992.

The emergence of an upcountry middle class was the result of the tremendous growth Thailand had experienced since around 1960; rapid economic development led to rising incomes and changes in

Table 9.7: Size of the middle class nationwide and in selected provinces, 1970 and 1990

	Absolute size (relative share of provincial population in parentheses)			
Province	**1970**	**1990**	**Absolute increase**	**Relative increase**
Patthalung	9,769 (6.3%)	28,995 (11.7%)	197%	86%
Nakhon Si Thammarat	36,942 (8.6%)	106,224 (14.7%)	186%	71%
Songkhla	35,483 (12.2%)	136,477 (24.1%)	285%	98%
Buriram	15,915 (3.9%)	59,062 (7.3%)	271%	87%
Sisaket	7,793 (1.8%)	46,607 (5.9%)	498%	228%
Chiang Mai	61,201 (12.5%)	185,295 (22.4%)	203%	79%
Nationwide	2,026,538 (12.2%)	6,015,992 (19.2%)	197%	57%

Source: *1970 Population and Housing Census, 1990 Population and Housing Census*, National Statistics Office. The composition of the 'middle class' is as in Table 9.5

occupational distribution and sectoral distribution of output in both Bangkok and the provinces. Middle-class expansion also resulted from specific government policies, such as the expansion of the higher education system. The establishment of institutes of higher learning in the provinces began by the 1960s; together with the extension in 1979 of the required length of schooling from four to six years, it created a large pool of upcountry students, teachers, and academics, who spearheaded the 1992 democracy movement in many places. In 1962, Thailand's 131,856 teachers and professors made up 0.97 per cent of the total workforce, while in 1990 the number of teachers, professors, and school administrators had grown to 630,394 people comprising 2.01 per cent of the working population.[83]

However, 1992 upcountry demonstrations also occurred in provinces like Sisaket, which was desperately poor and whose single higher

Table 9.8: Growth of the professions nationwide and selected provinces, 1970 and 1990

	Absolute size (relative share of provincial population in parentheses)			
Province	**1970**	**1990**	**Absolute increase**	**Increase relative to local pop.**
Patthalung	2,128 (1.4%)	8,639 (3.5%)	306%	150%
Nakhon Si Thammarat	6,652 (1.5%)	24,869 (3.4%)	274%	127%
Songkhla	5,262 (1.8%)	29,440 (10.2%)	459%	466%
Buriram	3,705 (0.9%)	17,668 (2.2%)	377%	144%
Sisaket	3,906 (0.9%)	16,074 (2.1%)	312%	133%
Chiang Mai	8,955 (1.8%)	38,193 (4.6%)	326%	156%
Nationwide	284,104 (1.7%)	1,326,589 (4.2%)	367%	147%

Note: The 'professions' refers to the category 'professional, technical, and related workers' employed by the National Statistics Office, and includes in part architects, scientists, engineers, doctors, nurses, teachers, academics, journalists, lawyers, artists, and accountants.

Source: *1970 Population and Housing Census, 1990 Population and Housing Census*

education institute housed in 1990 a mere 30 teachers and 291 students. Patthalung, although not as poor, boasts no institutes of higher learning whatsoever.[84] This points to a third factor crucial to the mobilization of provincial opposition to Suchinda's rule: organizations and social networks. NGOs, political parties, and ad hoc movement organizations formed from networks created by the PollWatch experience or ties among old student activists raised local political consciousness by disseminating information and strategies, and often led the anti-Suchinda protests. For the most part, the development and human rights NGOs only began to emerge in the 1980s, and were able to do so because of the availability of international funding and the increasingly liberal political atmosphere that prevailed under the prime ministers Prem Tinsulanonda (1980–1988) and Chatichai Choonhavan (1988–1991).

Middle-class provincial professionals played almost no role in the 1973 democracy movement, but took a leading position in the upcountry protest movements. On the other hand, we have noted earlier that provincial business people at best supported discreetly from behind. Several prominent provincial business people explained this choice by stating that local business people were uncertain of the outcome of the protests and were afraid that in the case of a Suchinda government victory, their enterprises would have trouble with state officials in the future.[85] The dependence of many provincial business people on either the provincial government or local officials for contracts, permits, or protection provides an economic basis for this fear.[86] It is unlikely that provincial business people will play a significant role in regime struggles until there are more upcountry enterprises whose survival is not so closely tied to the state. As businesses like hotels, department stores, and consumer goods production expand in the provinces, business people there may come to play a more politically assertive role.

BEYOND 1992

An immediate consequence of the provincial protests was that in the uncertain political atmosphere in the months following the May 1992 uprising, when there was a real possibility of a military counteraction, would-be coup-makers had to weigh the cost of suppressing resistance not only in Bangkok but upcountry as well. The size and breadth of the provincial protests also point to the emergence of a more sophisticated upcountry element which rejected the vote-buying and crude manipulation that political candidates were hitherto wont to deploy to mobilize rural support. The coalition of students, teachers, lawyers, doctors, business people, and NGO workers that turned out to oppose Suchinda in May 1992 formed the backbone of the PollWatch groups created three months later to maintain the integrity of the September parliamentary elections. Parts of this coalition remained active thereafter, working to deepen democracy by campaigning for the decentralization of state power through introducing the election of provincial governors. When this effort appeared to stall, the political focus in parliament, the press, and on the streets turned to amendment of the constitution and broader political reform. For the most part, however, the provincial middle class lapsed into quiescence after 1992. Since that time, small farmers have picked up the banner of provincial protest, agitating for land reform, commodity price supports, and, in the wake of the financial crisis of 1997, debt relief. The focus of upcountry protest activity has therefore moved away from more purely political concerns to material issues.

The election of Banharn Silpa-archa in July 1995 marked a return to the politics of patronage, vote-buying, and corruption. The victory of General Chavalit Yongchaiyudh in the 1996 elections seemed to confirm the restoration of rural-based patronage politics (though Chuan Leekpai's Democrat Party came in a very close second). The venality and inefficiency of the Banharn administration and its successor threatened to turn the middle class against not just the parties in power but against democracy itself. Bangkok opinion-makers began to make noises about changing the constitution to permit non-MPs to become prime minister. This is ironic in view of the fact that one of the main demands of the May 1992 protests had been for a constitutional clause requiring the premier to be an elected member of parliament. However, it is a reminder that for the middle class, it is clean and effective governance that counts in the end.

In the minds of the middle class, the resurgence of machine-style political parties in 1995–1996 underscored the need for political reform. Although parliament had begun to amend the constitution shortly after the May 1992 events, progress was slow as rural network politicians and conservative senators obstructed many of the more far-reaching proposals for reform. Only the onset of a severe financial crisis in 1997 created a sufficient sense of urgency in parliament to make possible the passage of a new constitution. This new charter, in addition to extending and deepening Thai citizens' rights, included rules about electoral competition, asset disclosure, conflict of interest, and the holding of ministerial portfolios. These rules were intended to reduce the role of vote-buying and the incentives and opportunities for corruption. The efficacy of these structures will remain untested until the next parliamentary election, which must take place by late 2000.

How the middle class will respond if the problems of corruption and ineffective government persist will have important implications for the viability of stable democratic rule. It is not likely that the middle class would soon support another coup, so its options would be either to push for a further round of reform, or to retreat towards a more limited model of democracy. The business-oriented segments of the middle class would probably favour a more restrictive solution, while academics and the NGO community would probably back an extension of democratic reforms.

The return of patronage politics in 1995–1996 also highlighted the deep rift between urban and rural Thais, a division that has political, social, economic, and cultural manifestations. Urban middle-class Thais have very different expectations of their politicians than do rural folk, and managing the resulting tension is one of the greatest problems facing the political system.[87] Time is ultimately on the side of the urban middle class, because the process of economic development is gradually creating a more educated and urbanized population. The expansion of the education system to make secondary and vocational education more widely available, the decline of the share of the workforce involved in agriculture, and the movement of the population off the farm and into the cities will slowly work to close the yawning urban–rural divide and create a larger social base for the kind of politics favoured by the middle class. In the meantime, however, the electoral system will very likely continue to reflect and reproduce the conflict between the urban middle class and the rural areas.

NOTES

1. Anek Laothamatas, *Mob muthu: chon chan klang lae nak thurakit kap phatthanakan prachathipatai* (Bangkok: Matichon Publications, 1993); Sungsidh Piriyarangsan and Pasuk Phongpaichit (eds) *Chon chan klang bon krasae prachathipatai* (Bangkok: Chulalongkorn University, 1993).

2. I use 'upcountry', 'provincial', and 'the provinces' to refer to all of Thailand outside of Bangkok and its environs. 'Urban' means any city or municipality, including all provincial capitals. 'Rural' means an area outside a city or municipality. Aside from civil servants, the upcountry middle class is located mostly in the provincial municipalities.

3. This definition of the middle class is very close to the definitions employed by Hewison (Kevin Hewison, 'Emerging Social Forces in Thailand: New Political and Economic Roles', in Richard Robison and David Goodman (eds) *The New Rich in Asia* (London: Routledge, 1996), p. 143), and Pasuk (Pasuk Phongpaichit, 'Botbat chon chan klang nai setthakit lae kanmuang khong prathet NICs lae thai: khonsangket buangton', in Sungsidh Piriyarangsan and Pasuk Phongpaichit (eds) *Chon chan klang bon krasae*

prachathipatai thai (Bangkok: Chulalongkorn University Political Economy Center, 1993) p. 91, n. 1).

4. In 1973 the Communist Party of Thailand (CPT) was not yet numerically significant; the insurgency would reach its peak five years later in 1978. See Sukhumbhand Paribatra, *From Enmity to Alignment: Thailand's Evolving Relations with China* (Bangkok: Chulalongkorn University Institute of Security and International Studies, 1987), pp. 20–21.

5. Benedict Anderson provides a superb analysis of the political about-face executed by the Bangkok middle class from 1973 to 1976 in 'Withdrawal Symptoms', *Bulletin of Concerned Asian Scholars*, 9 (July–September 1977): 13–30. On the 1973–1976 period generally, see David Morell and Chai-Anan Samudavanija, *Political Conflict in Thailand: Reform, Reaction, Revolution* (Cambridge, Mass.: Oelgeschalger, Gunn & Hain, 1981).

6. Anek Laothamatas, *Business Associations and the New Political Economy of Thailand* (Boulder, Col.: Westview Press, 1992), pp. 32–40.

7. On the rise of provincial businessmen and its political implications, see James S. Ockey, 'Business Leaders, Gangsters, and the Middle Class: Societal Groups and Civilian Rule in Thailand' (Ph.D. thesis, Cornell University, 1992).

8. Scott Christensen, 'Thailand after the Coup', *Journal of Democracy* 2 (1991): 99–101.

9. Anek Laothamatas, 'A Tale of Two Democracies: Conflicting Perception of Election and Democracy as a Source of Political Impasse in Thailand'. Paper prepared for the Social Science Research Center Asia Program on Elections in Southeast Asia, Woodrow Wilson Center, Washington, DC, 16–18 September 1993, pp. 10–12.

10. Ananya Bhuchongkul states that 'it was Chatichai's relationship with the military that was really his downfall'. ('Thailand 1991: The Return of the Military', *Southeast Asian Affairs 1992* (Singapore: Institute of Southeast Asian Studies, 1993), p. 316.

11. According to Prinya Thewanareumitrakul, who was the president of the Student Federation of Thailand and a member of the Confederation for Democracy in 1992, 'Few people opposed the coup, and those who did tended to be afraid to express their opinions'. Dr Pradit Charoenthaithawee, Rector of Mahidon University, stated that 'at that time, you could almost say that society had no difficulty accepting [the coup]'. Both quoted on p. 11 in 'Sewana-wiwatha: 1 pi hetkan duan phritsapha kap honthang khangna prachathipatai thai', *Chotmai khao kho. ro. pho.* 1, 7 (May 1993): 4–19.

12. For a detailed study of Chamlong and his military and political career, see Duncan McCargo, *Chamlong Srimuang and the New Thai Politics* (New York: St Martin's Press, 1998).

13. Chamlong received 703,000 votes, or about 62 per cent of the total, which was more than double the share of the runner-up (Rodney Tasker, 'Capital Gains', *Far Eastern Economic Review*, 18 January 1990: 9).

14. 'Anand in Review', *Bangkok Post* supplement, 13 March 1992: 5. In comparison, the elected legislature under PM Chatichai passed 108 laws in the two years and five months from 24 July 1988 to 31 December 1990 (Thinaphan Nakhata, 'Thahan kab kanphatthana khong thai', *Sayam rat sapda wichan* 40, 43 (1992): 22, fn. 3. As Anand discovered, there are definite advantages to authoritarian rule, such as insulation of policy-makers from societal pressures and the absence of squabbling coalition parties whose interests the prime minister must balance.

15. 'Anand in Review', pp. 15–18.

16. *Bangkok Post*, 23 June 1991, p. B3.

17. Later events would reveal the depth of support for Anand among the Bangkok middle and upper classes. In March 1993, with Anand out of office but facing criminal malfeasance charges for his handling of judicial appointments by a disgruntled judge, members of the Bangkok elite founded an organization called 'Friends of Anand' to support the former prime minister in his legal battle. Within a month and a half, about 20,000 people, mostly white-collar workers and bureaucrats, had signed up as Friends of Anand. David Peters, 'Paving the Way,' *Manager* [Bangkok], June 1993: 16–26.

18. Anek Laothamatas, 'Ru pen yak thi phoeng tun: chon chan klang kap kanmuang thai', *Mob muthu: chon chan klang lae nak thurakit kap phatthanakan prachathipatai*, pp. 78–80, 91.

19. Such was the case in the regional PollWatch coordinating committees covering provinces such as Songkhla and Patthalung in the South and Buriram and Sisaket in the Northeast. Interviews with Phichai Sisai, Songkhla high school teacher and southern region PollWatch committee member; Phitthaya Phutsararat (Patthalung); Niran Kulathanan, head librarian, Buriram Province Teachers College, northeast PollWatch committee member; and Suphan Sakhon (Sisaket), advisor to the northeastern PollWatch committee.

20. Based on the author's observations during visits to these offices in September before the elections.

21. On vote-buying, see Ananya Bhuchongkul, 'Vote-buying: More than Just a Sale', *Bangkok Post*, 23 February 1992; William Callahan and Duncan McCargo, 'Vote-buying in Thailand's Northeast: The July 1995 General Election,' *Asian Survey* 36 (1996): 376–392; and Daniel King and Jim LoGerfo, 'Thailand: Toward Democratic Stability,' *Journal of Democracy* 7 (1996): 112.

22. A survey of Bangkok residents conducted in May 1991 (n = 950) supports the contention that Bangkokians want a clean government that delivers economic development and modern infrastructure. Respondents were asked what issue the government should make its top priority: 57 per cent named the economy and basic problems, while 12 per cent named traffic problems. Thus, almost 70 per cent responded that the government should focus on the economy and local infrastructure. Another 12.4 per cent wanted the government to make the war against corruption its main

objective. Respondents were also asked what the NPC itself should do, and 38 per cent favoured a crackdown on vote-buying, while 25 per cent preferred it to prioritize economic issues. The social backgrounds of the respondents were not reported (*Bangkok Post*, 9 June 1991).

23. An exploratory survey of attitudes towards democracy among Bangkok and rural northern Thai conducted in late 1994 and early 1995 provides evidence that generally supports the assertion that Bangkokians (not differentiated by class) subscribe to this model. Asked what they thought a good member of parliament should do, Bangkok respondents stated that they expected their elected representatives to work diligently, be good party members, deliver material benefits to the locality, and ensure continued economic development for the nation as a whole. Jim LoGerfo, 'Attitudes toward Democracy among Bangkok and Rural Northern Thais: The Great Divide', *Asian Survey* 36 (1996): 904–923.

24. Ukrit Patmanan, 'Hetkan phritsapha thamin kap kansadaeng ook thang kanmuang khong nak thurakit thai', *Sangkhomsat parithat* 16, 1 (1992): 98.

25. Thailand. Ministry of Commerce, Department of Registration. The total number of businesses registered in these years was 42,943 in 1972; 96,620 in 1982; and 245,778 in 1992.

26. After the May crisis, with the military in disgrace, the second Anand government successfully restructured the terms of the project. At the signing ceremony on 2 July 1992, Anand stated that the state would have lost 200 billion baht over the 25 years of the concession if the contract had remained unchanged. Vuthiphong Priebjrivat, 'Politics of Privatization: Telephone Concession in Thailand', unpublished paper, 31 August 1992, pp. 16–23, and 'Anand in Review', p. 8.

27. 'Anand in Review', p. 9.

28. See, for example, Tai Ming Cheung, 'Officers' Commission', *Far Eastern Economic Review*, 2 July 1992, p. 13.

29. The term 'rural network politicians' refers to politicians 'who have build influence in a provincial district through distribution of money and business concessions' (Philip S. Robertson Jr, 'The Rise of the Rural Network Politician, ' *Asian Survey* 36 (1996): 924).

30. *Bangkok Post*, 17 November 1991. These included provisions which allowed active government officials to hold political posts and gave the NPC-appointed Senate the same number of members as the elected House along with the right to debate and vote in censure motions, and named the Senate speaker as president of parliament.

31. *Bangkok Post*, 19 November 1991.

32. Here a 'pro-military' party is understood as one that did not support the movement against the NPC constitution, and which was willing to support a non-elected former military officer (i.e., General Suchinda) as

prime minister. The pro-democracy parties were those that supported the movement against the NPC charter. This division is not perfect: Prachakorn Thai Party, which was a part of the government coalition, had actually given conditional support to the protests against the constitution. It was estimated that the parties spent a total of 3–5 billion baht (US$120–200 million) nationwide during the political campaigning. Gothom Arya, head of the election monitoring organization PollWatch, estimated that up to 50 per cent of the votes cast involved an exchange of money, and PollWatch officials and campaigners placed the figure at 70–90 per cent for the Northeast. Paul Handley, 'Where Money Talks', *Far Eastern Economic Review,* 2 April 1992, p. 12.

33. Rodney Tasker, 'Premier of Last Resort', *Far Eastern Economic Review,* 16 April 1992, p. 10.

34. After the junta had overthrown Chatichai, sending him fleeing to exile in England, it established an Assets Investigation Committee to uncover and seize the ill-gotten gains of Chatichai government ministers and their associates. It declared as 'unusually wealthy' a number of leading political party figures. Shortly before the March 1992 elections it seized assets totalling 206.5 million baht from three Chart Thai Party executives, 266.5 million baht from the exiled Chatichai Choonhavan, and 336.5 million baht from Social Action head Montri Pongpanich (Samrut Miwongukhot (ed.) *Kanyutsap nak kanmuang thai* (Bangkok: Siamban Chamkat, n.d.), pp. 50–61). The decisions of this committee were very likely the subject of political manipulation: for example, though it was known that Agriculture Minister Maj. Gen. Sanan Khajonprasan was involved in at least two deals thought corrupt (one concerning a eucalyptus plantation in Chachoengsao, and another concerning fertilizer), he was not charged with being 'unusually wealthy'. The committee did declare finance minister Banharn Silpa-archa and two others from the Chatichai cabinet to be 'unusually wealthy' but did not seize any of their property. It seized assets totalling 1,917,860,000 baht from ten people, but the post-military Chuan government returned every last baht.

35. The six 'unusually wealthy' politicians and their Suchinda cabinet positions were as follows: Montri Pongpanich, deputy prime minister; Watthana Assahawen and Suchon Champhoon, ministers without portfolio; Banharn Silpa-archa, communications minister; Sanoh Thienthong, deputy communications minister; and Chuchip Hansawat, deputy education minister. Scott Christensen and Ammar Siamwalla, 'Beyond Patronage: Tasks for the Thai State' (paper presented at the Thailand Development Research Institute 1993 Year-End Conference, Chonburi, Thailand, 10–11 December 1993), p. 28.

36. *Bangkok Post,* 8 April 1992.

37. Specifically, they required that the prime minister be an elected MP, the Senate's powers be reduced to simply screening legislation, the house

president as speaker of parliament, and permit MPs to introduce new legislation during parliament's second session.

38. See Chamlong Srimuang, *Ruamkan Su* (Bangkok: Thira kanphim, 1992), for his account of the 1992 crisis.

39. In 1992 there were 73 provinces in Thailand (there are currently 76). Much of the information I present on the upcountry protests comes from the *Matichon* daily newspaper, 6–22 May 1992. I have relied on *Matichon* because its political coverage was comprehensive. Another source used was a summary of the events from 5–23 May prepared by the Northern Coordinating Committee for the Development of Democracy (NCCDD). This document provides daily reports of movement activity from around the country, culled from such sources as television and radio broadcasts, information sent to the NCCDD by Campaign for Popular Democracy committees from other regions, and eyewitnesses at the demonstrations. The citation for this document is Khana kammakan prasanngan phua phattana prachathipatai phak nua, *Kan khluanwai khon prachachon khatkhan ratthathamanun thi mai pen prachathipatai lae tan nayok khon, wan thi 5–23, phritsaphakom 2535* (Chiang Mai, n.d.), hereafter cited as *Khana kammakan.* Finally, I obtained information from the *Bangkok Post,* which covered the provincial movements in much less detail than *Matichon.*

40. I define a 'protest action' as any form of expression by which non-officials make public a political opinion, either as individuals or as members of groups. Protest actions include issuing statements, submitting letters to government officials, and demonstrating in the streets. I consider as part of the democracy movement only those protest actions that called for Suchinda's resignation and/or pro-democratic amendment of the constitution, and unless otherwise stated, it can be assumed that 'protest action' refers to activity for democratic change. I do not include as part of the democracy movement those protests which condemned the use of violence or expressed grief at the loss of life in Bangkok without making demands for Suchinda's resignation or the amendment of the constitution.

41. *Matichon,* 7–11 May 1992; *Khana kammakan,* pp. 3–22; *Bangkok Post,* 9 May 1992.

42. *Khana kammakan,* pp. 20, 26–36; interview with Suphan Sakhon, lawyer, advisor to PollWatch Isan in January-March 1992, and advisor to the Sisaket Union for Civil Liberties, 2 June 1994.

43. *Matichon,* 16 May 1992; *Bangkok Post,* 16 May 1992.

44. *Matichon,* 18 May 1992; *Khana kammakan,* p. 51.

45. The sources for the provincial protest size are *Matichon,* 21 May 1992, and interviews conducted in 1994 with Phitthaya Phutsararat (teacher, Patthalung High School for Girls and committee member, Patthalung Confederation for Democracy); Prachote Siriwat (editor, *Taksin Times,* and committee member, Nakhon Si Thammarat Confederation for Democracy); Nipha Fangchonjit (editor, *Muang tai* [a Nakhon Si Thammarat newspaper]);

and Prof. Nongyao Yaowarat (Chiang Mai University Faculty of Education and committee member, Northern Coordinating Committee for the Development of Democracy). Where the estimates of *Matichon* and local activists have differed I have used the smaller figure. The Bangkok estimate is from Bangkok Post, *Catalyst for Change* (Bangkok: The Post Publication Co., July 1992) p. 15.

46. Many thanks to my research assistant Pawana Wiriyajaree for her help in gathering these data.

47. Interviews conducted in June 1994 with Dr Kittiphum Chuthasamit, director, Yangchumnon District Hospital, committee member Sisaket PollWatch (September 1992); and Suphan Sakhon, lawyer, advisor PollWatch Isan (March 1992).

48. See *Matichon*, 6–22 May 1992.

49. '[T]he main finding of the cross-national statistical work – a positive, though not perfect, correlation between capitalist development and democracy – must stand as an accepted result. There is no way of explaining this robust finding, replicated in many studies of different design, as the spurious effect of flawed methods. Any theory of democracy must come to terms with it.' Dietrich Rueschemeyer, Evelyne Huber Stephens, and John D. Stephens, *Capitalist Development and Democracy* (Chicago: University of Chicago Press, 1992), p. 4. In this study of political participation in Austria, India, Japan, The Netherlands, Nigeria, the United States, and Yugoslavia, it was concluded that 'those high on social and economic stratification hierarchies possess greater resources and motivation to be politically active. They, therefore, take greater advantage of political participatory opportunities than those lower on the socio-economic stratification hierarchy.' Sidney Verba, Norman Nie, and Jae-on Kim *Participation and Political Equality: A Seven-Nation Comparison* (Cambridge: Cambridge University Press, 1978), p. 4.

Larry Diamond argues that 'per capita income, or gross national product (GNP) is the development variable most often tested in association with democracy' (Larry Diamond, 'Economic Development and Democracy Reconsidered,' *American Behavioral Scientist* 35 (1992): 457). Diamond notes the flaws inherent in per capita income as a measurement of development, and uses the United Nations Development Program's Human Development Index (HDI) in his own statistical analysis. Since HDI figures are not available for Thailand, I used per capita income instead.

50. Thus a study of political participation in the United States found substantial disparities in the nature and extent of political participation among individuals at different levels of income and education, with those at the upper income range scoring much higher than those towards the bottom, and those in real financial need significantly less active; see Sidney Verba, Kay Lehman Schlozman, Henry Brady, and Norman Niew, 'Citizen Activity: Who Participates? What Do They Say?', *American Political Science Review* 87 (1993): 305.

51. The two exceptions were Songkhla and Nakhon Si Thammarat. The former saw protests both in Songkhla city and in the province's largest urban centre, Hat Yai. Songkhla is unique among Thailand's provinces in that its largest urban centre is not also its capital. Protest in Nakhon Si Thammarat in May 1992 occurred not only in the provincial capital but also in the district towns of Thung Song and Hua Sai; see *Matichon*, 14 May 1992; *Khana kammakan*, p. 52.

52. A unique survey conducted during the protest held in Bangkok on the night of 17 May documented the significance of the middle-class presence in the democracy movement. The Social Science Association of Thailand distributed 2,000 questionnaires at the demonstration, and found that 52 per cent of the respondents held bachelor's degrees, while 51.7 per cent were drawing comfortable middle-class incomes of 10,000 baht (US$400) or moresee *Phuchatkan* daily newspaper, 19 May 1992. The survey may be biased towards wealthier and better educated respondents, for those with lower education may have been unfamiliar with the concept of survey research and less willing to complete the questionnaire.

53. Worawit Charooenloet, 'Chon chan klang kab hetkan phrutsaphakhom: fai prachathipatai ru ratpatikan?', in Sungsidh and Pasuk (eds), *Chon chan klang bon krasae prachathipatai.*, pp. 125–126, 144–146. For details on lower-class participation in the 1991–1992 movement, see Somsak Kosaisuk, *Labor against Dictatorship* (Bangkok: Friedrich Ebert Stiftung, 1993), and Sungsidh Piriyarangsan, 'Lukchang, khon chon muang, kab hetkan duan phrutsaphakom', in Sungsidh and Pasuk (eds), *Chon chan klang bon krasae prachathipatai.*

54. Ockey, 'Political Parties, Factions, and Corruption in Thailand,' pp. 255–59; Daniel King and Jim LoGerfo, 'Thailand: Toward Democratic Stability', *Journal of Democracy*,7 (1996): 112.

55. Daniel King, 'The Thai Parliamentary Elections of 1992: Return to Democracy in an Atypical Year', *Asian Survey* 32 (1992): 1118.

56. After the military began the killing on 17 May, tourists around the country packed their bags, and hotels and travel agencies received a flood of cancellations. The scenes of military brutality broadcast on television screens around the world had a strong and immediate impact on the tourist industry. (*Catalyst for Change*, pp. 78–79; and interview with Sittisak Thapngam, chief administrator of the Association of Thai Travel Agents, May 1994). The Songkhla Chamber of Commerce commissioned a survey shortly after the crisis ended, which found that the Hat Yai tourist business was down by 40 per cent in May. In Hat Yai, the sudden loss of tourist income brought hotel owners, tour operators, and even nightclub singers out on the streets to demonstrate against Gen. Suchinda and the use of violence (interview with Chan Leelaphon, president, Songkhla Chamber of Commerce on 6 May 1994; and Phichai Sisai, president of the Southern Campaign for Popular Democracy on 5 May 1994).

57. If only MPs in Election District One (centred on the provincial capital) are considered, then Songkhla drops into the middle group. I have

also included figures on the share of MPs in Election District One from parties opposed to Suchinda because, given that protests almost invariably occurred in the provincial capital with participants drawn mostly from its own residents, party affiliation of MPs in other electoral districts might be considered irrelevant. When only District One MPs are considered, the share of MPs in opposition parties was 67 per cent or higher in five out of the six cases. On the other hand, strong protest movements occurred in other provinces with low proportions of Electoral District One MPs from opposition parties. In the northeastern province of Nakhon Ratchasima, for example, none of the District One MPs was from a party opposed to Suchinda, but that province was a major centre of protest. In a number of provinces all District One MPs were from opposition parties, but I have found no reports of protests (Chumphon, Krabi, Phangnga, Ranong, Sakon Nakhon, Samut Sakhon, Samut Songkhram, Tak, and Yala).

58. For an analysis of relative tie strength and its relation to processes of diffusion and mobilization for collective action, see Mark Granovetter, 'The Strength of Weak Ties', *America Journal of Sociology* 78 (1973): 1360–1380.

59. Interviews with Phichai Sisai (Songkhla), Phitthaya Phutsararat (Patthalung), Prachot Siriwat (Nakhon Si Thammarat), Niran Kulathanan (Buriram), Suphan Sakhon (Sisaket), Prof. Somphong Witthayasakphan (Chiang Mai University, member Northern Coordinating Committee for the Development of Democracy), and Prof. Nongyao Yaowarat (Chiang Mai). I did not obtain information about PollWatch in Nakhon Si Thammarat, but Prachot Siriwat said that the Nakhon Si Thammarat Union for Civil Liberties helped lead the movement there. Prof. Somphong Witthayasakphan stated that the Chiang Mai University professors who formed the core of the protest movement leadership in May mostly did not work for PollWatch in March because they considered it a 'paper tiger'.

60. Interviews with Phichai Sisai (Songkhla) and Suphan Sakhon (Sisaket).

61. In the Northeast, NGO-CORD and other networks of NGOs and people's organizations helped to gather and disseminate information about the political situation and mobilize local support for demonstrations. Niran Kulathanan, 'NGO Movements and Democratic Transition: View from the Northeast'. Paper prepared for the Fifth International Conference on Thai Studies, School of Oriental and African Studies, London, 1993, p. 8.

62. Interviews with Phichai Sisai (Songkhla), Nongyao Yaowarat (Chiang Mai), Somphong Witthayasakphan (Chiang Mai), and *Matichon*, 6–22 May 1992.

63. Predisposed against Suchinda and the NPC-sponsored constitution for at least two reasons: first, because a certain share of NGO workers had fought for years with the Communist Party of Thailand against the military; after the insurgency fizzled out in the early to mid-1980s they laid down their arms and took up the issue of rural development but retained their political awareness (interview with Prof. Saneh Chamrik, director, Local

Development Assistance Program, 19 November 1992). Second, because such NPC policies as the dissolution of state enterprise unions and the roundly hated Land Allocation Project for the Poor in the Degraded Reserve Forests (abbreviated Kho. Jo. Ko. in Thai) showed that protecting subordinate-group interests required democratic government. See Arom-phongphangan Foundation, 'Trade Union Rights in Thailand', paper presented at the Regional Conference on Trade Union Rights organized by the International Confederation of Free Trade Unions – Asia and Pacific Regional Organization, 24–28 October 1993, Phuket, Thailand, for information on the NPC assault on state enterprise unions and unions in general, and Niran Kulathanan, 'NGOs and Democratic Transition', for information on the Kho. Jo. Ko., local resistance, and the connection with the May protest movement.

64. Prof. Nongyao Yaowarat, secretary-general of the March PollWatch Region 5 Committee covering eight northern provinces, stated in interview (6 June 1994) that 'I know a lot of people in PollWatch who came to the protests. They felt like they had planted the tree of democracy with their own hands, and just a few months later the tree was destroyed. Those who had participated in PollWatch already had an interest in politics. PollWatch did not create their political consciousness, but it did give them an opportunity to come together.'

65. *Matichon*, 6–22 May 1992.

66. Information on business participation in the Hat Yai protests is based on interviews conducted in May 1994 with Chan Lilaphon, managing director, King's Hotel, The Thainam and Son Co., Ltd., Thainam Press, and Tawon Borikan Caltex Service Station, president Songkhla Chamber of Commerce, member Hat Yai Municipal Council ; Suphot Mancharoensin, director Hat Yai City Department Store; and Thamanun Salimin, manager Asian Hotel, executive committee member Democrat Party Hat Yai office.

67. Interestingly, the economy of Chiang Mai city is also heavily dependent on the tourist industry, yet local business people did not openly participate in the protests as in Hat Yai, nor did Chiang Mai business associations become involved in the fray. I made repeated but unsuccessful efforts to interview the head of the Chiang Mai Travel Agents Association, who was also prominent in the local branch of the Democrat Party and a former provincial councillor, in the hopes of obtaining an informed explanation of this.

68. Interviews conducted in May 1994 with Phichai Sisai, high school teacher, committee member Southern Teachers Federation, president Southern Campaign for Popular Democracy, committee member Songkhla Union for Civil Liberties; Phitthaya Phutsararat, teacher Patthalung School for Girls, committee member Patthalung Confederation for Democracy, Patthalung PollWatch.

69. Interview with Phitthaya Phutsararat (May 1994); *Matichon*, 20–21 May 1994.

70. Interview with Phitthaya Phutsararat. In May 1992 all three of Patthalung's MPs were from opposition parties (two from the Democrat Party, one from New Aspiration). The Democrat Party has dominated the Southern region in nearly every election since 1983.

71. The Communist Party of Thailand had been active in Patthalung as far back as 1959, and by the 1970s it had a strong presence there. In 1972, government forces developed a notorious method of eliminating suspected 'communists'. Soldiers would beat detainees, usually to unconsciousness, then put them in an oil drum, pour in gasoline, and set them alight. The 'Red Barrel' killings, as they were called, left tremendous bitterness among Patthalung residents towards the military. For details on the communist insurgency in Patthalung and the Red Barrel killings, see John Value Dennis Jr, 'The Role of the Thai Student Movement in Rural Conflict, 1973–76' (M.A. thesis, Cornell University, 1982), pp. 130–178. For the influence of these events on Patthalung demonstrations against Suchinda, interview with Parinam Saengthat, reporter in Patthalung for *Matichon,* May 1994.

72. *Khana kammakan,* pp. 19, 71.

73. *Khana kammakan,* p. 19.

74. Interview with a Chiang Mai NGO worker, June 1994.

75. Interviews, June 1994, with Prof. Nongyao Yaowarat and with Dr Phichet Wiriyachiet, professor of pharmaceutical sciences at Chiang Mai University and member Northern Coordinating Committee for the Development of Democracy.

76. Krom kanpokkhrong, Krasuang mahatthai, *Luaktang 22 minakhom 2535* (Bangkok: Kongwichakan lae phaenngan, 1992), p. 315.

77. Along with Major-Generals Pramarn Adireksarn and Chatichai Choonhavan, Banharn was a founding member of the Chart Thai Party. He first won a seat in parliament representing Suphanburi Province in 1976. Although he did not run in the 1979 election because he had been appointed to the Senate, he competed in the 1983 polls and has won every election from that time forward. One measure of Banharn's ability to bring home the bacon is the six schools, the clock tower, the park, the temple, and the numerous other sites in the province named after him and his wife. He was also responsible for the construction of the many paved roads that criss-cross Suphanburi, which are among the best in the country. See Bret Thorn and Sompong Suwantikul, 'In Power, but not in Office,' *Manager* (August 1993): 17–22; James Ockey, 'Business Leaders, Gangsters, and the Middle Class' (Ph.D. thesis, Cornell University, 1992) , p. 230.

78. *Matichon,* 21 May 1992.

79. *Matichon,* 21 May 1992.

80. The first protest action outside Bangkok occurred on 8 October, when students put up political posters around the Chiang Mai University campus,

and student protest spread to Ayutthaya, Chachoengsao, Chonburi, Chumphon, Khon Kaen, Lopburi, Mahasarkaham, Nakhon Pathom, Nakhon Ratchasima, Nakhon Sawan, Nakhon Si Thiammarat, Pattani, Phetburi, Phitsanulok, Phuket, Songkhla, Surin, Ubon Ratchathani, Udon Thani, Uttaradit, and Yala provinces (*Thai rat*, issues of 9–16 October 1973).

81. The sole exception was a newspaper report that attributed responsibility for putting up posts in support of the democracy movement around Trang city to 'members of the public', not to students (*Thai rat*, 12 October 1973).

82. Student representatives from every university in the country founded the National Student Centre of Thailand in December 1969 (Ross Prizzia and Narong Sinsawasdi, *Thailand: Student Activism and Political Change* (Bangkok: DK Books, 1974), p. 28. Furthermore, the transportation and communications infrastructure in 1973 was less developed than in 1992, so that Bangkok and the provinces were less integrated and people in the provinces might not have felt as close to the political struggles in the capital or as able to affect its outcome. In addition, expectations about the possibility of state repression might have been higher in 1973 than in 1992.

83. *National Population and Housing Census*, 1960 and 1990. The 1960 figure represents 'professors and teachers' while the 1990 figure includes school administrators as well, accounting for some of the increase.

84. *Report on Educational Statistics by Changwat [Province]: Academic Year 1990* (Bangkok: Office of the Permanent Secretary, Ministry of Education).

85. Interviews in May 1994 with Chan Leelaphon (Songkhla); Kosin Phaisansin, owner Toyota Patthalung, municipal councillor Patthalung, committee member Patthalung Confederation for Democracy; Nipha Fangchonjit, editor and manager *Muang tai* newspaper, president Nakhon Si Thammarat Mass Media Association, president, Phromsiri District Farmers' Group, and member Nakhon Si Thammarat Farmers' Central Committee. On the other hand, Bowon Janphodaphaiboon, secretary-general of the Patthalung Chamber of Commerce, suggested (interview, May 1994) that the political non-involvement of business people in his province was due to the fact that Bangkok politics had virtually no impact on their businesses, which are predominantly based on agriculture.

Photthawat Wilaihong, managing director, Lanna Supply Co., and secretary-general of the Chiang Mai Chamber of Commerce, stated that local businessmen did play a leading role in the protests. However, this was not confirmed by *Matichon* newspaper accounts (issues of 6- 22 May 1992) of the Chiang Mai demonstrations. My own interviews with members of the leading protest organization, the Northern Coordinating Committee for the Development of Democracy, do not bear him out (interviews in June 1994 with Prof. Nongyao Yaowarat, Prof. Somphong Witthayasakphan, and Dunyaphon Kittisalet).

86. 'When all is said and done, provincial businesses are very dependent either on Bangkok business (dealerships) or on the government (construction) or on government personnel (illegal businesses). Consequently, the political involvement of provincial businessmen have [*sic*] remained very strictly local except in a few rare cases, where an extremely powerful 'jao pho' [*chao pho*, or 'godfather'] have [*sic*] been able to extend his zone of influence over a few surrounding provinces.' Scott Christensen and Amarn Siamwalla, 'Beyond Patronage', p. 32.

87. Jim LoGerfo, 'Attitudes toward Democracy among Bangkok and Rural Northern Thais', pp. 918–920.

Select Bibliography

Amara Pongsapich (1976). 'Social Processes and Social Structures in Chonburi Thailand'. *Journal of the Siam Society* 64: 207–236.

Ananya Buchongkul (1985). 'From Chaonaa to Khonngaan: The Growing Divide in a Central Thai Village'. PhD thesis, University of London.

Anderson, Benedict R. O'G. (1977). 'Withdrawal Symptoms: Social and Cultural Aspects of the October 6 Coup'. *Bulletin of Concerned Asian Scholars* 9 (3): 13–30.

——— (1978). 'Studies of the Thai State: The State of Thai Studies', in Eliezer B. Ayal (ed.), *The Study of Thailand*. Athens: Ohio University Center for International Studies, 193–247.

——— (1990). 'Murder and Progress in Modern Siam'. *New Left Review* 181: 33–48.

Anek Laothamatas (1988). 'Business and Politics in Thailand: New Patterns of Influence'. *Asian Survey* 28: 451–470.

——— (1992). *Business Associations and the New Political Economy of Thailand: From Bureaucratic Polity to Liberal Corporatism*. Singapore: Institute of Southeast Asia Studies and Boulder, Col.: Westview Press.

——— (1992). 'The Politics of Structural Adjustment in Thailand: A Political Explanation of Economic Success', in Andrew J. MacIntyre and Kanishka Jayasuriya (eds), *The Dynamics of Economic Policy Reform in South-east Asia and the South-west Pacific*. Singapore: Oxford University Press, 32–49.

——— (1993). *Mob muthu: chon chan klang lae nak thurakit kap phatthanakan prachathipatai*. [The Mobile Phone Mob: The Middle Class and Businessmen in Democratic Development]. Bangkok: Matichon Publications.

——— (1994). 'From Clientelism to Partnership: Business–Government Relations in Thailand', in Andrew MacIntyre (ed.), *Business and*

Government in Industrializing Asia. London and Ithaca: Cornell University Press, 195–215.

——— (1996). 'A Tale of Two Democracies: Conflicting Perceptions of Elections and Democracy in Thailand', in R. H. Taylor (ed.), *The Politics of Elections in Southeast Asia*. Cambridge: Woodrow Wilson Center Press and Cambridge University Press, 201–223.

Anusorn Limmanee (1995). *Political Business Cycle in Thailand, 1979–1992: General Election and Currency in Circulation*. Bangkok: Institute of Thai Studies, Chulalongkorn University.

Arghiros, Daniel (1993). 'Rural Transformation and Local Politics in a Central Thai District'. PhD thesis, University of Hull.

——— (1995). *Political Structures and Strategies: a Study of Electoral Politics in Contemporary Rural Thailand*. Hull: University of Hull Centre for South-East Asian Studies.

——— (1997). 'The Rise of Indigenous Capitalists in Rural Thailand: Profile of Brickmakers in the Central Plains', in Mario Rutten and Carol Upadhya (eds), *Small Business Entrepreneurs in Asia and Europe: Towards a Comparative Perspective*. New Delhi, Thousand Oaks, London: Sage Publications, 115–146.

Bamrung Sukhaphan (1981). *Botbat khong chao chin nai prathet thai* [The Role of the Chinese in Thailand]. Bangkok: Thammasat University, Khana warasansat lae sueksan muanchon.

Bowie, Katherine A. (1992) 'Unraveling the Myth of the Subsistence Economy: Textile Production in Nineteenth Century Northern Thailand'. *Journal of Asian Studies* 51: 77–82.

Brown, Ian (1988). *The Elite and the Economy in Siam c. 1890–1920*. Singapore: Oxford University Press.

Callahan, William A. (1998). *Imagining Democracy: Reading 'The Events of May' in Thailand*. Singapore: Institute of Southeast Asian Studies.

Callahan, William A. and Duncan McCargo (1996). 'Vote-Buying in Thailand's Northeast'. *Asian Survey* 26: 376–392.

Chai-anan Samudavanija (1981). *Kanluaktang phak kanmuang, ratthasapha, lae khana thahan*. [Elections, Parliament, and the Military]. Bangkok: Bannakit Trading.

Chai-anan Samudavanija, Kusuma Snitwongse, and Suchit Bunbongkarn (1990). *From Armed Suppression to Political Offensive*. Bangkok: Chulalongkorn University Institute of Security and International Studies.

Chakrit Noranitipadungkarn (1970). *Elites, Power Structures and Politics in Thai Communities*. Bangkok: Research Center, The National Institute of Development Administration.

Chatchai Yenbamrung and Thamrongsak Phetloeanan (eds) (1987). *Banthuk kanmuang thai* [Thai Political Notebook]. Bangkok: Prachum chang.

Chatthip Nartsupha (1984). *Setthakit muban thai nai adit* [The Thai Village Economy in the Past]. Bangkok: Sangsan Publishing House.

Chatthip Nartsupha and Suthy Prasartset (1981). *The Political Economy of Siam, l851–1910.* Bangkok: Social Science Association of Thailand.

Christensen, Scott (1991). 'Thailand after the Coup'. *Journal of Democracy* 2: 94–106.

Clad, James (1989). *Behind the Myth: Business, Money and Power in Southeast Asia.* London: Unwin Hyman.

Coughlin, Richard (1960). *Double Identity: The Chinese in Modern Thailand.* Hong Kong: Hong Kong University Press.

Cushman, Jennifer W. (1991). *Family and State: The Formation of a Sino-Thai Tin-Mining Dynasty.* Singapore: Oxford University Press.

Dayley, Robert (1996). 'Entrepreneurs', in Bryan Hunsaker (ed.), *Loggers, Monks, Students, and Entrepreneurs: Four Essays on Thailand.* DeKalb: Northern Illinois University Center for Southeast Asian Studies.

Doner, Richard F. (1991). 'Approaches to the Politics of Growth in Southeast Asia'. *Journal of Asian Studies* 50: 818–849.

——— (1992). 'The Limits of State Strength: Toward an Institutionalist View of Economic Policy'. *World Politics* 44: 398–431.

Douglass, Mike (1984). *Regional Integration on the Capitalist Periphery: The Central Plain of Thailand.* The Hague: Institute of Social Studies.

Evers, Hans-Dieter, (ed.) (1969). *Loosely Structured Social Systems: Thailand in Comparative Perspective.* New Haven: Yale University Southeast Asia Studies.

Feeny, David (1982). *The Political Economy of Productivity: Thai Agricultural Development, 1880–1975.* Vancouver: University of British Columbia Press.

Galaska, Chester F. (1969). 'Continuity and Change in Dalat Plu, a Chinese Middle Class Business Community in Thailand'. PhD thesis, Syracuse University.

Girling, John L. S. (1981). *The Bureaucratic Polity in Modernizing Societies.* Singapore: Institute of Southeast Asian Studies.

——— (1981). *Thailand: Society and Politics.* Ithaca: Cornell University Press.

Hall, R. A. (1980) 'Middlemen in the Politics of Rural Thailand: A Study of Articulation and Cleavage'. *Modern Asian Studies* 14: 441–464 .

Hanks, Lucien M. (1975) 'The Thai Social Order as Entourage and Circle', in G. William Skinner and A. Thomas Kirsch (eds), *Change and Persistence in Thai Society.* Ithaca: Cornell University Press, 197–218.

Hawes, Gary and Hong Liu (1993). 'Explaining the Dynamics of the Southeast Asian Political Economy'. *World Politics* 45: 629–660.

Hefner, Robert W. (ed.) (1998). *Market Cultures: Society and Morality in the New Asian Capitalisms.* Boulder, Col.: Westview Press.

Hewison, Kevin J. (1981). 'The Financial Bourgeoisie in Thailand'. *Journal of Contemporary Asia* 11: 395–412.

——— (1985). 'The State and Capitalist Development in Thailand', in Richard Higgot and Richard Robison (eds), *South East Asia: Essays in the Political Economy of Structural Change.* London: Routledge & Kegan Paul.

——— (1986). 'Capital in the Thai Countryside: The Sugar Industry'. *Journal of Contemporary Asia* 16: 3–17.

——— (1989). *Bankers and Bureaucrats. Capital and the Role of the State in Thailand.* New Haven: Yale University Center for International and Area Studies.

——— (1989). *Power and Politics in Thailand: Essays in Political Economy.* Manila and Wollongong: Journal of Contemporary Asia Publishers.

——— (1992). 'Liberal Corporatism and the Return of Pluralism in Thai Political Studies'. *Asian Studies Review* 16: 261–265.

——— (1993). 'Of Regimes, State and Pluralities: Thai Politics Enters the 1990s', in Kevin Hewison, Richard Robison and Garry Rodan (eds), *Southeast Asia in the 1990s: Authoritarianism, Democracy and Capitalism.* Sydney: Allen & Unwin, 159–89.

——— (1996). 'Emerging Social Forces in Thailand: New Political and Economic Roles', in Richard Robison and David S. G. Goodman (eds), *The New Rich in Asia.* London: Routledge, 137–162.

Hewison, Kevin J. and Maniemai Thongyou (1993). *The New Generation of Provincial Business People in Northeastern Thailand.* Perth: Murdoch University Asia Research Centre.

Hirsch, Philip (1990). *Development Dilemmas in Rural Thailand.* Singapore: Oxford University Press.

——— (1993). *Political Economy of Environment in Thailand.* Manila and Wollongong: Journal of Contemporary Asia Publishers.

Holland, Stephen (1990). 'Development and Differentiation in Rural Thailand: A Case Study from the Central Region'. PhD thesis, University of Oxford.

Hong Lysa (1984). *Thailand in the Nineteenth Century: Evolution of the Economy and Society*. Singapore: Institute of Southeast Asian Studies.

Ingram, James C. (1971). *Economic Change in Thailand 1850–1970*. Palo Alto: Stanford University Press.

Jacobs, Norman (1971). *Modernizaton without Development: Thailand as an Asian Case Study*. New York: Praeger.

Johnston, David B. (1975). 'Rural Society and the Rice Economy in Thailand: 1880–1930'. PhD. thesis, Yale University.

——— (1980). 'Bandit, Nak Leng and Peasant in Rural Thai Society'. *Contributions to Asian Studies* 15: 90–101.

Kasian Tejaphira (1994). *Lae loet lai mangkon: ruam khokhian waduae khwampen chin nai siam* [Discerning the Dragon's Design: Collected Writings on Chineseness in Siam]. Bangkok: Kopfai.

Keyes, Charles F. (1967). *Isan: Regionalism in Northeastern Thailand*. Ithaca: Cornell University Southeast Asia Program.

——— (1989). *Thailand: Buddhist Kingdom as Modern Nation-State*. Bangkok: Duang Kamol.

——— (1991). 'The Proposed World of the School: Thai Villagers' Entry into a Bureaucratic State System', in Charles F. Keyes (ed.), *Reshaping Local Worlds: Formal Education for Cultural Change in Rural Southeast Asia*. New Haven: Yale University Southeast Asia Studies, 89–130.

Khana kammakan tittam lae sotsong dulae kanluaktang samachik sapha phutaen ratsadon (PollWatch) (1992). *Kanluaktang samachik sapha phutaen ratsadon* [The Election of Representatives to the National Assembly]. Bangkok: Khana thamngan fai wichakan.

King, Daniel E. (1992). 'The Thai Parliamentary Elections of 1992: Return to Democracy in an Atypical Year'. *Asian Survey* 32: 1109–1123.

King, Daniel and Jim LoGerfo (1996). 'Thailand: Toward Democratic Stability' *Journal of Democracy* 7: 112.

Korff, Rüdiger (1989). *Political Change and Local Power in Thailand*. Bielefeld: Southeast Asia Program, University of Bielefeld.

Kraiyudht Dhiratayakinant, 'Role of the Private Sector in the Thai Economy: Now and in the Future', in Suchart Prasith-rathsint (ed.), *Thailand on the Move: Stumbling Blocks and Breakthroughs*. Bangkok: Thai University Research Association, 1990.

Kramon Thongthammachat, Somboon Suksamran, and Pricha Hongkrailoet (1988). *Kanluaktang phak kanmuang lae sathienphap khong ratthaban.* [Elections, Parties, and Government Stability]. Bangkok: Chulalongkorn University.

Krasuang mahatthai, krom kanpokkrong, kong kanluaktang (1980). *Raingan wichai kanluaktang samachik sapha phuthaen ratsadon pho. so. 2522* [Research Report on the Election of Representatives to the National Assembly, 1979]. Bangkok: Krom kanpokkhrong.

——— (n.d.). *Raingan wichai kanluaktang samachik sapha phuthaen ratsadon pho. so. 2531* [Research Report on the Election of Representatives to the National Assembly, 1988]. Bangkok: Krom kanpokkhrong.

Krirkkiat Phipatseritham and Yoshihara Kunio (1983). *Business Groups in Thailand.* Singapore: Institute of Southeast Asian Studies.

——— (1989). 'Thailand: Industrialization without Development'. *East Asian Cultural Studies* 28: 91–100.

Leightner, Jonathan (1992). 'On the Periphery of Phenomenal Growth: Lampang, Thailand in 1981, 1991, and in the Future'. *Journal of Southeast Asian Business* 8: 47–58.

Likhit Diravegin (1985). *Thai Politics: Selected Aspects of Development and Change.* Bangkok: Tri-Sciences Publishing House.

——— (1992). *Demi Democracy: The Evolution of the Thai Political System.* Singapore: Times Academic Press.

LoGerfo, Jim (1996). 'Attitudes toward Democracy among Bangkok and Rural Northern Thais'. *Asian Survey* 36: 904–923.

MacIntyre, Andrew (ed.) (1994). *Business and Government in Industrializing Asia.* St Leonards: Allen & Unwin.

McVey, Ruth (1984). 'Change and Consciousness in a Southern Countryside', in Han ten Brummelhuis and Jeremy Kemp (eds), *Strategies and Structures in Thai Society.* Amsterdam: University of Amsterdam Antropologisch-Sociologisch Centrum, 109–137.

——— (ed.) (1992). *Southeast Asian Capitalists.* Ithaca: Cornell University Southeast Asia Studies.

Medhi Krongkaew (1995). 'The Political Economy of Decentralization in Thailand'. *Southeast Asian Affairs 1995.* Singapore: Institute of Southeast Asian Studies, 343–361.

Missingham, Bruce (1997). 'Local Bureaucrats, Power and Participation: A Study of Two Village Schools in the Northeast', in Kevin Hewison (ed.), *Political Change in Thailand. Democracy and Participation.* London: Routledge, 149–162.

Montesano, Michael (1994). 'Thap Thieng and the Wider World: Six Decades of Entrepreneurship and Economic Change in Trang Town', in Amara Pongsapich *et al.* (eds), *Entrepreneurship and Socio-Economic Transformation in Thailand and Southeast Asia.* Bangkok: Chulalongkorn University Social Research Institute, 307–321.

Montri Chenvidyakarn (1979). 'Political and Economic Influence: A Study of Associations in Thailand'. PhD dissertation, University of Chicago.

Morell, David and Chai-anan Samudavanija (1981). *Political Conflict in Thailand: Reform, Reaction, Revolution.* Cambridge, Mass.: Oelgeschlager, Gunn & Hain.

Murashima Eiji (1987). 'Local Elections and Leadership in Thailand: A Case Study of Nakhon Sawan Province'. *The Developing Economies* 25: 363–385.

Murray, David (1996). 'The 1995 National Elections in Thailand: A Step Backward for Democracy?' *Asian Survey* 36: 361–375.

Nakarin Mektrairat (1992). *Kanpatiwat sayam pho. so. 2475* [The Siamese Revolution of 1932]. Bangkok: Munnithi khrongkan tamra sangkhomsat lae manutsayasat.

Neher, Clark (1977). 'A Critical Analysis of Research on Thai Politics and Bureaucracy'. *Asian Thought and Society* 2: 13–27.

Nelson, Michael H. (1994). 'Administration and Politics in Rural Thailand: Internal Differentiation and Expansion of the Political System'. PhD thesis, University of Bielefeld.

Nidhi Aeusrivongse (1996). 'Chao pho withya kap khwam plianplaeng' [Change and the Study of Chao Pho] in Nidhi Aeusrivongse (ed.), *Song na sangkhom thai.* Bangkok: Phuchatkan, 105–108.

Nipon Poaponsakorn and Belinda Fuller (1997). 'Industrial Location Policy in Thailand: Industrial Decentralization or Industrial Sprawl', in Mayusama Seichi, Donna Vanderbrink, and Chia Siouw Yue (eds), *Industrial Policies in East Asia.* Tokyo, Nomura Research Institute, and Singapore, Institute of Southeast Asian Studies, 145–184.

Niran Thongban (1991). *200 setthi muang thai (phumiphak)* [200 Thai Provincial Millionaires]. Bangkok: Bonsai Group.

Nopalak Rakthum (1983). 'The Development of Branch Banking in Thailand'. MA thesis, Thammasat University.

Nopporn Ruengsakul, Chayawat Wibulswadi, and Duangmanee Wongprathip (eds) (1988). *Kanngoen kanthanakhan lae kandamnoen nayobai setthakit khong prathet* [Finance, Banking, and National Economic Policies]. Bangkok: Chulalongkorn University Press.

O'Connor, Richard A. (1986). 'Merit and the Market: Thai Symbolizations of Self-Interest'. *Journal of the Siam Society* 74: 62–82.

Ockey, James Soren (1992). 'Business Leaders, Gangsters, and the Middle Class: Societal Groups and Civilian Rule in Thailand'. PhD thesis, Cornell University.

——— (1993). '*Chaopho*: Capital Accumulation and Social Welfare in Thailand'. *Crossroads* 8: 48–77.

——— (1996). 'Thai Society and Patterns of Political Leadership'. *Asian Survey* 36: 345–360.

Pannee Bualek (1986). *Wikhro naithun thanakhan phanit khong thai, pho. so. 2475–2516* [An Analysis of Thai Commercial Banking Capitalists, 1932–1973]. Bangkok: Sangsan.

Pasuk Phongpaichit (1992). 'Technocrats, Businessmen and Generals: Politics of Economic Policy Reform in Thailand', in Andrew J. MacIntyre and Kanishka Jayasuriya (eds), *The Dynamics of Economic Policy Reform in Southeast Asia and the Southwest Pacific*. Singapore: Oxford University Press, 10–31.

Pasuk Phongpaichit and Chris Baker (1995). *Thailand: Economy and Politics*. Kuala Lumpur: Oxford University Press.

——— (1998). *Thailand's Boom and Bust*. Chiang Mai: Silkworm Books.

Pasuk Phongpaichit and Sungsidh Piriyarangsan (eds) (1992). *Rat, thun, chao pho thongthin kap sangkhom thai* [State, Capital, Provincial Godfathers, and Thai Society]. Bangkok: Chulalongkorn University Political Economy Center.

——— (eds) (1993). *Chon chan klang bon krasae prachathipatai thai* [The Middle Class and Thai Democracy]. Bangkok: Chulalongkorn University Political Economy Center.

Pasuk Phongpaichit and Sungsidh Piriyaransan (eds) (1994). *Corruption and Democracy in Thailand*. Bangkok: Chulalongkorn University Political Economic Center.

Pathorn Tamkam (1980). 'The Small Tractor Industry'. Master of Economics thesis, Thammasat University.

Phoemphong Chawalit and Sisomphop Jitphiromsi (1988). *Ha khanaen yangai hai dai pen so.so.* [How to Seek Votes to Be an MP]. Bangkok: Nititham.

Plai-oh Chananon (1987). *Phokha kap phatthanakan rabop thunniyom nai phak nua pho. so. 2464–2523* [Merchants and the Development of the Capitalist System in the North, 1921–1980]. Bangkok: Chulalongkorn University Social Research Institute and Sang Sawan Press.

Pornchai Trakulwaranont (1987). 'Wang Thong: A Study of History, Civic Identity, and Ethnicity in a Thai Market Town'. MA thesis, University of Kent.

Prachan Rakphong (1986). *Kansueksa kanhasiang nai kanluaktang 27 karakadakhom 2529 changwat Lampang* [A Study of Campaigning in the 27 July 1986 Election in Lampang Province]. Bangkok: Samakhom sangkhomsat haeng prathet thai.

Preecha Kuwinpant (1984). 'Marketing and the Management of Personal Relations in Wang Thong', in Han ten Brummelhuis and Jeremy Kemp (eds), *Strategies and Structures in Thai Society.* Amsterdam: University of Amsterdam Antropologisch-Sociologisch Centrum, 139–152.

Prudhisan Jumbala (1992). *Nation-building and Democratizaton in Thailand: A Political History.* Bangkok: Chulalongkorn University Social Research Institute.

Riggs, Fred W. (1966). *Thailand: The Modernization of a Bureaucratic Polity.* Honolulu: East–West Center Press.

Robison, Richard (ed.) (1995). *The Emergence of the Middle Class in Southeast Asia.* Perth: Murdoch University Asia Research Center.

Rozental, Alek A. (1968). 'Branch Banking in Thailand'. *The Journal of Developing Areas* 3: 37–50.

——— (1970). *Finance and Development in Thailand.* New York: Praeger.

Rujaya Abhakorn (1984). 'Ratburi, an Inner Province: Local Government and Central Politics in Siam, 1868–1892'. PhD thesis, Cornell University.

Rüland, J. and M. L. B. Ladavalya (1993). *Local Associations and Municipal Government in Thailand.* Freiburg: Arnold Bergsträsser Institut.

Saitip Sukatipan (1995). 'Thailand: The Evolution of Legitimacy', in Muthiah Alagappa (ed.), *Political Legitimacy in Southeast Asia.* Palo Alto: Stanford University Press, 193–223.

Seksan Prasertkul (1989). 'The Transformation of the Thai State and Economic Change (1855–1945)'. PhD thesis, Cornell University.

Sharp, Lauriston and Lucien Hanks (1978). *Bang Chan: Social History of a Rural Community in Thailand.* Ithaca: Cornell University Press.

Siffin, William J. (1966). *The Thai Bureaucracy: Institutional Change and Development.* Honolulu: The East–West Center Press.

Sirilak Sakkriangkrai (1980). *Ton kamnoet chon chan naithun nai prathet thai (pho.so. 2398–2453)* [Origins of the Capitalist Class in Thailand 1855–1910]. Bangkok: Sangsan.

Sithi-Amnuai, Paul (ed.) (1964). *Finance and Banking in Thailand: A Study of the Commercial System, 1888–1963.* Bangkok: Thai Watana Panich.

Skinner, G. William (1957). *Chinese Society in Thailand: An Analytical History.* Ithaca: Cornell University Press.

——— (1958). *Leadership and Power in the Chinese Community of Thailand.* Ithaca: Cornell University Press.

——— (1973). 'Change and Persistence in Chinese Culture Overseas: A Comparison of Thailand and Java', in John T. McAlister (ed.), *Southeast Asia: The Politics of National Integration.* New York: Random House, 399–415.

Sombat Chantornvong (1987). *Kanmuang ruang kanluaktang: sueksa chapo koranee kan luaktang tuapai pho. so. 2529* [Election Politics: A Study with Special Reference to the General Elections of 1986]. Bangkok: The Foundation for Democracy and Development Studies.

——— (1992). 'Botbat khong chao pho thongthin nai setthakit lae kanmuang thai: kho sangket buangton' [The Role of Provincial Godfathers in Thai Economy and Politics: Preliminary Observations]. in Pasuk Phongpaichit and Sungsidh Piriyarangsan (eds), *Rat, thun, chao pho thongthin kap sangkhom thai.* Bangkok: Chulalongkorn University Political Economy Center.

——— (1993). *Luaktang wikrit: panha lae thang ok* [Thai Elections in Crisis: Fundamental Problems and Solutions]. Bangkok: Kopfai.

Somkiat Wanthana (1993). 'Nak thurakit thongthin kap prachathipatai thai' [Local Businessmen and Thai Democracy] in Sungsidh Piriyarangsan and Pasuk Phongpaichit (eds), *Chon chan klang bon krasae prachathipatai thai.* Bangkok: Chulalongkorn University Political Economy Center.

Somphop Manarungsan (1989). *The Economic Development of Thailand 1850–1950: Response to the Challenge of the World Economy.* Bangkok: Chulalongkorn University Institute of Asian Studies.

Somrudee Nicrowattanayingyong (1991). 'Development Planning, Politics, and Paradox: A Study of Khon Kaen, a Regional City in Northeast Thailand'. PhD thesis, Syracuse University.

——— (1993). 'Thailand's NIC Democracy: Studying from General Elections'. *Pacific Affairs* 66:167–218.

——— (1993). 'Local Businessmen and Political Contest outside Bangkok'. Paper presented to the Fifth International Conference on Thai Studies, London.

Sondhi Limthongkul (1991). 'Chao pho: kankamnoet lae damrongyu yang pen rabop' [Chao pho: Origins and Persistence]. *Samut sangkomsat* 12 (January–July): 127–139.

Suchit Bunbongkarn (1987). *The Military in Thai Politics 1981–86*, Singapore: Institute of Southeast Asian Studies.

——— (1996). 'Elections and Democratization in Thailand', in R. H. Taylor (ed.), *The Politics of Elections in Southeast Asia*. Cambridge: Woodrow Wilson Center Press and Cambridge University Press, 184–200.

Suehiro Akira (1989). *Capital Accumulation in Thailand 1855–1985*. Tokyo: Center for East Asian Cultural Studies.

——— (1992). 'Capitalist Development in Postwar Thailand: Commercial Bankers, Industrial Elite and Agribusiness Groups', in Ruth McVey (ed.), *Southeast Asian Capitalists*. Ithaca: Cornell University Southeast Asia Studies, 35–64.

Sungsidh Piriyarangsan (1983). *Thai Bureaucratic Capitalism 1932–1960*. Bangkok: Chulalongkorn University Social Research Institute.

Sungsidh Piriyarangsan and Pasuk Phongpaichit (eds) (1993). *Chon chan klang bon krasae prachathipatai thai* [The Middle Class on the Current of Thai Democracy]. Bangkok: Chulalongkorn University Political Economy Center.

Surin Maisrikrod (ed.) (1992). *Thailand's Two General Elections in 1992: Democracy Sustained*. Singapore: Institute of Southeast Asian Studies.

——— (1993). 'Emerging Patterns of Political Leadership in Thailand'. *Contemporary Southeast Asia* 15: 80–97.

——— (1997). 'The Making of Thai Democracy: A Study of Political Alliance among the State, the Capitalists, and the Middle Class', in Anek Laothamatas (ed.), *Democratization in Southeast and East Asia*. Singapore: Institute of Southeast Asian Studies, and Bangkok: Chulalongkorn University Social Research Institute, 141–166.

Szanton, Maria Cristina Blanc (1982). 'People in Movement: Mobility and Leadership in a Central Thai Town'. PhD thesis, Columbia University.

——— (1983). 'Thai and Sino-Thai in Small Town Thailand: Changing Patterns of Interethnic Relations', in L. A. Peter Gosling and

Linda Y. C. Lim (eds), *The Chinese in Southeast Asia*, vol. 2. Singapore: Maruzen Asia, 99–123.

Tamada, Yoshifumi (1991). '*Itthiphon* and *Amnat*: An Informal Aspect of Thai Politics'. *Tonan Ajia Kenkyu* 28: 445–465.

Tej Bunnag (1977). *The Provincial Administration of Siam 1892–1915*. Kuala Lumpur: Oxford University Press, and Bangkok: Duang Kamol.

Thak Chaloemtiarana (1979). *Thailand: The Politics of Despotic Paternalism*. Bangkok: Social Science Association of Thailand and the Thai Kadi Foundation.

Tobias, Stephen F. (1973). 'Chinese Religion in a Thai Market Town'. PhD thesis, University of Chicago.

Trocki, David J. (n.d.) 'Big Men, *Naklaeng* and Power: The Politics of Violence in the Rural South of Thailand' (ed.) Carl Trocki, unpublished paper.

Ueda Yoko (1992). 'Research Note: Characteristics of Local Entrepreneurs in Nakhon Ratchasima City'. *Tonan Ajia Kenkyu* 30: 331–372.

——— (1994). 'The Development of Commercial Banking and Financial Businesses in the Provinces of Thailand'. *Tonan Ajia Kenkyu* 31: 385–411.

——— (1995). *Local Economy and Entrepreneurship in Thailand: A Case Study of Nakhon Ratchasima*. Kyoto: Kyoto University Press.

Van Roy, Edward (1971). *Economic Systems of Northern Thailand: Structure and Change*. Ithaca: Cornell University Press.

Vandergeest, Peter (1993). 'Constructing Thailand: Regulation, Everyday Resistance, and Citizenship'. *Comparative Studies in Society and History* 35: 133–158.

Vickery, Michael (1970). 'Thailand's Regional Elites and the Reforms of King Chulalongkorn'. *Journal of Asian Studies* 29: 863–881.

Visid Prachuabmoh and John Knodel (1974). 'The Longitudinal Study of Social, Economic, and Demographic Changes in Thailand: Review of Findings'. *Asian Survey* 14: 350–363.

Warr, Peter G. (ed.) (1993). *The Thai Economy in Transition*. Melbourne: Cambridge University Press.

Wijeyewardene, Gehan (1971). 'Patrons and Pau Liang'. *Journal of the Siam Society* 59: 229–234.

Wilson, David (1962). *Politics in Thailand*. Ithaca: Cornell University Press.

Witayakorn Chiengkul (1983). *The Effects of Capitalist Penetration on the Transformation of the Agrarian Structure in the Central Region of Thailand (1960–1980).* Bangkok: Chulalongkorn University Social Research Institute.

Wolters, O. W. (1998). *History, Culture and Region in Southeast Asian Perspective.* Singapore: Institute of Southeast Asian Studies.

Wyatt, David K. (1969). *The Politics of Reform in Thailand.* New Haven: Yale University Press.

Yoshihara Kunio (1988). *The Rise of Ersatz Capitalism in South-East Asia.* Singapore: Oxford University Press.

——— (1994). *The Nation and Economic Growth: The Philippines and Thailand.* Kuala Lumpur: Oxford University Press.

——— (1995). 'The Ethnic Chinese and Ersatz Capitalism in Southeast Asia', in Leo Soeryadinata (ed.), *Southeast Asia and China: The Politico-Cultural Dimension.* Singapore: Times Academic Press, 66–86.

Index

amnat (authoritative power) 5, 54, 131
amphoe (district) 4
Anand Panyarachun 40, 227
Arthit Kamlang-ek 183
Arthit Urairat 234
Arun Tangphanit 185
Asian economic crisis (1997) 17, 21, 146, 188, 257
Assembly of the Poor 44, 45
Assets Investigation Committee 106, 113, 261, 262 n. 34
Association of *Kamnan* and *Phuyaiban* 75, 84, 128
Ayutthaya 39, 64, 102, 103, 113, 124, 127, 145, 156, 235 table 9.2, 252

Bangkok 10, 31, 101, 102, 174, 180, 182, 183
Bangkok Bank 32, 33, 34, 35, 48, 82, 108, 109
Banharn Silpa-archa 17, 31, 36, 39, 40, 41, 47, 66, 88, 113, 262 n. 34, 252, 257
banks and banking 6, 10, 32, 80, 81, 108, 174, 208
Bank of Ayutthaya 102
Banyong Lotharaprasoet 184
barami (charismatic person) 7, 72 n. 37
Boonchu Rojanasathien 35, 38, 39, 48, 82
Boonsong Somjai 72 n. 29
Brick Manufacturers Association. *See* business associations
bureaucracy and bureaucrats 89, 102, 130, 131, 149, 198
bureaucratic polity 9, 12, 123, 148, 197
business associations 18, 97, 114, 124, 148, 179, 208, 219, 222, 225, 248, 253
  Brick Manufacturers Association 124, 128–149 *passim*
  Prasan Mit 185
businessmen 13
  as pariah capitalists 9
  and politicians 182, 183, 184
  in politics 184, 185
  replacement of patronage by monetary relationships 21, 22
  See also chao sua, tauke

capitalism
  businessmen and pariah capitalists 9. *See also* bureaucratic polity
  central importance of Bangkok 10, 11
  importance of banks 10, 11, 32, 33, 34
  provincial 36, 37, 196–214 *passim*
  role of military 10, 11, 33, 34, 35
  understanding 2
  See also businessmen
Central region 101, 235 table 9.2, 236, 237 table 9.3
chae (rotating credit society) 131, 173, 174
Chaichan Thianpraphat 103
Chalad Worochat 233
Chaloem Yoobamrung 66, 72 n. 29

Chamlong Srimuang 227, 233, 247
chamber of commerce 103, 177, 198, 209
Channel 7 101, 104
chao pho ('godfather') 18, 20, 21, 46, 97, 111, 141, 201, 212, 213
  defined 26 n. 17, 37, 55, 215 n. 12
  influence of 14, 53, 199, 201
  origins of 57, 80
  See also *nak leng*
chao sua (magnate) 30, 31, 33, 39, 48
chao thi. *See* peasantry
Charoen Phattanadamronchit. *See* *Sia* Leng
Charoen Pokphand 40
Chart Pattana Party 64, 67, 85, 113, 183, 186
Chart Thai Party (Thai Nation Party) 34, 35, 39, 63, 67, 72 n. 29, 74, 112, 226, 227, 233, 252
Chatchua Kannasut 102, 103, 105
Chatichai Choonhavan 31, 85, 113, 268 n. 77
  and businessmen 182, 183, 185
  and *chao pho* 40
  elected prime minister 13
  government 88, 106, 158, 195, 204, 226, 256
Chavalit Yongchaiyudh 17, 31, 45, 46, 63, 66, 72 n. 37, 201, 257
Chiang Mai 72, 167, 222, 229, 234–255 *passim*
Chiang Rai 37, 87, 234, 237 table 9.3
Chinese 47
  assimilation of 6, 16, 113, 115, 164, 171, 205
  China-born Teochiu 106
  economic activity of 57, 98, 99, 115
  See also Sino-Thai
Chinese associations 176, 208, 219
  Phitsanulok 107
Chomrom Mit 31 186
Chonburi 24, 37, 38, 46, 47, 61, 63, 67, 82, 84, 138, 176, 180, 235 table 9.2
Chuan Leekpai 31, 48, 63, 66, 105, 113, 210, 257
Chuan Rattanarak 102
Chulalongkorn, King 5, 22, 78
civil society 19, 91, 148, 221
'clean politics' 227
communist insurgency 43, 202, 225, 266 n. 63, 268
Communist Party of Thailand 71, 79
compradores (*khomprado*) 10, 81, 108
constitutional reform (1997) 17, 20, 232, 257
coup, military
  1976 (overthrow of democratic regime) 20, 225, 227
  1977 225
  1991 (overthrow of Chatichai government) 13, 17, 31, 35, 40, 53, 65, 72, 87, 91, 158, 159, 183, 186, 225, 226, 262 n. 34
criminal activity 14, 15, 80, 81, 90

democracy and democrats 10, 13, 39, 230
  democratic regimes 224
Democrat Party (DP, Prachatipat) 34, 74, 227, 233, 250

Ekkaparb. *See* Solidarity Party
elections 38, 83, 111, 125, 135, 140, 193 n. 45
  1969 86
  1988 13, 38, 63, 64, 84–88, 95 nn. 50 and 53, 112, 216 n. 16, 226
  1992 (March) 87, 228, 232, 243
  1992 (September) 87, 186, 229
  1996 87
electoral politics 59, 184, 200

foreign investment 145, 181

Green Northeast Project (Isan Khiew) 46, 201

hua khanaen (vote brokers) 60, 83, 112, 137, 140, 186

industry associations. *See* business associations
intellectuals 12, 222, 250
Isan Khiew. *See* Green Northeast Project
itthiphon (influence) 5, 54
Itthiphon Khunpleum 67

Joint Public-Private Consultative Committee (JPPCC) 198
Jongchai Thiengtham 63, 66, 72 n. 29. *See Sia* Jung

kamnan (head of village cluster) 7, 12, 26 n. 17, 74, 77, 128, 134, 138
Kamnan Poh (Somchai Khunpluem) 38, 46, 47, 61, 63, 64, 65, 67, 71 n. 24, 84

Kaset Rochananim 231
Khon Kaen 37, 55, 85, 195–214 *passim*, 219, 234–237 *passim*, 247, 250, 251
Khorat (Nakhon Ratchasima) 18, 37, 40, 154–189 *passim*
Kit Sangkhom. *See* Social Action Party
Kukrit Pramoj 63, 199
Khwan Wang Mai. *See* New Aspiration Party
kwangkhwang (well reputed) 108

Liberal Party (*Phak Itsara*) 110
lobbies and lobbying 132, 144, 147, 198

manufacturing 162, 165, 207
market society 99, 104, 107, 113, 115
middle class 18, 221, 223, 224
military 30, 39, 45, 102
 leaders 53
 rule by 12, 58, 224, 225, 226. *See also* coup, military; National Peacekeeping Council
'money politics' 13, 17, 27, 69, 98, 106, 112, 199, 200, 213, 214
Montri Pongpanich 39, 152 n. 24, 251, 262 n. 35
Muan Chon Party 66, 72 n. 29, 233

nai hua (patron in the South) 56
nak leng (strong man) 8, 54, 80, 142. *See also chao pho*
Nakhon Ratchasima 154–160 *passim*, 167, 176–189 *passim*. *See also* Khorat
Narong Wongwan 89, 232, 233, 251
National Development Party. *See* Chart Pattana
National Economic Development Board (NEDB) 198
National NGO Coordinating Committee on Rural Development (NGO-CORD) 247
National Peacekeeping Council (NPC) 69 n. 2, 106, 226, 228, 231
National Student Centre of Thailand 253
New Aspiration Party (NAP, Khwan Wang Mai) 63, 72 n. 37, 201, 227, 233
'New political economy' defined 149
Non-governmental organizations (NGOs) 223, 247, 255
Northeastern region 154–167 *passim*, 201–205 *passim*
 agriculture more significant 157, 158
 anti-Suchinda demonstrations (1992) 234–240 *passim*
 economic development 46, 157, 158, 203–205 *passim*
 electoral significance 202
 insurgency in 158. *See also* communist insurgency
 poorest, least developed region 156
 rural agitation 44
 traditional leadership 5
 See also Khorat, *Sia* Leng, vote-buying
Northern region 101, 235 table 9.2, 236, 237 table 9.3
Northern Coordinating Committee for the Development of Democracy (NCCDD) 263 n. 39

Palang Darma Party 87, 227, 233, 234
pariah capitalists 9
parliament 11, 31, 105, 112, 200, 214, 227, 231, 232, 233, 243, 256, 257, 261 n. 35
patrons and patronage 8, 14, 33, 58, 102, 130, 182
peasantry 4, 19, 23, 31, 41-46, 205, 225, 228, 247, 257
Phak Itsara. See Liberal Party

Phak Sangkhom Chartniyom. *See* Social Nationalist Party
Phetchaburi 64
Phichit 235 table 9.2, 237 table 9.3
Phitsanulok 75, 87, 105–113 *passim*, 235 table 9.2, 236, 237 table 9.3
pho liang (patron in the North) 56
phu mi itthiphon (man of influence) 54, 55 69 n. 2
phu yai 7
Phuket 234, 236, 238 table 9.3, 243, 267 n. 63
phuyaiban 7, 12, 54, 75, 128
Piya Angkhinant. *See Sia* Paeng
police 132
political parties 17, 59, 83, 112, 242
PollWatch 40, 87, 222, 228, 246, 250, 256
Prachakorn Thai 112, 226, 233
Prachatipat. *See* Democrat Party
Prachinburi 72 n. 29
Prachuap Khiri Khan 66
Pramarn Adireksarn 35, 112, 113, 268 n. 77
Praphat Charusathien 58, 102, 110
Prasit Kanchanawat 110, 111, 112
Prasut Minpraphan 179
Prem Tinsulanonda 31, 35, 65, 103, 256
'protest action' defined 263 n. 40
provincial capitalism. *See* capitalism
provincial council 28, 50 n.17, 87, 112, 128, 134, 135, 138–146 *passim*, 160, 236, 239, 249, 267 n. 67,
Puang Chon Chao Thai Party 183, 185
public contracts 13, 142

Ratsadorn 65, 74
rent-seeking 188, 231
revolution (1932) 32
'revolution' (1973) 10. *See also* student movement
Rotating Credit Society (*len chae*) 131, 147
rural network politicians 232

Samakkhi Tham Party (United Darma) 64, 67, 183, 186, 232, 233, 251
Sanan Khajonprasan 262 n. 34
Sarit Thanarat 8, 9, 58, 78
Sia (title of tycoon) 114
Sia Huat 82
Sia Jung (Jongchai Thiengtham) 63, 66, 72 n. 29
Sia Leng (Charoen Phattanadaronchit) 37, 55, 65, 81, 85, 86, 89, 201, 211 table 8.6, 212 table 8.7
Sia Oh (Udomsak Thangthong) 63, 66, 68, 71 n. 25, 72 n. 29, 73 n. 44
Sia Paeng (Piya Angkhinant) 72 n. 29
Sia Soh (Sompao Prachuabmoh) 72 n. 29, 73 n. 44
Sia Thoh (Thanit Trainsuwan) 72 nn.29 and 31
Sia Yae (Somchai Ruekwararak) 38, 60, 63, 64, 84, 85
Sino-Thai (Chinese ethnicity) 128, 135, 205
Social Action Party (SAP, Kit Sangkhom) 34, 38, 63, 152 n. 24, 226, 227, 233, 251
Social Nationalist Party (Phak Sangkhom Chartniyom) 111
Solidarity Party (Ekkaparb) 226, 233
Somchai Khunpluem. *See Kamnan* Poh
Somchai Ruekwararak. *See Sia* Yae
Sompao Prachuabmoh. *See Sia* Soh
Sonthaya Khunpleum 66, 67
Southern region 101, 104, 150, 235 table 9.2, 236, 237 table 9.3
student movement (1973) 34, 224, 241
students 241
Suchinda Kraprayoon 113, 221, 226, 231, 232, 233, 247
Suchon Champhunot (Tang Ui Chiao) 105–113 *passim*
Sunthorn Chanrangsi 178
Sunthorn Kongsompong 66
Suranaree Industrial Zone (SIZ) 158, 181, 182
Surin Tothapthiang 99–105
Sutham Tothapthiang100
Suwat Liptapallop 190 n. 9, 183, 185

talat (market place) 99
tambon (subdistrict, village cluster) 7, 12

tambon councils 28 n. 22
Tambon Development Fund 48
Tang Chung Yuai 106, 108
Tang Ui Chiao 106, 109. *See* Suchon Champhunot
tauke (merchant) 9, 11, 26 n. 17. See also businessmen
Thai Nation Party. *See* Chart Thai Party
Thanin Kraiwichian 225
Thanit Trainsuwan. *See Sia* Thoh
Thanom Kittikachorn 58, 102
Thanom-Praphat regime 224
Tothapthiang group 103
Tou Nguan Tiang 100, 107
tourism 223, 241, 243, 248
trade associations 177
Trang 99–108 *passim*, 238 table 9.3
Trat 72 n. 29
tycoon. *See Sia*

Udomsak Thangthong. *See* Sia Oh
Union for Civil Liberties (UCL) 222, 246, 250
United Darma. *See* Sammakkhi Tham Party
United Thai People's Party (UTPP) 110
Uthai Phimachaichon 73 n. 43, 96 n. 68

Vattana Assavahame 66, 72 n. 41, 73 n. 41
Vietnam War 34, 80, 157, 225
Vinyu Kuwanan 211 table 8.6, 212 table 8.7
vote-brokers. *See hua khanaen*
vote-buying 16, 85, 112, 136, 137, 141, 146, 226, 256

Wichai Choetchai 185
Wichian Bunnak 179
Wirasak Phromdi 179
Wirat Tanchindaprathip 186
Wittaya Khumpleum 67
working-class 19, 23, 171, 222–229 *passim*, 242, 247, 248, 250, 256, 266 n. 66

Yingphan Manasikan 112